# THE REHABILITATION COUNSELOR IN PROFESSIONAL PRACTICE

*WRITTEN BY*

GERALD K. WELLS

AND

ASHELEY D. WELLS

*WELLS & ASSOCIATES*

*STAUNTON, VIRGINIA*

*Published by*

ASPEN PROFESSIONAL SERVICES

63 DUFFERS DRIVE

LINN CREEK, MO 65052

2015

PUBLISHED BY
**Aspen Professional Services**
63 Duffers Drive
Linn Creek, MO 65052

The Rehabilitation Counselor in Professional Practice
[Written by] Gerald K. & Asheley D. Wells



Includes bibliographical references

ISBN 978-0-9853389-4-7

[Cover Layout by] M Jean Andrew, Esq.



**TO SECURE ADDITIONAL COPIES, CONTACT**

Aspen Professional Services
63 Duffers Drive
Linn Creek, MO 65052
jandrew@socket.net
573.317.0907
573.286.0418 Cell
573.873.2116 FAX

**aspenprofessionalservices.com**

# ACKNOWLEDGEMENT

Our Special Thanks

To Brian & Al

for opening the doors that made

this publication possible.

## TABLE OF CONTENTS

TABLE OF CONTENTS

# THE AUTHORS

**Gerald K. Wells, Ph.D. CRC** was one of the original 13 Directors of the Regional Rehabilitation Continuing Education Programs. Prior to coming to the Field of Rehabilitation, he served as Director of Continuation Education and Assistant professor of English and American literature at the University of Richmond. Dr. Wells holds a Bachelor of Science in Business Administration and Accounting, a Master's degree in English from the University of Richmond, a Doctor of English and American Literature from the University of South Carolina, and post doctoral studies in Higher Education Administration from the University of Virginia and rehabilitation counseling from Virginia Commonwealth University. He has been President of Wells & Associates, a private rehabilitation company located in the Shenandoah Valley of Virginia for over 30 years. As a Certified Rehabilitation Counselor, he has been directly involved in the placement of persons with disabilities for over 35 years and has served for 26 years as a Vocational Expert with the Office of Disability and Review (ODAR). His full-length publications in the field of rehabilitation, other than *The Rehabilitation Counselor in Professional Practice,* include *Shaping the Future*: *A Systems Approach to Human Resources Development in Vocational Rehabilitation Agencies* (1981), *Finding Jobs on Main Street* (1994), and The *Job Search Organizer* (2014).

**Asheley D. Wells, MS, CRC** has been in the Field of Rehabilitation for 9 years. She holds an undergraduate degree in Political Science and a Masters Degree in Rehabilitation Counseling from Virginia Commonwealth University. She has served as a rehabilitation counselor with George Moore and Associates in Richmond, Virginia where she counseled returning veterans of the Iraqi conflict. For the past seven years, she has served as an Associate with the rehabilitation counseling firm of Wells & Associates. With Wells & Associates, she has been involved in direct job placement of injured civilian employees for the Army and Air Force throughout the Eastern part of the United States. For the past five years, she has been serving as a Vocational Expert for the Office of Adjudication and Review (ODAR) in Roanoke, Virginia. She is the co-author of *The Rehabilitation Counselor in Professional Practice* and the *Job Search Organizer*.

In this publication, Asheley and her father Gerry bring to the practice of rehabilitation counseling two generations of formal university education and practical experience in helping persons with disabilities improve their lives and work. The main goal of *The Rehabilitation Counselor in Professional Practice* is to improve our understanding of our disabled clients, to help counselors manage the vocational aspects of counseling persons with disabilities, and to raise the level of participation of our clientele in the job search.

# THE AUTHORS, Cont.

**This is not just another how-to book. The foundation of this text is much broader. Whole chapters deal with insight into group and work identification, practical counseling to provide motivation and empowerment during a job search, applied behavioral counseling approaches designed toward helping clients become more involved in the job search, and practical approaches for identifying, locating, and securing appropriate work alternatives. The writing style has the toughness that comes from experience in the field, and yet, the caring of professionals working in an occupation that can make a difference in the lives of persons with disabilities.**

# TO STUDENTS AND PROFESSIONALS IN REHABILITATION

Some years ago, I accepted the position of Director of the Regional Rehabilitation Education Program (RRCEP) for Federal Region III. The purpose of the RRCEP programs was to create post-employment programs of continuing education for rehabilitation counselors and others in the state agencies and private facilities in each region of the Country. The funding for the grant to Federal Region III was unique in two respects: of the thirteen RRCEP programs created by the Rehabilitation Services Administration (RSA), the grant funding in Region III went to a state agency, the Virginia Department of Rehabilitation; each of the other RRCEP grants were administrated by institutions of higher education.

Even more unique, part of the funding was designated for the creation of a model program for the recruitment, training, and professional development of rehabilitation counselors. The results of the research were presented in a national conference in Chicago, Illinois in April 1980, under the sponsorship of the Office of Rehabilitation Services, Region V, and the Regional Rehabilitation Continuing Education Program, Region V. The research was published in book form titled, *Shaping the Future: A Systems Approach to Human Resources Development in Vocational Rehabilitation Agencies (1981).*

The model program was the "brain child" of Corbett Reedy, former Acting Commissioner of the Rehabilitation Services Administration to whom *Shaping the Future* is dedicated. Corbett Reedy had followed Commissioner Mary Switzer upon her retirement from the Rehabilitation Services Administration, but because of health problems, he also had to leave his position. He retired to Charlottesville, Virginia and became a special consultant to the state agency in Virginia.

Corbett Reedy long felt that there were significant gaps between the pre-employment education of rehabilitation providers in the universities and the professional practice in state agencies. As a result, following employment, the state agencies, in his words, had to "grow their own." Corbett Reedy envisioned the creation of a model program where higher education and state agencies would share information and create educational experiences more closely related to actual professional practice. The results, he believed, would provide better-educated and trained professionals for service to persons with disabilities. This book, *The Rehabilitation Counselor in Professional Practice*, directly addresses many of the same concerns. We are hopeful that it provides a partial answer to narrowing the distance between academia and the post-employment needs of the practicing professional.

First, the effort to bring education and training closer to the professional practice begins with the authorship. The book is the effort of practicing rehabilitation counselors, each of whom have formal education in rehabilitation counseling in recognized university degree programs, combined with current, private-sector experience in counseling injured workers and others, forensic rehabilitation, and job placement. As lead author, I have been in private practice in the field of rehabilitation for the last 33 years, following seven years of administration in public service with the Virginia Department of Rehabilitative Services. For the past 22 years, I have been involved directly in conducting labor market surveys and job placement of civilian workers injured at military bases throughout Eastern and Midwestern United States. In addition, for the past 26 years I have served as a vocational expert for the Office of Disability and Adjudication (ODAR) of the Social Security Administration. My principal publications include *Shaping the Future: a Systems Approach to Human Resources Development in Vocational Rehabilitation Agencies* and *Finding Jobs on Main Street*.

Joining me in the authorship of this book is Asheley D. Wells, BA, MA, CRC. She works as a rehabilitation counselor in private practice in the firm of Wells and Associates; and, like me, serves as a vocational expert with the Office of Disability, Adjudication, and Review (ODAR) of the Social Security Administration. She has an abundance of practical experience in counseling persons with disabilities, providing vocational guidance to injured veterans of the Iraq Conflict, and conducting labor market surveys and job placement of injured civilian employees from military facilities. Her contributions provide a fresh and youthful approach to the subject matter; and, as a research specialist in rehabilitation, she serves as a sounding board to update many of the ideas for this book.

Second, the practical applications in the text are given a sound basis in accepted traditions and theory, thus further narrowing the gap between academic education and professional practice. This text is about work and work in America. The title might suggest just another how-to book about finding jobs for injured workers. In one sense, this is true! Job search methods and techniques form the content of Part 3: "Finding Jobs for Persons with Disabilities in the Contemporary American Economy" and take up the last four chapters in the book as well as the separate publication, "*The Job-Search Organizer*." The remainder of the text, however, covers broad areas of professional practice. These broad areas of professional practice include the various roles and special interests in which rehabilitation counselors are engaged, identifying and describing populations served by the profession, motivational techniques for counseling clients in the job search, defining the diagnostics of rehabilitation, managing the case process, and exploring the social and political implications of work in a structured society.

Most of all, in the writing of *The Rehabilitation Counselor in Professional Practice* a conscious attempt has been made to focus upon professionalism in rehabilitation. Professionalism gives unity to the entire book. In this respect, the goals of the academic world and the practical world become one in the same. From the first chapter forward, the book defines professional practice, identifies areas of knowledge within the domain of the profession, and attempts to carry forward, in a deliberate manner, the ideals of a life of service to persons with disabilities. So often, in the absence of guiding leadership, professionals become bogged down in the frustration of having to deal with persons manipulating the system for their own benefit. This manipulation is by both professionals and clients, and with the legal maneuvering that seems to thwart case after case. Doubtless, each of us has played our part in compromising the ideals of the profession.

Nevertheless, rehabilitation is a proud profession, and we want those receiving education and training in the profession to know and understand the finer principles upon which our professional practice was founded. Through the years, professional practice in rehabilitation has helped thousands of disabled persons get back on their feet, support their families, and lead active and productive lives. Many have shared in this achievement. Through the years, literally thousands of dedicated counselors have served with quiet distinction. They believe in and act out a life of service. Dedicated lawyers and client representatives have spent their entire lives working for the rights of their clients, many times with only their private satisfaction to show for their efforts. Leaders (e.g., Dr. Estelle Davis, my mentor in rehabilitation, and Corbett Reedy, described as "a man whose life has always stood for quality in rehabilitation"), have taken their place in service to help clarify our needs and give direction to the rehabilitation program.

It is my hope that you, as students and professionals, reading and studying the chapters ahead will recognize the ideals that have guided most of us through the years; and in the process gain, or regain, a stronger sense of pride in your chosen profession. If that happens, our years of research and hundreds of tedious hours in writing will all seem worthwhile.

## WHAT THIS BOOK IS ABOUT

It has been 28 years since the initial research for *Finding Jobs on Main Street* was first presented as pre-conference training before an audience of rehabilitation counselors at the 1986 National Rehabilitation Conference in the District of Columbia. Over the following two years, this program of training and its revisions was presented in workshops in Orlando, Florida, Houston, Texas, Santa Fe, New Mexico, and New Orleans, Louisiana. The result was a publication in 1994 by Elliott & Fitzpatrick of Athens, Georgia entitled *Finding Jobs on Main Street.* The first edition was sold out in 2000.

In the years that followed, sections from *Finding Jobs on Main Street* were presented in featured conferences for state agency counselors and staff in Dover, Delaware, Minneapolis, Minnesota, and Pierre, South Dakota. The annual governor's conference in South Dakota was titled after the publication. Training and experience in rehabilitation practice since the first publication in 1994 have clarified many of these ideas and concepts. Indeed, some of concepts and ideas have fallen by the wayside while others, refined by practice and experience, have crystallized into new or expanded ways of doing business in professional practice.

Lessons learned during these years have shown that there are no gimmicks or special techniques to lead persons with limitations from a life of dependency to fully functioning individuals at work in society. When it comes to job placement, unlike the little boy in the nursery rhyme "Little Jack Horner," rehabilitation counselors cannot expect to "stick in a thumb, pull out a plumb, and say what a good boy am I." Success in the practice of rehabilitation is the result of a well-managed program of vocational counseling, knowledge of vocational principles and American occupations, and an understanding of the clients we serve and the nature of the jobs our clients perform in the workplace. *The Rehabilitation Counselor in Professional Practice* text seeks to provide students and counselors with at least basic knowledge used in professional practice. From the main features of this book, you will learn:

- THE PRACTICAL ASPECTS OF CASE MANAGEMENT
  For the rehabilitation counselor in professional practice case management is a process of discovery; discovery about the limitations and abilities of rehabilitation clients, discovery about the kinds of work clients can perform in spite of their limitations, and the identification of work suited to a client's abilities and interests. Much of the information can be gained from the case record and personal interviews, but the counselor must know how to discern important clues from what they hear and read. In this text, students and professionals will learn how to use their preparation to gain information they need, information that leads directly into finding jobs and job placement. *The Job Search Organizer*, a companion publication, provides students with an interactive format for managing the case process throughout the job placement process.

- CLASS DIFFERENCES
  Most rehabilitation clients come from the working class and a class of people we call in this study, baseline people. The interests, abilities, and occupations of clients are often very different from the background of their rehabilitation counselors. To be effective, rehabilitation counselors must know and understand occupations their clients typically perform and be able to help them transfer their skills and abilities to other occupations they are able to perform, given their functional imitations. Chapters Two & Three provide a basic understanding of class differences, occupations, and interests of each class, and vocational profiles that prepare counselors for job placement.

- PRINCIPLES OF MOTIVATION & EMPOWERMENT
  Rehabilitation counselors must know how to provide a motivational climate for job placement and empower their clients to make vocational decisions that lead to success in the world of work. Chapter Four offers students and professionals six (6) keys, based upon proven research in industrial psychology, for setting a motivational climate for their clients and empowering their clients throughout the job-seeking process.

- THE DIAGNOSTICS OF REHABILITATION
  The presence of a disabling condition makes rehabilitation counseling uniquely different from other counseling professions. Counselors must know how their client's functional limitations, both physical and mental, limit their clients' abilities to perform certain jobs. They also need to recognize the kinds of jobs their clients can perform in spite of their limitations. Chapter Five takes the student and counselor through the process for determining functional limitations and the impact these limitations have upon a client's ability to work. Chapter Six introduces rehabilitation counselors to ways to apply their knowledge about functional limitations and to assist administrative law judges within the Social Security Administration in making their decisions in disability cases.

- JOB PLACEMENT
  The term *job placement* is surely an antiquated term, suggesting that the rehabilitation counselor easily finds a source of employment for their clients. Furthermore, the

employment leads to a time when, using the quaint language of the Vocational Act of 1920, "the rehabilitated person is independent, confident, and happy, and all reports show he is producing at his maximum efficiency." Practicing rehabilitation counselors know that finding jobs suited to their client's abilities and interests is much different, with many unexpected twists and turns. Chapter Nine expands upon the old model of a counselor-guided job search, as defined in the literature. The chapter also shows that better success is now possible even with this antiquated model by using web sites and information provided by a computer search.

Chapter Ten of this text in conjunction with *The Job Search Organizer*, provides guidance toward involving the clients in the job search. Chapter Ten also shows that by using behavioral counseling techniques, rehabilitation counselors can effectively manage the case while increasing the involvement of their clients in finding suitable employment.

## THE AUDIENCE

*The Rehabilitation Counselor in Professional Practice* is addressed to those desiring to enter and those presently involved in the practice of rehabilitation counseling. The content of this book is meant to be an extension of the education and training received in college and university programs in rehabilitation counseling and address areas of knowledge counselors need to succeed in professional practice.

In programs of higher education, counselors learn many of the basic concepts of rehabilitation, such as counseling persons with limitations, medical and psychological aspects of disability, and unique ways to address the needs of special populations. As rehabilitation counselors engage in professional practice, the need for the knowledge learned in academic programs remains, but the emphasis changes; so much of the everyday activities in professional practice centers upon vocational and work-related issues.

To succeed in the professional practice, rehabilitation counselors need to be able to research and understand the requirements of a wide range of occupations, most of which a counselor may have little or no first-hand knowledge. If a rehabilitation counselor decides to become a vocational expert in Social Security and other courts, they will need to know, and be able to discuss, jobs appropriate to individuals with physical and mental limitations. In their counseling practice, counselors need to teach their clients vocational skills, and job-seeking skills, to help them succeed in finding and obtaining employment. Counselors need to learn ways for guiding clients through a job search to a positive outcome. Indeed, most of what you will be doing in professional practice is vocational in nature.

The authors believe that this publication provides a systematic plan and, to our knowledge, the only sequential approach for teaching the vocational aspects of the profession. Too often, it seems in rehabilitation, we throw away the accumulated knowledge of yesterday, and "reinvent the wheel." We have learned some things after 96 plus years of existence and several billion-tax dollars spent on education in the rehabilitation programs. The important contribution this new publication makes is that we take select academic research and some of the practical knowledge learned over the years and organize the information into a logical, usable format for educating students and professionals in the current practice of rehabilitation.

Happy Reading!

Gerald K. Wells, Ph.D., CRC
Senior Rehabilitation Consultant
Wells & Associates

## PART 1

# THE PRACTICE,

# THE PEOPLE,

# THE PROFESSION

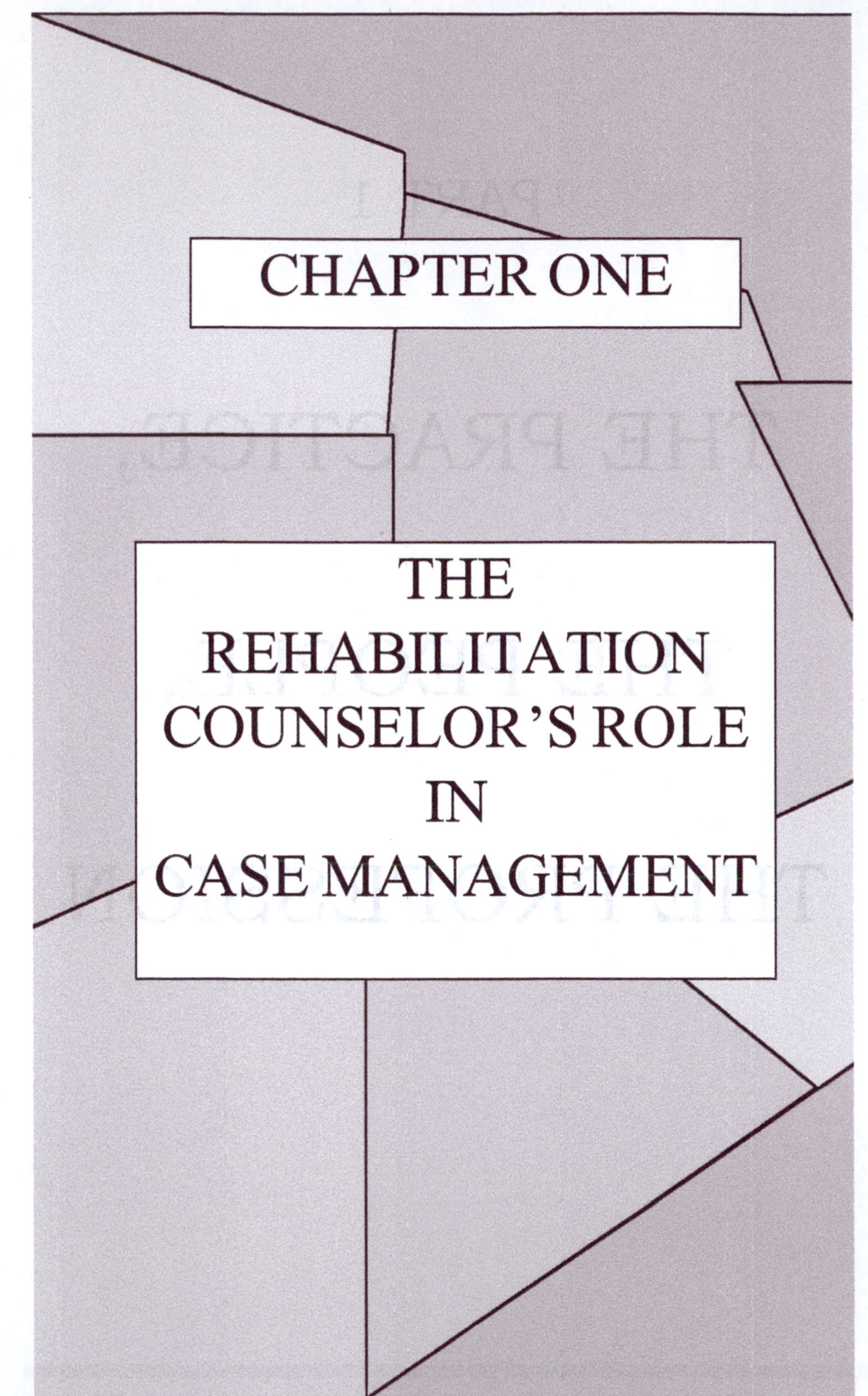

# CHAPTER ONE

# THE REHABILITATION COUNSELOR'S ROLE IN CASE MANAGEMENT

# PREFACE

To The Reader:

Paul Ellwood[3] wrote:

> *Rehabilitation is a profession of professions. From the very start, rehabilitation has attempted to organize itself to circumvent professionalized categories and to create a unified and synthesized program of management designed to integrate the skills of many professions. The essential quality that differentiates the rehabilitation profession lies in the dynamics of its multi-disciplinary, total concept approach to client service. Indeed, this represents a dominant aspect of rehabilitation's distinctive body of knowledge.*[pg. 21]

Interesting! A profession of professions. The people of rehabilitation have been struggling for years to clarify the professional identity of the rehabilitation counselor. Paul Ellwood[3] believes that the body of knowledge, that makes rehabilitation a distinct profession lies in the useful knowledge culled from the many professions with which we come in contact. The rehabilitation counselor has a fund of useful knowledge gained from many sources: from psychology, psychiatry, counseling and guidance, sociology, social work, law, education, medicine, and business. From time to time, the rehabilitation counselor is a combination of parent, doctor, psychologist, psychiatrist, teacher, politician, economist, public relations expert, personal manager, and jack-of-all-trades.

The knowledge demands of the profession require the rehabilitation counselor to be somewhat of a generalist, to have some knowledge of a wide variety of things. You cannot know it all. You are always learning! Moreover, much of the professional knowledge is learned by experience on the job. As Corbett Reedy, former Acting Commissioner of the Rehabilitation Services Administration after Mary Switzer, often said, and forty years later is still true, "In rehabilitation, we have to grow our own."

An important difference between rehabilitation counseling and other counseling occupations lies in the area of management. As Paul Ellwood[3] says, rehabilitation "has attempted to create a unified and synthesized program of management designed to integrate the skills of many professions."[pg. 21] In other words, the rehabilitation process, which is made up of "the integration of the skills of many professions," becomes "a unified and synthesized program of management" with the rehabilitation counselor serving many management functions. Among these functions are planning, organizing, coordination, directing, and evaluation. Unlike many other counselors in professional practice, rehabilitation counselors exercise an appropriate amount of managerial control throughout the rehabilitation process. In this regard, the field of rehabilitation bears a close resemblance to the field of social work, from which the case method approach was borrowed.

Chapter 1 concerns the rehabilitation counselor as manager:

- Why management has become such an important part of the rehabilitation process, with examples of some of the various management functions normally performed by rehabilitation counselors, and

- Ways to gain an appropriate amount of control over the case process.

This chapter concludes with a model for assessing control and determining appropriate amounts of managerial control rehabilitation counselors have in the placement of persons with disabilities in the work force.

The authors feel that one of the main contributions of *The Rehabilitation Counselor in Professional Practice* is the recognition of the complexity of the managerial role rehabilitation counselors have to play in working with disabled people, particularly in job placement. For the rehabilitation counselor, the whole case management process changes in midstream. In the early stages of case development, when counselors can exercise direct control, the main concern is motivation: what can a counselor do or say that will improve the chances of a successful outcome.

Chapter 4, Client Motivation and Empowerment, is devoted exclusively to motivation and motivational techniques counselors use during the early stages of case management. Once job placement begins, more and more clients have to function on their own, with less guidance, and make decisions independent of their counselor's direct control. This calls for a different kind of management control. Empowerment becomes the main managerial approach. In the world of work, we know of no other management system more complex with so many potential people problems.

Rehabilitation counseling has always been an evolving profession. From its beginning to the present, the direction of the program of service, public and private, has shaped the role and function of the professional. Today, we are seeing a new emphasis upon the management functions of the rehabilitation counselor. In fact, many rehabilitation counselors have taken on the name Case Manager, with its own certification, to emphasize the importance of management in their work, in preference to the more generic designation, Rehabilitation Counselor. This shift in emphasis goes to show the rising level of importance management has assumed in professional practice in the field of rehabilitation.

# INTRODUCTION
# THE EVOLVING ROLE OF THE REHABILITATION COUNSELOR

With the enactment of Public Law 236, Congress wrote into law the Vocational Rehabilitation Act of 1920. Set up within each state, and administered by each state under federal regulations, the State/Federal program became the first national program to serve persons with disabilities. While other programs assisting disabled persons have arisen since, (i.e., Goodwill) to serve specific functions, such as work adjustment and job placement, and others, (i.e., the National Federation for the Blind) to serve specific disabilities, the State/Federal program has been by far the most comprehensive and influential. At least up until the past two decades with the advent of private rehabilitation companies, rehabilitation in the United States for the past 90 years has followed the direction set by the State/Federal rehabilitation program.

Over the years within the State/Federal program, the title of the service delivery provider has changed several times. For the first eight or so years, the service delivery provider became known as a *Rehabilitation Agent*. Then, for approximately the next 30 years, rehabilitation service providers in most rehabilitation agencies became known as *Rehabilitation Supervisors*. From the late 1950's on, under the influence of education and with a growing sense of professionalism, the service delivery provider has been known as a *Rehabilitation Counselor*. Each of these changes reflect not only how practitioners and others view the role of the service delivery person at the time but also how these changes show a shift in emphasis of the rehabilitation program.

During the 20s, the focus of the rehabilitation program was upon physical disability, and the main goal of the services provided was employment of disabled persons. As the title *Rehabilitation Agent* implies, the service delivery person was seen as a government representative whose primary function was to bring together disabled people and a combination of service leading to employment. The term *Rehabilitation Agent* implies that the professional has no real control over the services or the clients. Truly, this is the purest example of a coordinator of service.

During the early period, the services provided were mostly vocational. As Robert Lassiter[5] writes, the guidelines for the professional administering the program were:

- to determine if the person met the guidelines to receive service,
- to decide upon a job objective and a tentative plan to meet that objective, and

- to follow up on the job training "until the disabled person is independent, confident, and happy, and all reports show he is producing at his maximum efficiency."[pg. 31]

# CASE METHOD APPROACH

Using the case method approach adapted from the field of social work, the rehabilitation agent, working one-on-one with the disabled person, provided vocational guidance and job placement. In this narrow role, the rehabilitation agent, like a real estate or insurance agent, served as a go-between to provide a variety of vocational services leading to independence in the world of work.

From the late 1920s until the middle 1950s, in many agencies of the State/Federal program the title for the front-line professional became *Rehabilitation Supervisor*. This change in title makes it clear that the agencies began to recognize the importance of a managerial role for the service delivery person.

By definition, a supervisor is an administrative officer who watches and directs the course of activities. This definition implies the front-line professional not only brings the client and the services together but also manages the whole rehabilitation process (i.e., the professional plans the process, organizes the resources, directs and coordinates the activities, and evaluates the effectiveness of the client's program). Over the entire process, the rehabilitation supervisor exercises appropriate control.

From the late 1950s, following passage of the "Vocational Rehabilitation Amendments of 1954,"[12] the rehabilitation provider took on a new title: *Rehabilitation Counselor*. The title Rehabilitation Counselor seems an appropriate designation for the role of the front-line professional since counseling is the one service that threads throughout the rehabilitation process and connects each of the services in the program. A more subtle change seems to have been taking place in the program. Slowly but surely, the rehabilitation program had begun, like other programs of education, to move toward a concern for the internal process of physical and mental restoration and preparation for work and away from its original objectives: vocational guidance and job placement. Two factors, one internal within the State/Federal program, and one external to the program, seem to have contributed to the movement away from employment outcomes.

By the early 1950s, the vocational rehabilitation agency had added new services, primarily medical and restoration services, and the caseloads had grown very large. For instance, the annual report from the state director of the vocational rehabilitation agency in Virginia at the end 1949 cites as the most pressing concern of the agency the need for more rehabilitation services providers to work with a burgeoning disabled clientele. The director notes at the time that the average caseload in the agency was 709. With caseloads this size, less and less time could be spent on an individual case. In effect, rehabilitation counselors had become more or less a "broker of services." With the huge caseloads the best counselors could do was to coordinate a program of service for their disabled clients. Any kind of effective management under these circumstances became physically impossible. The rehabilitation process had to make adjustments somewhere. Obviously, the direction chosen was to move away from employment outcomes.

The program also saw a shift in emphasis away from vocational matters in general. Robert Lassiter[5] writes about this period. He says,

> *Rehabilitation counselors became, during this period, coordinators who provided less and less vocational counseling and guidance services. These counseling services were not entirely forsaken by the staff, but the emphasis placed on providing medical services to large numbers of people meant that handicapped people who were in need of counseling services and job placements were many times referred to other agencies and professional individuals.*[pg. 47]

Externally, Congress sought to alleviate the pressing demand for more qualified rehabilitation workers. In 1954, with the passage of Public Law 565, often cited as the "Vocational Rehabilitation Amendments of 1954,[12] Congress authorized $30 million dollars in federal grants-in-aid to prepare students for careers in rehabilitation. Much of the grant money for the training of front-line professionals went to university departments of counseling and psychology. As pre-employment education and training became centered in the university system, the emphasis in the preparation of front-line professionals would naturally move toward counseling and the coordination of services in the internal process. For employment outcomes, the agencies were still in a position of having to "grow their own."

The title of the service provider has shown clear evidence of changes that had been taking place in the role and function of the front-line professional. Looking back over the 90 or so years of the state/federal program, we can see that the main role of the professional has been altered dramatically from an agent concerned almost exclusively with employment outcomes, to a supervisor managing the process of mainly vocational services, to a counselor concerned with client progress during restoration and preparation for work, and with less attention upon vocational matters, such as vocational guidance and job placement.

# THE EMERGENCE OF THE PRIVATE REHABILITATION COUNSELOR

What does the rehabilitation program look like today as we move into the second decade of a new century? The State/Federal program continues to be the primary source of employment of front-line professionals in the field of rehabilitation, hiring over 50% of the rehabilitation counselors. Large caseloads limit state agency counselors to managing clients during preparation for work. Counselors in the Virginia state agency indicate their caseload averaged about 150 cases. The agencies of the State/Federal program continue some emphasis on vocational outcomes, particularly through special initiatives, such as supported employment for their mentally challenged clients.

Outside the State/Federal program, the past three decades have given rise to several new specializations in the field of rehabilitation. Much of the growth in the field of rehabilitation since the early 1980s has been in the formation of private for profit companies made up of independent rehabilitation professionals and nurse practitioners working with insurance companies and lawyers to serve specific rehabilitation functions. The largest number of private rehabilitation counselors perform case management and job placement activities for insurance companies within each state's worker's compensation programs. Other private rehabilitation counselors make their living by doing a variety of things (e.g., serving as expert witnesses on vocational matters within the Social Security Administration, serving as expert witnesses for both defense and plaintiff attorneys in personal injury cases, preparing vocational assessments and labor market surveys for defense attorneys and insurance litigation teams).

Generally, the emphasis of rehabilitation professionals in private practice rehabilitation is somewhat different from the professionals serving the State/Federal program. These differences include:

1. *A primary focus in private rehabilitation upon the whole rehabilitation process, both medical management and vocational outcomes.*

The worker's compensation program is concerned with the return of the injured worker to employment. From the time the case is assigned, services provided to the client are directed toward returning the worker to his/her past work or alternative work. The rehabilitation professional offers guidance and direction to the client during the period of disability and provides a variety of vocational services, including vocational counseling, job seeking skills, and job placement, where necessary. In private rehabilitation, no case can be successful unless the injured worker returns to work.

When private rehabilitation companies first started in business in the late 70s and early 80s many of the cases were assigned to rehabilitation professionals only after the injured worker had remained on an adjuster's case role for long periods of time. The length of time may have been for two to four years. Job placement was the primary service. To say the least, these were difficult cases. Today, the typical case is assigned soon after the injury and the case manager can follow the case to completion. The typical case comes to the rehabilitation professional or case manager soon after injury and the rehabilitation practitioner is expected to make a vocational assessment, work closely with the insurance adjuster to oversee the medical management of the program, and provide the vocational services necessary for the transition from disability to work. Unlike counselors in the State/Federal program, private rehabilitation counselors have small caseloads and serve a limited number of clients.

2. *Private rehabilitation counselors exercise close, often tight control, over the case.*

In fact, most rehabilitation practitioners in private practice, as noted earlier, are case managers with a nursing background. These managers are the local watchdogs in the case. They perform regular management duties for the case, preparing the plan for a client's return to work, and overseeing the medical and physical rehabilitation phases of the program. The main functions of management in these cases are:

- to recognize potential problems (e.g., changes in the medical program), and to report rapidly and accurately to the case adjuster in the insurance company, and
- to alert the insurance carrier when clients have reached their highest attainment in their medical restoration (MMI) and are ready to return to work (RTW).

Since a return to work is the only goal, and the acquisition of future cases may well be based upon the attainment of that goal, the professional usually exercises a good deal of control over the case. The Selective Approach, explained more fully in Chapter 9, is usually the method of choice for managing the activities in job placement.

## OUTLOOK FOR THE REHABILITATION PROFESSIONAL

The direction of the rehabilitation program, both public and private, seems to be determined largely, by the demand of a growing activist disabled community and a Congress which is increasingly responsive to the expressed needs of persons with disabilities. The *Occupational Outlook Handbook, 2013-2014*,[2] is projecting a growth of 28% in employment for rehabilitation counselors from 2010 to 2020, faster than the average for all occupations in the United States. If that is so, then both the State/Federal program and professionals working in private rehabilitation will likely see an increased emphasis upon vocational services. Surveys have shown that disabled people come to rehabilitation agencies mainly because they want to work. Indeed, the recent "Ticket to Work" initiative has arisen mainly from disabled persons in Social Security Disability Programs saying that they would like to work if they had medical coverage and vocational assistance provided to them. The demand from Congress, plaintiff and defense lawyers, insurance companies, and others for greater efficiency and accountability in case management, private and public, would suggest a continued emphasis upon management in the counselor's role.

## MANAGEMENT AND THE REHABILITATION COUNSELOR

Is the front-line professional in rehabilitation a counselor or case manager? This subject has sparked a continuous controversy in rehabilitation for many years. At the level of personal contact with clients, the practicing rehabilitation counselor has often resisted being designated a case manager, preferring to be associated with occupations in other helping professions in the social science fields, like counseling, counseling-psychology, and psychology, rather than management occupations or social work. Indeed, those who consider themselves counselors have their point. As indicated earlier, counseling is the one function that occurs at all levels throughout the rehabilitation process and ties together all of the components of the rehabilitation program for the client. You cannot have much success helping a disabled person unless you can build a relationship with your client, and that requires continuous counseling. Moreover, as many front-line professionals have received their education and training among students in departments of counseling and psychology, they feel more of a kinship with others in the counseling fields. For these and other reasons, professionals in the field cling to the title of rehabilitation counselor for their professional identity.

We cannot settle this controversy here. However, it does not take long in professional practice to realize that in order to have any success serving persons having disabilities, the rehabilitation counselor has to perform a number of management functions. In the service role, rehabilitation counselors gather information from the case record and their client to make an evaluation of their client's vocational potential; prepare a plan outlining the services needed to reach the vocational goals; organize the program into an orderly sequence, with timetables; coordinate the program of services according to the client plan; and rehabilitation counselors direct the program and guide the program to completion. At the conclusion of the program, when clients, hopefully, are functioning independently in a job well suited to their abilities, rehabilitation counselors evaluate the results. Throughout the rehabilitation process, rehabilitation counselors guide, and, to a large extent, control the service delivery and events that take place during the client program.

Planning, organizing, coordinating, directing, evaluating, and controlling are all part of almost every service program rehabilitation counselors, public or private, put together for the disabled client; and all of these functions are part of any management definition. By definition, a manager is a person in charge of these very functions. Regardless of the title the professional uses, whether counselor or case manager, the professional in rehabilitation has to perform functions that are both case management and counseling. Let us look a little more closely at how these management functions are performed in the professional practice of rehabilitation.

## CASE PLANNING

Rehabilitation counselors engage in many forms of planning, from:

- overall caseload planning to determine actions for a given period of time for all their clients,
- case management planning and vocational planning with individual clients for physical and mental restoration and work, and
- personal daily office planning to make effective use of time and resources.

In professional practice, planning pervades almost every aspect of professional case practice.

Of course, the most important planning for the rehabilitation counselor is case planning with disabled clients. While each case is different, as each client is different, the information a counselor receives normally includes, along with standardized forms from the referral sources, the following: a file of records, including medical records concerning a diagnosed condition and treatment of that condition to date, vocational records showing achievements in education and training, and a history of past work. Based upon the information contained in the file and information gained from a personal interview with the client and others, the rehabilitation counselor forms a vocational profile to determine the functional level (residual functional capacity, RFC) of the client and the possible work the person can do. With this information, the rehabilitation counselor and the disabled client jointly decide what actions need to be taken to move the client from a condition of disability and dependence to independence in the world of work.

In other words, the counselor and the client prepare a rehabilitation plan. In the state agency, this plan goes by the name "Individualized Written Rehabilitation Program." In private practice rehabilitation, the plan may be a part of a formal or informal vocational assessment. Regardless of the name given to the procedure, the formal planning document is an attempt to reach into the future, chart a course to follow, identify potential problems and difficulties, predict the outcome in terms of the kinds of jobs the person can and cannot do, and determine the services needed to reach the goals of the plan. The goal may be a limited one, (e.g., elevating the client to independent living or sheltered employment), or a comprehensive one, (e.g., a return to former work, alternative work with the same employer, or new, competitive employment in the open job market). Services provided in the plan may include, among others, medical treatment, counseling, vocational adjustment, vocation training, job seeking skills, and job placement.

Forming the rehabilitation plan is an important management function. The plan sets the direction the case is to follow. Usually, the plan will include measurable steps with specific actions needed to reach the goal. When changes occur, or things go wrong, such as unexpected medical treatment, or the absence of employment opportunities in the area, the counselor and the client have a record of progress toward the goal, showing them where the case has been and the changes needed to put the plan back on course.

In the absence of a formal plan, the counselor is constantly caught up in crisis management, "kicking out brush fires." Without a record of past actions, various crises arise unexpectedly. Lewis Carroll in *Alice's Adventures in Wonderland* provides insight into the life of the crisis manager. In his novelette, the March Hair says to Alice, "Where are you going?" Her response is "I don't know." At this point The March Hair says to her, "Well, if you don't know where you are going, any road will take you there." Implied in his response is the idea that without a plan to guide your decisions and actions, the road you take may lead you to a place you may not wish to go.

## ORGANIZING CASE RESOURCES

The assumption that lies behind the whole concept of management is that the job to be done is larger and more involved than one person can do. Therefore, managers have to enlist others to help them get the job done. At the outset, professionals in rehabilitation have to:

- look at the job that lies ahead,
- decide what things need to be done and in what order of importance,
- make decisions as to what they have to do and what they can assign to others,

- delegate tasks and make assignments accordingly, and
- set up a system of communication so that they are able to maintain control over the process.

All of this is a management process called organizing; and whether or not organizing is done formally or informally, by agency counselors or counselors in private practice, organizing or ordering of the work activities is a critical function of management.

The management function of organizing in rehabilitation casework involves examining the activities to be accomplished, giving each of these activities its proper level of importance, and laying out the activities along the lines of the plan. Organizing may take the form of simply preparing for a day's work. This is often called time management. A counselor goes to the office and looks at what needs to be done on a particular day, setting up the daily tasks in some form of order or priority, deciding which things need to be done first, which things can wait for a while, and maybe which things do not need to be done at all. (Checking e-mail may be the first thing you do, but it is probably not the highest priority). Then, each of these activities is checked against the plan for the day, given a level of importance, and matched against the activities list to see how it fits into the overall program. Does this sound easy? Well, corporate America spends millions of dollars each year on training in time management. There is no reason to think rehabilitation counselors are very different, considering the amount of information, including paper work and electronic files that come across the desk in the average day.

Organizing the casework is more involved and, of course, more important than simply deciding on the activities of the day. How do rehabilitation counselors organize their case? Each counselor has their own special way of organizing the work, but all casework will have most of the same features. Following the formation of the plan, rehabilitation counselors make the decision about what needs to be accomplished to have a successful rehabilitation outcome. Then, counselors decide upon what things they have to do and what kinds of things can or need to be done by others. The diagnostics in rehabilitation (deciding the level of functioning and the kinds of work a person can do within that level of functioning) are always the professional responsibility of the counselor. Rehabilitation counselors cannot assign diagnostic responsibility to other people except for using others to help them sharpen their decisions, like obtaining a consultative report from a medical doctor or a psychologist,. Diagnostic determinations are, perhaps, the most professional activities performed by rehabilitation counselors.

Counselors frequently need to bring in persons from other specialties to help with the case. Medical specialists and treatment centers are often used to improve physical functioning; vocational schools and colleges provide education and training; work adjustment centers, (e.g., Goodwill Industries) are used for work adjustment training and work hardening to improve the client's physical and mental tolerance for competitive work; and employment agencies or placement specialists are sometimes used to help in job placement.

Yet, when assignments are made to other agencies or individuals, the counselor still retains the responsibility for the performance of these venders and must keep in constant communication to make sure the client is receiving the right service according to the vocational plan. One aspect of management that we emphasize repeatedly in this book is that while managers can assign work to others, called management authority, they maintain the ultimate responsibility for the successful or unsuccessful completion of the task.

Without proper organization of activities and tasks, virtually everything gets an equal value. Normally, a counselor who does not organize the workload takes things that come across the desk first-come-first-serve. However, counselors in professional practice soon find out that not all activities have the same level of importance. For instance, a directive from the commissioner in a public agency will have more importance than a note from the office secretary concerning a Friday birthday luncheon.

So how does an unorganized manager handle activities with different levels of importance? The manager deals with the most high-pressure concerns first and hopes time will allow for dealing with those things that have less pressure. In other words, to quote the familiar phrase, "the squeaking wheel gets the grease," but for these counselors, there is never enough time to get it all done. The solutions are regular overtime or leave it undone. This kind of management style is called crisis management.

Crisis management works against the counselor-manager in two ways:

1. Important tasks are left unfinished while unimportant tasks, many of which can be left undone, done later, or done by someone else, receive higher priority. Dealing with low priority tasks may give the illusion of movement and make the counselor feel a sense of accomplishment, but putting off time-consuming tasks or high-priority activities drive these activities toward a point of crisis, with the pressure mounting on the counselor.

2. Ultimately, the caseload controls the counselor. In managing anything, the person must be in charge, and feel in charge, of what is happening all the time. When a counselor leaves undone higher priority tasks, and the important decisions that go with the tasks, the pressures of the job mount, making the counselor feel overwhelmed. The expression "buried in paperwork" is frequently used to describe a manager overwhelmed with unresolved work. Usually, the feeling of having lost control comes about not from the volume of work but from the failure to take care of the important things in the job and organize the work properly. In our

opinion, most of the "burnout" among rehabilitation counselors comes not from large caseloads or external administrative turmoil but from failure in this all-important area of management called organizing.

## DIRECTING: MAKING DECISIONS IN THE CASE

In some ways, the management function of directing is closely allied to the management function of organizing. Organizing involves examining the work to be done and setting up the work activities in their order of importance. On the other hand, directing is making decisions and executing those decisions. In rehabilitation case management the term *organizing* means, arranging the activities and placing the activities in some order. *Directing* means making the decisions associated with the activities to keep the rehabilitation process moving. The two functions are like characters in the stage melodrama, "Dick Whittington and his Cat," where two actors each take one end of the cat as the animal appears on the stage. Organizing is the front end and directing brings up the rear but they are mutually dependent. You cannot have one without the other.

In the rehabilitation process, directing is separate from organizing. Here are three (3) important ways the two functions are very different.

1. *Directing creates movement in the case.* The rehabilitation process begins with counselors receiving the case file. The counselor examines the medical evidence, the vocational records and the past work performance, conducts an initial interview, organizes the resources of the case, and forms the planning document. From the beginning to the completion of the organizing and planning phases, the counselor has invested very little in the case except staff time. Possibly the counselor has written for additional information or sent the client out for a functional assessment, but all of this preliminary work has been part of the organizing and planning process. Now, in the directing phase of the process, the case begins to "heat up," to move in a specific direction; alternatives are eliminated as choices are made; passive functions now become more active.

2. *Directing brings about changes in control.* During the planning phases, which include planning and organizing, the counselor has almost complete control over the case. The counselor examines the file, sets appointments, interviews the client, obtains information to make an accurate functional assessment, and offers professional assistance in choosing the vocational objectives. The control of the case gradually begins to pass from the counselor to other people, especially the client. This happens once the

decisions are made about the things the client must do to reach the maximum level of functioning, other professionals are identified who need to be brought into the case, and the vocational pursuit is established.

3. *Directing brings higher risk.* Once the planning and organizing phases end, and until the case reaches conclusion, clients assume more and more control over the case. Counselors must depend upon their clients to make their way to appointments, to tell the truth, to relate information accurately to the counselor, to set up interviews, and to seek and follow up on job leads. The risk of failure rises as control passes from the counselor to the client. As a result, many more cases fail during the directing phase of the rehabilitation process than in the planning and organizing phases.

Part of the reason cases fail during the directing phase of managing the case may be that the action steps taken show up weaknesses in the planning process. For instance, the counselor and the client may have made the wrong decisions about functioning levels or the kinds of alternative work available. Part of the reason for failure may be from inaccurate information. Possibly the medical reports did not reveal situational depression which would affect the client's ability to take on additional authority.

More often than not, failure in the directing phase of case management comes from a counselor's reluctance to make timely decisions. Of course, all decisions carry a degree of risk, and every manager has to bear a certain amount of risk in making and executing decisions. Seldom does a manager require all the information to make a decision. An old adage in management is that it takes only 20% of the information to make 80% of the decisions. This adage also holds true in rehabilitation. All of the decisions a counselor makes are not life threatening. Lower level and low-risk decisions require less information. Counselors must train themselves to make decisions about their clients. A wrong decision is generally better than no decision at all and most failure is only temporary.

## COORDINATING CASE RESOURCES

As mentioned earlier, the basic assumption behind any kind of management is that the counselor's job is too great or too specialized for the manager to do alone. As a result, the manager must enlist help from others. For instance, the rehabilitation counselor has neither the time nor the expertise to conduct long-term therapy with a client. As part of the treatment plan, a client may be referred to a psychologist and/or a psychotherapist for testing and psychotherapy, or a client may need to learn work skills to become qualified for a particular occupation. As part of the vocational plan, counselors may refer their client for therapy or enroll their client in a school program for vocational training. The management function that involves soliciting the help of others is called *coordination.*

Making the assignment is only the beginning of the coordination process. While certain tasks are assigned to others to perform, the counselor-manager retains the responsibility for the quality of the work and the completion of the task. For instance, a counselor may refer a client to a vocational program for training as a locksmith; but if the client, for whatever reason, does not learn to perform work as a locksmith, the failure of the training falls back on the counselor-manager. The counselor may blame the vender, promise never to use that training program again, or simply "curse the.fates," but the counselor is stuck with a stalled rehabilitation plan and an unskilled client, with a considerable loss of money and time. Remember, in coordination, as in other management functions in the action phase, the counselor can only delegate authority–allow others to perform the function like training or therapy–but the counselor retains the ultimate responsibility for the success or failure of the task.

How can counselors in assigning work to others to help in the rehabilitation program be sure the work they have assigned is being done according to the plan? How can the counselor-manager identify potential problems in the rehabilitation program? The counselor has to know what is going on at all times. The client may be saying one thing while the treatment or training source says something very different, or the treatment/training sources may be providing information very different from what the client is saying. Only when the information counselors receive is true and accurate, can they manage the case. Therefore, the counselor has to figure out a way to manage the flow of information and perform periodic evaluations.

As before, the answer is communication with both venders and clients. The counselor must constantly initiate contact with the vender, ask for medical reports and progress notes or school records, and compare the information received with what clients report in interviews and other personal contacts.

This may seem simple, but most counselors with a number of clients to serve are inundated with paper work, and it is so easy for time to pass without any updated information to let them know how things are going. For instance, most doctors keep careful notes when they see a patient, but seldom do they routinely send this information to the case manager. Unless the rehabilitation counselor or case manager specifically asks for that information, and sends the doctor a release form signed by the client, there is no information to tell how the treatment is going. Incomplete information drives the counselor crazy. Consequently, case managers have to find a way to stay in contact with treatment sources and keep timetables to let them know when certain reports and other information are due. Most case managers in private practice would agree that inadequate communication with treatment sources is one of the thorniest problems for a private rehabilitation firm. In the management function of coordination, communication is the counselor's search engine.

## CASE EVALUATION

A rehabilitation plan seldom goes along the path the counselor and the client intend. Usually, there are changes in the plan presenting unexpected obstacles that require new decisions and different action (e.g., a client needs additional surgery or more recuperation time; a work adjustment program is not available in the area; the market for a particular occupation proves to be narrower than expected; or a client needs additional training). Any one of these or other unexpected events alter or delay the original plan, requiring new decisions and revisions. The management function of evaluation alerts the counselor to unexpected events that affect the plan and lets the counselor-manager stop the process at a moment in time to look at what has been going on and try to determine what can be expected to happen in the future. This "time out" allows the counselor, in conjunction with the client, to reassess the plan and set new directions.

Effective evaluation is like a lighthouse in the bay, alerting the ship to obstacles that lie ahead and pointing toward clear waters. With our limited ability to read the future and the rapid changes that always seem present in our society unexpected events will occur. Most practicing counselors know that something unforeseen is going on most of the time even when they have no information to the contrary. Call it experience! Call it a second sense! Call it paranoia! Therefore, every client plan has to have a built-in evaluation. So, how can counselors build a formal evaluation into their plans?

In the late 1970s, the state agency in Virginia employed a consulting firm to study ways for evaluating client plans to prevent potential problems. One of the suggestions that arose from this management study was to have every counselor examine each case at a designated point in time, one time a month, and decide upon appropriate actions for every case; no exception!

In truth, there is no way to legislate plan evaluation. The evaluation is only as effective as the counselor managing the casework is. Staying on top of the case work, exercising appropriate control, keeping careful records and organized, copious notes, and making a periodic examination of the case are a few of the ways counselors evaluate case performance. One thing is for certain, without some measures or techniques for evaluation, the risk of failure grows with each passing day, causing professional anxiety about both real and imagined problems, and a growing feeling of loss of control. As every professional counselor knows, the longer a case lingers in the case file, the less likely the case will be successful.

## MANAGERIAL CONTROL

Examine the management model on the next page. This management model is very similar to most models found in textbooks in the field of management. Notice that all of the management functions we have talked about are present. You will notice that each of the management functions is connected to the other, to suggest a continuous process flowing from planning to organizing, from coordination to directing, and from directing to evaluation. However, the order is not always the same. Any one of the functions may occur independent of other functions. For instance, the process may begin with client case planning, but, as we have seen, counselors may do many types of planning, from planning caseload actions to time management planning. In addition, with each evaluation of the case, the counselor is forced into new planning activities. The same is true about organizing and directing. New decisions in the case mean going back and making revisions in the case organization. Therefore, while the management functions do seem to follow a precise pattern in the model, each of the functions may be performed at any point in the case development.

CHART 1

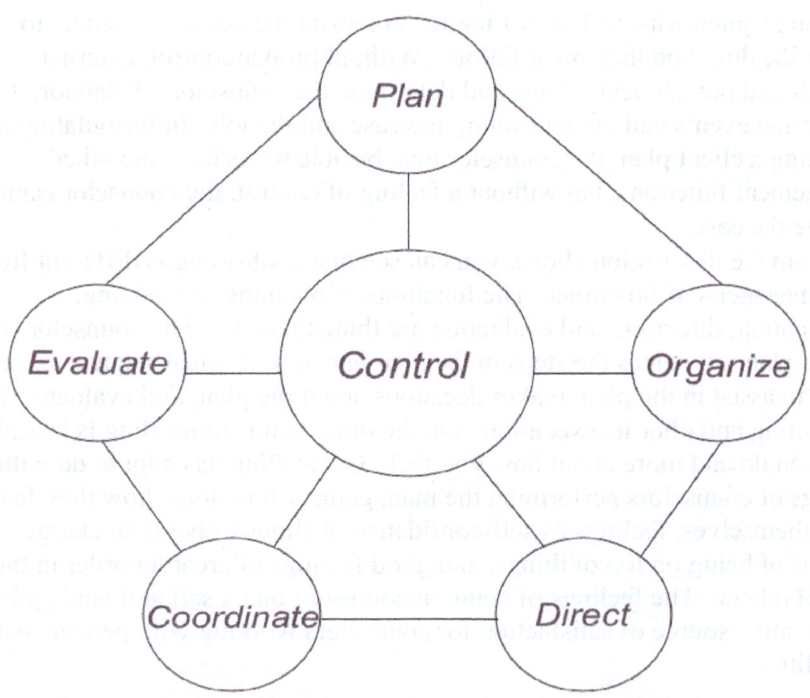

The management model shows a link between all of the management functions and the function of control. This linkage suggests that whether the functions are performed in a sequence or independently, they are all in some way tied in with control. We believe this is a proper relationship between the management functions and the function of control. In a management situation, you cannot perform any of the management functions without an appropriate amount of control.

Control pervades all management functions and relates directly to the knowledge, skills, and attitudes a counselor must possess to guide the process to a successful conclusion. Proper control places the counselor-manager in charge of the process and provides the personal power to make decisions and accept the necessary risks. Proper control provides the manager with self-respect, self-esteem, and the needed confidence to move the process toward conclusion, and proper control provides internal rewards to the counselor-manager with the feeling of a job well done and the knowledge that disabled people have been well served, even when the completion of a case is different from what was originally anticipated.

Without proper control, the job tends to run the counselor; things become confusing, resources become mishandled, and the clientele become permissive with the counselor's time and resources. Without proper control unrealistic fears, and sometimes realistic fears, sap the counselor's energy and create a feeling of ineptness as factors beyond the counselor's control dictate the direction of the case. Without proper control of the case and the job, counselors become plagued with feelings of inertia and await the actions of others to dictate the direction they must follow. Without proper control, external rewards and punishments shape and determine the counselor's behavior. Other people and events end up controlling the case and the job. In formulating and executing a client plan, the counselor may be able to perform the other management functions, but without a feeling of control, the counselor cannot manage the case.

From the description above, you can see that controlling is different from other management functions. The functions of planning, organizing, coordination, directing, and evaluation are things you do. The counselor sets in place a plan, organizes the steps in the plan into some logical sequence, seeks others to assist in the plan, makes decisions about the plan, and evaluates the plan during and after its execution. On the other hand, controlling is less about what you do and more about how you feel. Controlling has a lot to do with the feelings of counselors performing the management functions: how they feel about themselves, feelings of self-confidence, feelings of being in charge, feelings of being on top of things, and good feelings of creating order in the lives of others. The feelings of being in control of one's self and one's job can be a positive source of satisfaction for counselors working with persons with disabilities.

But while the management function of controlling may relate, on the one hand, to personal feelings such as the feeling of self-confidence, control is also about responsibility for others, making decisions that affect other people's lives, being the boss, and, in particular, controlling the actions–and sometimes the behavior–of other people.

On a personal level:

1. Using appropriate control is simply a matter of making sure the plan in force is going smoothly, according to the decisions you and your client have made.
2. Using appropriate control takes the form of verbal reinforcement and encouragement from the counselor that tells clients their behavior is consistent and productive. In this use of appropriate control, rehabilitation counselors become "value shapers," to use a term coined by Tom Peters[8] in his book, *In Search of Excellence*. (We will have more to say about "value shapers" in Chapter 4 on motivation and empowerment).
3. Using appropriate control involves gentle confrontation, (e.g., when clients have not followed through with assignments or other promises).
4. Using appropriate control may involve taking charge, re-assuming authority, and making tough decisions when the case needs to move in a different direction.

Controlling others may have negative connotations for many of us. As counselors, we do not like other people controlling us, and we do not like having the responsibility for controlling others. It makes us feel like some kind of despot. Somehow, controlling other people seems antithetical to personal counseling, the basis of our training, and the aims of any helping profession. When we realize that controlling other people is a big part of the counselor's job in rehabilitation, it is easy to see why professionals through the years have resisted the title of manager and have struggled to accept a managerial role in rehabilitation.

Most of the negative images that surround the function of controlling stem from examples of abuse of control wedged into our consciousness through the years. Nevertheless, in the practice of rehabilitation, a professional cannot be successful as a counselor without understanding and accepting an appropriate amount of control over the job and over the case process. Notice the use of the term *appropriate control*. Appropriate is the key word. Much of the conflict can be resolved once a counselor understands the differences between appropriate control and abuse of control and accepts appropriate control as part of the managerial role of the professional.

It is the position of this book's authors that rehabilitation counselors have to accept appropriate control is central to their role as a professional in setting the course of action for their injured and disabled clients. You are the professional, the expert in rehabilitation, the spokesperson for your agency or company. You may not always see yourself that way, but you possess the knowledge, the training, and the skill, as well as the authority, to make the system work for your client. In order to make the system work for your client, you must be able to exercise a certain amount of appropriate control. Rehabilitation does not just randomly happen in the lives of our clients; rehabilitation counselors make it happen with effective planning, careful organizing, coordination with others, careful appropriation of resources, good choices and good decisions, continuous attention to details and the progress of the case, and vigilant control over the events that take place in the process.

# "THE SHIFTING SANDS" OF CONTROL IN JOB PLACEMENT

In *To the Reader* at the beginning of this chapter, in referring to the counselor's role in rehabilitation casework, the authors made the statement, "I know of no other management system more complex than the rehabilitation process with so many potential people problems." Why is the management system so complex? What potential people problems make management in the rehabilitation process so difficult? Think about this! Here is our explanation.

For the counselor-manager the whole management functions of control changes in midstream, requiring very different management approaches. Slowly but surely, much of the direct control over the case passes from the counselor to the client. The counselor has to be primarily a motivator of clients at the beginning of the process, but later, the counselor needs to know and exercise the techniques of empowerment, all with the same client. The changing of the guard, so to speak, requires new management strategies on the part of the counselor.

Briefly, let us look in more detail at the dual-control function as it applies to the rehabilitation process. In the early stages of the case process, rehabilitation counselors:

- study to understand the case record, particularly as it relates to the physical and mental limitations the client may have,
- follow the progress of treatment and pinpoint what treatment outcomes mean in terms of client function,

- assist their clients in making the right vocational choices based upon their knowledge of the client's physical and mental functions and their knowledge of how jobs are normally performed in this country, and

- prepare a plan of action to enable the client to move from a state of dependence to fully-functioning individuals in society.

The plan becomes the culmination of the counselor's vocational assessment of the client's physical and mental functioning, the counselor's determination of the client's work potential, and the joint decision reflected in the selection of work alternatives that can be performed within the client's functional abilities.

In managing during the preparation stages in the case process, counselors exercise a large degree of control—setting counseling appointments, contacting treatment and training sources, and defining the dimensions of the planning process. Control over who does what is usually not an issue in the planning, organizing, and coordinating phases of the case process. Counselors make most of the decisions and perform most of the functions. These phases call for building a relationship and setting a learning climate of trust in which the client can progress and grow as an individual. Counseling in the early stages calls for one kind of management control: motivation.

Counselor control diminishes gradually during job placement until the counselor has little or less direct control over the case. If job placement is going to be successful, in most instances, clients have to assume more and more control over the events in the case and over their lives. They are the only ones in a position to perform so many of the activities necessary to make job placement work. Clients have to locate the jobs they desire and make decisions about which jobs satisfy their expectations; clients do the legwork to place applications with employers and set up interviews; clients have to network with family, friends, and acquaintances to locate job leads; and clients have to meet with employers to discuss job possibilities. While the amount of control counselors have may vary according to the managerial approach the counselor uses, the principle is essentially the same: counselors have a diminishing amount of managerial control over the placement activities as the case moves into the later stages of job placement.

Rehabilitation counselors cannot control the actions of their clients because, much of the time, they are not present during the performance of these activities. In many instances the counselor has to take a back seat and hope that the things the two of them have said and done in the preparation stage are sufficient to help the client make good decisions in job placement. The loss of direct control calls for a very different kind on management control: empowerment.

Empowerment places the counselor in new leadership roles. When much of the control passes to the client:

- Counselors serve as *a go-between* to bridge the gap between their clients, (i.e., most are from "the working people" and "the baseline people" in our society), and their middle-classed employers.

- Counselors serve as *advisors* and "value shapers" to help clients better understand and interpret employer needs and what employers expect of them.

- Counselors become *teachers* helping their clients to learn the job-seeking skills necessary to conduct an effective job search.

- Counselors serve as *agents of empowerment* reinforcing self-confidence and reassurance in their clients amid temporary failure and disappointment.

- Counselors become *advocates*, or sometimes even salespeople, when necessary to help employers see their clients' vocational potential in a favorable light.

Rehabilitation counselors still have to maintain control over the case process; the difference is that control becomes more indirect than direct. (Chapter 4: "Motivation and Empowerment" deals in more detail with influencing clients during these phases in the rehabilitation process and gives definition to relationship-building activities counselors may use during the latter stages of job placement).

The managerial control for the counselor in job placement does not cease. Control now becomes less direct and more indirect, and rehabilitation counselors take on a variety of new and different management activities, such as:

- updating the vocational plan as inevitable changes alter the initial work goals,

- monitoring client progress,

- advising clients about work options,

- counseling work-related behaviors, and

- teaching job-seeking skills, such as how to fill out an employment application, how to prepare and use a resume, a cover letter, and a thank you note.

# MANAGERIAL APPROACHES TO JOB PLACEMENT:

## A MATTER OF FREEDOM VS. CONTROL

Rehabilitation counselors truly remain the manager of the job placement process, and issues of control are central to the management role in job placement. The way rehabilitation counselors make decisions has to change once counselors move from having direct control over the case process into a more supported role with their clients. Well thought out, deliberate decisions with concern about how new ideas will affect client performance replace arbitrary decisions, or decisions made formerly by the counselor alone. Unilateral decisions, even in small things, become joint decisions. Counselors must consider the impact of each decision upon the person expected to carry out the action. Diplomacy, reinforcement, teaching, or simply "selling ideas" become more important than expediency, or telling the clients what you want from them.

Make no mistake! The counselor is still in control and is still in charge of making the decisions. Even though the counselor may choose to manage the case differently, and relax or pass on authority to the client, the rehabilitation counselor makes the decision about freedom and control. The counselor determines how much freedom will be allowed to the client in the pursuit of the vocational goals. Each client is different and each person a counselor works with has different expectations and capabilities. Likewise, the rehabilitation counselor determines how much control must be retained in a particular case. In other words, just because the way decisions are made changes or the communication process changes does not alter the responsibility the counselor has to make those decisions. Ultimately, the outcome of the case depends upon the counselor's ability to make decisions, and the success or failure of the case is most often the direct result of good and bad decision-making.

Standing at opposite ends on a continuum are freedom and control. Between these two polar opposites lie varying degrees of control and varying degrees of freedom, giving the rehabilitation counselor a lot of latitude to make choices. At one extreme, the counselor-manager may choose to give up control to their clients and allow them to make decisions on their own and find their own work. At the other extreme, in certain situations, counselors may decide to assume most of the control and conduct job placement themselves or, as normally happens, the two may share the job placement duties, each assuming an appropriate amount of control.

Following are three (3) managerial approaches to job placement that show varying degrees of counselor control and client freedom within the job placement process. The *Laissez-Faire Approach* presents situations with a low degree of counselor control and a high degree of client freedom.

The *Selective Approach*, on the other hand, presents the opposite situation with the counselor assuming most of the control. (Chapter 9: "The Selective Approach to Job Placement for Persons with Disabilities" expands upon ideas and techniques of a counselor-controlled job search and shows how the Internet has helped to make this approach more effective).

The *Client-Centered Approach* demonstrates shared placement responsibility. (Chapter 10: "Networking for Jobs in the Hidden Job Market: A Client-Centered Approach" shows effective ways behavioral counseling helps clients become more involved in the job search).

Each of these approaches to job placement has been used with varying degrees of success and each approach has its advocates. These models are designed to help students and practicing rehabilitation counselors examine the issues of authority, (i.e., issues of freedom and control). While these models present separate options to the placement counselor, we do not expect rehabilitation counselors to accept any one of these options in its entirety. Each client is different and has different needs and each client situation presents different circumstances. The determination about the use of the models remains a counselor decision, a deliberate decision that needs to be communicated to the client in strategy counseling sessions prior to beginning the job hunt. Nevertheless, these models highlight some of the key control issues that counselors face in job placement, and provide information to help counselors make the right decisions.

## THE LAISSEZ-FAIRE APPROACH

The Laissez-Faire Approach gives almost complete control to the client in job placement. Clients decide what jobs are best for them, make the necessary employment contacts, and secure the job. The counselor responds to the client's requests, such as funding for training or reimbursement for job-search activities, and completes the paper work necessary for a smooth transition into employment. Sounds like utopia for a rehabilitation counselor! Something you seldom see, but job placement situations do occur when the Laissez-Faire Approach is the right approach. Some of these are:

- *Large Caseloads.*
  Earlier in this chapter, we cited an example from the Virginia Department of Rehabilitation in 1949 where the Commissioner recorded that the average caseload per counselor in his agency in 1949 was 709. Obviously, to have any success at all, these counselors had to depend on their clients to place themselves in jobs with minimal counselor involvement.

- *Clients Returning to Previous Employment.*
  When clients are ready to return to work after an illness, injury, or period of medical rehabilitation (and most of them do), they may have already established rapport with their employer and do not need a counselor's intervention for job placement. The former safety director at the Lynchburg Foundry in Lynchburg, Virginia estimates that 85% of the injured foundry workers returned to work in the same job following injury. Injured workers in many of these industries receive case management services during physical restoration and no significant vocational services unless they need to find alternative work.

- *Fear That Counselor Intervention will Stereotype the Client.*
  Several studies have suggested that clients failed to receive normal promotions in situations where counselors secured the job for the client. Counselors working with disabled people must always be careful to avoid employer paternalism when placing clients in a job. Some employers feel that they are helping persons with disabilities by giving them a job and overlook superior performance of these workers when promotions arise.

- *High-Functioning Clients with Job-Seeking Skills.*
  In some locations, clients have a better command of the business community and resources within the community than the placement counselor does. The wise placement counselor will always use the knowledge and skills of the client, and the client's family, friends, and acquaintances to help in the placement process.

  This approach works particularly well when counseling some working people. These clients may have the ability to present their skills to employers without assistance. This is particularly true of working people in the trades when the hiring is done at a supervisory level in the organization. They may also be well established in the community and the client can network with ease in the "hidden job market," but the placement counselor needs to proceed with caution. Clients seldom have the breadth of knowledge it takes to function independently in the job market. This is especially true when the client requires new work or work alternatives.

These are legitimate reasons for using the Laissez-Faire Approach. Studies have shown that the more involved clients are in their own job search, the greater the job satisfaction and the longer they stay on the job. Nevertheless, the Laissez-Faire Approach has its pitfalls that may affect the outcome of job placement with some of these clients. As a counselor involved in job placement, it is helpful to remember these words of caution:

- You may be giving part of the job to the client without any way of determining the client's ability to accept that responsibility. When looking for new work, clients typically rely on resources that have a bad track record for permanent job placement, like the local newspaper, and become discouraged easily, resulting in few job contacts. Before relinquishing complete control to the client, it is often helpful to examine the past work record for consistency and length of time spent with previous employers.

- Research has shown that most clients are not adequately prepared to find their own jobs. A Minnesota Rehabilitation Center study[9] shows serious deficiencies in their client's job-seeking skills: "80% of the clients did not look for work frequently enough, 85% could not explain their skills to employers, and 90% could not explain their handicapping condition."[pg. 22]

The Laissez-Faire Approach is effective only when the placement counselor makes a conscious management decision to allow more freedom based upon the client's unique ability in securing employment and when the counselor conveys that decision to the client directly. The key words are *a conscious management decision*. Too frequently, counselors with multiple duties and a limited amount of time see themselves more as counselors than placement specialist. This role conflict, well documented in the literature, often leads them to make placement decisions by default. To compensate, they spend time in counseling and hope "the job placement thing" will go away. Experience tells us that items of top priority like job placement seldom manage themselves.

Chapter 8: "The Job Search" and Chapter 10: "Networking for Jobs in the Hidden Job Market: A Client-Centered Approach" provide guidance for helping counselors manage clients using the Laissez-Faire Approach in their job search. Moreover, the companion booklet The *Job Search Organizer* is designed to help counselors monitor the activities of clients using the Laissez-Faire Approach during their job search.

## THE SELECTIVE APPROACH TO JOB PLACEMENT

The Selective Approach to job placement had its origin in the practices of the employment service and, according to research sources, refers to the assessment of the capabilities, needs, and other relevant characteristics of clients and matching these to a compatible job. Under this concept, the counselor acts as a resource person and advocate in obtaining the job leads, making the employer contacts, and even accompanying the client to the interview.

In the Selective Approach, the counselor assumes almost complete control of the job placement. Counselors determine the right jobs for the client, locate the jobs, and play the primary role in securing the job. The client assumes a more passive role of attending appointments assigned by their counselors, performing the work, following the direction set by the counselor, and doing pretty much what the counselor tells them to do. Non-compliance on the part of the client can lead to a cancellation of benefits and severance of the placement services. Counselors using this approach evaluate the client's work potential, decide what jobs the client can do, and often prepare employment applications for their client, transport clients to interviews, and, where possible, observe client interaction with employers.

There are circumstances when the Selective Approach can be the necessary and the right approach for clients in job placement:

- *Low Functioning Clients*
  Clients with mental handicapping conditions often need close monitoring by the counselor. The 1980s gave rise to supported employment that has proven very successful for placing clients with mild mental retardation in competitive work. Under the supported employment concept, a supported employment specialist not only secures the job for the client, but most of the time, remains at the worksite for a time to assist the client in learning the job duties, often monitoring learning and performance, and intervening in the event of a performance breakdown.

- *Unmotivated Clients*
  Some clients do not want to work; some clients receiving benefits and other payments lack the incentive to work; some clients fear failure or suffer a lack of self-confidence; and for one reason or another, some just cannot seem to find work. These are the most difficult clients with whom to work. Motives are seldom very clear with these clients. The rehabilitation system, private and public, is based upon the assumption that if given the opportunity, most people want to work. Most experienced counselors believe that work is, in many ways, therapeutic for their clients; that is, a client's physical and mental condition actually gets better when they are engaged in productive activity like work. Unmotivated clients, for whatever reason, require close monitoring, cautious counseling, and continuous problem solving during job placement.

- *Clients Needing Job Consultation and Workplace Modification*
  Rehabilitation counselors are often needed to help employers redesign the work setting or otherwise show employers how jobs can be redesigned and job duties modified in such a way that persons with physical or mental difficulties can perform the needed work. Counselor intervention is often helpful to clients returning to their past work with additional functional limitations. In some work settings, to avoid performance breakdowns, counselors are helpful in checking out the exertion requirements of jobs obtained for clients with physical disabilities to make sure those jobs fit the restrictions set by treating doctors and other medical sources. Good rapport between counselors and employers and counselor ingenuity in job redesign or job re-engineering can create positions for their clients in some of the most improbable situations.

- *Older Workers aged 44 to 65*
  Studies of older, unemployed workers have shown these workers have serious adjustment problems. Many times they are hesitant to accept jobs that they feel are beneath the status of their prior employment; they often feel the job market discriminates against them; sometimes they do not know how to use networking techniques to find jobs; and they seldom know how to transfer their past work traits and skills to other employment. Research has shown that if an opportunity did not exist in the area of their training, older workers feel that they are qualified to do nothing else. In this study[6] of older, rural workers 85% of the participants needed help to locate a suitable job, 52% needed to learn what employers look for in older workers, and 44% needed to improve their self-confidence.[pp. 52-53] Intense counseling and teaching the appropriate job-seeking skills seems to hold the best solution for employment of these workers.

- *Clients with Poor Job-Seeking Skills*
  Some counselors consider job-seeking skills common sense, failing to realize that nothing in this world is more unevenly distributed than common sense. Job-seeking skills continue to arise as major educational deficits of disabled clients. Employers say poor appearance and inadequate job-seeking skills are two of the three most important criteria they use to screen out job seekers. In a Minnesota study,[9] cited earlier, 40% of the clients had poor personal appearance or inappropriate mannerisms and 85% of the clients seeking work could not explain their skills to employers.[pg. 22]

The Selective Approach has its advantages. It is the safest of all the approaches to job placement. The rehabilitation counselor takes almost no risk that after all their hard work clients will say or do something to cost them an employment opportunity. In addition, the counselor is able to determine if the job is within the client's capabilities. On their own, clients often find jobs that are not appropriate for their vocational abilities, or not within their functional limitations—situations that soon lead to frustration and failure.

Finally, one additional advantage to the selective approach to job placement: some employers appreciate the counselor intervention and like to be "sold" on the client's abilities by someone who knows the applicant's capabilities. In these cases, the counselor is there to answer questions employers would otherwise be afraid to ask, given the litigious environment in today's work settings.

Problems arise with this approach, however. First, as a passive partner in the job search, the client learns little or nothing about finding and securing a job. The Chinese proverb: "give a man a fish and you feed him for a day. Teach a man to fish and you feed him for a lifetime," describes the limitation of this approach. What happens if or when a client needs to make a job or career change later? The lack of involvement in this job search becomes a likely obstacle to future employment.

Moreover, this approach builds dependencies. Client's cease to act independently, thinking the counselor is responsible for the job search. In addition, when the counselor assumes pretty much all of the authority, job opportunities are missed which clients could uncover for themselves if they were more involved. Finally, much time is lost as clients await counselor job search and assignments. Olney and Salomone[7] had "designated selective placement as unsuccessful and resulting in poor job satisfaction, due to the controlling role of the rehabilitation professional and the non-participatory role of the job seeker."[pg. 42]

In spite of the criticism from scholars and practitioners, current practices in the marketplace are mostly variations of the selective approach. This is particularly true in private rehabilitation. Counselors in private practice most often locate the jobs and/or refer jobs to their clients. Clients are expected to set the time of the appointments, attend the interviews, and report the results. In some cases, the counselor will set up the appointments and even attend the interviews. To cover themselves, counselors, after the interview, may contact the employers directly for responses to their client's application and learn how the client performed in the interview.

This pragmatic job placement approach seems to have won out over approaches emphasizing more client involvement and vocational counseling. Experienced placement counselors report that many insurance adjusters and case managers prefer this method of placement because the selective approach reduces the chances that clients may sabotage the placement process willfully or unknowingly.

Chapter 9: "The Selective Approach to Job Placement" takes a closer look at ways to sharpen the techniques used in the selective approach. The chapter talks about the way to prepare the client for job placement, considers how counselors may use the internet in the job search, helps counselors read and understand websites for job clarification, and shows how rehabilitation counselors use telephone contacts for reaching the decision makers and relating functional information to employer contacts. This information comes from counselors experienced in job placement and conducting labor market surveys.

## THE CLIENT-CENTERED APPROACH

In the Client-Centered approach job placement becomes a shared responsibility. In client-centered placement, counselors act as a resource person, an agent, and an advocate, standing between the client and the employer. (Not unlike the way it used to be in the early days of rehabilitation when service providers were considered rehabilitation agents, as discussed at the beginning of this chapter).

In the client-centered approach to job placement, the client is the central figure and the primary actor. To this extent, the client-centered approach is closer to the Laissez-Faire approach. However, in this approach the counselor is more involved in the diagnostics, making sure the jobs considered are the right jobs, and providing information clients may need about the job market and the community to undertake an effective job search. While counselors may or may not be involved in the legwork, generally, they gather information, provide job leads, and set up appointments and interviews in situations where they have the most influence or personal contacts.

Moreover, the counselor remains close to the placement process, preparing clients for each step along the way. The counselor teaches clients job-seeking skills, such as how to:

- locate employer contacts,
- fill out applications, and
- present themselves well in an interview.

In addition, the counselor provides encouragement and support, stimulating motivation through a genuine working relationship that includes frequent client-counselor meetings, continuous job-seeking skill training, and planning strategies for the job search.

The client-centered approach utilizes the strengths of both the counselor and the client. The client maintains most of the control during the search for employment, but the counselor has the information needed to monitor the placement activities. Best of all, the client-centered approach opens doors to the "hidden job market" where 65% to 90% of the jobs, and most of the better jobs, are to be found.

The client-centered approach may be the right approach with

*Clients Well-Connected in the Community*

As we shall see later, most of the better jobs come through networking within the community. Once appropriate jobs are identified and locations determined clients could work with families, friends, and acquaintances to secure the jobs, calling upon the counselor to provide the needed information or assistance, such as answering questions about work restrictions.

*Self-Starting Clients*

The client-centered approach to placement requires a high degree of independence, motivation, and persistence on the part of the client. Self-motivation is a key factor in the success of this approach. Clients must regularly seek out opportunities, follow-up on job leads, and know how to use the expertise a counselor can provide. For these clients the client-centered approach can be very efficient because little time is lost between receiving the job leads and acting upon the information. Considering that the average job remains open only 15 days, the ability to act quickly can be a critical factor in the job search.

*Clients with Job-Seeking Abilities*

By profession, counselors know about counseling. They also determine vocational interests, physical and mental limitations, capabilities, and how these factors affect a client's ability to work. Most counselors have a good grasp of the world of work in general. Yet, for most counselors, whatever job-placement abilities they possess, they have gained from practical experience on the job. As a result, clients who have work experience may have higher-level job-seeking skills than their counselors do. The client-centered approach divides the tasks of job placement and assigns each task to the most capable and experienced party. Counselors who succeed best in this method will be those who ask themselves constantly "which of us is best suited to get the task done?"

The client-centered approach is meant to recognize the strengths and limitations of the primary participants in job placement. With this approach, the counselor and the client become a team, both working toward the same goal.

Chapter 10: "The Client-Centered Approach: Networking for Jobs in the Hidden Job Market" presents a model for managing job placement using the client-centered approach. Most rehabilitation counselors believe in the basic principles of this approach, (e.g., clients need to be the central actors in the job search; counselors believe that by having clients closely involved in their own rehabilitation they learn how to find jobs; and, by being more involved they find work that is more satisfying and long lasting). Nevertheless, in practice, counselors are reluctant to relax their managerial control without some way of keeping track of what is going on in the job search. Their fears and concerns are not without merit. One of the obstacles with using the client-centered approach has always been that counselors have few ways to monitor the activities of their clients in the job-seeking process. This problem is particularly apparent in worker compensation cases where clients are one-on-one with their counselors.

Chapter 10 also presents a discussion of how to use the *Job Search Organizer*, a communication tool designed to promote continuous dialogue between the counselor and client during the job search. This discussion takes the counselor and client step-by-step through a strategy for managing the job search, tracking progress, and recording each job contact. Additionally, the presentation in the *Job Search Organizer* shows clients how to involve family, friends, and acquaintances to assist in finding jobs, and leads them to ways for uncovering jobs in the "hidden job market" where most of the better jobs are found.

# TOPICS FOR GROUP DISCUSSION

1. Professions such as medicine and law are largely defined by their body of knowledge. What are the essential knowledge components for rehabilitation counseling? Make a list of what you consider the main job tasks of the rehabilitation counseling profession, then rank order the tasks; and, from the list, come to a group consensus on a definition. Compare your definition with the definition provided by Paul Ellwood[3] at the beginning of the chapter.

2. Chapter 1 begins with a discussion about how the role of the service provider in rehabilitation has changed through the years and how the name of the service provider has given evidence of the direction the program was taking at the time. How would the rank order of the job tasks you made in Question #1 change if the service provider were an agent, a supervisor, and a counselor? Which job tasks would rank higher and which job tasks would "fall from grace?"

3. Chapter 1 suggests that rehabilitation counselors have been reluctant to accept the role of manager in rehabilitation. Why has this been the case? Have times changed with the advent of professional case managers? Are today's rehabilitation

counselors reluctant to accept management in the counselor's role? What conflict exists between the role of counselor and the role of a manager? List several. In small groups, explore the dual role of the counselor in rehabilitation.

4. Divide the class or training participants into three (3) groups, and choose a leader to guide the discussion and a recorder to present the views of each group to the larger class or group. Each group will take one approach to job placement: Laissez-Faire, Selective, and Client-Centered. The assignment for each group is to make a list of the pros and cons of each of these approaches to job placement. Then, decide what counselors have to do to make that approach work in professional practice. Finally, come to a group consensus as to what you believe is the most desirable approach for working with disabled clients.

5. Does the rehabilitation process change in mid-stream as presented in Chapter 1? What is the difference between motivation and empowerment?

6. How important is managerial control in the case process? What potential dangers exist in exerting control over the process? What is appropriate control? Which management approach presented in Chapter 1 is most appropriate for rehabilitation counselors: Selective vs. Client Centered? (The beginnings of Chapters 9 and 10 provide definition and an historical approach to each).

# INDIVIDUAL EXERCISES

1. Locate and make a list of the many certifications presently offered by the Commission on Rehabilitation Counseling to the service provider in rehabilitation. Answer the following questions: Do you think there are too many or too few? Do the many certifications dilute the professional identity of the service provider?

2. Examine more closely the discussion about counselor control in job placement presented in Chapter 1. How do you feel about a counselor exerting control in a counselor-client relationship? This is an open-ended question. There is no definitive answer. Feel free to express your opinion about client freedom vs. counselor control and offer alternatives.

# REFERENCES

[1]Cull, John G. & Hardy, Richard E. (1972). "Vocational Rehabilitation: Profession & Practice," Springfield, Illinois: Charles C. Thomas, Publisher

[2]Department of Labor, *Occupational Outlook Handbook*, Winter, 2011-2012. US Department of Labor, US Bureau of Labor Statistics.

[3]Ellwood, P. M. Jr. (1968). "Can We Afford So Many Rehabilitation Professions," *Journal of Rehabilitation*, 34(3), pp. 21-22.

[4]Farr, J. M. (1990). *Job Finding Fast*. Mission Hills, CA. Glencoe/McGraw Hill, Educational Division,

[5]Lassiter, (1972). *Vocational Rehabilitation: Profession and Practice*. Springfield, IL: Charles C. Thomas.

[6]Myers, J. W. (1983). "Counseling the Older Rural Worker: A Report." *Journal Employment Counseling*, 20(2), pp.51-60.

[7]Olney, M. F. & Salomone, P. R. (1992). Empowerment and Choice in Supported Employment: Helping People to Help Themselves. *Journal of Applied Rehabilitation Counseling*, 23(3), 41-44.

[8]Peters, Thomas J. and Waterman, Jr., Robert H. (1982). *In Search of Excellence*. New York: Harper & Roe.

[9]Roessler, R.W. (1985). "Self-Starting in the Job Market: The Continuing Need for Job-Seeking Skills in Rehabilitation." *Journal of Applied Rehabilitation Counseling*, 16(2), 22-25.

[10]Tew-Washburn, S. (2001). Job Placement Methods and Models. Eleven unnumbered pages.

[11]Vandergoot, D. (1984). "Placement Practices in Vocational Rehabilitation." *Journal of Applied Rehabilitation Counseling*, 15(3), pp.25-27.

[12]Vocational Rehabilitation Amendments of 1954, Public Law 565.

# THE AMERICAN CHARACTER: LIFE AND STRUCTURE IN THE AMERICAN SOCIETY & THEIR IMPLICATIONS FOR JOB PLACEMENT

# PREFACE

*There were grades of society, people of good family, people of unclassified family, people of no family. Everybody knew everybody and was affable to everybody and nobody put on any visible acts; yet the class lines were quite clearly drawn and the familiar social life of each class was limited to that class. It was a little democracy which is full of liberty, equality and the Fourth of July, and sincerely so, too; yet you perceived that the aristocratic taint was there. It was there and nobody found fault with the fact, or even stopped to reflect that its presence was an inconsistency.*

Mark Twain [On Hanibal, MO]

To the Reader:

The purpose of chapters two and three is to bring about a better understanding of the different groups of people or classes which make up our complex society in America and to show how class behavior affects job placement of persons with disabilities. Most Americans share certain values, such as those spelled out in our Constitution: life, liberty, and the pursuit of happiness. Nevertheless, there are vast differences in the way individuals and groups think about their place in society; and, in particular, their work and preparation for work.

Rehabilitation counselors are a primary link between employers–the people with the jobs–and our clientele–injured workers or persons with disabilities in need of help to enter/return to work or to find a work alternative. The employers we meet are primarily entrepreneurs and managers who run private or public businesses. Most of the entrepreneurs and managers come from advantaged homes where education is a prerequisite within the family and upward mobility in a business or an occupation is a hoped for and expected goal. Career development usually means seminars, workshops, and college degrees to learn new knowledge that will lead to higher levels of achievement. They value ownership and wealth accumulation. These people make the everyday decisions that lead to success or failure in their chosen business or occupation.

On the other hand, our clientele in rehabilitation come mostly from the "working class" or a group we are calling in this study "baseline people" where work skills are more important than formal education. Learning work skills and lateral movement within occupations are more likely than upward mobility, where training and education lead to higher levels of work skills within an occupation. Where physical and often heavy work is usually the norm. They work for someone else and normally have little or no authority over business decisions.

Most of us who provide rehabilitation service to injured workers and persons with disabilities come from middle class America. While we share some of the values of both groups, generally, we have not been employers nor have we experienced the jobs, first-hand, done by our clientele. To be effective in what we do, we must acquire knowledge about jobs, how they are performed, the job duties required, the preparation necessary to perform the jobs, and understand the people doing the jobs, both the workers and their employers.

Chapters 2 & 3 are about the people of rehabilitation: namely, the people we serve and the people who hire them. These chapters seek to provide a foundation for understanding the groups within communities throughout America; and, in particular, how each group views work and the workplace. Chapter 2 looks at some of the sociological research on American community life and presents a composite view of five main groups within our society. Chapter 3 gets into more specifics about work and the workplace.

# INTRODUCTION

The search for open and available jobs usually begins by looking for the right system–the system that leads clients to a level of employment suited to their talents and career aspirations, yet employment that lies within their skills and abilities as well as, in the case of persons with disabilities, their functional limitations. Unfortunately, the search for a reliable system usually ends in failure. The reason for this is, as Richard Bolles[1] has so aptly stated in *What Color Is Your Parachute,* "the job system in this country is no system at all."[pg.10] If there were a fool-proof job system, one that everybody could go to in locating the ideal job, be assured that your state employment office would have the system in place, eliminate all of the competition, and grow to unheard-of bureaucratic excellence. Nevertheless, the truth of the matter is that the state employment system makes only seven (7%) percent of the job placements in this country and roughly forty (40%) percent of those are vacated within thirty days or less.

In a country like ours where employers are free to choose those who work for them, finding jobs is not about systems, but about people, in particular, people meeting people, and people helping people, though the search for the right system goes on endlessly. Over seventy (70%) percent of the successful job seekers in the United States find their jobs independent of any system; working through others, on their own, or going directly to the employer. In smaller communities and in rural areas, estimates of people networking and making independent contact with employers runs as high as ninety (90%) percent. Most of us know these facts are true because most of us have gotten our jobs in this way. Often, what we do not know is how to get from A to Z, which employers to see, what the people with the jobs are like, or how we can reach the decision-makers.

There is no set direction for a job search; no predetermined path to follow that will take a job seeker directly from unemployment to a job. Still, there is a place to begin, and that is in getting to know the community and its people. Before settling down with a cup of coffee and flipping through the want ads or making cold calls to local employers, counselors must take a few minutes to try and understand the social and economic structure of the community. In a nutshell, people, like ourselves, helping others find jobs in a community, need to take a glance at the "big picture."

Seeing the "big picture" is what Chapters 2 and 3 are all about. In these chapters, we do this by using the American small town as a microcosm of America as a whole. That is, we talk about life and work in the small town and ask you to accept what we say about small towns as typical of life and work in most settings across the country. As a result, you will be able to apply the concepts and strategies for job placement almost anywhere you may work. You are not limited to small towns. While there are obvious differences between cities and small towns, we have found that social patterns and the way people interact with one another are really not very different from place to place in this country. Using the small town as a microcosm to reveal the character of the people is more useful in contemporary America than ever before because:

- Today, the workplace in small towns and cities bears remarkable similarities. Access through the Interstate highway network and advances in communications have brought about dramatic shifts in work and the work environments of small-town America. The internet has replaced much of the agrarian culture that once characterized this country and created a new economy with job opportunities for over half the population.

- The sociology of the small town gives us an understanding of how Americans think and act as individuals and as a people. This allows us to focus our attention upon real people in real communities. This reality breathes life into dry job placement and management concepts, and gives meaning to otherwise empty words like networking and community development. After all, we are talking about people; and in particular, people meeting people and people helping people.

- Using the small town allows us to place community life in America "under a spyglass," so to speak, in order to test concepts and illustrate ideas about job placement. From these concepts and ideas, we draw conclusions about the worker and the workplace. We know that what we say is based not only upon counselor experiences but is firmly rooted in established social research by observers of the American scene that takes us back a hundred years and beyond.

- Finally, the best research we have about how Americans as a people feel about their social and political systems come from the fiction of creative writers of the Realistic Period in America, (e.g., Mark Twain, and Sinclair Lewis), and from research sociologists, (e.g., A. B. Hollinshead, Arthur Vidich, and Joseph Bensman, to name a few). In what has come to be known as the "Revolt from the Village," creative writers explore the American culture, showing the character and values of the people, the strengths and weaknesses of the culture, and the attitude of local citizens toward the workplace in their society. The small town serves as a backdrop for their social research and their satire. Likewise, using the small town as a setting for their landmark studies, *Elmstown Youth* and *Small Town in Mass Society*,[8] research sociologists look at factors that have shaped the American culture and its people yesterday and today.

# THE SMALL TOWN: AMERICA IN MICROCOSM

The American small-town is used in this text in order for us to better understand community life in America and discern individual and group patterns of behavior that give insight into the "American Character." The following behavior patterns are critical to our understanding and success in job placement.

- how American people view their community,
- how they act toward each other in social situations,
- how they organize themselves, and, in particular,
- how they view work.

Locating common threads in the behavior of people within the community is helpful as counselors become more comfortable in their interactions with people in the community and make employment outcomes more predictable for their clients.

*It is all tied together! We cannot overemphasize the importance of Chapters 2 and 3. You will find that research from these chapters forms the foundation for many job placement concepts and techniques suggested later.*

The Authors

The sections that follow present two (2) major themes frequently associated with American community life. Theme 1, "The Best of All Possible Worlds," looks at both the ideal and the reality of life, work in a democratic society, and the values we hold as a people. Theme 2, "The Myth of Equality: The Small Town Stratified," examines the class structure that calls into question the democratic ideal while showing characteristics commonly held by each class or group of people and suggests how the class structure shapes the concept of work for all its citizens. Each theme concludes with practical guidance for the rehabilitation counselor. In each of these sections the writings of social scientists, creative writers, and other observers of the American scene, "bring to life" the concepts associated with life and work in America.

# THEME ONE: "THE BEST OF ALL POSSIBLE WORLDS"

Observers of the national scene have long noticed that people living in small towns often display an exuberant and optimistic pride in their community. They tend to believe that they are a close-knit people where "everybody knows everybody," a closeness that can be shared by all who chose to participate. They believe that they really get close to people and involved in the lives of their neighbors in a positive way that gives added meaning to everyone. To most villagers, their community may aptly be described as "the best of all possible worlds."

The youthful energy that is so much a part of the character of these people may be found just about anywhere in America; but this youthful energy takes form and expression in almost every small town. We see it in the Fourth of July celebrations, such as the Staunton, Virginia, "Happy Birthday USA" with its patriotic parades, fireworks, and live country music concerts featuring hometown favorites, the Statler Brothers; in the hoopla that surrounds the homecoming football games in towns in the Fall on Friday nights all across the country; and, occasionally, we find this small-town community celebration spilling over into the cities, like the excitement surrounding the Minnesota Twins, Atlanta Braves World Series of 1991 with its "homer hankies" and "chop shops." This youthful energy is not limited to small towns. More recently, we saw this kind of youthful exuberance displayed in the way people all around the country rallied around the people of New York following the September 11, 2001 terrorist disaster.

Cynics may call this display of civic emotion foolishness; psychologists may consider this release of emotional energy as "the child unleashed"; and sociologists may see these displays of community feelings as examples of an immature society that never seems to grow up. The feelings are, nonetheless, real and in many ways positive. Beneath this surface emotion seems to lie a basic faith in human potential; a restoration of renaissance humanism, that believes most things are possible through striving and hard work and accepts human error and shortcomings as temporary and changeable. We see this exuberance in the peoples' attitude toward each other, in their political systems, in their moral values, and in the workplace.

## AMERICAN DEMOCRACY AT WORK

Using a quaint, provincial term, "just plain folks," is the way people living in small towns look upon themselves. "Folks" include everyone in the community, including rich or poor, for everyone can share equally in the genuine qualities of town life. It does not require money, status, family background, learning, nor refined manners to be one of the "folks." In short, as seen through the eyes of the townspeople, small towns are democracies at work, just the kind of place our ancestors had in mind.

Equality among local citizens carries over to the political system as well, giving the town what its defenders consider the perfect example of applied democracy. Expressing the attitude of the people of Springdale, Vidich & Bensman[8] say,

> *Whenever they can, community leaders encourage broad participation in all spheres of public life: everyone is urged and invited to attend public meetings and everyone is urged to "vote not as a duty, but as a privilege." The equality of all men at the ballot box, each according to his own conscience, in a community where you know all the candidates personally, where votes cannot be bought and where you know the poll keeper is the hallmark of equality that underpins all other equality.*[pg. 41]

There are classes that create social divisions and, as we shall see, most townspeople recognize that divisions do exist between people. But community people believe that these "little democracies" possess a community *esprit de corps* based upon a morality composed of friendliness, human understanding, and concern for one's neighbor which transcends class lines and provides all the people ready access to the whole town, regardless of their social position.

## JUST PLAIN FOLKS: THE MORAL COMPONENT

Equality is only one aspect of the small-town concept. Implied in the term "folks" is also a whole set of moral values, (i.e., fair play, trustworthiness, good-neighborliness, helpfulness, sobriety, and clean living, "where a spoken word is as good as a contract. . .where everybody knows everybody. . .where you say hello to anybody").

These values arise from the personal, daily contact people have with each other, giving folks a closer identification with the town and a deeper commitment to the people of the town. Describing the people of Hillsboro in her novel, *Hillsboro People*, Dorothy Canfield Fisher[3] says, "If you live in the country, you're really married to humanity, for better or worse, not just on speaking terms with it."[pg.11] The author of this statement knows these people are no better or worse than those living in the city; in fact, she realizes that by urban standards, their lives may seem dull and insignificant. The slower pace of life and the opportunity to stop their daily routine and to notice others gives townspeople a deeper commitment to life.

American writers have provided numerous examples to show the way townspeople care for people and rally in support of each other in times of crisis. For example, the narrator in Zona Gale's,[4] *Friendship Village*, recalls such an incident outside the town of Friendship one night.

> *A train carrying children from a nearby orphanage derailed and overturned, killing the matron in charge and injuring several children. Upon learning about the incident the townspeople pitched in and worked together to rescue the children from the wreckage. While some attempted to alleviate the suffering of the injured, others took the remaining children into the church where they fed, comforted, and entertained them throughout the night. The next morning, after the orphanage had sent representatives to escort the children to their destination, the narrator summarizes her impressions of the generosity and benevolence of her neighbors. In her simple brogue, she says, "if you want to love folks, just get into some kind o' respectable trouble. . .an' you'll see so much loveableness that the trouble'll kind o' spindle out an' leave nothin' but the love doin' business."* [pg. 93]

We would expect any group of Americans, or people from any country, for that matter, to act in much the same way if a train overturned carrying orphan children. Most townspeople would say this behavior is typical of the way their neighbors act in times of distress, even when the recipients may not always be deserving. In just such a situation, Hamlin Garland[5] in *Main Traveled Roads*, illustrates the openness and acceptance the town of Bluff Siding showed in the treatment of the Bloom family, newcomers to the small community.

*To get out of the rat race of Chicago, Robert Bloom moved his family to the small Wisconsin town of Bluff Siding. On his first day in town, Robert Bloom makes the mistake of treating as common laborers the movers he has hired to transport the belongings from the train depot to his new home, as he had been accustomed to doing in the city, without realizing these movers were, in actuality, his new neighbors.*

*Through his oversight, Robert offends the simple pride of the townspeople; and, for the next several months, they will have nothing to do with him: "They suspected him. They had only the estimate of the men who had worked for him; and while they were civil, they plainly didn't need him in the slightest degree, except as a topic of conversation." Reacting to the town's assessment of him, Robert Bloom and his wife decided that the townspeople were living caricatures of dullness and pettiness and "their squat little town was a caricature of themselves. But, when one afternoon Robert Bloom has a slight stroke on the street of Bluff Siding, the town demonstrates its willingness to forget former resentments by showing him and his family kindness and attention. As he experiences the combined display of friendliness, human concern, and neighborliness, Robert Bloom learns the meaning of "folks" in a small town. In his final appraisal of Bluff Siding, Robert Bloom affirms "they will never be caricatures again–to me."* pg. 316

People helping people lies at the core of the American small town value system. It transcends class lines and narrow social prejudice. These people see themselves as living close enough together to share ideas and information intimately. The closeness results in a deeper commitment to both the community and to each other. If, indeed, changes are needed in the governing political system, an informed representation is present to accommodate the flexible democratic process.

## THE ETHIC OF WORK

The public ideology of equality and the private, underlying morality also has its economic correlates. The inequality of income and wealth do not go unnoticed; indeed, they are closely watched. Nevertheless, such differences are not publicly weighed and evaluated as an assessment of the person. What makes a difference, say the researchers of *Small Town in Mass Society*[8] "is not wealth but the character behind it." In Springdale, for instance, "The measure of a person's worth, for all public social purposes is the diligence and perseverance with which a person pursues their economic ends: "the worker," the "good worker," the "hard worker" in contrast to the "fly-by-night schemer" or the person who tries to get in with the better people by aping them in dress and possessions which only money can buy. The good person, therefore, is the person who works; and in the public estimation, the fact of working transcends, even explains, economic differentials. In Springdale, as in many other towns, "work has its own social day of judgment and the judgment conferred is self-respect and respectability." [8, pg. 42]

# THE BEST OF ALL POSSIBLE WORLDS: A COUNSELOR'S SELF-FULFILLING PROPHESY

The profile that emerges shows a people with a deep love for their community and their neighbors, a strong attachment to the democratic ideal, and a value system based upon fair play and a practical work ethic. Right or wrong, fact or fiction, the profile is reasonably accurate in portraying the way provincial people, and Americans in general, view themselves and their community.

If these conditions are true, then the small town sounds like a comfortable place to conduct a job hunt, and it can be. An awful lot depends upon the attitude and expectations of the rehabilitation counselor. To feel the sense of community may require you, as a counselor, to be closer to people, strangers, if you will, than you typically are, or wish to be, particularly if the surroundings are unfamiliar. Social distance may be the most visible difference between small towns, small cities, and large metropolitan areas. Perhaps Robert Tournier[7] in his article, "Small Towns at the Crossroads" states it best by saying,

> *Many of our attitudes toward small towns are a fundamental outgrowth of characteristics of urban life, for one of the ways we have learned to survive in cities is to wall ourselves off, both physically and emotionally, from each other. As we have done so, our attitudes toward interaction have changed. For to extend the hand of friendship in many of our cities is to risk losing one's watch if not one's hand, and interaction with others is not seen as rewarding but as incurring unwanted obligations. To people unaccustomed to this situation, life in small towns is threatening indeed: people there talk to you and by so doing raise the specter of a kind of clannishness threatening to those who pride themselves on their independence.* [pg. 31]

Job placement in a community where people have close personal ties to one another does mean getting closer to people and the uneasiness Robert Tournier[6] describes can be very unsettling to some counselors as social distance narrows. By training and education, we learn to have our clients open themselves emotionally to us; but, all too often, we remain the people asking the questions, revealing very little of ourselves.

For some counselors, openness can be difficult. Distancing yourself socially during job placement can be a problem in any sized community, large or small, but "playing your cards close to your chest" can pose special problems for job placement. In most communities, the people you meet will see themselves as opening to you:

- Go to the local Chamber of Commerce and you will likely find a representative, possibly the director, who is proud of the community and will readily give you free material and tell you about the general outlook and the progressive plans their town has for future growth.

- Talk to local employers about jobs and the way these jobs are performed, and you will likely find them friendly and receptive, even when you quiz them about specific jobs for your client. In fact, the information you gain about jobs from local employers is generally more accurate and reliable than the information you gain from the statewide services, including the employment offices and vocational rehabilitation agencies.

- Tell community people (i.e., desk clerks at the local motel where you may be staying, waitresses in nearby restaurants where you may dine, or just about anybody), what you do for a living–find jobs for persons with disabilities–and you will likely find them interested and willing to be involved, much like we saw in the earlier illustration from the citizens of Friendship Village. In fact, many of your colleagues in rehabilitation surface their best job leads in this way, leads that often result in successful placements.

Be aware that they will expect the same openness from you. Foremost, the people you meet will want to know who you are and what brought you to their town. They will want to know something about you–where you are from, your family linkage, if any, to the community, and possibly some personal details about you and your occupation.

If you expect to be successful in their town, you must be prepared to reveal some personal information about yourself. Furtive behavior on the part of the counselor is the death knell to job placement in small communities. Even if you are shy and reserved, you must be willing to self-disclose, to provide some degree of self-revelation, and to be measured, as the community is apt to do, as sincere and doing purposeful work.

Your self-disclosure only provides a momentary beginning to dialogue, getting your foot in the door, so to speak. Your long-range success may well depend upon your attitude toward the town and its people. You see, the message to you as a counselor in job placement is that in a small town, or in any community, you will find a self-fulfilling prophesy at work. If you believe that the people of the community are friendly and open in their communication with you, that they care about one another, and that they possess a democratic community with a positive social and work ethic, then they will likely reinforce your assumptions with incredible responsiveness.

On the other hand, if you hold negative beliefs about the town, seeing them as clannish and provincial, backward and indifferent to change, and stereotypical small-town types, as did Robert Bloom in the earlier example, you will likely get that response from them, and leave the town disgruntled and unsuccessful.

The self-fulfilling prophesy–what you give is what you get–is not unique to small towns. It is hard to imagine your succeeding in any sized community in this tough business without getting involved with people. What is different is that being in a community where everybody knows everybody, the kind of person you are perceived to be (particularly if you are a newcomer to the town) is quickly determined and transmitted, and your openness and attitude toward people in the town spells success or failure in your job placement efforts.

# THEME 2: THE MYTH OF EQUALITY: "THE TOWN STRATIFIED"

Supporters of the village way of life have perpetuated the long-standing belief that the American small town stands as the last bulwark for the true democratic ideal. They recognize obvious social and economic differences in the little communities; but they believe small towns possess a social equality based upon the close contact among people that transcends class boundaries. The town where "everybody knows everybody" precludes any fixed and rigid boundaries.

To support their democratic ideal, supporters cite examples of how newcomers, like the Robert Blooms, were greeted on the streets with friendly salutations from complete strangers; how in churches and at the polls, everyone regardless of social and economic circumstances receives identical treatment; and how, even in tightly-stratified towns, like Gopher Prairie from the novel *Main Street* by Sinclair Lewis,[6] the immigrant Miles Bjomstam feels it his privilege to stop the wealthy mill owner on the open street and debate with him issues of local and national significance.

America is a nation of classes. No matter how we choose to deal with the inconsistencies, American society is caste along economic and social lines, even more so than ethnic and racial lines. Casually, we talk about "middle class values" and refer to the people who work with their hands as "the working people." The "rags to riches" dream in America holds out the hope that anyone, regardless of class position, can rise above their circumstances. Moreover, the concept of class that structures society throughout America is perhaps even more pronounced in small towns. The evidence is abundant. As we shall see, the class system in small towns, as well as elsewhere in America, shapes the economic as well as the social outlook of the people.

## CLASS STRUCTURE IN THE SMALL TOWN

The class profiles that follow are not meant to perpetuate small-town stereotypes or to suggest that all people living in towns are going to conform to the patterns of behavior suggested here. The class profiles are not meant to "pigeon hole" anybody. Nor are you going to find that the characteristics suggested here apply across the board to every individual or group you find in a community. An analysis of class groupings will help you understand group behavior in a community, behavior that you will find relatively universal in community life throughout America, and help you draw conclusions from the class analysis that will be helpful to your job placement activities in any community.

The following class profiles are a group composite from several sociological studies of small town life; all the statements in quotation marks come directly from these studies. Our belief is that you will find the profiles provide a reasonably accurate picture of the social groups in most small as well as large communities. Knowledge of these groups and the values they hold should give you a frame of reference for your case planning.

The five (5) class profiles considered here are in descending order based upon their prestige within the town:

*Class 1: The Aristocracy.* The aristocracy is the least visible, and, in many ways, exerts the least influence upon the community. Their influence, if any, lies behind the scene. You know them as "the old families," "the society class," or the "top four hundred." Their prestige is based upon three characteristics:

1. *money*: "Nobody is in this class without money, but it's not money alone,"

2. *family connections*: "You can rate if you have enough money and little or no family," and

3. *acceptance*: "They are accepted by the people in the group as equals; if they are not accepted, they don't belong."

Newer communities, those lacking a significant tradition, may not have an aristocracy and, in these towns, persons from Class II stand at the top of society and receive the status and prestige of an aristocracy. Their ranking is based upon wealth and having achieved material status worthy of admiration. Gopher Prairie of Sinclair Lewis', *Main Street*[6] is just such a town.

> *In Gopher Prairie, the second generation of inhabitants, the author explains, "were more materialistic then their forebears." The prosperous banker living in the "largest residence" was their provincial sage; but the townspeople had elevated Percy Bresnahan, the president of an automobile concern in Boston and the only individual to achieve recognition outside of the town, to the level of a national hero.* [pg. 43]

In the novel, every member of the elite society in Gopher Prairie attempts to identify with Percy Bresnahan, the business magnate, because he represents the "rags to riches" fulfillment of the American Dream to which most citizens aspire.

Older, more established towns, however, often have an aristocracy whose immediate prestige comes from neither wealth (though wealth may have gotten them there) nor power. They serve more or less a ceremonial function in the town, giving the town roots and a link with the past.

Among aristocrats, leisure, not labor, is dignified; and travel is an avidly followed pursuit. As little time as possible is devoted to earning a living. To them education is not highly regarded either for knowledge or for the tools of a professional career. Their young people finish high school and go on to attend a "good" college or university; but if these young people have a successful career, they will likely spend it elsewhere, usually not returning to their hometown except, possibly, during vacation or holiday.

Members of the aristocracy typically live on a depleted income derived from home ownership, securities, and annuities, and a small income from "acceptable jobs," like a bank clerk or court reporter, a small, deviant farm operation, or the operation of a small family business. In keeping with their recognized function, much of their limited income is spent on preserving the homestead, but not modernizing it with new appliances or up-to-date home decorations. Obviously, they are not conspicuous in their consumption or their expansionist attitude. Their dominant behavior patterns are hoarding family funds earned in the past.

Aristocrats tend to remain socially aloof from the rest of society and are a threat to no one. Characteristically, they seclude themselves, limiting their personal associations to persons within their small group. Personal publicity in the newspaper is regarded as a social weakness; and, for the most part, to be avoided, but their aloofness from the main stream and their social position often give them the advantage of:

- knowing just about everyone in the town,
- seeing, accurately, the relationships between groups and individuals within the community without threatening their own class or anyone else, and
- being able to cut across class lines–to reach out and touch just about anyone.

What a valuable contact local aristocrats can become to the perceptive counselor in job placement.

*Class II: The Oligarchy of Respectability.* These are the prominent, upper middle class business and professional people of the community. Typically, they have family connections, but not much money. Although they are likely to have small accumulations of savings, it takes most of the income to live and maintain their life-style within the community. Security rather than wealth seems to be their economic goal.

While most have achieved their position in society from their own efforts (some from inheritance), they hold a strong link with the town's past, revering the homes of the "old families" and the "halo" of past glories. Much of their time is spent in community service projects that improve the town and restore traditional symbols. They often try to identify with the aristocracy; but they are keenly aware of the social distance standing between the two classes.

These people are the "movers and shakers" in the town, the community leaders, the decision-makers at the top level of society. Members normally include the president of the local bank, manager of a public utility company, personnel manager of the mill, most lawyers, several doctors, owners of large, family-owned farms; and owners of family-owned businesses and agencies. Their incomes are derived from personal participation in an independent profession, such as law, medicine, engineering, architecture, or dentistry; in the operation of a family-owned business; from a salaried executive position in a business owned by a member of a Class I family; from a salaried, professional position in a public office; or from the administration of the local school system: principal or superintendent.

To most of the town, these people are society. They dominate the prestigious clubs: the country clubs, the book clubs, and certain service clubs; they provide leadership to the community through membership in power-wielding organizations, like the chamber of commerce or local political parties; and they are the employers, the class of people you and your client must approach to secure the better jobs in the town.

These middle-class citizens believe that their social position and financial success come from self-improvement and expansion of appreciable assets. To them, education is the prime requisite. It is no wonder, then, that this class contains the most highly educated individuals. Moreover, most of the economic activity is directed toward the enhancement of possessions that increase in value, such as buying homes, adding acreage, and increasing propriety equity. In the past, usually all of their income was derived from the father's work. Now, however, work for women and youth in this class is becoming more common and accepted.

Class II people are also the "culture bearers" of the community, setting the standards for taste and culture. As decision-makers and as working leaders of the community, they have borne the brunt of the attacks from the critics. Sinclair Lewis,[6] in his satire, *Main Street,* labels this group the Oligarchy of Respectability indicating that he feels Class II people control the small-town value system; and, therefore, they are the only class of people capable of making the changes he feels are needed in their provincial values and life-style.

*Class III: The Social Aspirants.* Of all the classes, this "fringe middle-class" exhibits the strongest social feelings. They look to the Class I aristocrats for leadership and social direction; but they actually receive all of these from Class II. Most of these people in Class III come from blue-collar backgrounds, and consider themselves to have risen in society: not because of family connections and inherited money like Class I: "few have social connections outside of the churches and lodges"; or because of education like Class II: "few have a four-year college education (though this has changed somewhat in the last several decades as children from working-class backgrounds have obtained college educations). Class III people attribute their rise in society to personal abilities and hard work. The only limitation in their social progress, they believe, results from the upper classes "keeping us down."

The "Social Aspirants" are owners of small businesses or farms; independent professionals: school teachers, many counselors, nurses, vocational teachers, stenographers, secretaries, seamstresses, beauticians, some managers, and clerks in the mines, mills, banks, retail establishments, and public services. Notice, unlike in Class II, this list includes occupations normally performed by women. This is because, typically, both husband and wife work, and, as a rule, see to it that their children work as well, if for no other reason than to learn the value of money.

Work with the "Social Aspirants" knows no limits. In fact, much of their self-esteem as a group comes from the belief that their success, their having "lifted themselves above the masses," can be directly attributed to hard work, industriousness, and frugality. As a result, it is not unusual to find a husband in a full-time job and his wife operating an independent business, shop, or farm. Unfortunately, the income they make, while providing enough money for life's comforts and conveniences, leaves little for investment. Nevertheless, they are frugal, often delaying their buying or restricting their buying to the absolute necessities. Yet, when they do buy, as in their home furnishings, they will likely seek value, quality, and durability.

Members of this class of people are ardent joiners, and most of their leisure time is involved in some kind of organized activity. For men, it is membership in lodges, and veterans and civic groups. Women are members of the auxiliaries, social clubs, and church groups. They attend church with the same kind of zeal that they approach work, feeling regular attendance at church demonstrates a kind of moral responsibility, and for their social activities, they seek "respectable publicity." Unlike Class I that avoids publicity in the local media and Class II that avoids mention "too frequently," the social aspirants avidly advertise their activities in the social columns and in other parts of the newspaper.

*Class IV: The Working People.* The Working People have few social aspirations, regarding themselves as 'living right but never getting anywhere." Typically, they are very conscious of the class structure. They distinguish sharply between "people like us" and the solidly ambitious higher classes. The working people almost despise those below, referring to them as "the reliefers, the loafers, and the criminal element." The upper classes look upon the working people as "poor but honest, hard-workers, who pay their taxes and raise their children properly, but never seem to get ahead." Generally, the working people regard themselves as the backbone of the community.

These people do mostly skilled and semi-skilled labor in the local trades, or in the mills, factories, and mines. Some are clerks in local stores; some own small service businesses in the skilled trades, such as plumbing, heating, and air conditioning. Their education is usually high school or below. In practice, they often discourage their young people who aspire to continue their education beyond high school because they cannot see the value in education unless it enhances their skills. (Their biases toward additional education for their young people does not seem to be as strong today as in the past, as many young people from working-class families are receiving education through the community college systems across the country to obtain additional skills and training).

Unlike the social aspirants, they are not joiners. Generally, they do not belong to the civic organizations; however, they do associate with others in certain social clubs where people of their own class congregate, such as the Elks and the Moose clubs. Many are not active churchgoers; and, generally, they limit their associations to intra-class relationships, having little social contact with persons in either Class III "The Social Aspirants" or Class V "The Baseline Villagers."

Both husband and wife work, as a rule, but their earnings are required to support the family. Little remains for investment. When they purchase durable goods, their practice is to use store credit available to them in the town. Their leisure is spent at home or in activities offered to the public, such as the community swimming pool at the park, little league baseball, or the Quarterback football program for kids. At home on weekends they spend time "fixing things up" or "working around the house." Little time is spent reading magazines or newspapers, except those printed in the town.

*Class V: The Baseline Villagers.* "The Baseline Villagers" are the only group that does not fall within the town's conception of "just plain folks". They are identified in the literature as "the shack people," as most often they live in a special section of the town, the "Poles" or "Irish", though the group is made up mostly of native Americans, often among the oldest inhabitants of the town. Almost all of "the baseline villagers" perform jobs that are unskilled or semi-skilled: laborers, machine operators, factory workers, farmhands, waiters, dishwashers, cooks, domestics, janitors, etc. If the families contain both husband and wife, they usually both hold jobs outside of the home.

It is not their nationality or their occupations, but their behavioral patterns as a group, and the response of the community to their behavior, that place them in the lower ranks of society. It seems that everything the baseline villagers do in life leads to failure. Their parents do it to them, setting an example with fractured relationships; the community does it to them, branding them and their families as outcasts and keeping them from the wealth of the community; and they do it to themselves, living up to the expectations of the community with self-defeating work behavior, poor school performance, an erratic work history with mostly unskilled jobs of short duration, and problems of adjustment to work and life in the community.

From direct contact with people in the communities, researchers have concluded that the general outlook of most "baseline villagers" is passive and fatalistic. Baseline villagers realize that they occupy the bottom rung on the social ladder; but they believe that there is nothing they can do to improve their status. They give the impression of being resigned to a life of frustration in a community that despises them for their disregard of morals, lack of "success goals," and dire poverty.

Their appraisal of the attitude of the community toward them is generally accurate. The community impression: "they cannot be trusted; they steal you blind; if you are friendly toward them, they will take advantage of you; if you lend them something, you will never see it again; they're bad, live like animals...families who are not worth a damn and don't give a damn." To many in the town, the only function they are seen as serving is as a baseline against which individuals in other classes can make favorable comparisons of themselves.

Their work history is likely to be unstable with a record of high turnover, instances of quarrels with supervisors and co-workers, and long periods of idleness or illness. Some leave their jobs casually, often without notice. Failing to come to work on time, walking off the job, and other loose work habits are common. For these reasons unless there is a labor shortage, employers do not like to hire "baseline villagers." Even then, employers place them in the most menial and temporary jobs available.

The family work history of "the Baseline Villagers" is generally known to the employers in the town; and when hiring takes place, employers act upon this knowledge. It is not uncommon for young people from this group to have their application stigmatized by the past family work history.

Husbands and wives frequently live in an unstable relationship. They marry young and bear their children young. Normally, the mother-to-child is the strongest and most enduring family relationship. Illegitimate births and abandonment by the father is high among "baseline villagers." For this reason, many of their homes contain one-parent families.

Their incomes commonly yield only the meager necessities of life. Their furniture is often second-hand or abused, and their purchases of durable goods are regularly at yard sales and rummage sales. Because of diminished earnings and frequent low financial ratings, a fact well known in the community, credit in stores and banks is difficult to obtain. Without capital accumulation or credit, home ownership is virtually impossible, making them perpetual renters.

"Baseline villagers" are regular recipients of various forms of relief from state and federal programs, such as welfare and family-assistance programs, SSI, and from benevolent people in the upper classes. As expected, the education level of "the baseline villagers" is limited, for the most part, to elementary school. Socially, they are set apart from the rest of society; few attend the churches regularly or participate in other community activities. Moreover, their misdeeds are reported and circulated about the community in the local newspaper on a regular basis.

## CLASS ANALYSIS FROM A REHABILITATION COUNSELOR PERSPECTIVE

Some of the best rehabilitation counselors have a difficult time accepting class profiles. Such profiles do not allow for the individuality of the person, and, in many cases, these counselors are right. Making easy classifications can be a problem. The dangers always exist that an unprofessional caseworker will take class frameworks and apply the boundaries indiscriminately to their client, thus stereotyping the client and limiting the vocational exploration.

Professional rehabilitation counselors can never allow themselves to forget that each client is a unique individual and each client possesses qualities that do not fit the molds we would invent for them. Caution needs to be taken to avoid substituting the class profiles for proper diagnostic assessments.

Counselors with the hope of being successful in the local job market must understand each of the groups in society–the values and motivations held by each group– and how the classes interrelate. In most communities, the business owners and managers come from the middle class. These are the decision-makers, the people with the jobs. On the other hand, most of our clients come from among "the working people" and "baseline villagers." The reason rehabilitation counselors are needed to help disabled persons from among these two classes find jobs is:

- persons from these classes work in the trades, often at heavy levels of exertion, and are subject to injury, and
- people from these classes are generally employed by persons in other classes and they have little or no direct influence over the local job market.

Our intervention–if we do the job right–helps re-connect them to work and the mainstream of society and gives them a chance to transcend social obstacles.

Class analysis can be a helpful tool for rehabilitation counselors in job placement. A lot depends on how you view the information you receive about the community and how useful this information is in clarifying the vocational objective for your client. Let us suggest several ways class analysis can help rehabilitation counselors in case planning and in their vocational counseling.

### IDENTIFYING EDUCATIONAL AND ADAPTIVE LIFE SKILLS

People tend to group themselves voluntarily along lines of common interests. Persons from the middle class, for instance, share interests in community projects, like landscaping to beautify the town and attract visitors; in leisure endeavors, such as attending local concerts and drama; and in educational activities, such as local workshops and conferences, to improve their general knowledge and lead them to higher levels of professional and managerial expertise. Interests commonly associated with the working class of people are automobiles and automobile racing, home cooking, country music, and just about anything that involves doing things with their hands and improving their work skill.

Group interests can be the basis for skill identification. In counseling and case planning, rehabilitation counselors locate many of the education and adaptive skills, skills that expand the vocational potential of their clients, by exploring with their clients individual and group interests. The class profiles presented in this chapter form a backdrop to help counselors understand the significance of the information they are receiving from their client.

*Reconnecting clients to the community.* When people become disabled from work, many things happen in their lives that tend to separate them from others. The loss of a job and the financial support the job brings is but one result of disability. When disability occurs and a person cannot do the things they used to do, even temporarily, they begin to feel a loss of purpose, a separation from their co-workers, and generally a loss of identity as fully functioning individuals in society. As disability lingers on, these people disconnect from the community and even isolate themselves from family, friends, and other sources of support. The result of this separation is what psychologists have labeled "situational depression."

Almost every client you encounter in professional practice will have situational depression to some degree. While rehabilitation counselors are not therapists, or trained adequately to engage in psychotherapy, in their counseling and case planning, counselors must consider the whole person. That includes their client's family complex, personal and work interests, and their place in the community. An understanding of community grouping and the interests of the group can broaden a professional's horizons and help the counselor deal more effectively with some of the more global issues of their clients.

*Job placement vs. career development.* The terms career development and job placement may seem to be interchangeable, and, indeed, are often used that way. The same college or university program may contain instruction in both subjects. While these terms may have similar definitions in theory, they have a very different connotation in practice.

Career development is defined as "a profession or occupation that one trains for and pursues as a life's work." In career development we normally think of long periods of educational study that lead upwardly mobile people along career paths toward their career goals. Continuing education has become a key factor in the process of career development. Career development is more appropriately assigned to the educational process for middle class members of society, classes II and III.

Job placement, on the other hand, is associated more with the working class of people, classes IV and V as defined earlier. The working people develop both physical and mental work skills on their jobs and in vocational programs, which they use in their trade or occupation throughout their work life.

Movement among occupations is likely to be mostly laterally, where working people can use the same or similar work skills in a number of jobs or work locations. When making a job change, for whatever reason, their interest is more in a job using the same or similar work skills than in preparing for a different career. If a new career becomes necessary, through skill obsolescence or disability, they will normally desire to seek employment that allows them, if possible, to transfer their work skills to another occupation. That is why analysis of transferability of work skills is so important in job placement. If vocational training to learn new work skills becomes necessary, the learning period is normally short.

*Finding the right job for your client.* Job placement is more complex than simply finding a job. In narrowing the job base and identifying appropriate jobs, rehabilitation counselors have to take into account such things as a person's age, education, work experience, their transferable skills, and their physical and mental limitations—things a person can no longer do as the result of their disabling condition.

Of equal importance in locating alternative work is determining the kinds of work suited to a client's class and group. Thus, to find the right employment alternative, rehabilitation counselors have to understand a person's place in the community. Class identification helps counselors get beyond the general information they gather in the interview, such as the vocational aspects of age, education, and work experience, and examine broader concerns of the individual, such as the appropriateness of the work to the individual's lifestyle and class, work of others within the family complex, and the impact of alternative work on their client's self-image.

# CONCLUSION
# LOOKING FORWARD

In using the small town as a microcosm of the nation as a whole, Chapter 2 sets forth the proposition that job placement of persons with disabilities improves as rehabilitation counselors gain an understanding of groups and group behavior within a typical American community. While trying to avoid stereotyping groups and individuals, the analysis and group composites allow us to focus our case planning on work that is appropriate for our clients. Chapter 3 takes a harder look at work in the community and those factors that influence the flow of jobs within the community as well as pinpointing work-related issues among the people in the community with whom counselors interact directly: Class II, the people with the jobs and Class IV "the Working People" and Class V "Baseline People," people in need of a job.

# TOPICS FOR GROUP DISCUSSION

1. Chapter 2 makes a strong argument for the small-town as a microcosm of America. This chapter suggests that a student or

professional can take the research about people in small-towns and apply the assumptions and conclusions drawn from that research to people living just about anywhere in America. Do you agree? From a work perspective, how are towns and cities similar and different from each other?

2. Chapter 2 contains a section called "The Best of All Possible Worlds" which provides American attitudes toward their political system, their social order, and their work. Are these an accurate depiction of American values today? When politicians speak of "American Values," are these the values they mean? On a chart, have a class member list what the group would consider qualities that best characterize the American culture using the information from this section, from the class profiles later in the chapter, and from those surfacing from the group.

3. The chapter makes a bold statement that America is a nation of classes, is that true? Are the class profiles reasonably accurate in the characteristics and features assigned to each class?

4. The chapter suggests that an understanding of class profiles is essential to rehabilitation counselors involved in job placement. Characteristics of each class are given at the end of the chapter. Divide the class into three groups with each group taking one of three classes: the middle class, the working people, and the baseline villagers. Have each of the groups prepare a presentation defining their subject and listing at least five characteristics of the class. The instructor may choose to have group leaders make the presentation to the class.

5. This chapter argues that social distance can be a problem in the job placement phase of the rehabilitation practice. What do you consider an appropriate "professional distance" in rehabilitation counseling between:

   - your client;
   - your colleagues; and
   - the community where you work?

Identify the issues involved and come to an agreement on a proper relationship that professional counselors need to have with their clientele.

6. The chapter makes a strong statement that in order to be successful in job placement, a counselor has to become involved with the community. List some of the ways rehabilitation counselors can become involved, appropriately, in their community and at the same time improve their performance in job placement.

## INDIVIDUAL EXERCISES
## THE CASE OF PAUL SILAS

*Paul Silas is a 42-year-old man from Peterstown, West Virginia, a rural community of less than 500 people. Peterstown is located about 30 miles from Harrisonburg, Virginia, a city of 35,000. Paul attended school through the 9th grade and later obtained his GED at the local vocational technical center. He can read, write, and perform math calculations at a high school level. After leaving school, he started working in the coalmines, but after the mines had a permanent layoff, he got a job as a stock clerk at Foodland, a chain of grocery stores in southwest Virginia and Tennessee. He became the produce manager at Foodland in 1999 and worked in that capacity until 2008 when he slipped on a wet surface at the store and hurt his back. He has been on workers compensation since that time. He had surgery on his back in 2009 at the University of Virginia Medical Health Center in Charlottesville, Virginia.*

*Paul's treating doctors have now said that he can return to work, but he has permanent restrictions for light work only (light work as defined in the DOT meaning he can lift 20 pounds occasionally, 10 pounds frequently, and stand and walk at least 6 hours in an 8-hour day). He cannot do the work he had done in the past because as a produce manager; he had to lift boxes of produce that sometimes weighed over 50 pounds. His insurance company has asked you–a rehabilitation counselor–to help him find new work that he can do.*

1. What kind of work do you think Paul can do given his vocational profile? Would knowledge of class association help you in your case planning? How? Does Paul have work skills and abilities he may be able to use in other work? List some of these and discuss.

2. What obstacles would you expect to encounter when you attempt to place Paul in a job? Make a list of these problems. How would you deal with these problems in your counseling with Paul?

3. What resources do you as a counselor have at your disposal to help in locating employment for Paul? List these resources. Discuss the case with other classmates if you wish.

## REFERENCES

[1]Bolles, R. N. (1991). What *Color Is Your Parachute?* Berkeley, CA: Ten Speed Press.
[2]Bolles, R. N. (2007). What *Color Is Your Parachute?* Berkeley, CA: Ten Speed Press.
[3]Canfield Fisher, Dorothy (1915). *Hillsboro People.* New York: Henry Holt & Company.
[4]Gale, Zona (1910). *Friendship Village.* New York: The Macmillan Company.
[5]Garland, Hamlin (1899). *Main Traveled Roads.* New York: Harper & Brothers.
[6]Lewis, Sinclair (1920). *Main Street.* New York: Harcourt, Brace and Company.
[7]Tournier, Robert E. (1983). "Small Towns at the Crossroads: Outcome Scenarios in Non-Metropolitan Change" in *Change and Tradition in the American Small Town.* New York: John Wiley and Sons, Inc.
[8]Vidich, Arthur and Bensman, Joseph (1958). *Small Town in Mass Society.* Garden City, NY: Doubleday and Company.

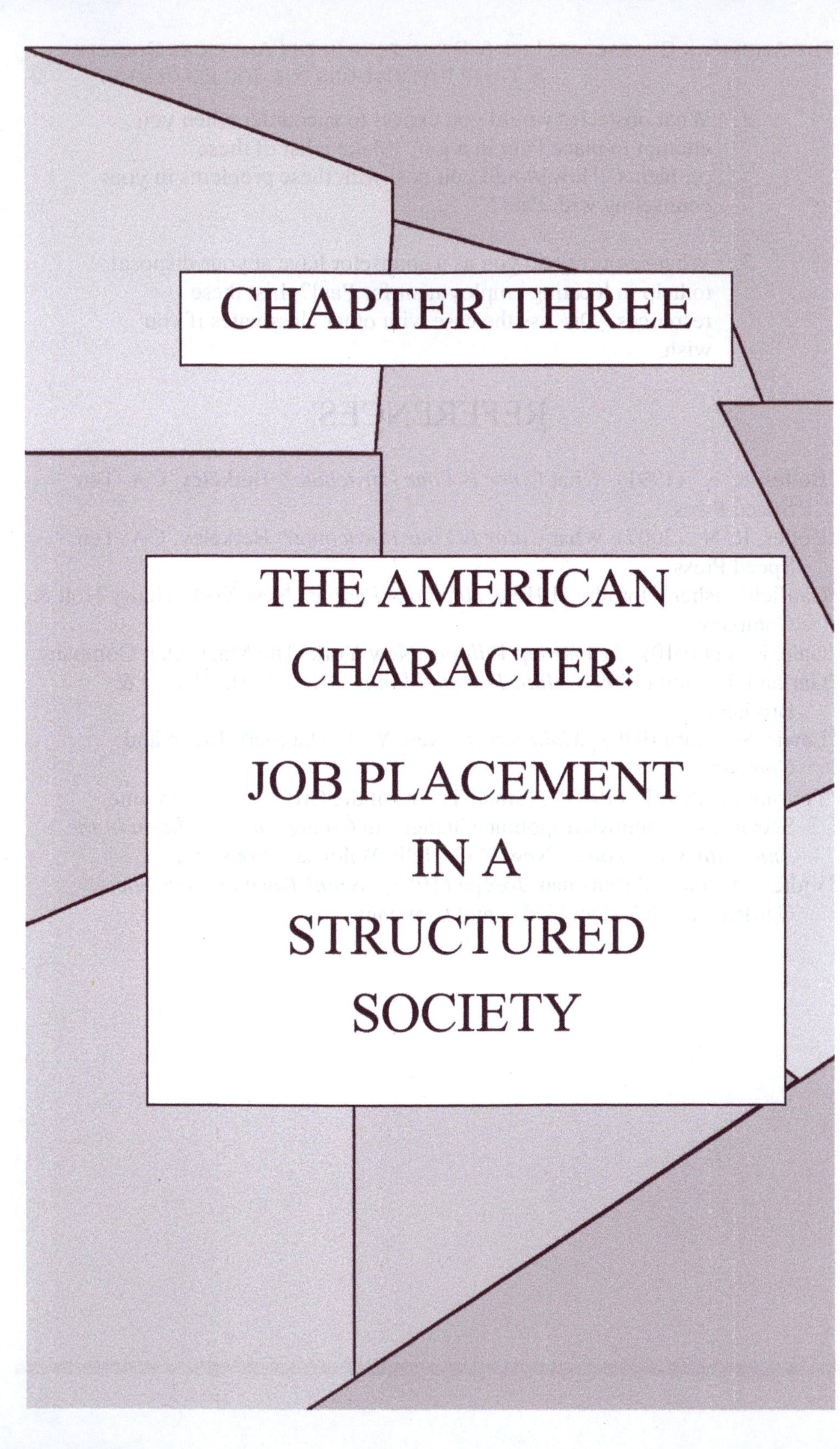

# CHAPTER THREE

# THE AMERICAN CHARACTER: JOB PLACEMENT IN A STRUCTURED SOCIETY

*"The evidence is abundant that the class system shapes the economic as well as the social outlook of the people. Very early in life, people in small towns, and likely in most places, begin to conform to the expectations of adults and peers in the class."*

A. B. Hollingshead

To the Reader:

In chapter two (2), we provided a breakdown of the social grouping in the small town in America and listed some of the characteristics of each group as noted by a variety of American critics and authors. We used the small town as a microcosm to show how Americans view community life, how they organize themselves into groups, and how patterns of social behavior affect the life of a community. Using social research from observers of the American scene, we were able to make our own observations and provide counselors with suggestions they may use to interface with the community in job placement. Class differences or stratification becomes even more important as we turn our attention to the workplace in the typical American community.

In order to be effective in job placement, rehabilitation counselors have to know the structure of the community and its people. Traditionally, many rehabilitation counselors have a family background with characteristics similar to that described in the past chapter as Class III. In other words, from their family affiliation, many counselors already have an acquaintance with management functions, particularly at the middle management and supervision levels, and some understanding of working people and the kind of jobs working people perform. When selecting a career goal in their college program, it is natural that many students with a working-class background would be interested in the social sciences, particularly the field of rehabilitation where work is a central feature. Their background is especially helpful once they join the profession because these students come to the profession with an understanding of their clients and the kinds of work their clients have performed.

Rehabilitation counselors, to be effective in professional practice, need an in-depth knowledge of occupations, how the work is performed, and managed. In-depth knowledge, for most of us, comes only from experience on the job, but all of us have to start somewhere. Our belief is that the knowledge about work our professionals need in order to become expert in job placement and in the courtroom, and in other phases of the profession, begins with gaining a general knowledge of group relationships within the community and learning how these relationships interrelate. This knowledge forms a framework for specific learning about jobs and their function.

As we turn our attention to Chapter 3, our investigation into the American character becomes narrower in scope. Again, we use the social research from our small-town investigation as a background from which to make our observations and analyses, particularly the social groupings or classes, but our focus of attention centers exclusively upon vocational issues. Much of the content for Chapter 3 comes from social science research and from experience gained through the years in counseling clients on vocational issues.

To begin Chapter 3, we look first at some of the family and social influences that affect vocational choice and vocational selection. Then we profile the main players with whom counselors interact in job placement–the employers, the people with the jobs, and the clientele–the people needing the jobs. From the profiles, we are able to draw inferences about employers and the people counselors serve that we feel will improve the effectiveness of rehabilitation counselors in service to persons with disabilities and as experts on vocational issues.

## HOW CLASS SHAPES VOCATIONAL CHOICE

Writers of exposé fiction and social critics of the small town have focused their interests upon the social aspects of the town structure. In their works (i.e., Grace Metalious' *Peyton Place*), we see people frustrated because others hold them down, not allowing them to participate in certain exclusive groups or clubs; we see class prejudice, often based upon race or nationality; and we see condescending attitudes that belittle and ridicule aspiring villagers. Oddly enough, in their writings we see little of the economic suppression, "the dollar," upon which the whole social system relies. Recognizing the economic inequalities created and sustained by the class system is necessary to our understanding of work not only in small towns but also throughout our whole society.

The evidence is abundant that the class system shapes the economic as well as the social outlook of the people. Very early in life, people in small towns, and likely in most places, begin to conform to the expectations of adults and peers in the class. For instance, youth from the working class adjust their ambitions to occupations working with their hands; and youth from Class II begin early to prepare for further education. By adulthood, townspeople are well entrenched in vocational selections suitable to their class system.

In preparation for A. B. Hollingshead's[2] research for *Elmstown Youth*, he posed this question to his adolescent study group: "Name the job or occupation you would like to follow when you reach maturity."[pg. 282] This question was designed, he writes, to determine the relationship between adolescents' ideas of desirable vocations and their class position. The answers to the question were predictable. Adolescents in each class tended to name the types of vocations with which they were most familiar. Class II youth knew most about business and the professions; Class III were more familiar with small business, management, clerical pursuits, and the crafts; Class IV youth were mainly interested in clerical work and the skilled trades; and Class V youth were oriented toward the unskilled service occupations. Many of the Class V youth were indecisive or named dramatic, romantic, or freak occupations, such as a wild animal trainer, bareback riding in a circus, or a six-day bicycle racer, indicating that they had not given much thought to a vocation and were receiving little guidance at home.

It was the opinion of the researchers that by adolescence lower-classed youth in both Class IV and Class V had already adjusted their job goals to what they may hope to achieve. By so doing, they had limited their horizons to class horizons, and in the process unconsciously placed themselves in the position that they would occupy in the class system–at the same level as their parents. In short, they were either being forced to accept or they were willing to accept the vocational patterns the class system held out to them.

## Family Influence Over the Local Job Market

Research has also found that family influence plays a dominant role indirectly in shaping the vocational outlook of their adolescents and directly in manipulating the local job market to secure jobs for their family members and children. The findings indicate that parent and family influence lies in direct proportion to the class in which the adolescents belong. Accordingly, the higher classes place their young men–and now their young women–in strategic positions that will lead to financial, managerial, and legal control of the major portion of the community wealth. As a rule, Class II youth often do not work, but if they do, the work has to be dignified, that is, physically clean. Work is essential to the Class III family complex. Therefore, with full encouragement of their parents, most of the Class III youth work. In fact, most owners and managers in local businesses are in Classes II and III and give preference to these youth in hiring. Class IV youth take what Class III leave them, since their parents have little direct influence upon the flow of jobs. Finally, Class V youth in the lowest class of community prestige take what they can after the higher-class children have taken the desirable jobs.

The work of Hollinghead[2] and his research team have shown clear linkage between work and the class system, a much closer tie than most of us ever believed possible, or want to believe. They suggest that class attitudes affect vocational choice. He says, "We believe that the adolescent's idea of desirable jobs is a reflection of their experiences in the class or family culture complexes. And that families of the top three classes use direct and indirect influence to make the job market conform to their choices: "the net results is that the assignment of 'good jobs', such as office and clerical work, go to Class II and Class III; and the respectable jobs to Class IV. The Class V youth get the 'bad jobs', such as helping in the junk yard and hauling garbage and ashes."[pg. 282]

If this strong a relationship exists between work and the class system–and the evidence is certainly persuasive–then every phase of the job placement process becomes affected. Case planning with clients must account for class attitudes and the client's social position in the community; placement counseling must recognize clients' attitude toward what they perceive as appropriate work; and the job search must overcome, or in some cases take advantage of, the extraordinary influences "the right connections" have over the local job market. You cannot counsel the work needs of your client without accounting for these factors within the class structure that are almost certain to exist in every community.

## JOB PLACEMENT AND THE CLASS STRUCTURE

When we turn our attention to work and the workplace in these small communities, we are faced once again with having to deal with the class structure. The middle-class people are the employers–the people with the jobs. They own and manage most of the local businesses. In order to be successful in job placement, counselors must know the skills required in local jobs and have a working knowledge of the human qualities employers look for in hiring their employees. This knowledge can only be acquired by having a networking relationship with middle-class employers. (As we have seen, the aristocracy has little to do with local business and seldom exert a direct influence over the local job market. As a result, no further attention is given to the aristocracy in this study).

At the same time, most of the placement opportunities counselors receive are from the Class IV Working People and the Class V Baseline Villagers as defined in this book. The working people are often in the heavy trades and they are more susceptible to injury and the need to reshape their work lives. These people often have a strong work motivation and a variety of hidden work skills or "adaptive skills" that provide them with a basis for other work, but they are often inflexible toward change and rigid in their attitude toward other work. Counseling with injured workers from this class will provide them work alternatives and how they can use their transferable skills to continue their work life.

On the other hand, baseline villagers often have three strikes against them:

1. their work background and work habits,
2. their attitude toward work and "success goals", and
3. a community that has formed a negative opinion about their worth.

Generally, they have no direct or indirect influence over the local job market. To place them in anything more than menial jobs require a very different kind of vocational counseling and ingenuity in job placement. These cases present the greatest challenge to the rehabilitation counselor. Perhaps the most important vocational contribution we, as rehabilitation counselors, can provide is empowerment–believing that behavioral change is possible, having faith in our clients in spite of self-defeating behaviors, reinforcing positive work values, and encouraging them to rise above their circumstances.

To conduct job placement, the rehabilitation counselor interfaces primarily with these three groups of people:

1. the middle-classed employers–the people with the jobs,

2. the working people, and

3. baseline villagers–the people in need of a job.

We will take a closer look at each group and how they function in the work place.

## A PROFILE OF THE DECISION-MAKERS: THE PEOPLE WITH THE JOBS

By now, you should be able to identify small-town employers by their class association. If the people you meet are managing fast-food restaurants, or they are supervisors in the local factory, their class identification may be difficult to determine. In all likelihood, they are working people on the rise; if, however, they are in management or they own their own business (unless it is a business in the trades), you can bet that some of the characteristics we describe as "middle class" apply to them.

Middle-classed people are the decision-makers at the top levels of society. Normally, members include, but are not limited to, the presidents of local banks, managers of the public service companies, personnel managers of the local mills or large private corporations, most professional people, doctors and lawyers, owners of large, family-owned farms, and owners of prestigious local businesses, such as local insurance companies and real estate agencies. Their incomes are derived from personal participation in an independent profession, such as law, architecture, or dentistry; in the operation of a family-owned business; from a salaried executive position in a business often owned by a member of a Class I family; from a salaried professional position in a public office; or from administration of the school system such as superintendent or principal.

If you accept the group profile presented earlier in Chapter 2 as reasonably accurate, several of the characteristics of the middle-class provide clues to the way middle-classed people think about work and the worker. Knowing how this group as a whole regards work provides the rehabilitation counselor with a common ground for dialogue with employers in the community. Let us expand upon some of the group characteristics of middle-classed citizens and draw a few inferences that might help counselors understand better the behavior and attitudes of this group of employers.

*They have pride in their community.* Likely, much of their time away from work is spent participating in community projects. They are on the boards of directors for most community projects, human services agencies, and local and statewide banks. They know the history of the town and they have an interest in preserving established traditions within the community. As a result, they will likely respond with interest to any knowledge you have gained about the town and its people or any other questions you may have that will help you better understand the community and the local work environment. They will likely respond with pride to a few well-placed, sincere compliments or "strokes" about the town, things you have noticed in your initial observations, like recent improvements or the friendliness of the people, especially if you show you care about the community and its people. Since you are helping persons with disabilities find jobs, and bringing money and financial resources into the community, you are a natural object of their affection. They are unlikely to respond favorably to your views of their backwardness or how great life is in other towns or cities.

*They will likely show an interest in people who "want to get somewhere in life."* Most middle-class people have acquired an education and are in pursuit of appreciable assets that will yield a measure of security. They work hard and strive to better themselves and they appreciate the same qualities in others. Therefore, in presenting your client and/or your client's employment credentials, you may consider leaning heavily upon the educational background of your client, particularly if your client's education indicates progression along a vocational path. For instance, as an icebreaker, you may point out that your client has prepared for the job you are seeking with an employer:

> *Mr. Hopkins, John wants to be a welder like his brother Joseph; to learn the trade of welding; he has taken a six-month program at Valley Vocational Technical Center.*

You can relay to the employer some of your client's work history or career aspirations, knowledge you have gained in your interviews that show commitment to the trade, employer loyalty, or just a steady work history:

*Mr. Humphrey, Fred had two jobs previously and stayed with his employers for more than ten years. This is good because you know the way people leave their jobs these days.*

As the middle-class sets the standards for custom and taste in the community, *they will likely have respect for those who have the wisdom to follow their example*. For instance, most people in business dress in a conservative manner; and, when you come into their business, they expect you and your client to dress accordingly. They will not tell you how to dress directly, but their response to you is sufficient indication. (A conservative dress code is not peculiar to small towns; several surveys among employers nationally have shown that appearance is one of the three top reasons for rejecting applicants to employment).

One local business owner shared with us a bias about job placement people he had met. He said he could always tell human service people who came into his business by their shaggy beards and jeans. He said that whenever they showed up at his door, he asked one of his salespeople to answer their questions and send them away. Obviously, if this attitude is representative of the way business owners regard us, rehabilitation counselors are not going to be successful, if for no other reason than that they are unable to talk to the decision-maker. In recent years, rehabilitation counselors have become more professional in their appearance. They have shown more concerns about their own and their clients' dress, raising the image of rehabilitation counseling in the eyes of employers and making the rehabilitation clients acceptable candidates for employment.

## How Decision-Makers Conduct their Business

The prominent locally-owned businesses in most towns and small cities include the local automobile dealerships, auto parts distributors, and service stations; farms, farm equipment sales, farm service businesses, and farm cooperatives; small manufacturing concerns and food processors; furniture and appliance dealers and other retail shopkeepers; wholesale operations, such as oil and beer distributors; hardware stores, independent grocery stores (although independent hardware stores and independent grocery stores even in small towns are rapidly vanishing under the pressures from Walmart and other nationwide chain stores); business and professional service agencies, such as real estate and insurance firms; restaurants and other food establishments.

Perhaps nowhere in America can you find a better example of the protestant ethic at work than among small, independent businesses. (Small independent businesses are important employers. You may wish to see Chapter 7: "The Counselor's Introduction to the World of Work in The New American Economy," that states American Express has advertised that in America today, 99% of all businesses are classified as small businesses). Local employers may not belong to the Protestant faith; most do, but they will likely be involved in the local churches, service clubs and lodges, and community celebrations, if for no other reason than personal exposure is good for business. They may not be Republican; most are, but they subscribe to Republican business principles, such as wealth accumulation, managerial status, and a desire for less interference from governmental bodies, local, state, and federal. They may not be archconservatives; most are, but they run their businesses in a conservative manner, working long hours with direct, personal involvement in the business.

Their conservative approach to business is due in part to prevailing economic conditions. Independent businesses have to compete with the chain operations. Yet, for them, administrative costs, except for staff or "people costs," are higher as they cannot spread their expenses, like advertising, warehouse, and delivery, over a number of locations. Because they have to buy in smaller quantities than the chains, the selling price and profit margins on the items they sell or distribute have to be higher. To compete effectively, owners of small businesses hold expenses to a minimum, work long hours in the business, advertise as little as possible, offer extraordinary service, permit short-term credit, patronize each other, and prospect for business within the informal network, particularly among persons of their own class.

As might be expected, for retail businesses that compete directly with the chain operations, locally-owned businesses are most successful in the specialty or high end markets, with items that appeal to members of their own class, where personal and professional service become part of the price consideration. These include quality furniture retailers with handcrafted furniture and custom manufacturing, fine jewelry stores, and specialty boutiques. You will find that most of the chain stores appeal to the mass market with their primary patronage among the working people and the lower-middle class.

Richard Lingeman[3] in "*Caste and Class in the American Town*" describes the local businessperson as tight-fisted, spending as little as possible on advertising, redecoration of their stores, new lines of goods, and so on; instead of plowing their profits back into the business, they buy real estate. These shopkeepers work long hours and operate on a tight margin. "Their world view is similarly parsimonious: cost cutting and saving are their twin gods."[pg. 435]

Under existing market conditions, with stiff external competition, comparatively high expenses and reduced profit, it is easy to see how Richard Lingeman[3] draws such a harsh conclusion about business owners in a small town. The businesses seldom yield incomes sufficient to create an abundance of wealth; most often the business, if well managed, does provide security and a reliable livelihood for the family. In addition, the business does offer a measure of social status in the town, but the legacy for all those years of hard work and financial stress is often only the real estate in which the business is conducted.

Security rather than wealth seems to be the economic goal of the business. Security goals are very different from goals directed toward wealth accumulation or expansion. Security seekers tend to hold on to what they have rather than take risks necessary to expand their business. As Vidich and Bensmen[4] discovered in their research of Springfield in *Small Town in Mass Society*, owners of small businesses spend as little as possible on advertising and other business expenses. During slow seasons and recessive periods of economic slowdown, owners tend to ride out the bad times rather than remodeling, extending a merchandise line, or reaching out to customers with advertising in an attempt to capture new business.

Moreover, security seekers will normally make slow and methodical business decisions–decisions with less risk. Employee decisions are no different from other business decisions. Not long ago, one of my clients was the successful candidate for a job in a print shop and was told that he had the job. The employer, however, waited for almost two months before adding my client to his staff, waiting for a single contract to come through. Another counselor friend of mine had almost the identical experience with a security firm where the owner waited for a month before hiring a new person to find out if his firm had a security contract with a new manufacturing firm in town.

As indicated earlier, the income from the business is derived from personal participation in the business. Owners and managers work long hours and hire only when the workload becomes too great for them to take care of the business themselves. In order to hold down the expenses, other family members are often used temporarily in the business instead of hiring new people.

Absentee ownership in the independent business seems to be the exception rather than the rule. The profits are simply not sufficient to support non-participation. As a common practice, small business employers tend to keep their workers "lean and hungry," barely having enough people on board to maintain the necessary production levels or level of service. They tend to pay less than larger businesses and have many add-on responsibilities, often making the physical level of exertion greater than similar jobs in the national economy or those listed in the *Dictionary of Occupational Titles*.[1] Fear of over-expansion and narrow profits rather than greed seems to predominate in hiring decisions.

The business practices of independent owners explain some of the problems rehabilitation counselors have in finding jobs for their clients. These owners frequently make low-risk decisions, often delaying hiring beyond what would seem reasonable for business planning, as cited in the above examples. Then in a state of crisis, they "shoot from the hip," and hire new people on impulse. The hiring comes only after they have exhausted all the temporaries from among acquaintances, family, and other relatives. With the smallest number of employees possible, all of the staff must take on additional work with levels of exertion beyond what would normally be expected of these jobs.

However, there are compensations. Look for these in your job placements:

1. *The owner is in the place of business.* You do not have to go through several layers of management to see the person making the hiring decision, and they are accessible to you with the right introduction.

2. *Owners do hire local people.* In fact, most of the time, they know when a hiring situation is coming along, even if they are not ready to add to their staff. They may not do a lot of formal planning but, likely, they carry a lot of what they plan in their heads. You just might convince a business owner that your client is the right person for the job–if you have their trust and you know what motivates an owner. Incentives from the state and federal government, or worker compensation programs, such as payment for trial work periods, can lower the risk to the employer and may give your client an edge in the open job market.

3. *Their conservative approach can become a form of job security.* Typically, these employers hire only the number of employees needed to do the job. As the employer works side by side with his or her employees, the employees they hire often become more like family members. As a result, when business is slow or the economy is in recession, these employers tend to wait longer to lay a worker off.

4. *Small businesses do have jobs.* As you will see in Chapter 7, "A Counselor's Introduction to the World of Work in the New American Economy," many of these small businesses are among the fastest growing occupations in the national economy. The Department of Labor projects this trend will continue in the future.

# PROFILE OF THE WORKER
# PEOPLE IN NEED OF A JOB

Most clients whom counselors are asked to assist in job placement come from Class IV and Class V as previously defined. As we have discussed, working people and baseline villagers need our assistance in locating work in a job market over which they have very little influence. In most cases, their primary interest is in the job, not a career. Working people develop skills for their trade. They may have several job changes with other employers, but they will likely work in the same or similar capacity with each employer, using their acquired work skills, unless, they become injured and can no longer perform their past work. That is when they need the help of a rehabilitation counselor.

Baseline villagers, on the other hand, tend to have a variety of unskilled jobs, and stay in entry-level work throughout their work lives. In job placement, rehabilitation counselors provide clients from each of these groups with the knowledge about themselves and the job market that enables them to make a work adjustment and to overcome some of the disadvantages of their physical and mental limitations as well as their class position.

It is important to understand that persons from each of these classes have very different attitudes toward work and the workplace. Recognition of these differences in class attitudes and group behavior will help determine the right counseling approach; and, for the most part, a rehabilitation counselor's success in job placement. Therefore, we appropriately end this chapter with a close look at these two groups.

## REHABILITATION COUNSELING AND THE WORKING CLASS

Normally, working people perform the work with their hands in the unskilled, semi-skilled, and skilled trades within the community. Some, like millwrights and maintenance mechanics, are employed at the mills, in the factories, or in the mines. Some are automotive mechanics in local automobile and farm equipment dealerships. Some, like pipe fitters and steamfitters, are employed in the skilled trades and service occupations, (e.g., construction and heating and air conditioning). Some may occupy clerk positions in the stores that relate to the trades, such as auto parts clerks, or hardware salespeople. A few may even own their own businesses, usually in the area of their skills, and some, such as brick masons, and carpenters, may be in a variety of other trades in the field of construction. In addition, these people operate the heavy equipment, drive the 18-wheelers, and manage the nation's warehouses. They make things work, manage the product, build the structures, and keep things running.

Unfortunately, much of their work is performed at a heavy or more level of exertion, placing them at greater risk to injury. Once injury occurs, or they reach an age when they can no longer perform work having high physical demands, they are forced to change from their regular occupations to lighter, less physical jobs. This may mean an entire career change, as they are no longer able to use their customary work skills. In the absence of any transferable skills, skills that they can use in less-demanding occupations, they often qualify only for low-paying, entry-level work. Self-employment is seldom an option, as only a few have the background and experience to start a business.

Counseling by a rehabilitation specialist is critical to helping working people make the vocational adjustment to new work. Rehabilitation counselors can make a difference in the lives of their working class clients in a number of ways:

- *Adjustment counseling* helps these disabled workers overcome the emotional trauma and situational depression that normally accompanies the end of a work phase. Adjustment counseling provides hope to replace the despair in their emotional state. In everyday practice, seldom can vocational counseling and job placement be separated from adjustment counseling with this group.

- *Analysis of the worker's employment background* locates work skills from past work and provides identification of life skills or adaptive skills that may be used in other occupations to give them a competitive advantage in the job market.

- Listening to what the client has to say about personal interests, such as hobbies and what they do in their spare time, reveals *personal traits* that can be useful in empowering clients and locating new work alternatives.

- *Advocacy* occurs during the job placement activities, when rehabilitation counselors give working people a voice as well as a go-between among middle-class employers upon whom they must rely for their future livelihood.

A rehabilitation counselor's knowledge of work and the variety of jobs in the workplace offers working people hope for a new vocational beginning in the area of their lives, their occupation, where most working people find the greatest meaning. (You may recall from the class profile in Chapter 2 that the pride of the working people lies in their work and their work skill).

For the rehabilitation counselor, working people are among their most motivated and rewarding clients. As we have seen, the pride of working people is less in their community than the work that they do. Their work, as they see it, makes them "the backbone of the community." They often possess a strong work ethic and normally want to work. Indeed, their whole self-image as people and contributing members of society is wrapped up in the confidence they have in their work skills, in their desire to work, and in their feelings about the value of work. Does counseling people disabled from their usual and customary work seem meaningful and rewarding to you? Many of us feel the opportunity to provide vocational counseling, job-seeking skills, and job placement service to injured workers who want to continue working offers special rewards many other professions lack. On the other hand, special characteristics, unique to working people, make case management for this category of people more challenging.

Injured working people may have an abundance of skills from their past work. Some of these skills may be found in the jobs they have done in the past; and some may be found in hobbies and special areas of interest. Many of these skills are transferable to other work or occupations. Clients, however, seldom know about transferability of work skills, or adaptive skills, and how these skills may apply to other work. Rehabilitation counselors need to be able to identify skills that can provide these clients with a competitive advantage in the open job market and show these clients how to use these skills in locating new work.

As a rule, working people are concrete in their thinking, with little patience for rhetoric, and take a very practical approach to most things, particularly when it comes to work. The case needs constant attention and to show constant movement. (This is one of the reasons private rehabilitation counselors only handle a small caseload).

Many of the working people have limited people skills and become passive when it comes to dealing with employers and human resource managers, requiring rehabilitation counselors to be more direct in their counseling approach when involved in job placement. Rehabilitation counselors must be aware of the perceptions of working people, particularly about the kind of work that is appropriate for working class people. Let us look more closely at each of these areas of vocational exploration.

## Analyzing Past Work Skills

Sometimes rehabilitation counselors have difficulty in analyzing skills from a client's past jobs that would transfer to other occupations. Don't worry! Even experts in the field have difficulty with the concept of transferability of work skills. Sometimes we look for too much.

Generally, if work tasks can be learned in 30 days or less, they are not transferable to other occupations. The work is considered unskilled; unskilled work has no skills to transfer. A client who can operate a cash register or package goods on an assembly line will find that this skill is not much help when they are looking for new work, unless they are considering a job in the same or similar occupations.

Work skills, even those that were learned on the job, (e.g., caring for convalescent patients or serving food in a restaurant), often give the client a competitive advantage in the open job market. Job tasks that deal with people have wide application in other work, particularly in the services sector of the economy. A close examination of the work records and the information gained from interviews with clients can yield work skills that are useful in jobs you may be considering for your client.

One way of looking at transferability of work skills is to take a semi-skilled or skilled job and divide the job into job tasks. Ask yourself how each of these tasks might be used in other work; visualize how each of these tasks might appear on a resume. Then, see how many of these tasks are involved in the work you might be considering. The closer the skills needed to perform the job or jobs considered are to skills used in jobs done successfully in the past, the more likely the client will be a good fit in the new work.

Transferable skills are important to employers only if the employer recognizes their importance. Do not take for granted that an employer knows about your client's skills just because you placed them on the resume. You must communicate your findings about transferable work skills to your client, and he or she must understand the importance of their own skills and be able to communicate those skills to employers in an interview. All the analysis in the world a counselor does is of no value unless both the client and the employer recognize the skills and understand their importance in the job to be performed.

## HIDDEN SKILLS OF THE WORKING PEOPLE

In the exploration of the work background with clients from the working class, a rehabilitation counselor will find these clients often possess many hidden skills or adaptive skills, skills that they have acquired from "fixing up things", that may give them a vocational base for other work. These adaptive skills can often be applied to work alternatives at a lighter level of exertion than their past work. For instance, fixing up old cars and building additions to their houses may provide the product knowledge to sell and inspect property or automobiles or advise customers in the selection of hardware, tools, or building supplies. With a little imagination and a good resume, a client may be shown to have demonstrated skills that can be used to perform such jobs as auto parts clerk, rental agents for equipment and leasing firms, or inventory clerks, all jobs that are normally performed at a lighter level of exertion than their past work. All of these jobs are likely to exist in most communities, and all of these jobs in the services industry have something to do with the trades or occupations suited to the background of these working people.

In an interview, counselors may ask clients to explore some of their hobbies or the part-time work they have done in the past, what they do with their spare time on a typical day, or if they are in the habit of helping their neighbors. Listening to the "small talk" clients have with you may often reveal these life or adaptive skills. Done correctly, a counselor will frequently uncover some real gems among their client's hidden skills.

So many clients among the working class of people truly believe that if they cannot do their past work, which is frequently medium to heavy in exertion, they have no skills for other work. Research has shown that as workers age, this tendency to believe they can no longer work grows. To them, Social Security benefits and other forms of relief become an acceptable way of life. They just do not see the importance of all of the sidelines they have undertaken through the years (e.g., fixing up things around the house, helping neighbors with weekend projects, or volunteer work at their club or church). In most cases, however, both for their mental state and for their economic well-being, these people are better off working. Continuing to work reinforces their personal and class identity, making them feel they are still a vital part of things and giving them an income that is usually much larger than they can receive from benefits. Many counselors and even some psychologist believe that work has its own therapeutic value.

It is up to you as their counselor to interpret for these clients the value of these hidden or adaptive skills and to show them ways their life skills can become the basis for new work alternatives. There is possibly no area of rehabilitation counseling more professional than analyzing a person's work skills, both learned job skills and adaptive skills, and counseling new work behaviors. What a source of empowerment a rehabilitation counselor can become and what a contribution a counselor can make to the lives of persons with disabilities!

## The Need for Case Movement

When counseling working class people, and any others whom you identify as having a strong work ethic, it helps to keep attentive to the movement of the case. Our experience is that these people have a high regard for a rehabilitation counselor's ability to create miracles in their lives, and they are generally cooperative in doing what you ask of them. Unfortunately, all too often, injured people from the working class become too dependent and rely too much upon the counselor's expertise. (Too often, they rely upon the counselor to find the jobs for them when they should be participating directly in the job placement activities). They become impatient when the case stalls; and if you have formed a good relationship with someone, they may "bug the life out of you." More than most, these clients need to see progress toward work goals and become actively involved in the job hunt. Normally, they are well suited for "grass roots" job exploration as described in Chapter 10: "Networking for Jobs in the Hidden Job Market: A Client-Centered Approach."

For many years, the field of rehabilitation has recognized that the longer clients stay dormant on the caseload, the less likely they will be successful in job placement. This rule is particularly applicable to these working-class clients. In fact, as many counselors relate, long layoffs and the lack of movement tend to create additional problems with situational depression, client discouragement, and feelings of worthlessness, making placement success even less probable. The key words here seem to be *keeping these clients active and involved.* If you are their case manager or job-placement specialist, show them the way jobs are found through your knowledge of the job market. If rehabilitation counselors can "keep the waters stirring" with lots of continuous activities on the client's part, using good job-seeking skill counseling with continuous assignments, many of these clients will find jobs on their own. The motivational approaches described in Chapter 4: "Client Motivation" generally works well with these clients. Moreover, the management approach provided in "The Job-Search Organizer" is designed especially for this kind of client.

## THE CONCRETE THINKER: OVERCOMING THE LACK OF PEOPLE SKILLS

As we have seen, working people are often skilled in the work they do and take a lot of pride in their occupations. These people make things work, manage the product, build the structures, and keep things running. Indeed, these people are the backbone of our society. Without them, the American economy would come to a rapid standstill.

In most cases, the lives of the working people have been spent in occupations where they were able to use their learned skills; and if they were in a management role, it was as a supervisor or lead worker for people in the same or similar trade. Likely, they have been involved in taking orders from managers and supervisors, and doing the job that has been laid out for them by others. While they may be highly skilled in their work, many of the working people we meet lack skills in dealing with people or do not have what we often refer to as "people skills."

Unfortunately, the work they do often places them in hazardous work environments at a greater risk for accidents. When work-related accidents occur, many times working people are unable to return to the same type of work they had done in the past. If they are to return to work and continue to be contributing members of our society, they will likely have to find alternative work. Finding new work can become a real challenge for these people. So often, working people become uncomfortable in dealing with others, particularly managers and human resource administrators, and take a passive stance. Such behavior can be, and is often, interpreted as lack of motivation by managers and interviewers.

Rehabilitation counselors may make the same observation and draw a similar conclusion. When a rehabilitation counselor is assigned to the case these clients typically take little initiative on their own. The counselor may get the idea that the client expects the professional to do all the work. Too often, this passiveness is misinterpreted as laziness, unwillingness to work, or a deliberate attempt to extend payments of worker's compensation. Sometimes this is the correct conclusion.

Our experience has shown that much of the time passiveness can be overcome by using good communication skills and a more direct counseling approach. In their initial interviews, counselors have to:

- Sort out the roles each participant is going to play in the job exploration, clear up any misunderstanding about the client's desire to work, and set forth what the counselor expects the client to do in the job search.

- The counselor must identify the transferable work skills and take the time to show clients how the transferable work skills can be presented in the interview with employers. An employment resume that prominently shows the work skills can be a guide for the client in the interview and serve as a written document to place before the potential employer during the interview.

- While the counselor encourages these clients to use networking and make application to employers on their own, much of the time the counselor has to identify jobs that lie within the client's functional restrictions, explain to these clients how they can do the job, and set appointments with employers.

To illustrate with a live example:

> Our office accepted the case of a 57-year-old forklift driver. He injured his hand and shoulder when he lost his balance while pushing a pressure washer down a ramp. No surgery was necessary and he was released to light and medium work with limited reaching above his shoulder.
>
> The insurance adjuster had assigned the case to our office from a counselor in another part of the state who had conducted an initial interview and determined the functional level for alternative work in job placement. About once a month, the former counselor would meet with the injured worker, update the records, and lay out possible jobs the client can do, always encouraging the client to search the newspaper and go to places where possible jobs could be found. After the counselor left, nothing happened. For the better part of a year, there was no movement in the case. In fact, there was a statement in the record that the client had told the previous counselor he did not want to work.
>
> When the case was assigned to our office, the insurance adjuster reiterated what the record said about the client's lack of

desire to work, and suggested the issue in the case may be non-compliance if the client failed to actively search for work. The greatest problem here seems to have been the physical distance between the counselor and the client.

In our initial interview, the client said that he wanted to work and needed to work. In meetings close to that time, our rehabilitation counselor examined the client's past work for possible work skills, but most of his past work had been semi-skilled with no transferability. Contacting the injured worker daily and discussing potential work alternatives kept the client active and involved. Within a week, our office canvassed the community, locating over 16 job possibilities. Assignments were made to the client with the expectation that the client would actively seek employment by following-up on these job leads. The next month, the injured worker was hired as a maintenance man by a local cemetery. What was the difference? Rapid movement in the case, staying close to the client on a daily basis, and keeping in touch with the community where the work alternatives were being located.

It is always possible, and all too often true, that clients who come to us do not want to work or have disincentives that get in the way of finding appropriate work. Experienced counselors are always aware of that possibility. But before reaching the conclusion that the client does not want to work, consider the possibility that passiveness on the part of a client may be a lack of people skills, skills which need to be addressed in job seeking skill sessions and considered in the selection of placement alternatives.

## WORKING PEOPLE AND THEIR PERCEPTIONS OF WORK

In selecting work alternatives with these very class-conscious clients, a rehabilitation counselor needs to take into account the perceptions of what these clients consider "appropriate work." So often, we pay attention to our client's willingness or unwillingness to pursue jobs, their functional capacity to do certain jobs, and ignore their perceptions of work. Of course, functional abilities and work motivation are important, but if our class profile, presented earlier, is reasonably accurate, then we have to consider the types of jobs that are normally associated with this class of people.

So often in job placement clients from the working class are cooperative and attentive as long as the jobs named fit their perception of work, but conflict arises, openly or not, when counselors identify jobs that fall outside of the range of work normally performed by their class. These job options may not only pose a threat to working-class clients because they offer something new and untried, surfacing fears about change and the fear of failure, but also these jobs may threaten a client's class identity. When a conflict exists between a client's perception of appropriate work and the work alternatives offered, resistance is the logical result.

For instance, suppose your client has been a truck driver for most of his working life, and, as the result of a back injury, he can no longer do that type of work. In your job counseling, you indicate several job possibilities that may lie within his functional capabilities, restaurant work or retail sales that he rejects without any real consideration. If you can eventually find jobs in one of these vocational areas, even if these are good jobs with compensation equal to or above that of his last employment, your client is unlikely to accept employment unless you can reconcile the job with his perception of work.

Perceptions of work have a lot to do with job satisfaction in some areas of the country. For example, in West Virginia and in the Appalachian regions of Virginia and Kentucky, the fastest growing employment is in the service industry. This is nothing new. Most sections of the country are experiencing growth in services jobs as America continues to move toward a services economy. Most service sector jobs springing up in these poorer, mountainous sections are unskilled, often food service jobs, and there always seem to be plenty of them. Counselors working these regions may find these jobs easy pickings when they need to show progress in a worker's compensation case.

In these regions coal mining, manufacturing, and construction industries, the traditional job base for this section of the country, are on the decline. Jobs are being lost in occupations related to these industries. Yet, the vocational aspirations of many working class people still lie in these occupations. When they think of work, they think of jobs in these industries: "manly work." (*A side light*! Don't things that go around come around? In recent years, the federal government began a federally assisted training program to train young people for the mining industry since there is a real shortage of miners in the Appalachian Regions).

Rehabilitation counselors doing job placement in these states report having a difficult time with workers injured in the heavy trades making a vocational adjustment to lighter jobs in the services industry. In frustration, some counselors have interpreted their client's resistance to a macho attitude toward such work. Their clients say that work is heavy or "manly" work; and when they can no longer meet the demands of the heavy trades, they do not believe they can work. It is the perception of many of these counselors that their clients are saying they prefer accepting state and federal assistance or worker's compensation to working in the service jobs. Of course, counselors can never rule out that possibility.

For many of us, this kind of resistance is difficult to understand. Employment in the service sector usually offers cleaner jobs and careers that, at least above the entry level, pay as well or better than their previous work, and these jobs are normally within their functional capabilities.

Situations do occur when counselors find themselves asking, are these clients unable to make a vocational adjustment to lighter work? Are they poorly motivated? Do they have a welfare mentality? Often, conclusions drawn from this speculation are legitimate and each of these conclusions may be possible. Nevertheless, before a counselor selects one of these alternatives, it may be necessary to consider an additional possibility; that is, that there may be a conflict between certain jobs that may be readily open and available and the perception of work held by this class of workers. With more investigation, a counselor may find that their client's resistance lies not in their unwillingness to work but in the conflict that results when the type of work available runs counter to their idea of "appropriate" work. These clients may see work in the service jobs as performed by people in Class V and "manly work" as jobs normally performed by their class.

What can counselors do when they suspect the presence of this conflict among their working-class clients? First, it is important to recognize the types of jobs that fall within a client's perceptions of work. As we saw in the last section, not all of these jobs are heavy in exertion. Some of these occupations are related to the trades and require knowledge of the trades, but do not require heavy lifting or excessive standing and walking. Such jobs are rental clerk, plumbing, lumber sales, service station attendants, and light parts delivery. Even security occupations and other jobs in the protection industry are normally acceptable. Many times, if the worker has the product knowledge, employers are willing to make reasonable accommodations for the physical limitations.

Second, a client may have some hidden skills, adaptive skills that would serve as preparation for many lighter jobs that are acceptable to their class and peers. Exploration during an interview may uncover skills and knowledge clients may have of which even they are unaware. Working on cars or home improvement may provide a basic knowledge for occupations like equipment rental clerk or lumber and hardware sales. When using adaptive skills as a job base, however, it helps to prepare a short resume with your client present that shows these skills prominently, and then review the resume with the client carefully, convincing them of the importance of the skills and preparing them to voice the adaptive skills in their interviews with employers. Too often, they have a difficult time grasping the significance of these skills when talking with employers. In many cases, employers, particularly small employers, may not have actually thought through the requirements of a job themselves. These employers may find that a client's presentation of adaptive skills during an interview to be rather impressive.

Third, if counselors cannot expand the job base or locate other skills, such as skills from past work or adaptive skills, they may look to the family and friends for help. (Forming covenant groups is discussed at length in both Chapter 10 and in the companion booklet, The *Job Search Organizer*). Some counselors have taken the time to gather family groups or groups of friends for a conference to:

- explain a client's situation,
- tell them what your client can do functionally,
- go over the kinds of jobs that may be available, and
- provide them with brief, job-seeking skills highlights.

In this way, a rehabilitation counselor can enlist a whole new group of committed job seekers to help in the job search. The jobs that come out of these sessions will almost certainly be acceptable to the family complex and thus reduce the possible resistance to the jobs identified. If a counselor is successful in expanding the job base, finding new skills among the client's adaptive skills, or locating friends and/or relatives to assist in recognizing other job alternatives, these counseling efforts will reduce your client's resistance and result in an easier job placement experience.

A final suggestion for dealing with client resistance to work alternatives is to meet the matter head on with some kind of gentle confrontation. Gentle confrontation can be effective when conflict is first suspected. Gentle confrontation is part of most rehabilitation counselor's repertory of counseling skills, and too lengthy to discuss in detail, (i.e., except to point out some of the advantages of using gentle confrontation when your client's perceptions run counter to the market realities).

First, gentle confrontation allows a counselor to establish the existence of the conflict by letting clients know you suspect their understanding of the jobs they can do is getting in the way of their considering new job options. Second, gentle confrontation allows counselors to check out their own perceptions with those of their client. Service jobs may be the only jobs or the best jobs available. Third, gentle confrontation allows the counselor to maintain an even pace in the dialogue. Experience tells us that most of the time an injured worker will appreciate your honesty and your perceptiveness, and will sincerely look inward, though not necessarily immediately; to examine the way they feel about the conflict.

## Rehabilitation Counseling and the Baseline Villagers

We have no interest in offering a social commentary on a person's group classification within a community. People in the lower ranks of the community do, as a rule, have less wealth and social standing in the community, but remember, as we saw earlier in Chapter 2, "the steady worker," "the good worker," and the "hard worker" is usually "the measure of a person's worth in the community." Nor are we classifying people by their occupation. Baseline villagers do perform jobs that are unskilled or semi-skilled in the community. These include jobs for laborers and helpers to the trades; machine operators; factory workers; farm hands; cooks, waitresses, dishwashers, bus persons and other food service workers; domestics; janitors; and grounds keepers and gardeners. Do not be deceived, however, by the job titles. Some of the most respected workers in the community hold these jobs. We would not mislead you to believe that you can look at a person's job or their social standing in the community and draw conclusions about their behavior or their worth.

Our concern is the pattern of nonconforming behavior that leads certain individuals to, what we believe, are repeated personal and work failure, void of success and achievement, which alienates them from the community and sources of help. It is what these people do, their behavior, not what they are as people, that poisons the attitude of many insurance adjusters and case managers. This causes these professionals to lose faith in dealing with injured people, to "hate their jobs" believing that all clients are manipulative and unmotivated, and to exercise excessive caution in dealing with injured workers. Problem behaviors are the source of most of the bad experiences and failure for practicing rehabilitation counselors in job placement. Therefore, it is important that a study of this kind recognizes these behaviors and offers some guidance in handling problem behavior.

*Baseline villager* is a term chosen to describe persons or groups of persons who keep themselves and their families in the lower ranks of society because of a pattern of learned, self-destructive personal and work behavior. The term was adopted from the sociological study by Hollingshead. In this section, our intention is to:

1. identify behavior that we believe is unproductive and destructive in a social or work setting,

2. to discuss how rehabilitation counselors can recognize and deal with these behaviors; and

3. to offer suggestions as to how these behaviors can be changed.

## IDENTIFYING PROBLEM BEHAVIOR

It seems that everything baseline villagers do in life leads to failure. Their parents do it to them, setting an example with fractured family relationships; the community does it to them, branding them and their families as outcasts. "They cannot be trusted; they'll steal you blind" employer perceptions keep them from the "good jobs" and the wealth of the community. In the final analysis, they do it to themselves, living up to the expectations of the community with self-defeating work behaviors, poor school performances, an erratic history of unskilled jobs of short duration, and problems of adjustment to work and life in the community. It is the behavior not the occupation or the class standing that places a person among the baseline villagers. These behaviors include:

- *Dysfunctional families*, with fractured, often one-parent families, and a home life frequently characterized by alienation and conflict.

- *Poor school performance*. Typically, they have a marginal or limited education, generally dropping out of school before graduating from high school, or in many cases, elementary school. Their school performance is often characterized by fighting, truancy, poor grades, and other performance problems.

- *History of unskilled work*, with many jobs of short duration. The work record is often erratic with frequent absences due to presumed illness and other medical problems.

- *Problems at work*, often caused by an inability to get along with supervisors and/or co-workers.

- *Frequent changes in employment*, often the result of excessive absences, walking off the job casually, quitting without notice, or being fired for sub-par performance.

- *Low motivation to work*, typically with performance problems, such as underachieving or trouble completing tasks, thus requiring excessive control and supervision on the part of the employer.

- *Docile compliance with authority* that keeps them in entry-level work throughout their work life. Docile compliance often shows up in job placement by an unwillingness to complete assignments and follow up on work possibilities.

## Recognizing Client Problem Behavior in Rehabilitation Counseling

What we have said in this chapter about how the working people value work is likely accurate when we look at the group profile but, individually, each client is different. Just because they belong to a class of people who value work does not automatically mean an individual client believes they can work, that they are willing to work, or that there will be no problem behaviors that get in the way of a successful transition to new work. Moreover, we cannot assume that because a person from what we call "the baseline people" have a history of working in poor paying, unskilled, entry-level jobs means that they perform that kind of employment because of problem behavior at work. In other words, in determining how a person will adjust to a work setting, a counselor cannot rely upon previously formed assumptions about an individual, the class to which they belong, or their previous jobs or occupations. Many other, more subtle, factors go into determining successful work behavior.

Regrettably, even if a person responds favorably to questions about work behavior, you cannot entirely rely upon what your client is saying to you. Sometimes clients accept work alternatives without ever considering the most important question of all: do they want to work, believe they can work, or do they fear the consequences of non-compliance. To complicate matters, many clients apparently do not see their own behavior as limiting their work potential. For these reasons, if job placement is going to be successful, the rehabilitation counselor must recognize the problems, employ tactical measures to minimize the problems, and identify ways to limit or change the behavior.

Warning signals or "red flags" that will likely doom the job placement process need to be recognized early in the placement process. Nothing can be more frustrating to a rehabilitation counselor than to begin looking for work only to have the client sabotage an interview with negative thinking or for counselors to find themselves in vocational counseling with a client deep into the classic Eric Berne game of "yes, but" when you begin identifying appropriate work alternatives.

How do counselors recognize early signs of "bumps in the road" that may later wreck the placement process? How can counselors ever be sure they are not involved in "games people play" with a client during an interview or when setting up a job contact? How can counselors be sure that their client will make a sincere effort to obtain a job? In truth, you can never be sure, but there are frequently clues lying around that indicate which problems will appear on the horizon, patterns of behavior that counselors can recognize as sources of conflict. Some of these clues may be found in interviews, others may be found in the case records, in the family background, or in a discussion about the kinds of jobs the client is asked to consider.

In looking for early signals, rehabilitation counselors cannot forget the purpose of their investigation–to identify patterns of problem behavior that will allow them to anticipate later problems in job placement. The word pattern is very important. Few clients or members of their family will have a spotless record. There are nearly always some discrepancies when a counselor sees the same problems emerging repeatedly, forming a pattern of behavior. If this happens, it should raise a "red flag" and alert the counselor to a potential problem. These patterns may begin appearing in the following ways.

*An Interview*. A rehabilitation counselor can discern a sense of how a client feels about work from the information gained in the initial or subsequent interviews, particularly in gathering a history of past work. Most counselors look for continuity in the work history; that is, how many different places a client has been employed; how long a client has been with one employer; reasons why a client left one employer and went to another; the number of jobs a client has held, and length of employment with each employer. Discrepancies disclosed in any one of these areas may suggest how well a client has adjusted to a past work situation, and how well the client has gotten along with bosses, supervisors, and co-workers.

*The Case Records*. There are often positive or negative indications of work behaviors found in the case file, particularly in vocational records. In the initial examination of the records, most counselors examine past work experiences for the skills level and the likelihood of transferable skills from a particular job, the kinds of skills it takes to do the job, and how many jobs an individual has had over his or her work life. Many positive and negative work behaviors are suggested by reading between the lines, behaviors that give the counselor an indication of what the future holds.

Rehabilitation counselors may find evidence of a worker's behavior in any one of the following areas:

- The kinds of skills learned on the job, the progression in skill development through on-the-job training, continuing education courses workers have taken to improve work skills, and certifications a client might have obtained that suggest a client's appreciation for education or training and how willing an individual is to learn new things.

- Advancement to more responsible positions within the business or organization may suggest the willingness of a worker to take on new responsibility, and

- The length of time spent with one employer, in one occupation, or in one location may help predict loyalty to the workplace, continued loyalty to one's skill or occupation, or even how far a worker is willing to travel to locate new employment.

*The Family Education and Work History*. The family education and work history will not likely be found in the records a counselor receives on a case. The rehabilitation counselor usually has to obtain the information in the initial interview or later. Taking the time to obtain a profile of your client's background and the background of family members is usually well worth the effort. In addition to understanding your client and soliciting sources of help, a profile of the education and work of each family member can uncover work-related problems and locate sources of trouble that may lie within the family complex.

For instance, how long members of the family have been with their current employer may suggest how well members of the family get along with others in the work environment and the general work stability of the family as a whole. The achieved educational level of family members, both individually and collectively, may suggest how the client's family view education in general or the vocational training needed to learn new work skills. The occupations of the family members may indicate the level of achievement in work pursuits that is expected within the family complex.

This discussion and the presentation of covenant networks in Chapter 10 is for the purpose of helping counselors reach an understanding of the family complex. This discussion also suggests how the family complex as a covenant group can play a key role in determining the kinds of employment a client will accept, the level of achievement that can be expected at work, the willingness of clients to undertake vocational training, and the extent of their outreach into the employment community.

As mentioned above, the family can be a valuable resource in job placement as well as provide a reliable way to predict potential problems in the placement process. For this reason, many rehabilitation counselors ask their clients to make a list of the education achieved by each family member, including parents and siblings, the current occupations of each member, and the length of time each member has been with their current employer. The list provides a snapshot of the social environment in which your client lives, helps the counselor get to know the personal lives of family members, and suggests how work is viewed within the family complex.

*The Kinds of Jobs Desired.* In many rehabilitation practices, counselors do not do very much testing, even vocational testing. The focus of rehabilitation counseling is mostly upon what the person has done in the past (education, life, and work skills) and how the things they have learned fit other occupations (transferable skills). In the counseling process rehabilitation counselors look forward to trying to match up what the client can do with what the person wants to do. How do counselors determine what a person wants to do? They ask them. It may sound over simplified, but there has been no measure found that is a more reliable predictor of vocational outcomes than simply asking a person what they want to do. For this reason, at the outset of the client/counselor relationship, many counselors ask their clients to make a list of the kinds of jobs that interest them. The normal list of jobs is 10 or less.

This list is important in identifying potential problems that may arise in job placement.

- **The list tells the counselor how far along the client is in rehabilitation after an injury by showing how much thought has gone into vocational expectations.**

- **The kind of jobs on the list indicates how much thought a client has given to work in general. (Recall the research of Hollingshead earlier in this chapter about work perceptions by various classes of youth).**

- **The list gives an indication of the kinds of jobs a client is likely to accept during job placement.**

- **The job list shows how realistic a client's vocational aspirations are. When used in concert with the vocational information about the family, a counselor has a good idea about the appropriateness of the vocational selections.**

- **The kinds of jobs listed give an indication of the level of commitment a client is willing to make to a vocational selection. Do they want a job? Do they want an occupation with possible advancement? Do they want a new career? An analysis of the jobs on this list also provides an indication of work motivation and a way for beginning the job search.**

In trying to identify potential problems that may arise in a particular case, it is important not to become involved in negative thinking. Counselors must keep a positive, but realistic, attitude toward each case. Just because you are dealing with people who have made mistakes or seem to have lacked success behaviors in the past does not mean the job placement is doomed. Each case is a new experience and each client affords new opportunities. Change can occur and rehabilitation counselors must always believe in the human potential of each client.

## The Baseline Villagers: Do People Really Change Their Behavior?

Identification of potential behavior problems in the job placement process is essential to a later successful outcome. As we have discussed, recognizing these problems early saves the counselor a lot of grief later down the road. Nevertheless, identification of problem behavior is only the beginning. The essential question, once you have identified problem behavior, is what you as a professional, can do about it! Can the pattern of non-productive behaviors we have identified be changed to allow our clients to have a successful work experience? To what extent can rehabilitation counselors, charged with job placement responsibilities, ill equipped for psychotherapy, and with little time for long therapy sessions, be expected to provide behavioral-changing solutions?

In many ways, rehabilitation counselors are uniquely suited by philosophy, by education, by experience, and by circumstance to help change non-productive behavior—behavior that gets in the way of a successful work experience. Here are some suggestions:

- Rehabilitation counseling is one of the few helping professions with a primary emphasis upon work; and work in itself has its own therapeutic value. Moreover, the rehabilitation counselor sees both sides of the employment picture: the problems of unemployment and the whole-life benefits of a successful work experience. Thus, by philosophy and experience, the rehabilitation counselor learns from experience what it takes to be successful at work.

- Rehabilitation counseling is rich in applied counseling theory. Most rehabilitation counselors see their clients in a one-on-one relationship in a variety of real settings that allow for practical counseling solutions. Thus, the counselor is in a unique position to influence change.

- Most important, rehabilitation counselors meet their clients in crisis situations, at a time when they are most vulnerable. These are the very times when behavioral change is most likely to take place. For many, past behaviors have not worked; and, if they are to find any measure of success in their lives, they must find new behaviors. Many clients are at a crisis in their lives when they are willing to try new behaviors and accept the guidance of a person with whom they have confidence and feel they can trust. This places rehabilitation counselors in a position to become change agents and empower their clients. Is change possible? The real challenge for the professional may be in believing that people really do change.

# LOOKING FORWARD

The next chapter, Chapter 4 "Client Motivation," extends this discussion. We will examine ways rehabilitation counselors can take advantage of their unique position to help create positive change in the lives of their clients. The chapter on client motivation presents some of the latest research in the field of industrial psychology. Many of the ideas and solutions determined by this research are well suited for setting a productive environment for behavioral change.

# TOPICS FOR GROUP DISCUSSION

1. The statement is made in this chapter that work has its own therapeutic value, suggesting that work provides an environment in which a person's physical or mental condition actually gets better because of work. Do you believe work can be therapeutic? Are people not better off on benefits, such as Social Security, than having to work with difficult physical or mental problems? Discuss the merits of work and how your philosophy of work relates to your career in rehabilitation.

2. Approaching employers seems to have always been a difficult part of the job for rehabilitation counselors. Many RC's tell us that they do not like job placement because it involves meeting employers. Why is job placement not a desirable assignment for some colleagues in our profession? What is your perception of an employer? How many in your group have been employers or had parents who were employers? This chapter suggests some "ice breakers" rehabilitation counselors may use in meeting employers. Discuss your perception of employers, identify some of the problems, and possible fears counselors may have in meeting employers, and suggest ways counselors may become more comfortable in meeting employers.

3. Do you really believe that people can change their behavior? Is our behavior so welded in us by the time we are adults that we never really change our deep-seated behavior? Can you suggest conditions under which behavior change may occur? Does an RC's attitude toward changing behavior affect their job satisfaction? What is our attitude toward using confrontation?

## INDIVIDUAL ASSIGNMENTS

1. Research has shown a linkage between a person's perceptions of work and their place in the social system. Do you think a person's perception of work is important in your consideration of work alternatives? As a rehabilitation

counselor, how can you determine if your client's perceptions of work are consistent with the work alternatives they have identified and the possible jobs you are thinking about for them?

2. In what ways are injured workers from the working class among the most rewarding clients for a rehabilitation counselor? What are some of the reasons these clients are difficult to place in light and sedentary jobs?

3. What are some of the problem behaviors counselors may find among rehabilitation clients? How can a rehabilitation counselor identify patterns of problem behavior? Suggest ways you feel problem behavior may be overcome in counseling.

4. Research has shown that family connections can have both a positive and a negative influence in the job market. Identify both the positive and negative effects of family influence in the local job market. What are some of the tools you can use to offset the negative impact of family influence?

# REFERENCES

[1]*Dictionary of Occupational Titles*, 4th edition. US Department of Labor.

[2]Hollingshead, A. B. (1965). *Elmstown's Youth.* New York: John Wiley and Sons, Inc.

[3]Lingeman, Richard (1988). *"Caste and Class in the American Town" in Small Town America: A Narrative History 1620–Present.* New York: G.P. Putnam's Sons.

[4]Vidich, A. and Bensman, J. (1958). *Small Town in Mass Society.* Garden City, NY: Doubleday and Company.

[5]Wells, Gerald K. (1972). Caste and Code in the American Village, 1870–1920. An Unpublished Dissertation, University of South Carolina.

# CHAPTER FOUR

# CLIENT MOTIVATION & EMPOWERMENT: SETTING A RECEPTIVE CLIMATE FOR JOB PLACEMENT WITHIN THE COUNSELOR–CLIENT RELATIONSHIP

# PREFACE

> *I firmly believe that any organization, in order to survive and achieve success, must have a sound set of beliefs on which it premises all its policies and actions. Next, I believe that the most important single factor in corporate success is its faithful adherence to those beliefs. And, finally, I believe if an organization is to meet the challenges of a changing world, it must be prepared to change everything about itself except those beliefs as it moves through corporate life.*
>
> Thomas Watson
> President of IBM
> (From *In Search of Excellence*[8, p. 280])

To the Reader:

In the section "To The Reader:" in the opening chapter, and at several other points in the early chapters, we have referred to the definition coined by Paul Ellwood that rehabilitation was a profession of professions. That is, that the body of knowledge that gives rehabilitation its distinct professional identity lies in the selection of useful knowledge culled from the many professions with which we come in contact. In other words, we pull useful concepts from many professions to form the basis of our identity.

Perhaps, the idea of a "profession of professions" is no better exemplified than in Chapter 4: "Client Motivation and Empowerment." Theories of motivation at work abound in the literature and pop culture in our society. The popularity of the movie "Office Space," the television series "The Office," and the cartoon series "Dilbert," arise from situations about workers and the workplace in our society. They are about office production, about office relationships, about boss and employee conflicts in the work setting, and about how managers treat their people in the workplace.

In this chapter we take only a few of these theories and concepts, explain how we think the ideas are useful in our field, with examples, and show how these theories and concepts apply to our relationship with clients and, in particular, persons with disabilities seeking work. The practical applications we are able to make are the guiding principles in our selection of the motivational concepts and theories chosen for discussion in this chapter.

At the outset, we ask to what extent is a rehabilitation counselor responsible for the motivation of his/her clients? Is motivation something you say? Is motivation something you do? We know motivation is real. It really happens because we have seen changes in ourselves and others, changes that promote action, make a person want to do things differently, and give new directions to life and work. The word motivation suggests a whole set of intangibles–thoughts, feelings, attitudes, and motives–which cannot be seen or measured by any scale or paradigm. How can one expect results from something you cannot even see or measure?

Better yet, to what extent can one person really motivate another person? Some theorists take the position that a person–a rehabilitation professional–cannot really motivate their client and place the burden for creating change entirely on the client, relieving the professional of all responsibility for motivation. This is certainly the easy way out for the professional and provides the professional with a way to explain away past failures. Most of us know that in professional practice there are things a counselor can do and say, good and bad, which influence the behaviors of their clients and help or hinder the outcome of the case process. Chapter 4 explores the concepts of motivation and suggests six (6) ways counselors can build positive, empowering attitudes and behaviors into the counselor-client relationship.

Chapter 4 begins with a search for a definition that takes us to a brief discussion of some of the major theories of motivation prevalent in the United States and other industrialized countries over the past 100 or so years. The main substance of our discussion is inspired by research from the field of industrial psychology and set forth in Tom Peters' book, *In Search of Excellence*.[8] This publication becomes the backdrop for our discussion of motivational theories and practice in the field of rehabilitation. Much of the research that forms the basis of this chapter was conducted and first presented for counselors and supervisors from the Minnesota Department of Rehabilitation at the "Finding Jobs on Main Street" workshop in 1998.

## MOTIVATION AND THE REHABILITATION COUNSELOR: A SEARCH FOR DEFINITION

Gregory Smith, President of "Chart Your Own Course,"[10] defines motivation in this way. He says,

> *Motivation describes a process or a set of forces that cause a person to behave in a certain manner. These forces or motives can be social, spiritual, financial, or psychological. These forces can be a set of basic needs, wishes, desires, or dreams. These forces are called either motivators or de-motivators. The resulting behavior can be either positive movement toward a goal, or negative movement away from a goal. Motivators move us toward a goal, while de-motivators move us away from a goal."*[pg. 248]

This is just one of many such definitions of motivation that have been penned over the years, all of which contain many of the same elements or key words. Let us look for a moment at some of the key words found in the way Gregory Smith[10] defines the term motivation.

First of all, "motivation is a process or set of forces."pg. 248 Gregory Smith[10] suggests that motivation does not arise from just one thing or a single act. For instance, a counselor seeking to build motivation into the counselor-client situation cannot expect to have many quintessential or "Ah ha" moments when the lights go on and the bulbs flash and life changes before their very eyes. Indeed, there may be moments when things do become clear and pathways seem to lead in obvious directions; such moments are described by the poet Robert Frost as "a clarification of life." The Apostle Paul says that at such moments "old things are passed away; behold, all things become new."

We know from experience these life-changing moments are rare and their effect is often short-lived. Gregory Smith[10] sees motivation as a process occurring over time that involves many intended and unintended actions, "a set of forces."pg. 248 In other words, throughout a process, motivation is the result of many small actions, "baby steps" so to speak. In the practice of rehabilitation counseling some of the actions may seem small and insignificant, such as returning a phone call promptly or complimenting the client on the way they dress for an interview. Over time, positive attitudes and actions accumulate, influencing client behavior and affecting the outcome of the case. As a case develops, rehabilitation counselors have to ask themselves: "What can I do in my client contacts to effect in small ways positive thoughts and actions?"

Second, motivation, according to Gregory Smith,[10] comes from the performance of "*a set of forces or motives*" that can be "*social, spiritual, financial, and psychological.*"pg. 248 Most of us have been to so-called motivational seminars. Typically, speakers, well known for accomplishments in their field of endeavor, come to tell us how they became rich or famous or both. During the training, I have often been amazed by the insightful comments from these dynamic speakers. They always seem to have the right answers and say the right things at the right times. The events are frequently amusing and spectacular.

The implication of what these speakers have to say is that if each of us can say or do the right things at the right time, we too can affect positive change in the attitude, thoughts, and behavior of the people we serve. However, when the seminar is over, I somehow sink into a momentary state of subdued reflection when I realize that I cannot do it like the speaker. I am a guy who seldom has the right answer at the right time in social situations and later, upon reflection, when the lights finally go on, I find myself saying "Oh, I wish I had said ....". Truly, I would like to be Johnny-on-the-spot and always say and do the things that clarify life experiences for my clients, causing them to see the world, even temporarily, as I do. Unfortunately, I realize my inspiration is partial and I have to be me all the time.

In thinking more about it, I know motivation and empowerment do not work that way. The orations of these speakers just expose the enormous gap between the speaker's world and the world of the average Joe. The set of forces that bring about real and lasting motivation involve much more complex issues, (i.e., social, spiritual, financial, and psychological), many of which are beyond our control or the scope of the counselor-client relationship. In fact, many of the things that affect a client's motivation have nothing to do with the counselor at all.

Some of the things important in motivation like trust, confidence, an improved feeling of self-worth, and a desire to change can evolve from a wholesome counselor-client relationship. A rehabilitation counselor cannot always have the right answers for their client nor be the miracle worker the client wants the counselor to be. Rehabilitation counselors can provide a receptive climate where good things, positive life-shaping events, happen in the lives of the people they serve. Without a doubt, good things are much more likely to happen in a receptive climate where "positive regard" is the order of the day and "change" becomes a hoped-for result rather than a feared condition.

Finally, as Gregory Smith[10] says "*the forces are called either motivators or de-motivators. The resulting behavior can be either positive, movement toward the goal, or negative, movement away from the goal. Motivators move us toward a goal, while de-motivators move us away from the goal.*"[pg. 248] In motivation, like in love, there are two ways to fall, in or out. There can be positive action and communication that build and strengthen motivation, or there can be negative action and communication that weaken and destroy motivation. To go one-step further, one can say that there are few actions or interactions that occur in our contact with clients that do not, in one or the other, increase or decrease motivation. Counselors are seldom on a level plane. In any dynamic relationship, things are going on all the time; changes occur constantly with virtually everything going into the mix. Effective rehabilitation counseling recognizes those forces within the control of the counselor and builds those forces into positive motivators. So much depends upon the attitude of the counselor as well as the attitude of their client.

As used in this study, motivation concerns setting a receptive climate in which a client begins to "grow independent, confident, and happy" to quote a statement of the goal of rehabilitation from the Vocational Rehabilitation Act of 1920. What can rehabilitation counselors do or say in their client contacts that encourage trust and cooperation? How can a rehabilitation counselor build a relationship with a client that encourages growth, enthusiasm, and a willingness to change?

These are all questions motivational studies have sought to answer. In our discussion and examples on the subject of motivation, we turn to American industry where industrial psychologists have long sought answers to these questions. The authors have drawn heavily from the McKinsey Studies on motivation conducted by Tom Peters[9] and his staff of researchers and recorded in their book, *In Search of Excellence*. The findings of these industrial psychologists, we infer, have direct application to the field of rehabilitation.

# MOTIVATION THEORY: PAST AND PRESENT

Chapter 1 "The Rehabilitation Counselor's Management Role in Job Placement" began our discussion of management control. The idea, as presented, is that management control affects each phase of the management process: planning, organizing, coordinating, directing, and evaluation. Without appropriate control over the management process, case management becomes disorganized and confusing. So much of the success in achieving appropriate control depends upon the way rehabilitation counselors think about their clients, the degree to which they are willing to assume the responsibility for the things under their control, and the way they go about their position as managers of the case process.

Appropriate control involves thought processes as well as feelings and actions, thinking about the case process as a whole as well as doing things to make positive things happen in client's lives and work. This is particularly true in the early going, during the planning, organizing, and coordinating phases of the management process, when most of the management control lies in the hands of the counselor. From the outset, counselors must feel they are the professionals, the experts, and they have the responsibility to set the direction and determine the necessary amount of freedom and control between counselor and client.

The issues of freedom and control have been the main concern of business and industry since the beginning of the Industrial Revolution. For many decades, industrial psychologists have observed workers, primarily in a factory setting, and asked how much control does management need over workers to keep production and morale high? How much freedom can management allow workers, and, yet, get the same or higher production levels? The search for answers to these questions, and a determination of the best organizational structure to provide the right degree of freedom and control, have formed the core of the motivational research available to us today.

Outcomes from these motivational studies in industry have provided us with the knowledge of how to treat people, and not to treat people, in a work setting. How does this apply in our field of rehabilitation? These studies provide guidance for the things we can do as counselors to provide our clients with a climate that fosters growth and goodwill during the transition in their lives from disability to independence.

We have selected three (3) major studies in motivation that speak to our concerns in rehabilitation about freedom and control in the case management process. Fortunately, these are major studies, all of which were dominant in management theory and practice during the past century. These studies appeared at different times, yet almost consecutively over the past 100 years, and provide us with a progression of thought that has led to current, prevailing motivational theories and practices in American business and industry.

## BUREAUCRACY: "THE ORGANIZATIONAL SIDE OF MANAGEMENT"

We begin our journey into motivational studies with the bureaucratic model. This model dominated the thinking about motivation from about 1900 to 1930, and never completely died away. The two main spokespersons for this model were Max Weber, a German sociologist, and his American disciple, Frederick Taylor. (You may recall the film "Cheaper by the Dozen" which is about the life and times of the American industrial psychologist, Frederick Taylor).

The bureaucratic model presented management control in its absolute form, with total emphasis upon maximizing production and organizational efficiency. The bureaucratic management theory was all about the organization; the model showed little or no concern for the worker. Like other management theories that preceded it, the bureaucratic model mainly considers the organization and maximizing its workers efforts. Unlike today, management theory did not worry about the environment, foreign competition, the marketplace, or anything external to the organization. The view centered upon what could be done to "optimize resource application" inside the company or plant. The model was based upon the idea that in the right kind of organization, positions and workers would become, for the most part, interchangeable.

Underlying the Weber-Taylor school of thought was the idea that "if a finite body of rules and techniques could be learned and mastered–rules about breakdown of work, about spans of control, about matching authority and responsibility–then the essential problems of managing large groups of people would be solved."[10, pg. 92] Max Weber doted upon bureaucracy. Its rule driven, impersonal form, he said, was the only way to assure the long-term survival for an industrial organization. Frederick Taylor, the source of the time and motion approach to efficiency, felt that "if only you could divide work up into enough discrete, wholly programmed pieces, and then put the pieces back together in a truly optimum way, you will have a truly top-performing unit."[10, pg. 5]

While the impersonal, rule-driven bureaucratic form for managing people has lost some of its luster as research has revealed its basic flaws, many of the concepts persist today. Most organizations use some form of bureaucratic model. In fact, as an organization matures, and the management problems increase, there seems to be a tendency to search for more form and rigidity, and the impersonal bureaucratic monster raises its ugly head once again. In addition, the greater the power at the top of the organization, the more likely the bureaucratic model will find a home. This is evident today in many corporations, as mergers and consolidations make conglomerates larger and larger. In human service agencies of government, there is an ever-present search to find a system, a pert chart, an impersonal form, or a psychological instrument, to replace the personal touch and all human judgment.

## THE HUMAN RELATIONS MOVEMENT: "THE HUMAN SIDE OF ENTERPRISE"

Like so many movements in this Country, once a widely accepted dominant model is challenged, the pendulum swings too far to the other side and managers have the tendency to "throw out the baby with the bath water," so to speak. This was the case with the bureaucratic model. New research in the 1930's began to reveal that attention to workers and their needs might actually yield higher levels of production and many side benefits. This body of research ushered in what has come to be called the Human Relations Movement with its outpouring of evidence that the treatment of workers and improved working conditions has something to do with productivity. (The 2001 *Wall Street Journal* National Business Best-seller, *Practice What You Preach: What Managers Must Do To Create a High Achievement Culture*, is an extension of this kind of thinking. The author, David Maister has attempted to show that the human touch statistically can be shown to increase productivity).

The Human Relations Movement had its beginning in the late 1930's with Elton Mayo and the now-famous Hawthorne Studies at the Western Electric plant in Hawthorne, New Jersey. These investigations started out inauspiciously as ordinary fieldwork, consistent with the Weber-Taylor bureaucratic tradition. The research data were intended to be just a bunch of straightforward studies on industrial hygiene factors. The experiments, which took place in the bank wiring rooms of the Western Electric plant, were designed to show improved working conditions could actually have an effect on productivity.

During the experiments, however, a surprising series of events intruded on the theoretical background and continued to persist as stubbornly as the stubbornly held beliefs that preceded them. A good example, and the one most-often given, is about lighting levels in the plant. When the lights were turned up, productivity went up. However, when the lighting was turned down, surprisingly, productivity went up again. What had happened? The events of these experiments were interpreted to mean that the simple act of paying attention to workers, as well as better working conditions, has a great deal to do with productivity.

Based upon these and other studies, Mayo and his followers at Harvard University established the field of Industrial Psychology. World War II spurred growth in the field and by the end of the War such related areas of study as group training and leadership selection were beginning to flower.

One major contribution to the Human Relations Movement was made by Douglas McGregor.[8] We chiefly remember Douglas McGregor[8] for his development of the Theory X and Theory Y construct, contrasting the opposing views that workers are lazy and need to be driven (Theory X) alternately with the view that workers are creative and should be given responsibility (Theory Y). McGregor's[8] influence was sweeping, according to the Preface of his landmark book, *The Human Side of Enterprise*. In the Preface to his research study, he writes, "This volume is an attempt to substantiate the thesis that the human side of enterprise is 'all of a piece' that the theoretical assumptions management holds about controlling its human resources determines the whole character of the enterprise."[pp. vi-vii]

The Theory X–Theory Y hypothesis is meant to show that the positive attitudes management holds toward its workers translates directly into increased productivity and more satisfied workers. McGregor [8] termed Theory X "the assumption of the mediocrity of the masses." Its premise is:

- that the average human has an inherent dislike for work and will avoid work if he can,

- that people, therefore, need to be coerced, controlled, directed, and threatened with punishment to get them to put forth effort toward the organization's ends, and

- that the typical human prefers to be directed, wants to avoid responsibility, has relatively little ambition, and wants security above all.

Theory Y, by contrast, assumes:

- that the expenditure of physical and mental effort at work is as natural as in play and rest–the typical human doesn't inherently dislike work,

- that external control and threat of punishment are not the only means for bringing about effort toward the company ends,

- that commitment to objectives is a function of the rewards associated with the achievements–the most important of such rewards is the satisfaction of ego and can be the direct product of effort directed toward an organization's purposes,

- that the average human being learns, under the right conditions, not only to accept but to seek responsibility; and that the capacity to exercise a relatively high degree of imagination, ingenuity, and creativity in the solution of organizational problems is widely, not narrowly distributed.[pg. 34]

McGregor's[8] theories and the work of other theorists in the Human Relations Movement have fallen out of favor over the past few decades. During the heyday of the Human Relations Movement the group was credited with giving impetus to management experiments, such as T-Groups, Bottom-Up Planning, Democratic Management, Management by Objectives and other forms of "feel-good" notions in the work environment. The Human Relations Movement did help to solve some communication problems in the organizations where the techniques were employed. However, the pendulum moved too far to the left, in favor of freedom for the worker, and many of the main issues management has to deal with became lost in the democratization of the corporate workplace.

## IN SEARCH OF EXCELLENCE: "A BALANCED APPROACH TO WORKER MOTIVATION"

The underlying problem with the human relations approach to management was that the Theory X–Theory Y positions were seen as mutually exclusive. Seemingly, the manager had to choose between the two polar opposites, either Theory X or Theory Y, or, in other words, between control and freedom, depending upon the manager's general attitude toward subordinates. What was needed was a balance between management controls or authority, offered by the bureaucratic model and the freedom provided the worker in the human relations model.

With their 1982 publication, *In Search of Excellence*, Tom Peters and Robert H. Waterman, Jr.[9] codified many of the more moderate ideas prevalent at the time and demonstrated in their research a balanced approach to managing workers. Perhaps the exuberance of the writings, professional jealousies, or the fact that many of the companies labeled "excellent" have not fared so well in recent years has led some critics to discount the importance of *In Search Of Excellence*.[9] Yet there can be little doubt that this publication was a landmark study in the field of industrial psychology during the 1980's and 1990's and has made a significant contribution to contemporary theory and practice in worker motivation. The McKinsey Global Institute continues as a major consulting firm today.

The original design of the McKinsey "Studies in Excellence" was an attempt to look at management practices in large corporations and determine the qualities that made them stand out in their industries, keeping them "alive, well, and innovative." The authors asked such questions as, "Why were these companies successful?" "Was it their corporate culture, their leadership, or their people?" For their sample population the researchers chose 62 corporations, most of which had sales of over one billion dollars annually and a successful history of over 20 years. The findings or data provided by the McKinsey studies and the publication of *In Search of Excellence*[9] give research validity to many current management practices in both government and industry.

The ideas about worker motivation voiced in the publication *In Search of Excellence*[9] were not all new concepts at the time. What Tom Peters has to say about the work environment is consistent with other books, such as *The Five Minute Manager* by Ken Blanchard and other spin-off, how-to, "pop" culture books published about the same time. Tom Peters[9] and his associates provide research data that others lack and argue the motivational concepts convincingly. Since the research project that led to the publication, Tom Peters[9] has built a successful consulting career advising organizations in employee relations and has written other books on the same and similar subjects.

# SIX (6) KEYS TO MOTIVATION AND EMPOWERMENT

In our opinion, many of the ideas from *In Search of Excellence*[9] easily translate into correct ways rehabilitation counselors can set a motivational climate for their clients during the case process. We have chosen to present six (6) principle ideas from *In Search Of Excellence*[9] to serve as a backdrop for discussing motivation in rehabilitation. The examples we have chosen from the work of Tom Peters[9] and his associates give the topics on motivation a more universal application and suggest that if they have worked in business and industry, they are likely to work in rehabilitation as well. (Counselors in state rehabilitation agencies may find several of the ideas presented here familiar, having been exposed to the ideas, in different ways, in such popular training programs as "Counseling Skills" and "Effective Caseload Management" which the lead author of this publication had a part in creating for the Regional Rehabilitation Continuing Education Programs).

## KEY # 1: COUNSELOR ATTITUDE TOWARD CLIENTS

In his research, Tom Peters[9] postulated, "all of us are self-centered, suckers for a lot of praise, and generally think of ourselves as 'Winners.'"[pg. 56] In other words, most of us are more right-brained than we care to admit, with "wildly irrational opinions about ourselves." We make decisions more on hunches than on facts, and most of us "shoot from the hip rather than follow a rational approach to solving complex problems, human or otherwise."

Tom Peters[8] uses the following social science questionnaire to show how adults feel about themselves. In one psychological study with a random sample of adult males, one hundred percent (100%) of the respondents rated themselves in the top half in their ability to get along with others. Seventy-five percent (75%) considered themselves in the top 25% in leadership skills; only 2% rated themselves below average. Sixty percent (60%) rated themselves in the top 25% in athletic ability; only 6% believed themselves below average.

If we take these self-reports at face value, most of us would live in relative harmony at work and in our homes. There would be an abundance of leaders to fill needed positions at all levels in corporations and government; (unfortunately, there would be few followers to do the menial tasks like counseling clients). The majority of Americans would be in tip-top physical shape; and obesity would never reach the headlines in the national media.

Tom Peters[9] says that a major difference between the successful companies they studied and others they examined was in the attitude successful companies held toward their people. He believes any large population sample would look much the same as the one provided above. He says in the successful companies, "their populations are distributed around the normal curve, just like every other large population." The difference is that their systems recognize in their philosophy and the way they run their business that their workers have the need to stand out, to feel important, even if the opinions workers held of themselves may be exaggerated. "These companies promote and reinforce degrees of winning rather than losing."pg. 77

The main statements Peters[9] makes are directed toward the ways leaders look upon the performance of their followers. He argues,

> *If leaders consider their followers abilities rather than their limitations, and if leaders have high expectations of their employees or followers, people at all levels of the organization will respond with a higher level of performance.* pg. 82

To support this contention, Tom Peters uses the findings of Warren Bennis' *The Unconscious Conspiracy: Why Leaders Can't Lead.*[1] In his book, Warren Bennis draws attention to a study of schoolteachers giving IQ tests. Bennis found that when teachers held high expectations of their students, that alone was enough to cause an increase of 25 points in the students IQ scores.

*Can the attitude of counselors have a positive effect upon client performance?* Can we construe from these psychological studies and from the way Tom Peters[9] and his associates apply the results of the study to the management of employees that we need to consider our clients winners? If we look upon our clients with positive regard and have high expectations of them and their abilities, will they reward us with increased cooperation and a higher level of motivation to accomplish the tasks needed to achieve a successful rehabilitation?

If the past serves as an indicator, some rehabilitation counselors have voiced opinions that show they do not always view their clients in the same way they view themselves. In "Effective Caseload Management" workshops, rehabilitation counselors rated themselves, using the McGregor[8] Theory X–Theory Y descriptions, stated earlier. Without exception, all counselors placed themselves in the Theory Y camp. In general, counselors did not believe that people in their profession had an inherent dislike for work, and had to be externally controlled and threatened with punishment to get them to make an effort toward the goals of the program. They believed that professionals in their jobs accepted and sought out responsibility; and that rehabilitation counselors, as a rule, display a high degree of imagination, ingenuity, and creativity in the solution of problems. In hypothetical situations, the attitude of these practicing counselors toward their clients was, for the most part, positive with high praise for their client's ability to overcome their disabling condition. After all, they said, this is our reward for being in this profession!

Yet, when it came to their clients seeking work, many counselors indicated that clients dislike work (even though surveys have shown that clients come to rehabilitation for finding appropriate work), and clients will avoid work if they can. Many felt that the typical client needed to be directed, wanted to avoid responsibility, had relatively little ambition, and above all, sought security, such as third-party payments, over the opportunity to go back to work. Their responses implied that because of these factors, counselors needed to coerce, direct, and threaten clients with punishment, such as cutting off compensation checks, to get them to put forth the effort to find a job. So it seems, by placing themselves in the Theory Y category, counselors showed that they consider themselves winners, and by placing their job-seeking clients in the Theory X category, they showed by their responses and actions that they consider their clients losers.

In all fairness, when it comes to job placement, counselors have ample justification for their skepticism about a client's willingness to work. The problems are real and the rate of client success in job placement is considerably lower than it should be, given the level of support available to them. Seemingly,

- Some clients do not want to work, preferring to receive some form of compensation rather than returning to work, particularly if the option is alternative work.

- Often they display self-defeating behavior that gets in the way of success.

- Many times the disincentives in the system reinforce idleness and compromise a client's work ethic.

- Many clients do not look for work often enough, creating long and costly delays in the job search.

- Many clients interview poorly and sabotage their own placement plans.

- Some clients continue substance abuse habits that somehow show up only in the final days before they are ready to begin employment.

In addition, legal representatives enter the picture and compound the problems for counselors. As a result, large portions of a counselor's time is spent in guarding against abuse of the case process and in trying to handle problem cases, causing many counselors to lose faith in the system and their clients. No wonder counselor attitudes toward clients in job placement demonstrate frustration and skepticism.

American industry has encountered many of the same frustrations and skepticism about worker motivation. Problem employees are a fact of life in the work place wherever the location. As a result, many of the companies, Tom Peters[9] says, have designed their whole system of personnel management to remedy the problems caused by what he calls a "few bad actors." These measures taken to minimize the disruption have the unfortunate effect of demoralizing the rest of the workers. *In Search of Excellence*[9] records this statement made by a manager at General Motors:

> *Our control systems are designed under the apparent assumption that 90% of the people are lazy ne'er-do-wells, just waiting to lie, cheat, steal, or otherwise screw us. We demoralize 95% of the work force who do act as adults by designing systems to cover our tails against the 5% who are bad actors. By designing the control system to handle abuses, the companies create a low-risk work environment that undermines the company philosophy.*[pg. 57-58]

Tom Peters[9] goes on to say about these companies:

> *They call for risk-taking but punish even the tiny failures; they want innovation but kill the spirit of the champion; they design systems that seem calculated to tear down their workers self-image. When companies view their workers negatively and*

> *actively promote policies to counteract the disruption caused by a few, they, in effect, create additional bad actors. Label a man a loser and he'll start acting like one.*pg. 57

It seems what can be taken from motivational studies and translated into rehabilitation counselor attitude toward clients is this: counselors cannot allow themselves to get caught up in the trap of thinking that problem cases, or "bad actors" as Tom Peters[9] describes them, are the norm in rehabilitation. As one experienced rehabilitation counselor in private rehabilitation told us,

> *I have had plenty of failures, and I will probably have a lot more. It often seems that about the time my client is ready to go to work, I get a call about failing a drug test or a letter from a lawyer saying my client cannot work because he/she is in too much pain. I cannot let incidents like these affect the way I feel about other clients or disabled people in general. If I do, I am finished in this business.*

A positive counselor attitude toward clients and belief in their client's potential for success makes an important contribution toward setting a receptive climate in the initial stages of rehabilitation. Numerous research projects in verbal and non-verbal communication in recent years have shown clearly that a counselor's attitude in the counselor-client relationship, both good and bad, is hard to conceal from their clients. What research in industrial psychology has shown is also true in rehabilitation counseling. As Tom Peters[9] points out, observations of their research team among leaders in industry have shown clearly that "actions speak louder than words; and that we really cannot fool any of the people any of the time." Those who rely upon us for direction watch patterns of behavior in our most minute actions. They are wise enough to distrust the words that in any way mismatch our deeds." The same results have been demonstrated by research in related fields and ours. Studies of verbal and non-verbal behavior have demonstrated that when others notice the inconsistencies between verbal and non-verbal behavior, they tend to trust the non-verbal behavior more. If counselors hold negative attitudes toward their clients, there is little or no hope that they will be able to conceal them from their clients. Clients know how a counselor feels about them most of the time.

## KEY #2: INTRINSIC MOTIVATION

In his research for *In Search of Excellence,* Tom Peters[9] was looking for evidence that would explain what it was that made the people in the successful companies committed to their job and the goals of the company. Part of the answer, he became convinced, was that inwardly people have a strong need for meaning in their lives. He says, "We desperately need meaning in our lives and will sacrifice a great deal to institutions that will provide meaning for us."[pg. 56] What Tom Peters seems to be saying is that people need to derive some kind of meaning from the work they do; and if a company wants to create a work environment that motivates its workers, administrators will look for ways to show their employees the significance, or meaning, of what they are doing for the company. Very little has changed from the time of the publication of *In Search of Excellence* to today. In their research for writing *Generation Entrepreneur,* Stuart Crainer and Des Dearlove[3] found that skilled people seeking employment want to work for a company that, in some way, contributes to better the lives of other people. As a result, many companies at their web sites and in their publications make it a point to show that the company is engaged in meaningful work.

Tom Peters[9] goes on to say that for people to build lasting commitment to a task or a goal, the task or goal must be inherently worthwhile. He mentions the numerous experiments of Edward Deci at the University of Rochester which have demonstrated that lasting commitment to a task is engendered only by fostering conditions that build intrinsic motivations, conditions coming from inside the person that spur them on to higher levels of achievement. In other words, he says, "people must believe that a task is inherently worthwhile if they are really to be committed to it."[9, pg. 72]

How do people in these companies find significance in what they are doing? What enables them to see their contribution as important and build within themselves intrinsic motivation that helps them rise to a higher level of purpose? Tom Peters[9] says "making meaning" for workers is the function of leadership:

> *The role of the leader is one of orchestration and labeler: taking what can be gotten in the way of action and shaping it–generally after the fact–into lasting commitment to a new strategic direction. In short, leaders make meaning.*[pg. 75]

This one statement seems best to summarize the content of his entire book, *In Search of Excellence*. So much of the content of *In Search of Excellence* is really an elaboration upon ways various leaders, CEOs, managers, and supervisors within the successful companies have found to make meaning for their employees. Engendering intrinsic motivation has resulted in higher levels of achievement and commitment to the goals of the companies they serve.

*"Making Meaning" for Clients in Rehabilitation.* How may the ideas of Tom Peters[9] concerning intrinsic motivation translate into working with clients in counseling and job placement? Let us look first at the early stages of case development. Whether or not counselors are planning to use some form of the selective approach or the client-centered approach, the beginning case

development is much the same. Most cases in rehabilitation start with an assignment of the case and a review of the medical, vocational, and other information for a history of diagnosed conditions, treatment outcomes, prognosis, and residual abilities and limitations.

Then the counselor conducts an initial interview to gain an understanding of the client's personal and work history and what effect their medical problems have on a day-to-day basis. From the review of the case file and the interview with the client, rehabilitation counselors begin to:

- develop a vocational profile,
- determine the functional limitations, both mental and physical, and
- identify personal assets, such as work skills, educational achievements, and life experiences that will help their client in making the transition from disability to independence in work.

From this exploration, the counselor and the client begin to build a plan that will carry them through the rehabilitation process.

That is where motivation becomes a concern of paramount importance. Every practicing rehabilitation counselor knows that a plan, even when jointly developed and containing agreed-upon goals, is only as good as the client's commitment to the plan. At some point in the initial evaluation of the client's abilities, a counselor must ask the question: "What can I do or say that will cause my client to believe what we are doing is worthwhile and to follow the plan through to the end?" In keeping with the research, another way of phrasing this question may be to ask ourselves, "How am I able to build meaning and value for my client that will lead to greater commitment to the program to which we have both agreed?" You cannot be successful in our field unless you have a commitment on the part of the client to the rehabilitation plan.

Building meaning and value for clients is a way of thinking a little differently about the things you do routinely in professional practice. The thought process of building meaning and value for clients can lead to a re-examination of our role as counselors, casting ourselves in the position of a leader whose main role may be as:

- a manager and orchestrator of the rehabilitation process,
- a teacher and interpreter of meaning for their clients, and
- a value shaper, identifying important concepts and ideas (values) that result in actions that lead toward the goals of rehabilitation.

*Manager* has become a term with which we are now familiar. Teacher is just another day at the office for most practicing counselors, but orchestrator, interpreter, value shaper. These are unusual terms used to describe the counselor position. Contemporary discoveries in motivational research would lead us to believe these designations are an accurate description of the counselor's leadership role in the rehabilitation process. We will look more closely at how these terms used in motivational research may apply to professional practice in rehabilitation.

*Manager/orchestrator*. Here, and at other places in this book, the position taken is that the rehabilitation counselor is a manager of the case process. That is, rehabilitation counselors assist clients in planning, organizing, coordinating, and directing the action of the case. Counselors usually take an active role in preparing resumes and determining which jobs are right for their clients, and regardless of the job placement approach, counselors remain active in evaluating the progress and adjusting the actions of the case to the realities of the job market.

In this scenario the rehabilitation counselor is, in many ways, like an orchestra leader directing a concert, interpreting musical scores for the players, determining which players perform at a given point according to the musical composition, and choosing which instruments are to perform at a given point to create a unified effect. Much like orchestra leaders, counselors become the orchestrators of the case process. Clients are like the musicians, playing out their parts and contributing to a successful outcome.

*Teacher/Interpreter*. In the discussion of job placement and in the examples used in the text, readers may get the idea that most of the teaching and interpreting comes in the empowerment phase of job placement where, routinely, counselors teach job-seeking skills, review the results of employer interviews with their clients, and assist clients in selecting job opportunities. Teaching and interpreting is just as important in building the counselor-client relationship and in setting a receptive climate for job placement.

Assuming the role of teacher and interpreter may make some counselors feel uncomfortable. They do not view themselves as competent to fulfill the lofty roles of teacher and interpreter. Rehabilitation counselors have a wide exposure to knowledge from many sources, and in two areas of knowledge, disability and the world of work, rehabilitation counselors are the expert. They may not feel like experts, but those seeking our help and professionals in other fields look to us for expertise in at least these two areas of knowledge.

There is no other professional specialty that ties together disability and work and looks at such things as physical and mental limitations, residual functional capacity, the impact of disability upon a person's ability to work, and what skills are required to perform appropriate work activity. In these areas, rehabilitation counselors are the experts. Indeed, that is why rehabilitation counselors are in demand as vocational experts by the Social Security Administration and by attorneys litigating personal injury cases. In working with clients, counselors must gain the confidence to fulfill the role of an expert. Much of what goes on during the rehabilitation process needs interpretation, and it is the duty of the counselor to share their expertise in their areas of knowledge.

Feeling nervous in the role of expert is nothing new. We have all had our moments. I recall my early experiences as a Vocational Expert in Social Security hearings. During the hearings, I would watch the clock waiting to hear the Administrative Law Judge or the hearing reporter say the magic words "the hearing is closed." Unfortunately, before the close of the hearing, the ALJ would usually say the dreaded words "let's now hear from the vocational expert." I remember feeling uneasy, even frightened, at these words and wondering to whom the judge could be referring, calling me a vocational expert. Surely, at those moments, I felt like anything but an expert. I found out later from my discussions with other experts on vocational matters that my reaction was normal. Many times in those moments of despair, I would roll over in my mind the words of Philip Bussey, one of my mentors in rehabilitation: "remember, you are the expert!"

How do rehabilitation counselors take on the role of teacher and interpreter? You will recall the discussion in chapters 2 and 3 about the class position in society of the people we serve. Most employers come from the middle-class of society while most of our clients in rehabilitation are working people and come from social classes that have little or no influence over the flow of jobs. The "world of work" is the domain of the rehabilitation counselor. It is the responsibility of our profession to enlarge the concepts of work for our clients; to teach and interpret issues that face them in seeking work in the American economy; to show them how jobs are found in their society; and to expand their horizon in order for them to see possibilities for resuming work or seeking alternative work.

Sometimes teaching and interpreting involves challenging the misconceptions clients have about work. The reader may recall the research project among older, unemployed workers discussed in Chapter 3. Researchers found these workers believed that if they could no longer do their past work, they felt unable to perform any work at all. This research applies particularly to older, skilled trades workers. When rehabilitation counselors are trying to place an older, injured worker in alternative work, they cannot ignore the validity of this research replicated so often in so many settings. For clients to overcome their fears or false perceptions and have them consider returning to work requires interpretation and teaching, expanding upon the idea that age makes little or no difference in today's economy where 25 million or more workers are over 65, and showing them that there are other opportunities in the job market for them. Let us work our way through a typical case example of how rehabilitation counselors look upon the results of a vocational assessment and interpret the results for their clients.

> *The client is a 55-year-old carpenter on worker's compensation with a degenerative disc problem in his lower back. The treating physician has given him permanent restrictions of lifting no more than 25 pounds.*

Question # 1: *Can he do his past work as a carpenter?* The answer is generally no. Carpentry, as it is normally performed in the national economy, and as it is described in the *Dictionary of Occupational Titles,* is medium to heavy work, requiring the lifting levels of 50 pounds occasionally. Therefore, this carpenter is left with either seeking alternative work or retiring on some form of disability.

Question # 2: *Which is the better choice?* Most counselors believe alternative work. As we have seen, so much of the identity of working people is tied up in their work skills and in their ability to work. The inability to work usually results in loss of identity with situational depression as a normal by-product of this condition.

Question # 3: *Does the client have transferable skills to help him find work in other fields?* The answer may be yes. Perhaps an examination of his past work and his life skills would lead, for example, to work as a counter clerk in a retail lumber establishment. Before a worker would accept the possibility of other employment his rehabilitation counselor would need to enlarge his perspective to include work other than carpentry and interpret for him the benefits of continued employment. Careful interpretation, letting clients know exactly what you expect from them, is essential in sound behavioral counseling.

*In Search of Excellence*[9] quotes from the book *Morale* written by Thomas Watson, Jr.,[11] the President of IBM. In the section "A Business and Its Beliefs" Watson says,

> *I firmly believe that any organization, in order to survive and achieve success, must have a sound set of beliefs on which it premises all its policies and actions. Next, I believe that the most important single factor in corporate success is its faithful adherence to those beliefs. And, finally, I believe if an organization is to meet the challenges of a changing world, it must be prepared to change everything about itself except those beliefs as it moves through corporate life.* [pg. 280]

Thomas Watson, Jr.[11] believes the basic philosophy, spirit, and drive of the organization have far more to do with its relative achievements than do technological or economic resources, organization, structure, innovation, and timing.

Most businesses would measure success by what happens on the bottom line of the income statement. In the secular world of business, results are all that matter. Here the president of one of the long-standing and most powerful corporations in America, one that continues to fare well in the long economic recession today, is saying that he feels success at the IBM Corporation has more to do with their philosophy and basic character, what they believe, than material assets, technology, and management strategies.

Can the same thing be said about our profession? In a helping profession, such as ours, are our beliefs about the value of people overcoming disability and the value of work important motivators for staff and for our clients? Is what we believe included in the messages we send to our clients as we take them through the rehabilitation process?

With the above interpretation, accepting the terms orchestrator or interpreter may be an easier task when defined in the context as things counselors are likely to do regularly with any client.

*Value Shaping*. To some, the term may suggest some form of psychotherapy, getting into the heads of their clients, something few rehabilitation counselors have the ability or the time to do. To others, value shaping may suggest an expansion of the role of the counselor to include some form of "shepherding" with clients, attempting to change behavior by replacing a client's value system with one of their own. Still others, at a time when the nation is attempting to define moral values, may see the term value shaping as equivalent to advancing the conservative theology of the so-called "moral majority."

That is not the intension here. Value shaping in this context means an examination of the values you hold as a counselor and the philosophical principles about your profession that you in some way convey to your clients, whether in counseling, in reinforcement, or in the manner of conducting the case. In rehabilitation, we do not talk much about values and beliefs anymore.

Maybe we have become too sophisticated. Leadership gaps and politics may have had something to do with it. When I came into the field of rehabilitation, philosophy and belief were central to our professional identity. I recall the leaders in rehabilitation referring to the profession as "the bridge over which a person with disabilities passes on their journey from dependence to independence;" leaders then talked about the goal of each professional in practice as one "to insure the right of disabled citizens to rise to their highest level of achievement" and using terms such as "the dignity of work;" and I recall the pride rehabilitation counselors felt serving in a profession which affords a professional the opportunity to participate in a meaningful process that serves persons with disabilities. This example may help to clarify the concept of value shaping.

At the beginning of each conference, the training staff passed out a questionnaire to the counseling audience. This was a discussion document to generate interest in the program and involve the audience in talking about their practices in job placement. The first question on the list asked, somewhat ambiguously, "Do you believe that work is therapeutic?" with an explanation that went something like this: "Do you believe that people actually get better medically by working." The discussion that followed always came down to a self-examination of the importance of work and how members of the audience felt about work. The discussion was stimulating because most of the attending counselors had not really thought much about the philosophy of their profession, even though work was central to their professional pursuits.

## KEY # 3: BUILDING COMMITMENT THROUGH POSITIVE REINFORCEMENT

How counselors feel toward their client and the values they hold as professionals give them a foundation upon which to build a professional counselor-client relationship. There are also things counselors can do, deliberate actions, which affect, and to a certain extent, shape behaviors that build commitment toward mutual goals. The remaining ideas, with examples drawn from the research of Tom Peters[9] and his associates, expand upon things counselors can do to enhance motivation and build commitment to the rehabilitation process.

The first of these is the concept of Positive Reinforcement. The theories of positive reinforcement stem from the original research of B. F. Skinner, the Father of the Behavioral School of Counseling, and later refined by many other behavioral scientists, prominent among them includes John Krumboltz. For the most part, behavioral counselors consider client problems mostly as problems of learning. In the event that a person has a personality disorder or behaviors that are not working for them, the problems lie in the effects of faulty learning. These counselors view the task ahead of them in counseling as an attempt to help those who come to them to learn new, more adaptive behaviors.

Observation and practice are their usual methods. In the practice of rehabilitation, counselors who give their clients assignments, have their clients make lists, and have them heavily involved "doing things" to advance the goals of their personal rehabilitation are probably using methods pioneered by behavioral scientists.

One of the "laws of learning" as postulated by B. F. Skinner was the theory of operative conditioning. That theory says that, if a behavior is followed by an environmental event that brings satisfaction to the individual, then the probability of that behavior's recurrence is increased. In other words, if the performance of a particular action or behavior (giving a few coins to a beggar) results in some kind of satisfaction or reward (the warm feeling of generosity) the person is likely to learn the happiness of charitable giving and repeat the action. The contrary is also true. If the performance of a particular action or behavior (touching a hot frying pan) results in some kind of dissatisfaction (burned fingers), the person is likely to avoid such behavior in the future. Finally, if an action or behavior is not recognized or reinforced, that behavior tends to diminish, and, ultimately, become extinguished.

The conclusions reached in the study, *In Search of Excellence*,[9] are that positive reinforcement works as a powerful tool for leaders in the corporate world and most effective leaders in the successful companies use positive reinforcement in some form or another. In fact, the writers of *In Search Of Excellence*[9] carry Skinner's theory of operative conditioning a step further. These writers postulate, with scientific research to back them up, that if we as people learn that we have done something well, and are told we did well, we tend to do even better.

In one experiment reported by the writers of *In Search of Excellence*,[9] adults were given ten puzzles to solve. All ten were exactly the same for all subjects. The participants worked on them, turned them in, and at the end received the results. In fact, the results given were fictitious. Half the exam takers were told they did well, seven out of ten correct. The other half were told they did poorly, seven out of ten wrong. Then all were given another ten puzzles (the same for each person). The half who had been told that they had done well in the first round did even better in the second round; the other half really did worse than they had done previously. In subsequent replications of this experiment, similar results were obtained.

The authors of *In Search of Excellence*[9] say that the results of studies like these appear to show that personal success, reinforced appropriately, leads to persistence, higher motivation, or something that makes us do even better. Half of the people who thought they did well really did do better. Everyone, it seems, has the need to be recognized and has the need to achieve something between the time they are born and the time they die.

What motivational studies tend to show us in the field of rehabilitation is that through careful use of recognition and rewards based upon actual, identified achievements, counselors can increase desirable behavior and decrease undesirable behavior. Suppose, for instance, you have a client in the process of developing a vocational plan. You have given him the assignment of coming up with a list of jobs that may use the skills he has learned in his past work. Several days later, he comes to your office and tells you that last evening he invited several friends over to his home to help him identify some of the skills he had learned in his last job that may have application to other work. Instead of saying "well, let's see what you came up with" and judging the accuracy of the effort, you recognize him for taking the initiative to define his work-related skills and let him know the importance of using family, friends, and acquaintances to help in defining appropriate work. You think that because you have recognized the effort, your client will try harder and take even greater responsibility in the future. Studies in motivation would support that notion.

Studies have shown conclusively that positive reinforcement does work, but counselors have to be very careful not to use the technique of positive reinforcement as a way to manipulate their clients. The wise counselor will recognize that our presentation here is a brief outline, intended to point out the logic of positive reinforcement. Before using this technique as a counseling tool, however, counselors need to perfect their reinforcement skills through training and understanding all of its ramifications. Guidelines for counselors in the proper use of positive reinforcement would normally include these words of caution: *Be sincere and reinforce behavior based upon earned achievements.* Positive reinforcement is a sensitive and powerful tool of human psychology. Used correctly by responsible counselors, it leads to higher levels of motivation; used incorrectly and irresponsibly, it becomes a tool of manipulation. The motives of the counselor must be sincere, and reinforcement must be based upon recognizable achievements.

To show some of the benefits of positive reinforcement as well as some of the complexities counselors may have in using positive reinforcement, we will consider two contrasting examples. One rather simple example is where the counselor is able to use positive reinforcement in the correct way, based upon recognizable achievements. Another example is a more difficult situation where a counselor is faced with deception, where reinforcement would likely reinforce the wrong actions and behaviors.

## EXAMPLE ONE

*Your client is a 35-year-old former over-the-road truck driver, Ned Bayshore. Ned has had a back injury that resulted in fusion surgery at the L4-L5 levels. The recovery has gone well. His treating surgeon does not believe Ned can do his past work but has released him to return to some kind of work with a lifting restriction of no more than 25 pounds. In your last session with Ned, you have talked with him about the restrictions and asked him to go home and make a list of 10 jobs that he thinks he will be able to do. This morning he returns with the list, showing he has spent considerable time making the list and looking over possible work alternatives.*

*As his counselor, you praise Ned for his thoughtful work in compiling his list. The list not only provides possible jobs that may be appropriate for him and suggests the kinds of work that may be of interest, but also the list becomes a discussion document for both of you to use in the job search. Your initial praise and recognition of this achievement reinforces positive work behaviors (i.e., he was given and completed his assignment). Just as important, your use of the list as a foundation for a job search provides reinforcement for actions he has taken to become independent. At some other point in his life, when he has the need to find new work, he will likely begin his job search by making a list of possibilities (instead of running off to the newspaper), looking over the list to determine things he can actually do, and seeking only those jobs he can actually perform within his abilities and limitations. It is the old adage "teach a man to fish and he eats for a lifetime" popping up once again.*

## EXAMPLE TWO

*We are still using the 35-year-old injured truck driver, Ned Bayshore. This time the counselor receives a different result from the assignment. To get an idea of the kind of jobs that might be of interest to your client, you have asked him to make a list of 10 jobs that your client thinks he would be able to perform within his limitations. Several days later, he returns with a few job titles scratched on a note card. You immediately detect that he had spent little time in preparation, and had not given much thought to the assignment. What do you do? Do you praise Ned, thinking that by using positive reinforcement he will do better the next time, as the theory of operative conditioning may suggest? Will a well-placed compliment, "well I'm glad you took the time to do the assignment" erase the counselor's suspicion, relax the client, and allow the relationship between the two of you to continue?*

Hardly. First, your reinforcement will not be sincere as you already detect he is trying to deceive you. Moreover, the reinforcement is not based upon actual accomplishments, but upon the client's pretense. So what would your praise of your client reinforce? More than likely, suspicion and doubt in the eyes of the counselor and deception "he knows he got away with it" on the part of the client, weakening rather than strengthening the role of the counselor as a leader. You will also have reinforced poor performance and likely, that performance will be repeated in the future. In this case, gentle confrontation may have been a better counseling technique.

*Be specific.* What these motivational studies seem to suggest to us in rehabilitation is that through positive reinforcement—the use of recognition and rewards based upon actual identified achievements—counselors can increase desirable behavior and decrease undesirable behavior. If clients offer personal insights that show clarity in their understanding or, even better, they do something to advance their own progress toward growth and independence in their rehabilitation program, and you as their counselor notice this achievement and tell them about it, you will likely see behavior that is even more adventurous in the future.

In order to shape success behavior, counselors must identify the exact actions that they feel point in the right directions. Praise in a general way "you look nice today" may be sincere and make clients feel good about themselves, and, at the same time, serve as a good warm-up to your interview. However, compliments like this would be what the counseling theorist Carl Rogers would consider "unconditional positive regard," offering a general recognition of their clients as important human beings in their own right. Make no mistake, however! Compliments of this kind are important, but these kinds of compliments do not provide direction or really tell clients anything much about themselves or their behavior.

Compliments about how one looks in general are not specific enough to reinforce behavior. In the same situation, if you were to say "You look nice today. I like the way you are dressed. If you dress that way for your interviews, potential employers will likely have a favorable impression of you. That may help you get the job you want. Interviewers have told us that how a person dresses is one of the three most important things they look for in judging a candidate." Now you, as your client's counselor, have reinforced a particular behavior, appropriate dress, a specific behavior you want repeated when your client meets employers. This behavior is likely to be repeated at a more crucial time in the job-seeking process.

*Be Immediate.* The sooner reinforcement occurs, the greater power the reinforcement has in shaping future behavior. The theory of operative conditioning states that any behavior that is immediately reinforced will tend to be repeated. What this means is that when you recognize something good your client has done, your client will associate your reinforcement with what he/she has just done, and your client will likely repeat that action again. As the theory goes, the closer the reinforcement to the time the behavior occurs, the more impact the reinforcement has upon future acts or behaviors.

In the above example, you noticed your client was well dressed for an interview with you; you paid the client a compliment for the way your client is dressed on that day; then, you told your client how important dress is to the employers they meet, giving the client a job-search technique substantiated by proven research evidence. Such specific reinforcement increases the likelihood that when dressing for an interview in the future, at a time the counselor will probably not be present; the client would recall what you had said about dress and take the time to dress appropriately. Just as important, the reinforcement you provided to the client was both spontaneous and immediate, increasing the chances that the behavior would be repeated.

*Be conditional*. As we have discussed, reinforcement can be unconditional, based upon your recognition as clients for what they are "I enjoy working with you." "Working with you is fun." "You are really a fine person." As we have seen, unconditional reinforcement may bring about warm feelings and make both the counselor and the client feel better, but unconditional reinforcement is not directed toward specific behaviors. Moreover, unconditional reinforcement does not improve learning; unconditional reinforcement does not help clients know what they need to do or not to do. Unconditional reinforcement does not provide direction in telling the client what desirable actions or behavior to use in future situations. Therefore, unconditional reinforcement does not significantly improve the chances that desirable behaviors will be repeated.

Positive reinforcement must be conditional. In the use of conditional reinforcement, you are recognizing the behavior or action for what it is. If the behavior is productive and represents a behavior you feel is important to repeat, you reward the behavior with recognition. For instance, suppose your client has had a problem coming on time to an interview with you. In the last session you told your client that you would like him to come to appointments on time (a specific behavior you want him to repeat) and provided him with reasons why being on time is important in a job situation. You say to him on his arrival (an immediate reinforcement) "It makes me happy when you show up for your appointment on time."

When you reinforce behavior conditionally, you are also implying that you may disapprove of a different behavior later. As in the above example, you are saying what your client did this time was good; but you are also reserving the right to disapprove future behavior that is off-task and non-productive. Now, suppose your client is 10 minutes late for the next interview, saying that he had car trouble and could not make it on time. The first question is, *is his excuse acceptable?* No! Your client could have notified you that he was having difficulty with his automobile ahead of time. Your client has wasted your time. You are a professional and your time is the most valuable resource you have to offer. You cannot tolerate behavior of this kind. Moreover, repeated tardiness will affect your client's ability to sustain employment. You must prevent this behavior from becoming a chronic problem through conditional reinforcement during the initial preparation, the job search, and employment.

The second question: *Is he telling you the truth?* Maybe, but what you are dealing with here is not the question of your client's credibility. It is possible that credibility may be an issue in the future, but your reinforcement is based upon his present behavior, repeated tardiness, a behavior that cannot be tolerated. If you question the credibility and suggest or imply that he may not be telling you the truth, you could confuse the issue, and the behavior you want to change becomes lost in dealing with the larger issue of credibility. Stay with the behavior you want to be changed, for now at least.

A third question: *Does it really matter?* After all, it is only 10 minutes. Absolutely! Each contact you have with a client is a training session in rehabilitation. Through conditional reinforcement, you are trying to bring about behavior that will lead clients to success in the workplace. You are the leader, the value shaper, and the teacher. As we have seen, in reinforcement what you expect of your clients is usually what you get. Counselors need to hold expectations of their clients high, with little tolerance for off-task behavior. Little things often become big things; occasional late arrivals at an appointment become chronic if not dealt with by counselors.

What do you say in these situations? Something like this: "I can understand you having car trouble; I have sometimes had the same problem, but I want you to be on time. Being on time is important now, as I have other clients who need my time; and being on time will become even more important to you in the future as your employer is not going to allow you to be late to work. If you are going to be late, let me know ahead of time so that I can readjust my schedule." In such a reply, you have identified automobile trouble as a possible problem that could happen to anyone; you have also said that under certain conditions, the behavior is acceptable; but you have left no doubt about what you want from your client.

Conditional reinforcement says, in effect, that you may approve desirable behavior, but you reserve the right to disapprove behavior in your clients that is non-productive and self-defeating. Clients will likely see your gentle confrontation on issues like these as a way of helping them develop behaviors they can use in the future. Moreover, they will respect you for "calling a spade a spade." Furthermore, clients will tend to recognize conditional reinforcement for what it is and seek out behaviors that will result in positive reinforcement.

## Key # 4: Action vs. Contemplation

A theory still hotly contested in the field of psychology is the ordering of perceptions, attitudes, and actions. Theorists have long believed that perceptions (attitudes, beliefs, strategies) precede actions. They believe that the way you look at things determines the way you act, that thinking precedes action. To illustrate, in the popular rehabilitation training program "Effective Caseload Management" developed by the Region III Regional Rehabilitation Program, the instructors used a film titled, "You Pack Your Own Chute," directed and produced by Eden Rile.

In the film the author and speaker, Eden Rile, narrates this event. She relates feelings of peace and contentment while sitting on a beach overlooking the Pacific Ocean. Under those conditions, she is willing to enjoy the peaceful surroundings. She says, suppose a chasm developed on the beach before her and a great groundswell of water shoots into the air. Under these new conditions, she would feel differently, unsafe, and consider the beach to be a dangerous place. She would then get up from her peaceful resting place and hurriedly flee the premises. In the film, this narration was meant to show that the way people look at things (a peaceful or a hazardous beach) determines their behavior (staying and enjoying the setting or fleeing the possible dangers). From her standpoint, thinking clearly precedes action.

In the workshop "Effective Caseload Management," in reinforcing the concept that thinking precedes action, we often used games to expand counselor perceptions in the hope that they would change their old ways of looking at things and examine something a little different. One of these games was the familiar 9-Dot Test. In the training exercise, participants had before them the following group of nine (9) dots and they were asked to connect the dots with four continuous straight lines. Of course, you cannot connect the dots with the lines without going outside of the perceived box that the order of the dots seems to suggest. The correct answer is indicated on the diagram at the right:

The only way to join the dots with four connecting straight lines is to alter your perceptions that the nine dots form a box, and go beyond the box to make the connection. By making the right choice our trainers believed that the participating counselors might alter their perceptions, begin to accept the idea that things are not necessarily the way they seem, and expand their learning horizons. Clearly, the message was that if you looked at things differently, you would act in a different way.

According to Tom Peters,[9] recent research has shown little relationship between explicitly stated belief and mundane actions. In fact, these studies have shown the exact opposite. They show that if you get people acting, even in small ways, they will come to believe in what they are doing. Doing things and not thinking about them leads to "rapid and effective learning, adaptation, and commitment." Tom Peters[9] says that Harvard professor Jerome Bruner[2] captures the spirit when he writes, "You are more likely to act yourself into feeling than feel your way into acting."[pg. 73]

The research is not saying that important decisions should be made without thought and consideration. Major decisions, such as choosing a vocational goal require information, market research, and a lot of consultation and deliberation. The key word here is mundane, a word that characterizes most of the actions in the counselor-client relationship. Counselors who use these motivational practices get their clients involved in the activities of their own job placement. From the very beginning, even before extensive initial counseling, the counselor makes assignments, has them look at job options, seeks out job leads, and networks among friends, relatives, and acquaintances. As their clients become more involved in their own job placement, even through trial and error, they build intrinsic (or internal) motivation and personal commitment to their job search. If they make mistakes, looking at occupations with too great an exertion level, for instance, it really does not matter. These mundane actions are easily corrected as shown in the following example.

*In a typical case assigned to counselors in private rehabilitation, the case folder comes to the office containing the personnel form with the name of the client, the employer, the insurer, and usually a note from the insurance company stating the boundaries of the assignment: case management, a labor market survey, and/or job placement. The file folder will normally include accident reports and medical records from treating doctors. Following a review of the records, counselors usually set up the first interview to obtain a vocational profile, a history of past work, and a statement from their client as to how their medical problems affect them on a day-to-day basis. Usually the initial interview takes several hours to obtain the information counselors need to write the first report to the company.*

*The temptation is always present to just gather the information and allow clients to go off on their own and wait until the counselor gets around to calling them in for counseling and preparing the rehabilitation program. Those counselors who believe clients are "more likely to act themselves into feeling than feel their way into acting" get their clients involved from the beginning. If the clients are considering going back to their past jobs, the counselor has them contact their employer on a regular basis to stay involved, get with co-workers in and outside the work place so that they can stay connected, and ease the transition back into employment. Moreover, these counselors have clients ask their employers about skills and knowledge they can learn while getting over the injury. Research has shown conclusively, and these counselors know, that the longer clients stay*

> *dormant on the caseload, and not doing things, the less likely the rehabilitation will be successful.*
>
> *From reading the case records, counselors can usually decide at the beginning if a client will be able to do his or her past work. If alternative employment, requiring job placement, is the case direction, these counselors immediately find ways to have their clients involved in the job search. At the outset, these counselors have their clients consider employment options, make lists of persons who might help them in finding a job, and obtain an employment history from them of family members, friends, and acquaintances to determine the types of employment acceptable within the family complex.*

All of these things can be done while the counselor is finalizing the initial preparations. If the motivational research is correct, and we believe it is, then the clients of these counselors are doing things that lead toward "effective learning, adaptation, and commitment" during their own rehabilitation program. Learning by doing things keeps clients actively involved in their rehabilitation and prevents the erosion of their spirit.

## KEY # 5: SELF-DETERMINATION: GAINING CONTROL OVER ONE'S DESTINY

As we have seen, getting workers "doing things," and taking action on their own behalf, leads to effective learning, adaption, and commitment. Doing things not only gets workers involved, but also gives them a sense of control over their own destiny. As a result, workers begin to take greater ownership in what they are doing, become committed to the results, and are willing to put forth more time and energy toward a successful outcome. The reason this concept works, say the writers of *In Search of Excellence*,[9] is that greater control meets the need most workers have for self-determination. Tom Peters[9] says their team of researchers observed, "time and again, extraordinary energy exerted above and beyond the call of duty when workers, from the bottom of the organization to the top (shop floor workers, sales assistants, desk clerks) are given even a modicum of apparent control over their destiny."

*In Search of Excellence*[9] cites this experiment to demonstrate how a greater sense of control increases self-determination. In the experiment, adult subjects were given some complex puzzles to solve and a proofreading chore. In the background was a loud, randomly occurring, distracting noise; to be specific, it was a combination of two people speaking Spanish, one speaking Armenian, a mimeograph machine running, a desk calculator, a typewriter, and street noise producing a composite, non-distinguishable roar. The subjects were split into two groups. Individuals in one set were told to work the task under prevailing circumstances amid the distractions. Individuals in the other group were provided a button to push to turn off the noise, "a modern analog of control–the off switch." The group with the off switch solved five times the number of puzzles as their cohorts and made a tiny fraction of the number of proofreading errors. Now the kicker: none of the subjects in the off switch group ever used the switch. The mere knowledge that one can exert control, says the writer, "made the difference."

This motivational research from *In Search of Excellence*[9] would suggest to us in rehabilitation that our clients also have the need for self-determination. If given a degree of control over their program (helping to make decisions, completing assignments given them by their counselor, assisting in conducting research in the local job market, working with their counselors in determining vocational choices, helping set vocational goals, and helping to select work alternatives) clients will become more closely involved in their own rehabilitation. They will learn from doing; they will become better adjusted to the goals of the process; and they will take a degree of ownership over their program. Involvement by the client in the rehabilitation process meets the human need most people have for self-determination. The self-determination gained from this involvement leads to a greater sense of control and improves performance.

This evidence would suggest that most of the time a managed approach to job placement is the right approach. This is particularly true of higher functioning clients. (The Client-Centered approach detailed in Chapter 10 using the *Job Search Organizer* seems to help meet the self-determination needs of these clients). In setting a receptive climate in the early stages of the client program, counselors using a managed approach help their clients to understand (value shaping) that the program is theirs. The counselor using a client-centered approach, whether or not the one suggested in this text, will say something like this to the client: "this is your rehabilitation; what we are doing here today is shaping your future, and the choices you make are important and may affect you for a lifetime. My job is to help you make the right choices and I am here to do just that."

Such a statement at the outset of the program:

- sets forth the roles each will play (you own the program; I am the manager and teacher),
- lets clients know that most of the actions will be taken by them, under the counselor's guidance,
- that much of the success or failure of the program depends upon their hard work, and

- prepares them for the time during job placement and beyond when the counselor's control over the process becomes diminished or when rehabilitation is complete.

## Key # 6 REDUCING RISK THROUGH SELF-DETERMINATION

The proposition suggested by motivational research in the previous section is that if people think they have even a modest personal control over their destinies, they will persist in the tasks. They will do better at them. They will become more committed. However, regardless of the experiments in motivation, textbook solutions may not always be the answer. Relinquishing control to clients often does not work. For instance, clients may not become motivated by becoming involved and having greater control over their program. Moreover, they may not show a need for self-determination, believing the counselor's role is to do it all for them As is often the case, they may become overwhelmed by the fears of failure that go along with the risks they are asked to take. Under these circumstances, some form of the selective approach, where the counselor maintains most of the control, may be the only feasible approach. Of course, role identification at the outset can avoid some of the confusion; but, even then, uneasy feelings remain as clients assume more and more of the risks.

Risks can be reduced somewhat by understanding some of the principles of probability. *In Search of Excellence*[9] offers a partial solution in the authors' discussion of "cognitive biases," a concept illustrated during experiments in the very specialized field of "Illusion Control." In a typical experiment, subjects estimate their probability of success at future tasks after they have had experience doing the same sort of activity. The results are pretty consistent, the author says, whether the subjects are adults or college sophomores. They over-estimate the odds of succeeding at an easy task and under-estimate the odds of succeeding at a hard task. In short, they regularly distort estimates of the possibilities of events. If their proven past record is, say, 60% success at an easy task, the subjects will likely estimate their future odds of success at 90%. If past experience demonstrated ability at the hard task of 30%, the subject will estimate the odds of success at this task in the future at 10%.

According to the research, in looking ahead at the probability of success (trying to determine the amount of risk involved in what lies ahead) people tend to under-estimate the difficulty of doing tasks that in some way relate to things they have done well in the past, seeing them as easier tasks or tasks with which they have some familiarity: "I think I can; I think I can" says the Little Engine That Could. However, when it comes to trying to predict the difficulty of doing tasks they believe more difficult, or tasks with which they have little or no familiarity, they tend to over-estimate the difficulty, viewing the task as too hard. In other words, the harder or more difficult people believe the task to be, the less confidence they have in their ability to achieve success.

Much of what we do in rehabilitation is have our clients look into the future, plan ahead (select vocational alternatives, set goals), make some estimate of their interests, skills, ability, and willingness to learn new things (skill analysis, vocational training, job readiness), and, consciously or unconsciously, project their success at future tasks and jobs (vocational guidance, job placement).

The motivational research would suggest to us that we carefully examine the assignments we make, and the decisions and choices we are asking our clients to make, for their levels of difficulty. The amount of risk may be different for each client. What one client may see as an easy task and rate their chances of success high, other clients may view the very same task as difficult or unachievable. For instance, one client might view such things as contacting an employer or making a list of jobs as easily achievable. On the other hand, deciding on relocation or changing occupations might be viewed as very difficult unless the client has moved often or changed occupations several times.

In counseling sessions, a counselor may openly point out the potential problem areas and ask clients how they feel about the risk involved and receive their responses. Pointing out likely problem areas may not mean a change in strategy; recognizing potential risks and dealing with these risks openly in counseling sessions may "let some air out of the balloon" and, in itself, reduce the risk involved. Research would suggest to us that if in their dialogue counselors and clients can somehow relate the choices clients need to make with identified past achievements or areas of familiarity, the more likely the clients will feel their options are achievable.

## Recent Research in Motivation Studies

The selections we have taken from *In Search of Excellence*[9] have been directed toward answering one question central to our professional practice in rehabilitation. That question is what can rehabilitation counselors say or do that will create a receptive climate for their clients and bring about situations that will motivate action on their part and cause them to become more committed to the goals of their rehabilitation? With the support of practical research done in over 80 successful corporations, we have discussed how a positive attitude toward clients and belief in a client's worth and potential can raise the commitment level of clients. Furthermore, we have looked at new ways to value clients and create an environment receptive to intrinsic motivation by broadening the counselor's role to include orchestration, interpretation, management, and teaching. In addition, we have looked at specific things and deliberate actions counselors can take, (e.g., positive reinforcement, getting clients involved early in the process, having clients become more self-determined, and taking calculated risks to enhance motivation and build commitment to the rehabilitation process).

As mentioned earlier, most of the ideas and concepts Tom Peters[8] and his associates used in writing *In Search of Excellence* were not new to the workplace. How people manage themselves and relate to others in the workplace is central to classic management theory on motivation. From the early 1970s onward, many of these concepts were available in the widely read pop-psych literature written by such writers as Abraham Maslow, Frederick Perls, Robert Carkhoff, Eric Berne, William Glasser, and Muriel James, just to name a few. The focus of these writings has been upon managing feelings so that they are expressed appropriately and effectively. This enables people to live and work together. We may also define the ability to manage feelings as basic counseling skills.

What is new and more recent in work motivation, says Daniel Goleman,[4] is the data. He says, "We now have thirty-five years of empirical studies done mostly by social scientists that tell us with previously unknown precision just how much the pop theories and "soft skills" matter for success in business and life itself."[pg. 7] During the period of time since the earlier studies, additional support for these empirical studies have come from the field of neuroscience that looks at the brain and its functions.

> *The emotion part of the brain, neuroscience tells us, learns differently from the thinking part of the brain. And unlike IQ, which changes little after the teen years, the emotional side of the brain continues to develop as we go through life and learn from our experience, allowing us to grow in competence and change when things go wrong.* [p.7]

Perhaps the most influential of the recent writing dealing with managing feelings has come from the writing of Daniel Goleman,[4] the author of *Working with Emotional Intelligence*. Goleman[4] uses the all-inclusive term emotional intelligence for the process of managing feelings. In his book, from which the quote above is taken, he tells how he coined the label. He says "talked about loosely for decades under a variety of names, from "character" and "personality" to "soft skills" and "competence," there is at last a more precise understanding of these human talents, and a new name for them: *"emotional intelligence."*

Goleman[4] goes on to define what he means and does not mean by emotional intelligence. He says,

> *Emotional intelligence does not mean "being nice." At strategic moments it may demand not being nice but rather, for*

> *example, bluntly confronting someone with an uncomfortable but consequential truth they've been avoiding... emotional intelligence does not mean giving free rein to feelings–letting it all hang out. Rather it means managing feelings so that they are expressed appropriately and effectively, enabling people to work together smoothly toward common goals.* pg. 6

Daniel Goleman[4] states that emotional intelligence counts more than IQ or expertise for determining who excels at a job–any job. He points to the results of two surveys that show what employers want in their employees. First, a 1991 "Survey of American Employers" conducted by The Harris Education Research Council, reveals that more than half the people who work for employers in America lack the motivation to keep learning and improving in their job; four in ten are not able to work cooperatively with fellow employees, and just 19% of those applying for entry-level jobs have enough self-discipline in their work habits.

Goleman[4] references a second survey of observations employers have made of the persons they employ. Goleman[4] says that a national survey of what employers are looking for in entry-level workers conducted by the Department of Labor Employment and Training Administration in 1989, shows that specific technical skills are now less important than the underlying ability to learn the job. After "ability to learn the job," employers list the next five items in order of importance as follows:

1. ability to learn the job,

2. listening and oral communication,

3. adaptability and creative responses to setbacks and obstacles,

4. personal management, confidence, motivation to work toward goals, and pride in accomplishments,

5. group and interpersonal effectiveness, cooperativeness, and teamwork, skills in negotiating disagreements, and

6. wanting to make a contribution toward the effectiveness of the organization. pp. 12-13

The Department of Labor in 1996 conducted a follow-up study of what employers are looking for in the people they hire. In this survey, employers listed the two most highly sought-after skills in new hires as oral communication and interpersonal abilities. Goleman[4] points out that with the exception of specific technical skills, all of the qualities desired by employers in the two surveys fall under the heading of emotional intelligence.

# CONCLUSION THE IMPACT OF EMOTIONAL INTELLIGENCE UPON PROFESSIONALS IN THE FIELD OF REHABILITATION

Recent research on motivation, such as the two surveys mentioned above, call into question at least one established practice in rehabilitation. That is the identification of transferable work skills. During the rehabilitation process, counselors spend much of their time examining a client's past work to identify work skills, skills transferable from one occupation to another that would give their clients an advantage in seeking alternative work. Indeed, elaborate systems have been devised by educators to assist counselors in identifying transferable work skills.

If the recent research on motivation can be trusted, the soft skills or adaptive skills are more important to employers hiring people than work skills. In other words, the human traits that a person brings to the job may be more important than what they have done in the past. We expand our discussion of adaptive skills later in Chapter 9, "The Selective Approach to Job Placement for Persons with Disabilities." This chapter presents ways transferable work skills are identified and used in the job search and shows how counselors can use emotional intelligence or the adaptive skills in preparing and presenting their clients to employers.

Recent research on motivation also speaks to the need for teaching emotional intelligence to our clients in rehabilitation, making the teaching of the soft skills part of the job-seeking skill-training format. If employers are judging the abilities of prospective employees on the basis of their nonverbal behavior and active listening skills, we need to prepare our clients for this kind of experience during interviews, job-seeking training, and self-help workshops.

# TOPICS FOR GROUP DISCUSSION

1. In "To the Reader," we raised questions about motivation and in the early part of Chapter 4, we dissected one of the definitions of motivation to examine its parts. Do you believe that a person can motivate another person? Do you think that rehabilitation counselors can motivate their clients? What risks lie in attempting to motivate others?

2. Research and write a Short Biographical Report on one of the following on their contribution to the field of motivation. The instructor may wish to have students or a group of professionals in their seminars, make a short presentation to the group on the contribution of one of the following scholars to the field of motivational theory:

    1. Muriel James
    2. Jerome Bruner
    3. B.F. Skinner
    4. Eric Berne
    5. Frederick Perls
    6. William Glasser

3. Chapter 4 sets forth the proposition that clients become more motivated and committed to their program of rehabilitation when they are involved in the job search. Divide into sub-groups, choose a leader and recorder, and prepare a list of ways clients can become more involved in their own rehabilitation program.

# INDIVIDUAL ASSIGNMENTS

1. Read Chapter 3: "Man Waiting for Motivation" from *In Search of Excellence* by Thomas J. Peters, et al.[9] Select one idea for class discussion which you consider is important in building a counselor-client relationship.

2. Research and write a short description or biographical sketch on one of the following and present a five-minute presentation of the topic to your work group or class. Include pros and cons of how the topic you choose may affect the motivation of workers in today's work environment. Do you believe the contribution of these models or thinkers is still relevant today?

    The Bureaucratic Model
    The Human Relations Movement
    Max Weber/ Frederick Taylor
    Douglas McGregor

# SELECTIVE REFERENCES


[1]Bennis, Warren G. (1976). *The Unconscious Conspiracy: Why Leaders Can't Lead.* New York: AMACON

[2]Bruner, Jerome S. (1973). "You More Likely Act" from *On Knowing: Essays For The Left Hand.* New York: Atheneum.

[3]Crainer, Stuart and Dearlove, Des (2000). *Generation Entrepreneur.* London: Pearson Education Limited,

[4]Goleman, Daniel (1998). *Working with Emotional Intelligence.* New York: Bantam Dell.

[5]Hagner, David, Kelly McGahie, Heidi Clouter, (2001). "Model Career Assistance Process for Individuals with Severe Disabilities." *Journal of Employment Counseling,* December, 197-206.

[6]Hansen, James C. (1982). *Counseling: Theory and Process.* Boston: Allyn and Bacon.

[7]Hansen, James C. & et al. (1982). *Counseling: Theory and Practice.* Boston: Allyn and Bacon, Inc.

[8]McGregor, Douglas (1960). *The Human Side of Enterprise.* New York: McGraw-Hill.

[9]Peters, Thomas J. and Waterman, Jr., Robert H. (1982). *In Search of Excellence.* New York: Harper & Roe.

[10]Tracey, William R. Editor (1994). *Human Resources Management & Development Handbook.* New York: American Management Association.

[11]Watson, Thomas, Jr. (1963). *A Business and Its Beliefs: The Ideas That Helped Build IBM.* New York: McGraw-Hill.

[12]White, W. A. (1937). *Forty Years on Main Street.* New York, NY: Farrar and Rinehart.

# PART 2

# AN INTRODUCTION TO FORENSIC REHABILITATION

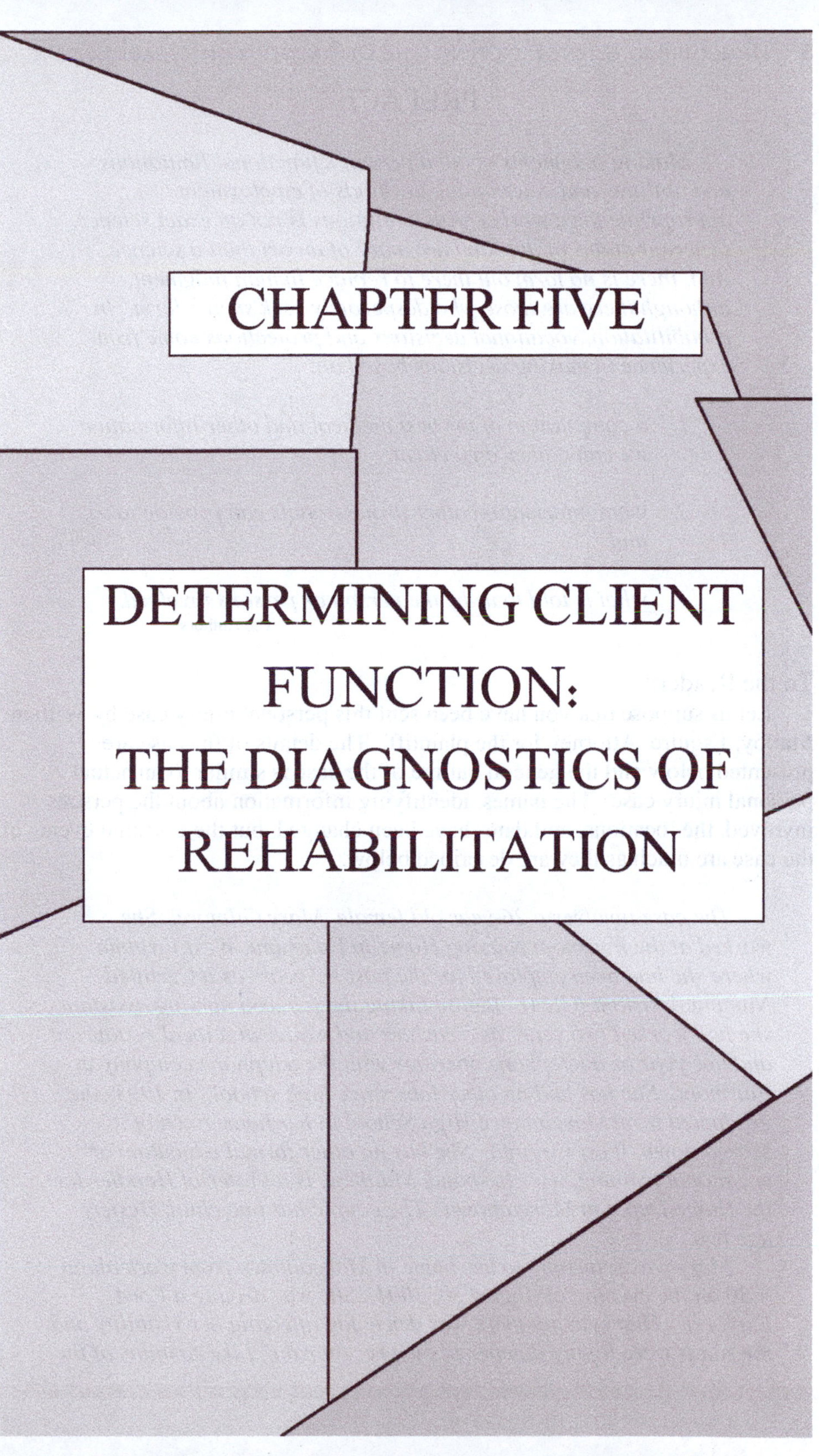

# CHAPTER FIVE

# DETERMINING CLIENT FUNCTION: THE DIAGNOSTICS OF REHABILITATION

# PREFACE

*Making judgments about a person's functional limitations and abilities and determining the kinds of employment appropriate for a worker with limitations is not an exact science. Determinations of this kind are more of an art than a science. And, there is no form out there to replace human judgment, although there are those who desperately seek such a form. In rehabilitation, vocational decisions and projections come from experience in making decisions based on:*

1. *a compilation of the best medical and other information we can gather on a client,*

2. *what information other professionals can provide to us, and*

3. *what is told to us by the person or persons involved.*

The Authors

To the Reader:

Let us suppose that you have been sent this personal injury case by William Malloy, Esquire, Attorney for the plaintiff. The details of the case are presented below and the general outline of the case is similar to an actual personal injury case. The names, identifying information about the persons involved, the locations, and dates have been changed, but the essential events of the case are much as they are described below.

*The case involves a 26-year old female, Mary Gilmore. She worked at the Fairmont Nursing Home in Fairmont, West Virginia where she had been employed for the past six years as a Certified Nursing Assistant (CNA). Before taking the job as a nursing assistant, she had worked two years as a cashier and waiter at a local restaurant and one year as a telephone operator with the telephone company in Fairmont. She has had no other jobs since high school. In 1993, she graduated from Morgantown High School in her home town of Morgantown, West Virginia. She has no other formal education or vocational training. Her husband, Matthew, is a Material Handler for the Home Depot in Morgantown. The couple has one child, Hester, age two.*

*Mary was returning to her home in Morgantown from work about 8:30 on the evening of August 30, 2001. She was driving a Ford Explorer. That evening there was dense fog affecting her visibility and the roads were lightly dampened by a recent rain. Like so many of the back roads in the mountainous state of West Virginia, the highway was narrow and winding. She was able to drive only about 35 miles an hour. As she came around a turn in the road, she noticed the pathway before her appeared slick and rather treacherous, but she did not know why. She slowed down even more. All at once, she saw an overturned oil tanker in the middle of the road. The oil spill had caught fire and the blaze was coming toward her. (The driver of the truck from the Fly-By-Night Trucking Company later died from injuries received in the accident). Before Mary was able to stop, however, the flames were all around her vehicle. She was able to escape from her vehicle, but as she was fleeing, she received third degree burns on both of her ankles. She was treated for burns over the next two years by Dr. Paul Nolan in the burn ward of the Cumberland County Hospital. In spite of treatment, her legs and ankles never returned to normal and she had recurrent swelling in her ankles upon prolonged standing and sitting, when she had to sit with her feet flat on the floor. Dr. Nolan said in his deposition that she would have to elevate her legs every 30 minutes while sitting.*

*The attorney, Mr. Malloy, has filed suit on Mary's behalf with the Morgantown Circuit Court against the Fly-By-Night Trucking Company. The doctors responsible for Mary's treatment have provided evidence through oral deposition, providing the court with a history of her treatment and their opinions about the care she will need in the future. The doctors, from a physical standpoint, have also provided their best estimate of her residual abilities and limitations.*

*Now, the attorney, William Mallory, wants the rehabilitation counselor (VE) to provide an expert opinion to the court about how the accident has affected Mary's ability to work. These are some of the questions the attorneys, both plaintiff and defense (as the trucking company will certainly have representation) are likely to ask rehabilitation counselors during the court proceedings.*

1. *Can Mary return to her past work as a Certified Nursing Assistant without limitations?*

2. *If not, can she return to that kind of work with a limited amount of work accommodation?*

3. *If not, can she do a similar job that the company may make available to her?*

4. *If not, can she do any of the work she has done in the past?*

5. *If not, what residual abilities does she have to do any work?*

6. *Does she have any skills from her past work that would be useful in any other work and give Mary a better chance of finding alternative work?*

7. *If she has no work skills or other skills from her past, is Mary a candidate for vocational training that would equip her to go back to work?*

8. *Is Mary disabled from any sustained work activity?*

9. *How much has Mary lost in wages as a result of the accident?*

Each of these issues is vocational in nature, and all of these issues relate to client function. The attorneys on the case are not going to ask rehabilitation counselors about Mary's medical condition. The medical questions are the domain of the medical professionals. In personal injury cases such as this, medical doctors will usually testify about Mary's medical condition. Moreover, the attorneys will not ask rehabilitation counselors about the amount of pain she has suffered or how her injuries have affected her mentally. These questions are addressed to other professionals, such as psychologists, psychiatrists, or pain management doctors. What information the attorneys and the court want to know, and only a rehabilitation counselor serving as a vocational expert can provide, is how her medical condition, her pain and suffering, and her possible depression have affected her ability to work. In other words, rehabilitation counselors are asked to address only the main areas of their knowledge and expertise: disability and work.

Chapter 5 is about how practicing rehabilitation counselors typically gather information, a few of the sources they consult, and the way they put together information to determine the level of client function. This information helps rehabilitation counselors:

1. determine the limitations in function affecting their clients,

2. give guidance to the rehabilitation process, and

3. identify the kinds of work persons with functional limitations are likely to be able to perform.

The content of this chapter should be seen as an introduction to determining a client's vocational potential. Other books in our field deal with the subject of determining client potential in more depth. However, the content of this chapter, with numerous illustrations and examples, should give the reader and student an accurate picture of how practicing professionals develop the typical forensic case on a day-to-day basis.

Remember our earlier statement that making judgments about a person's functional limitations and abilities and determining the kinds of employment appropriate for a worker with limitations is not an exact science. Determinations of this kind are more of an art than a science. In rehabilitation, vocational decisions and projections come from:

- experience in making decisions,
- a compilation of the best medical and other information we can gather on a client,
- what information other professionals can provide to us, and
- what is told us by the person or persons involved.

# THE DIAGNOSTICS OF REHABILITATION: PRIVATE AND PUBLIC REHABILITATION

As mentioned earlier, perhaps the most professional activity in rehabilitation is making a determination of a client's vocational potential. This determination represents a combination of a person's residual functional capacity (RFC), the level at which a person can perform work activity given their physical, mental, and vocational limitations and abilities, and their employability; can the person perform work activity, and if so, what kinds of work can this person do given their residual functional capacity. Residual functional capacity (RFC) and employability are the main diagnostic questions under consideration in vocational rehabilitation.

Whether or not the rehabilitation counselor is with a private company or a public agency, the primary professional activity undertaken is much the same:

- determining a person's residual functional capacity (RFC), and
- making an assessment of their employability.

Let us look briefly at the circumstances under which a diagnostic evaluation often takes place in each of these rehabilitation settings.

Public rehabilitation agencies in each state work within guidelines from the federal government as these agencies are part of a state/federal program. The federal laws and regulations state that the agency must accept for service, first, the most severely disabled persons. Therefore, many of the rehabilitation clients served by the public rehabilitation agencies have never worked or they have been declared unable to work by other agencies, (e.g., the Social Security Administration or Veteran's Administration). The main focus of professional service in the public sector is, as with other vocational rehabilitation programs, assessing the functional level of their disabled clients, and given their functional limitations, determining to the fullest extent their employability.

During the rehabilitation process, public agencies provide medical and vocational services that will improve the person's ability to live and work; and, as a result, raise their employment potential. (Public rehabilitation agencies do provide independent living services to handicapped individuals unable to work, and a variety of other services, such as vocational evaluations, to other agencies. These services are not considered in our study).

In private rehabilitation, when a person is injured, whether in a work-related accident or an accident away from work, such as an automobile accident, the injured person is provided with medical treatment. Typically, the injured person receives treatment and in a short time returns to their normal work routine. In situations where the injuries are severe, the treatment may be much longer, and afterward, the person may not be able to do the things they have done in the past.

If the injury is a work-related injury, the injured worker may be taken off work, temporarily or permanently, and provided with worker's compensation payments. These worker's compensation payments may extend for a period of time as long as ten years. Worker's compensation is obviously expensive, both in lost productivity to the company or in actual cash payments (cash payments are usually made by the insurance company). It is imperative, therefore, for the company and/or their insurance carrier to have the injured worker return to work as soon as possible. Many insurance companies today have found it cost effective to employ rehabilitation case managers to monitor the medical and other treatment and return the worker to their regular job, or, if they are unable to return to their past job, to place them in alternative work. In order to manage the case and to address work-related questions, the counselor in private practice must first have a firm understanding of the client's level of functioning (RFC)and the kinds of jobs that person can do (employability).

On the other hand, when an injury is not work-related, or when an accident occurs outside of the work setting, such as a person injured in a motor vehicle accident, by using a faulty product, or during medical treatment, the only recourse available to the injured person may be to seek damages for their losses through the court system. Typically, the injured person will hire legal representation to file a suit for the damages incurred. (The person filing the suit is known as the *Plaintiff*; the party being sued is known as the *Defendant*. In the illustration opening this chapter, Mary Gilmore is the Plaintiff; the Fly-By-Night Trucking Company is the Defendant). A vocational expert (usually a rehabilitation counselor) may be brought into the case proceedings by either the plaintiff or the defendant to serve as an independent witness or vocational expert.

Naturally, the parties employing the independent vocational expert hope the testimony of the vocational expert will improve their side of the argument. For instance, a plaintiff attorney will want to demonstrate that the injury has resulted in diminished residual functional capacity and limited employability with lost wages. On the other hand, the defendant will want to show limited damages and a limited loss of employability as the result of the injury; and, through expert testimony, and possibly a labor market survey, show that there are actual well-paying jobs a person can do, in spite of the injury. In either case, the vocational expert is independent of the litigation process and, ethically, must render professional judgments based upon the experts own expertise and assessment of the case.

Thus, in most rehabilitation case work the main issues concern the diagnostics of rehabilitation:

- the residual functional capacity (RFC); that is, given the physical, mental, and vocational limitations, at what level can the client function in the open job market, and

- employability, what kinds of jobs, if any, can the client perform on a sustained basis within these functional limitations?

This chapter concerns the diagnostic procedures, the information gathering and interpretation, and the vocational criteria used by rehabilitation counselors in making judgments about these two primary issues.

# THE RESIDUAL FUNCTIONAL CAPACITY: DEVELOPING A MEDICAL PROFILE

The case file coming to the rehabilitation counselor almost always contains medical information relating to the diagnosis and treatment a person has received. The case file may contain, among other things, a report of an accident and initial treatment, letters of referral to a primary treating physician, hospital records, records from physical therapy, possibly reports from a pain management center, independent medical examinations (IME) from other doctors, and functional capacities evaluations (FCE). For the rehabilitation counselor, the case begins with the examination of the case file, and sorting through the information to determine what may be useful in making a vocational evaluation of the client.

The residual functional capacity (RFC) is the determination made by medical professionals. Rehabilitation professionals rely upon the medical community to provide the work-related limitations of the person. Once the work-related limitations are set forth in the medical records, the rehabilitation counselor can make the determination of how these limitations impact the person's ability to work and point to the kinds of jobs a person can perform, given these limitations. These work-related limitations can be physical and/or mental. Both are considered below.

## RESIDUAL FUNCTIONAL CAPACITY: PHYSICAL LIMITATIONS

As the authors of *Vocational Assessment: Evaluating Employment Potential*[3] have aptly pointed out, the determination of a residual functional physical capacity evaluation begins with the treating physician. Why is this? Most of the time, the treating doctor(s) has (have) compiled the medical records and seen the person on a regular or scheduled basis. These doctors are in the best position to know the patient's present medical condition. Thus, treating physicians are able to make an up-to-date assessment of the individual's functional capacity. Administrative Law Judges with the Office of Disability Adjudication and Review (ODAR) of the Social Security Administration, in their disability determinations, likewise, give the greatest weight to the opinions and assessments of treating physicians.

In the case of a work-related injury or other accident, a client over time may have several treating doctors. At the time of an accident, the treating physician may have been the emergency room doctor, but after initial diagnosis and treatment, the emergency room doctor may refer the injured person to a family doctor or other specialist, such as an orthopedic doctor or neurologist. Another doctor, such as a physician in a pain management center, may take over the case for a period of time. In any event the rehabilitation counselor or case manager has to determine which doctors are in the best position at any given time to provide information about the person's condition and the level at which the person is able to function. Usually, the opinions of doctors currently or recently providing treatment are the most helpful.

The issues that the treating physician must address for the rehabilitation counselor or case manager are:

- The client's progress in recovery and an assessment of whether or not the client has reached maximum medical improvement (MMI); (i.e., has the client's recovery reached maximum potential and can you consider work as a possibility).

- If the client has not reached maximum medical improvement, the treating doctor needs to provide an explanation of the treatment being delivered, and the expected time and date when the individual will likely reach maximum medical improvement, and

- If the client has reached MMI, what are their current work-related limitations?

If the person is able to work at some capacity, the report from the treating doctor may contain a notice of a release to return to work (RTW) and a statement about the person's physical and mental limitations (RFC).

To be useful in formulating the residual functional capacity of a particular client, the medical information from the treating physician must be placed in functional terms. When requesting such information, it is important to remember that physicians are generally not trained in worker trait nomenclature. Their office notes and reports may provide a diagnosis of the condition, the course of the medical treatment, the physical systems reviewed, the various tests done on their patient, the medications prescribed for the patient, and a general appraisal of the person's progress toward recovery. Unless treating doctors are specifically asked, many times they fail to provide much information about the person's functional ability.

In recent years, medical doctors have become more aware that other professionals need to have medical evidence placed in functional terms, and such assessments have become more common. Even then, the doctor's assessment of the functional condition may need clarification. Consider this example.

> *In an examination of the records, the rehabilitation counselor reads a letter the insurance adjuster has written to an orthopedic specialist asking for functional information that would enable the counselor to begin a job search. Below is the doctor's full, actual response:*
>
> *Thank you for your letter regarding Sheila Handy. Regarding Ms. Handy's current right knee condition, it is my opinion that she has done well after knee replacement surgery. In relation to the report of July 11, 1998, I feel that she has reached maximum medical improvement. With regard to estimating her future medical needs, it is my impression that this knee replacement has the potential benefit of lasting 20-30 years or longer. There is a risk of a potential need for revision of the polyethylene liner or a complete revision at some point in her future; however, it is difficult to predict with any certainty the likelihood of multiple procedures and is based upon her activity level as well as determined factors with regard to the type of polyethylene that was placed in her knee. She can indeed return to work with restrictions of prolonged standing excluding any significant squatting, bending, or lifting over 20-30 pounds.*

In preparing to serve this client, what can the rehabilitation counselor glean from this response to help in understanding the client's functional abilities? First, the doctor has told the counselor that his patient has reached maximum medical improvement (MMI); and as far as the knee replacement is concerned, the patient is not likely to improve to a level beyond this point. Thus, she is as ready as she will be to go back to work. Second, the doctor has provided some information about her ability to function: "She can indeed return to work with restrictions of prolonged standing excluding any significant squatting, bending, or lifting over 20-30 pounds." However, the functional abilities are too vague and insufficient for the counselor to proceed with job placement without some clarification. The doctor seems to have left out the very important word *no* before prolonged in the restrictions. In addition, the doctor has not really told the counselor enough about the level of work suggested.

In this case, the rehabilitation counselor wrote a follow-up letter of clarification to the doctor, stating:

> *The purpose of this letter is to clarify these restrictions before they are presented to our employer contacts. The limitations you have provided for Ms. Handy in your letter are: "she can indeed return to work with restrictions of prolonged standing excluding any significant squatting, bending, or lifting over 20-30 pounds." In an earlier letter, you expressed the thought that a sedentary job would be reasonable. May I assume that you consider her able to function at a sedentary level of exertion; that is, sitting most of the day, lifting 10 pounds or less, and standing and walking as needed, but no prolonged standing? Within these limitations, she would be able to do light work as well, lifting in the range of 20-30 pounds as long as she did not have to squat or bend and had the opportunity to sit when needed.*

Tactfully, the rehabilitation counselor has requested the doctor to reexamine the work restrictions and the counselor has asked the doctor to consider the vocational implications of his restrictions, providing for the doctor the definitions of light and sedentary work. (These definitions are discussed in more detail later in the chapter).

Many times the records do not contain any functional information from the treating doctors. When the record is absent of functional information, it may become necessary to request a "medical source statement" in the form of a functional assessment from treating physicians. Such an assessment would tell the counselor their client's ability and limitation, if any, to meet the

1. *physical demands of work-related activity*, such as standing, walking, sitting, lifting, pushing and pulling;

2. *postural activities,* such as climbing, balancing, stooping, kneeling, crouching, crawling;

3. *manipulative demands of work activity,* such as reaching, handling, fingering, feeling;

4. *communicative limitations and abilities,* such as talking, hearing;

5. *sensory limitations and abilities,* such as tasting/smelling;

6. *visual limitations and abilities,* such as near acuity, far acuity, accommodation, depth perception, color vision, field of vision; and

7. *environmental restrictions,* such as the ability to work around heights and moving machinery, the ability to tolerate temperature extremes, and the ability to work around chemicals and dust, noise, fumes, humidity, and vibrations.

On the next page is an example of a work-related physical capacity evaluation form used by rehabilitation professionals and others to solicit functional information from treating doctors.

Notice the Note at the top of the form says "In an 8-hour workday" occasionally equals 1% to 33%; frequently equals 34% to 66%; constantly equals 68% to 100%." These are vocational terms. Without these definitions printed on the form, a treating physician may not be able to understand the way in which these terms were used. Providing these definitions helps the treating physician make an assessment of the client's ability to perform the work-related physical functions (i.e., sitting, standing, walking, lifting, carrying, pushing, and pulling) and, at the same time, to rate how long on a given day the client can perform these strength activities.

TABLE 1

## ESTIMATED WORK CAPACITY FORM

Patient:
File #:

Dear Dr.

We would appreciate your cooperation in completing the following items on this form. It is important to our efforts in determining this person's work *potential*. Any item that you do not believe you can answer should be marked N/A.

Thank you.

**Note**: In terms of an 8-hr. workday, "Occasionally" equals 1%, to 33%, "Frequently" equals 34% to 66%, "Constantly equals 67% to 100%.

1. In an 8-hour workday, person can: (Circle full capacity for each activity)

Total at one time: (hours)

| | | | | | | | | | | |
|---|---|---|---|---|---|---|---|---|---|---|
| Sit | 0 | ½ | 1 | 2 | 3 | 4 | 5 | 6 | 7 | 8 |
| Stand | 0 | ½ | 1 | 2 | 3 | 4 | 5 | 6 | 7 | 8 |
| Walk | 0 | ½ | 1 | 2 | 3 | 4 | 5 | 6 | 7 | 8 |

Total during entire 8-hour day: (hours)

| | | | | | | | | | | |
|---|---|---|---|---|---|---|---|---|---|---|
| Sit | 0 | ½ | 1 | 2 | 3 | 4 | 5 | 6 | 7 | 8 |
| Stand | 0 | ½ | 1 | 2 | 3 | 4 | 5 | 6 | 7 | 8 |
| Walk | 0 | ½ | 1 | 2 | 3 | 4 | 5 | 6 | 7 | 8 |

| 2. Person can lift: | Never | Occasionally | Frequently | Constantly |
|---|---|---|---|---|
| Up to 10 lbs. | | | | |
| 11- 20 lbs. | | | | |
| 21- 50 lbs. | | | | |
| 51- 100 lbs. | | | | |
| 100+ lbs. | | | | |

| 3. Person can carry: | Never | Occasionally | Frequently | Constantly |
|---|---|---|---|---|
| Up to 10 lbs. | | | | |
| 11- 20 lbs. | | | | |
| 21- 50 lbs. | | | | |
| 51- 100 lbs. | | | | |
| 100+ lbs. | | | | |

| 4. Person can push / pull: | Never | Occasionally | Frequently | Constantly |
|---|---|---|---|---|
| Up to 10 lbs. | | | | |
| 11-20 lbs. | | | | |
| 21-50 lbs. | | | | |
| 51- 100 lbs. | | | | |
| 100+ lbs. | | | | |

5. Person can do repetitive movements as in operating controls:

| Right Hand / Arm | Right Foot / Leg | Left Hand / Arm | Left Foot / Leg |
|---|---|---|---|
| ____Yes ____No | ____Yes ____No | ____Yes ____No | ____Yes ____No |

| 6. Person can | Never | Occasionally | Frequently | Constantly |
|---|---|---|---|---|
| Climb | | | | |
| Balance | | | | |
| Stoop | | | | |
| Kneel | | | | |
| Crouch | | | | |
| Crawl | | | | |
| Reach (all directions) | | | | |
| Handle (gross manipulation) | | | | |
| Finger (fine manipulation) | | | | |
| Feel | | | | |

| 7. Any difficulties involving: | None | Mild | Moderate | Severe |
|---|---|---|---|---|
| Talking | | | | |
| Hearing | | | | |
| Tasting / Smelling | | | | |
| Seeing (near, far, depth, Accommodation, color, or Field of vision) | | | | |

| 8. Any restriction of activities Involving: | None | Mild | Moderate | Severe |
|---|---|---|---|---|
| Exposure to cold, heat, wet, Or humidity | | | | |
| Noise | | | | |
| Vibration | | | | |
| Exposure to fumes, odors, Dusts, mists, gases, or Chemicals | | | | |

Moving mechanical parts ____ ____ ____ ____
Unprotected heights ____ ____ ____ ____
Operating automotive equipment ____ ____ ____ ____

9. Is this person involved with treatment and/or medication that might affect his/her ability to work?
____ Yes ____ No Describe: ________________________________
________________________________________________

10. Has this person reached maximum medical improvement?
____________ Yes (indicate when) ____________ No (indicate when)

11. Can this person return to work according to restrictions defined above?
____ Yes ____ No

If not, give estimated date for return to work: ____________
Work full-time? ___ Yes ___ No Work part-time? ____________ Hrs./Day

12. Additional Comments: ________________________________
________________________________________________

Physician's Signature: ________________________ Date: ____________

(The work-related physical capacity evaluation form is from a form designed and published in1992 and used in the 1994 publication, *Vocational Assessment; Evaluating Employment Potential*).[3]

In the event that functional information cannot be obtained from a treating source, an attorney may seek a medical source statement from another professional in the medical field to help the rehabilitation counselor make a vocational assessment. Usually, this information is obtained from a medical specialist with credentials related to the condition of the injured person. For instance, if the injured person suffered a back injury, the medical source statement will likely be obtained from an orthopedic specialist; if the person has a brain injury, the medical source statement will likely be obtained from a neurologist or a neuro-psychologist.

To provide this information, the medical specialist will read the relevant medical information, read the conclusions from the patient's treating doctors, examine the patient before rendering an opinion about the medical condition, and provide functional limitations. The statement from the consulting specialist is known as an Independent Medical Examination (IME). An IME often does not carry the weight of an assessment from a treating source but may be useful as a second opinion when questions arise about the reliability of the primary information or when the record lacks all or part of the essential information on a client's function.

In recent years, physical therapy departments in hospitals and independent physical therapy groups provide formal functional capacity evaluations (FCE). During these evaluations, injured or disabled persons are given a series of physical exercises to test their endurance in strength factors such as walking, standing, sitting, lifting, carrying, and pushing and pulling. The exercises also test the use of the client's body to perform postural activities, such as climbing, balancing, stooping, kneeling, crouching, crawling, reaching, handling, and the use of the fingers for gross and fine fingering activities. Normally, a physical therapist is placed with the individual, one on one, during the exercises. As a rule, the functional capacity evaluation report includes a statement from the therapist about the amount of effort a person has put forth during the testing, to provide information about possible malingering, and the degree of pain experienced during the exercises.

The purpose of the functional capacities evaluations (FCE) is usually to provide factual information about a person's current functional ability and to determine at what level of functioning the person could sustain work activity (i.e., sedentary, light, medium, heavy, or very heavy). The FCE is an attempt to take some of the subjectivity out of trying to appraise a person's functional abilities. Many physicians find the formal functional capacity evaluation attractive because it gives them a more factual basis for estimating a person's abilities and limitations. Attorneys also find the FCE useful in the litigation of personal injury cases to substantiate or refute claims of disability.

## Residual Functional Capacity: Mental Limitations

As seen earlier in this chapter, the residual functional capacity (RFC) is based upon functional assessments made by the treating doctors, assessment centers, specialists, and other consulting doctors. The section before dealt only with physical functioning. As a rule, before any consideration is given to returning to past work or alternative work, the counselor must determine the physical functioning of their client. The physical functioning of the client is based upon the opinions of the treating doctors and other physicians about the physical capabilities of their patient. To reiterate the main point made in our earlier discussion, the opinions of these physicians and others must be stated in functional terms.

The same is true regarding the client's mental functioning. An individual client:

- may be clinically depressed, the depressed state may have occurred because of changed circumstances in their life,
- may have an anxiety condition as evidenced by such things as headaches or panic attacks,

- may have a bi-polar disorder, with mood swings affecting their stability, or

- may have suffered brain damage and display erratic behaviors as a consequence of a motor vehicle or other accident.

All of these mental and emotional conditions may have altered the person's ability to sustain work activity; but to what degree and just how limiting is the mental impairment? Again, this is where the medical community, psychiatrists, other treating physicians, and related professionals, (e.g., clinical psychologists, psychiatrists, and neuro-psychologists) must step in and provide a determination of the person's mental functioning for the counselor.

At what point may rehabilitation counselors need assistance from a mental health professional to make a determination of a client's mental residual functional capacity? The authors of *Vocational Assessment: Evaluating Employment Potential*,[3] have provided this guidance. They say the assistance of a mental health professional is needed when:

- the client's limited work history does not truly reflect the capabilities of the client,

- when cognitive dysfunction as a result the injury is suspected,

- when a determination is needed to substantiate the existence of mental illness,

- to establish interpersonal coping and skills,

- to determine work-related adjustment problems, and

- to help clarify family and support systems.

The kinds of information psychiatrists and psychologists can provide include *Psychometric Testing* to clarify a client's residual functional capacity for worker traits, such as general educational development in reasoning, mathematics, and language; *Clinical Interviews* to help predict on-the-job behaviors, stressors to avoid in the work place, ability to perform simple, repetitive tasks. A variety of other information and *Personality Tests,* such as the Minnesota Multiphasic Personality Inventory (MMPI), may be provided to help assess the degree and nature of a client's emotional condition.

While mental health professionals can provide a wide variety of testing and assessments to measure a client's mental and emotional condition, more often than not, rehabilitation counselors have to rely upon some form of medical source statement in determining the mental residual functional ability of their clients. If the counselor determines a client has a mental impairment that affects his/her ability to work, or there is evidence of such impairment, a psychiatrist or psychologist needs to provide some kind of statement about how prepared mentally the client is to return to work. Once again, if the client has a treating mental health professional, this specialist becomes the primary source of information.

As with the physical abilities and limitations, to be useful, this information needs to be placed in functional terms. That is, the information from the treating source or other sources must tell the rehabilitation counselor how and to what degree the mental impairments limit the person's ability to manage the activities of daily living and to function in the workplace. A widely accepted way in which the mental health community has attempted to assess the mental functioning of their patients is using the "Global Assessment of Functioning" (GAF) Scale. This rating of overall psychological functioning using a scale of zero - 100 was created by L. Luborsky.[4]

TABLE 2

## Global Assessment of Functioning (GAF) Scale

(From DSM-IV-TR, p. 34.)

Consider psychological, social, and occupational functioning on a hypothetical continuum of mental health-illness. Do not include impairment in functioning due to physical (or environmental) limitations.

| Code | (Note: Use intermediate codes when appropriate, e.g., 45, 68, 72.) |
|---|---|
| 100<br>91 | **Superior functioning in a wide range of activities, life's problems never seem to get out of hand, is sought out by others because of his or her many positive qualities. No symptoms.** |
| 90<br>81 | **Absent or minimal symptoms** (e.g., mild anxiety before an exam), **good functioning in all areas, interested and involved in a wide range of activities. socially effective, generally satisfied with life, no more than everyday problems or concerns** (e.g. an occasional argument with family members). |
| 80<br>71 | **If symptoms are present, they are transient and expectable reactions to psychosocial stressors** (e.g., difficulty concentrating after family argument); **no more than slight impairment in social, occupational or school functioning** (e.g., temporarily failing behind in schoolwork). |
| 70<br>61 | **Some mild symptoms** (e.g. depressed mood and mild insomnia)<br>**OR some difficulty in social, occupational, or school functioning** (e.g., occasional truancy, or theft within the household), **but generally functioning pretty well, has some meaningful interpersonal relationships.** |
| 60<br>51 | **Moderate symptoms** (e.g., flat affect and circumstantial speech, occasional panic attacks)<br>**OR moderate difficulty in social, occupational, or school functioning** (e.g.. few friends, conflicts with peers or co-workers). |
| 50<br>41 | **Serious symptoms** (e.g.. suicidal ideation, severe obsessional rituals, frequent shoplifting)<br>**OR any serious impairment in social, occupational, or school functioning** (e.g., no friends, unable to keep a job). |
| 40<br>31 | **Some impairment in reality testing or communication** (e.g., speech is at times illogical, obscure, or irrelevant)<br>**OR major impairment in several areas, such as work or school, family relations, judgment, thinking, or mood** (e.g., depressed man avoids friends, neglects family, and is unable to work; child frequently beats up younger children, is defiant at home, and is failing at school). |
| 30<br>21 | **Behavior is considerably influenced by delusions or hallucinations**<br>**OR serious impairment in communication or judgment** (e.g., sometimes incoherent, acts grossly inappropriately, suicidal preoccupation)<br>**OR inability to function in almost all areas** (e.g., stays in bed all day; no job, home, or friends). |
| 20<br>11 | **Some danger of hurting self or others** (e.g., suicide attempts without clear expectation of death; frequently violent; manic excitement)<br>**OR occasionally fails to maintain minimal personal hygiene** (e.g., smears feces)<br>**OR gross impairment in communication** (e.g., largely incoherent or mute). |
| 10<br>1 | **Persistent danger of severely hurting self or others** (e.g., recurrent violence)<br>**OR persistent inability to maintain minimal personal hygiene**<br>**OR serious suicidal act with clear expectation of death.** |
| 0 | Inadequate information. |

The instructions for the "Global Assessment of Functioning" (GAF) scale say,

*This assessment considers the psychological, social, and occupational functioning on a hypothetical continuum of mental-health-illness. The ratings do not include impairment in functioning due to physical (or environmental) limitations.*

Notice, this assessment not only presents a scale rating of zero-100, a description of the severity of the rating "moderate symptoms" and the kind of things psychiatrists look for in making the assessment "flat affect, circumstantial speech, or occasional panic attacks," but also provides descriptors to tell how these conditions affect a person's ability to function in society and at work: "moderate difficulty in social, occupational or school functioning" with examples of how these conditions manifest themselves on a daily basis: "few friends, conflicts with peers or co-workers."

The GAF rating is only one of several tools mental health professionals use to assess the mental and emotional functioning of their clients. Certainly, the GAF scores are helpful to rehabilitation counselors and other professionals in gaining an understanding of a client's ability to function. Often the GAF rating scores appear in the medical records following a narrative statement outlining a patient's mental condition and is the only statement, or one of few, in the narrative about their patient's mental functioning. In many reports from mental health professionals, the GAF score does not appear at all. Moreover, for the purposes of litigation, disability determination, and job placement, the information provided by the GAF score may be insufficient to make a determination of a person's mental functioning. In these instances, the professional may need to obtain a functional capacity assessment of the mental functioning of a client from the treating specialist.

The form on the next two pages titled "Mental Limitations Assessment" is one example of a mental residual functional capacity (MRF) assessment. There are many variations, but almost all of these mental assessments focus upon the same or similar mental concerns:

- concentration,
- reliability,
- social interaction, and
- understanding and memory.

The example assessment asks the evaluator to rate in seventeen areas the severity of their patient's mental limitations on a continuum from *None/Slight* "generally functions well," to *Extreme* "No useful ability to function in this area." The definitions at the top of the page tell the degree of limitation each rating term suggests. For instance, in this mental RFC the term *Moderate* says "significant limitation, but still able to function satisfactorily." This definition would suggest that symptoms would likely be noticeable to the individual; nevertheless, the person should be able to carry out assigned job duties. *Marked*, on the other hand, says "serious limitations, such that performance in this area would be unsatisfactory." This definition would suggest serious symptoms affecting a person's effectiveness in a work setting and this person would likely experience some deterioration or breakdown in performance over time.

The rehabilitation counselor will find that while the terms used in these mental assessments are much the same, the definitions assigned to the rating terms may vary from form to form. Most of the forms contain an explanation of how the terms are used and are similar in the terms names (i.e., *None, Mild, Moderate, Marked*, and *Extreme*). The definitions of these terms may be very different among assessment forms, giving a completely different interpretation to the psychological instrument.

CHART 1

## MENTAL LIMITATIONS ASSESSMENT

---

NAME:
SSN:
EVALUATOR:

To help determine this individual's ability to do work-related activities on a day-to-day basis in a regular work setting, please give an opinion–based on clinical findings–of how the individual's mental/emotional capabilities are affected by the impairment(s). Consider the medical history, the chronicity of findings (or lack thereof), and the expected duration of any work-related limitations, but not the individual's age, sex, or work experience. The assessment should be exclusive of any limitations caused by current substance abuse. If it is not possible to separate the effects of substance abuse, please so indicate where applicable.

For each activity shown below, please describe the DEGREE OF LIMITATION resulting from psychological factors on a continuum using the terms defined below:

NONE/SLIGHT: Absent or mild limitation; generally functions well.
MODERATE: Significant limitation, but still able to function satisfactorily.
MARKED: Serious limitations such that performance in this area would be unsatisfactory.
EXTREME: Severe limitations. No useful ability to function in this area.
UNKNOWN: Unable to assess based on available information.

A. IMPAIRMENT IN ABILITY TO SUSTAIN CONCENTRATION AND ATTENTION

| Degree of limitation | None/Slight | Moderate | Marked | Extreme | Unknown |
|---|---|---|---|---|---|
| 1 Ability to carry out short and simple instructions throughout an 8 hour workday | | | | | |
| 2 Ability to maintain attention and concentration for *extended* periods | | | | | |
| 3 Ability to maintain customary work pace and complete tasks in timely manner throughout an 8 hour workday | | | | | |
| 4 Ability to adhere to a schedule throughout an 8 hour workday without special supervision | | | | | |
| 5 Ability to sustain an ordinary work routine throughout an 8 hour workday without special supervision | | | | | |
| 6 Ability to work in coordination with or in proximity to others throughout an 8 hour workday without being distracted by them | | | | | |
| 7 Ability to make simples work-related decisions consistently throughout an 8 hour workday | | | | | |

B. IMPAIRMENT IN RELIABILITY

| Degree of limitation | None/Slight | Moderate | Marked | Extreme | Unknown |
|---|---|---|---|---|---|
| 8 Ability to maintain regular work attendance on a full-time basis without absence of more than 2 days per month | | | | | |
| 9 Ability to tolerate ordinary work stresses (e.g., decisions, attendance, schedules, pace, interactions with supervisors and peers), without decompensation or deterioration in work performance throughout an 8 hour workday | | | | | |
| 10 Ability to respond appropriately to changes in the work setting | | | | | |

C. IMPAIRMENT IN SOCIAL INTERACTION

| Degree of limitation | None/Slight | Moderate | Marked | Extreme | Unknown |
|---|---|---|---|---|---|
| 11 Ability to interact appropriately with the general public | | | | | |
| 12 Ability to ask questions or request assistance as needed | | | | | |
| 13 Ability to accept instructions and respond appropriately to criticism from supervisors | | | | | |
| 14 Ability to get along with coworkers throughout an 8 hour workday without distracting them or exhibiting inappropriate behavior | | | | | |

D. IMPAIRMENT IN UNDERSTANDING AND MEMORY

| Degree of limitation | None/Slight | Moderate | Marked | Extreme | Unknown |
|---|---|---|---|---|---|
| 15 Ability to remember locations and work procedures | | | | | |
| 16 Ability to understand and remember short and simple instructions | | | | | |
| 17 Ability to travel in unfamiliar places or use public transportation | | | | | |

E. Please state or reference, as applicable, the clinical findings that support your assessment, and describe any other limitations on mental function.

EVALUATOR DATE

# EVALUATING PAIN AND THE EFFECTS OF PAIN

A medical expert said recently in a disability hearing for the Social Security Administration, "If I could devise a way to rate accurately a patient's degree of pain, I would be an immediate candidate for the Nobel Prize." The reason for his exasperation and vagueness in trying to deal with the effects of pain is that pain is a subjective matter; and the only way to determine the degree of pain is to ask an individual to describe the pain, tell where it hurts, and have them explain, as best they can, the severity of the pain. Yet, unless the degree of pain is understood, it is difficult to assess the person's functionality in daily activities or at work. This is true not only for the litigation of disability cases but also for job placement. Rehabilitation counselors must be able to assess the effects of pain upon their client's functional abilities to be able to determine how well, and at what level, a client will be able to sustain employment.

Professionals have used the Pain Rating Scale as one method to determine pain in their clients. The normal procedure in the use of the "Pain Rating Scale" is simply to ask a patient to rate pain on a scale of one (1)-10 with one being "no significant pain" and 10 being "excruciating pain." The Pain Rating Scale is presented below.

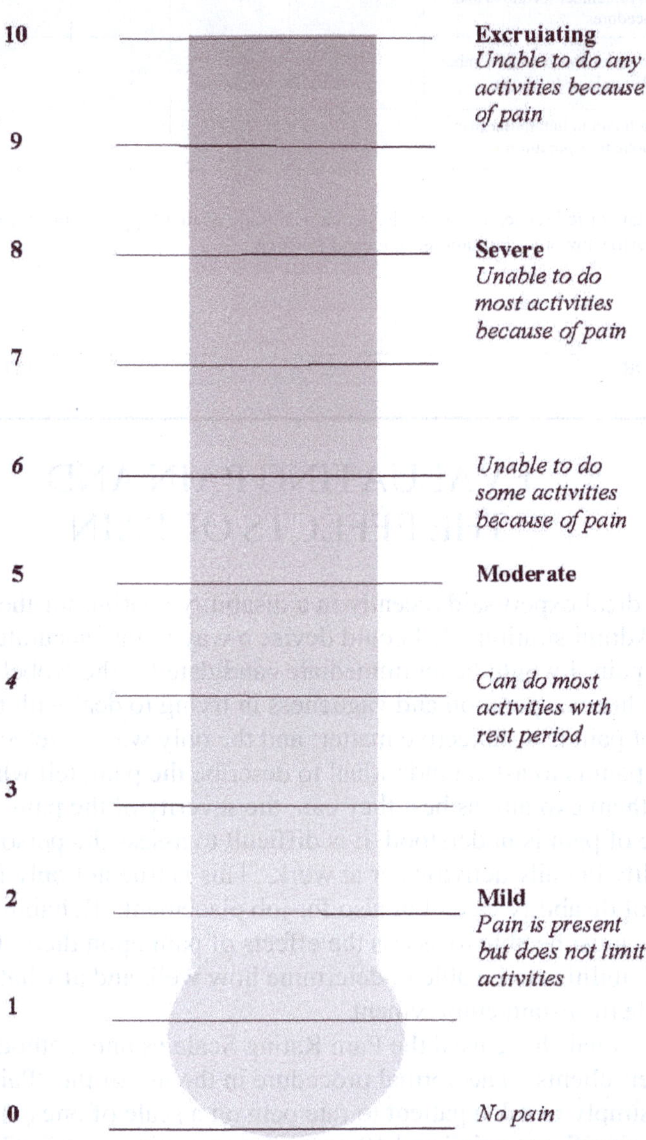


*McCaffery and Pasero[5] "Pain Rating Scale" published in the Pain Clinical Manual, 1999 at Martha Jefferson Hospital in Charlottesville, Virginia.*

The pain scale (above) shows the numbers associated with the pain level on the left side of the scale and the pain level and a description of the functional limitations caused by the various degrees of pain on the right. For instance, pain is defined in functional terms (i.e., *Mild* pain is when "pain is present but does not limit activity;" *Moderate* pain is defined as "can do most activities with rest periods;" *Severe* pain is defined as "unable to do most activities because of pain;" and *Excruciating* pain is defined as "unable to do any activities because of pain"). The Pain Scale is helpful in trying to assess the degree of pain and the functional descriptions help in trying to assess the way in which pain limits the person's activities.

Many rehabilitation counselors use the pain scale in their interviews with clients to gain an idea of how pain may limit their client's ability in daily activities and at work. Counselors have also found it helpful to carry the discussion of pain further by asking how their clients deal with the pain on a daily basis. Counselors may ask their clients to tell them what things they can do to make the pain better. Some familiar answers are lying down, sitting in a recliner, or taking pain medication. This question may be followed with "what things do you do that makes the pain worse." Familiar answers are driving long distances, sweeping or vacuuming the floor, or standing or sitting for prolonged periods. From the verbal responses to the numbers on the pain scale and follow-up questions, the rehabilitation counselor gains an understanding of the way pain limits a client's activities.

To gain a more refined picture of how the pain affects a client's mental functioning, counselors often compare the responses their clients have given to the pain scale with what clients tell them about their activities of daily living (ADL's). Activities of Daily Living are what the client does on a typical day. The rehabilitation counselor may ask their clients what time they rise in the morning and what kinds of activities they do around the house, (e.g., making meals, doing the dishes, sweeping floors, dusting furniture, doing yard work, driving the family vehicle, shopping, and taking the children to and from school). From these kinds of questions, the rehabilitation counselor learns the kinds of activities their clients are able to do in spite of the pain and obtains a better understanding of how accurate their clients have been in estimating their pain on the pain scale.

Taking this a step further, the counselor may ask their clients to estimate their functional abilities to perform certain work-related physical functions. For instance, the counselor may ask about a client's ability to stand and walk: "how long or far can you walk on a smooth, level surface without stopping? How long can you stand in one place at one time, like behind a counter, without having to sit down?" In an 8-hour day, how long can you walk and stand? These questions may be followed by a related question about a client's sitting capacity: "How long can you sit at one time without having to rise? What causes you to need to get up? How many hours can you sit during an 8-hour work day?" These questions would normally be followed by questions about lifting and carrying, such as "How much can you lift at one time? How far can you carry this weight?"

After the counselor has gained an understanding of the strength factors, walking, standing, sitting, and lifting, an estimate follows concerning non-exertion limitations and abilities, (e.g., climbing, balancing, stooping, kneeling, crouching, crawling, reaching, handling, the use of fingers for fine activities), and whether or not the pain is affected by changes in the weather. From these interview questions concerning exertion and non-exertion abilities and limitations, the counselor gains an understanding of how pain is likely to impact the type of settings in which the client has to work.

# EMPLOYABILITY: DEVELOPING A VOCATIONAL PROFILE

As we have seen, the medical community sets the medical residual functional capacity (RFC) for their patients, providing rehabilitation counselors with the medical information about:

- the diagnosis and treatment of their patients and the outcome of the treatment,
- the patient's ability to perform physical activities, if any,
- when the patient has reached maximum medical improvement (MMI), the date the patient can return to work (RTW), and
- the functional limitations a person will have when returning to the work setting.

The primary source of this information is the treating doctor or doctors, but occasionally other specialists may be asked to provide functional capacity assessments as well.

Much of the medical information is contained in the file a rehabilitation counselor reviews upon receiving the case. However, if the information is unclear or certain information is missing from the file, (as we saw earlier in this chapter in the example of Sheila Handy) the rehabilitation counselor must request this information before proceeding further with the diagnostic procedure and toward the development of a vocational profile for job placement. At the very minimum, before proceeding, the rehabilitation counselor must have in the client file:

1. a statement that the patient has reached maximum medical improvement (MMI),

2. a release from the medical doctors saying that the client is able to return to work (RTW), and

3. a clear statement of the functional limitations (RFC).

The better and more complete the information, the better understanding the counselor will have of the client and the more accurate the counselor can be in helping the client select vocational choices.

Once the medical residual functional capacity (RFC) and the mental residual functioning is established, the rehabilitation counselor examines the medical information to see what effect, if any, the work limitations will have upon the client's ability to work, and the kinds of jobs a person can perform given these limitations. In other words, the rehabilitation counselor now becomes concerned with the client's employability. *Employability is a determination made by the rehabilitation professional.*

Determining employability involves creating a vocational profile of the client and determining the kinds of work, given their functional limitations, this person can perform. In making a determination of employability, the rehabilitation counselor will address these questions:

- Given the client's functional limitations, as provided by the medical RFC, is the client capable of returning to their past work? This determination may involve talking with employers or former employers and, possibly, conducting a job analysis.

- If returning to past jobs is not an option, then the rehabilitation counselor will address the question of what alternative work, given the work limitations, this client can do.

To make a determination of employability, the rehabilitation counselor will normally examine the vocational information in the file, gather any additional information from the research, and conduct a personal interview with the client. To establish a vocational residual functional capacity, the counselor must consider a number of vocational factors.

## VOCATIONAL FACTORS

Years ago, in the formation of its disability program, the Social Security Administration wisely recognized that the three most important vocational factors affecting a person's residual functional capacity were the combination of a person's age, their education, and their work experience. The wisdom of using these three factors to make a determination has withstood the test of time. Age, education, and work experience are the three (3) key factors that go into making up a person's vocational profile. Rehabilitation counselors use a combination of these same three factors in assessing their client's ability to work and a determination of the kinds of jobs that person can perform. Let us look at these three factors in more detail.

*Factor 1: Age, and the ability to adjust to alternative work.* "Age" refers to an individual's chronological age and the extent to which age affects the ability to adapt to new work situations and to do work in competition with others. The research that went into designing the regulations recognized that as persons grow older; their ability to adjust to a work setting becomes more difficult. Recall the research on older persons with disabilities cited in Chapter 2 that found that many older individuals believed that if they could not do their past work, they considered themselves unable to do any work. Professional experience tends to bear out the assumption that as people age, vocational adjustment to new work becomes more difficult. Sections 404.1563 and 416.963 of the regulations governing disability under the Social Security program separates age into these categories:

- **Younger Person**–if an individual is under age 50, the regulations provide that generally an individual's age will not seriously affect the ability to adapt to new work situations.

- **Person Approaching Advanced Age**–if an individual is closely approaching advanced age (50–54), along with a severe impairment and limited work experience, age will be considered to possibly seriously affect an individual's ability to adapt to a significant number of jobs.

- **Persons of Advanced Age**–advanced age (55-59) is considered to be the point at which age significantly affects a person's ability to engage in substantial gainful activity. If an individual is severely impaired, they may be found disabled unless the individual has skills that can be used in (transferred to) less demanding jobs.

- **Persons Close to Retirement**–if an individual is close to retirement age (60-64) and has a severe impairment, they will be considered unable to adjust to sedentary or light work unless the individual has skills that are highly marketable.

The criteria used by the Social Security Administration to determine the effects of age upon a person's ability to work do not mean a person with a severe impairment at any age cannot work. The criteria do set forth some of the conditions rehabilitation counselors need to consider regarding their clients. The regulations basically say that a younger person, less than 50 years of age, should have no significant difficulty in adjusting to new work. With clients between 50 and 54, age may be a factor and seriously affect their ability to adjust to a "significant number" of alternative jobs. With persons approaching advanced age, rehabilitation counselors need to take into account their client's age and, when making a vocational choice, consider how well their client can make a vocational adjustment. For clients over 55, age significantly affects a person's ability to work. This is true unless they have work skills that can be transferred to other occupations. At age 55 to 59 rehabilitation counselors need to not only consider vocational adjustment but also the kinds of work skills their client can carry over to new work. For persons age 60 and above, transferable work skills should be "highly marketable."

*Factor # 2: Formal education and vocational training.* In making a determination about a person's employability, age is only one of the vocational factors rehabilitation counselors need to consider. Age is generally used only with regard to the ability of a person with impairments to make a vocational adjustment to alternative work. Age should not affect a person's ability to perform their past work unless other factors exist, such as the intrusion of a disability reducing a person's RFC, a lengthy time period between the present and when the work was performed, or changes that may have occurred in the way the work is normally performed in the national economy. Occupational changes would become a consideration if, for instance, a person had been a retail clerk in an electronics store in the 1980's. The product knowledge learned in the remote past would be of little benefit to them in the same retail setting today.

A second factor in the determination of a vocational profile is the client's education and/or vocational training. Education primarily means formal schooling or other training that contributes to a person's intellectual ability to meet the requirements of a job and the demands of competitive work. The kinds of skills a person likely learned in a formal school setting include reasoning, communication skills, and arithmetical ability. A lack of formal schooling does not necessarily mean that a client is uneducated or lacks the abilities in reasoning, communication, and arithmetic. Duties and responsibilities from work done in the past may demonstrate intellectual abilities, although a client may have very little formal education. Also, adaptive or life skills, such as hobbies and daily activities, acquisition of certifications, vocational training off or on the job, or the results of testing may also demonstrate intellectual abilities that a client can use in vocational planning or the selection of alternative work.

How do rehabilitation counselors determine the reasoning, mathematics, and language requirements of a particular job? The *Dictionary of Occupational Titles*, pp. 1009–1012[8] provides what is known as the *General Education Development Scale (GED)* that lists the general intellectual abilities required of a worker for a satisfactory performance of a particular job. The categories provided are Reasoning Development, Mathematical Development, and Language Development. The intellectual requirements are described on a scale of one (1) to six (6), with one being the lowest level and six being the highest level. (The "Scale of General Educational Development" can be found in Appendix 8:3 of the *Dictionary of Occupational Titles*).[8] Below each of the job descriptions listed in the DOT are references to each of the three categories. For instance, a Dining Room Attendant or Bus Person (311.668-018) needs to have a commonsense understanding to carry out detailed but uninvolved written or oral instructions (R2), add and subtract two digit numbers, as well as perform simple multiplication and division calculations (M1), and be able to read and speak simple sentences (L1).

The usefulness of a client's educational background may depend on how much time has elapsed between the completion of the formal education and the onset of a physical or mental impairment, and what the person has done with their education at work or in life. Formal education that the person completed many years before, or long, unused skills and knowledge that were part of a person's formal education may no longer prove meaningful or useful in terms of their ability to work, (e.g., suppose you are in an interview and your client, a construction worker, tells you he is a high school graduate. Since graduation, he has worked only as a laborer, reads very little, and engages in few activities that involve reading, math, or communication ability.) Intellectually, can he still function at the level of a high school graduate? In preparing a vocational profile and selecting job alternatives, the counselor must make this determination. The client may need additional testing.

The client's simple statement about the numerical grade completed: "I completed the fifth grade" is normally sufficient to determine the client's educational abilities, unless there is evidence in the file to the contrary. A review of the responsibilities assumed in the past work, acquired skills, daily activities, hobbies, as well as the results of testing (information normally gathered at the time of the personal interview) might show or suggest a client's level of reasoning, communication, and arithmetical ability to be higher than the level of formal education. Therefore, the person may meet the criteria for elevated levels of work. An insightful counselor may convey this information to potential employers through a carefully crafted resume.

The Social Security Administration (SSA) has listed educational categories in their regulations governing their disability programs. These categories reveal the functioning of persons at various educational levels and the kinds of work–unskilled, semi-skilled, and skilled–the person is likely able to enter given the level of intellectual functioning. (Classification of jobs as to their skill level is considered later in this chapter). Without evidence to the contrary, most rehabilitation counselors find these categories useful in conceptualizing job requirements as well as their client's intellectual abilities. (The federal guidelines make these categories binding on a Vocational Expert in disability hearings, (i.e., a Vocational Expert (VE) in a disability hearing must consider the educational categories, listed below, in their evaluation of jobs and in a determination of jobs that a claimant can do). The categories and the descriptive information for our discussion are taken from the "Vocational Expert Handbook[(6)]. The Social Security Administration's educational categories are:

1. ***Illiterate or Unable to Communicate in English***: A person is illiterate if he or she cannot read or write a simple message such as instructions or inventory lists, even though they can sign their name. Generally, an illiterate individual has little or no formal schooling. A person who does not speak and understand English may find it difficult to perform a job, regardless of the amount of education the individual may have in another language. Therefore, the counselor should consider a person's ability to communicate in English when evaluating what work, if any, the client can perform. Typically, the identity of another language that the person speaks fluently is immaterial.

2. ***Marginal.*** This category refers to formal schooling at the 6th grade level or below and the acquisition of reasoning, arithmetic, and language skills that permit performance of simple, unskilled work.

3. ***Limited***. This term denotes formal schooling at the 8th grade through 11th grade level and reasoning, arithmetic, and language skills that do not permit performance of most of the more complex job duties needed in semi-skilled or skilled jobs.

4. ***High School Education or More***. Generally speaking, this category is used for individuals who have completed the 12th grade or have earned a high school equivalency diploma. Persons in this category have acquired the reasoning, language, and arithmetic skills that permit performance of semi-skilled and skilled work.

5. ***High School Graduate or More - Provides for Direct Entry into Skilled Work***. This category applies when a short period of time has elapsed since the completion of formal education, that enables the individual with a minimal degree of job orientation, to begin performing the skilled job duties of certain identifiable occupations with their residual functional capacity (RFC).

*Factor # 3: Work experience*. Most of the information pertaining to the client's past work is gained during client interviews. The file may contain an employment application, and other information, such as the client's past employer or the company making the referral. To gain any insight into the past work, the counselor generally asks the client to describe his/her past work. To refine this information, counselors compare what clients tell them about their past jobs with the work described in the *Dictionary of Occupational Titles (DOT)*.[8]

Using the DOT to compare the job performed by the client and related to the counselor during the interview, with the way a job is normally performed in the national economy is useful to rehabilitation counselors in several ways.

1. *Clients are not always accurate in their descriptions*. This kind of comparison helps counselors make sure everybody is on the same page; that is, counselors and their clients are both talking about the same job.

2. *Clients do not always provide complete information.* They are likely to relate their daily work routine, the things they do on a regular basis, but in relating this information to their counselor, ignore some of their most important and skilled activities. In looking at the job skills and transferable skills, a comparison between what the client says in the interview and the job as described in the DOT gives the counselor a more complete picture of the total job, and perhaps, most important,

3. *The comparison between the interview information and an examination of the job description in the DOT provides documentation and makes any vocational assessment or report more complete and professional*.

Report documentation essentially says to the reader, "OK, here is the way my client has described the job to me, and here is the way our best research presents that job. In my analysis, to get a clear picture of the job, I have examined both of these sources of information." The DOT listing with the number designation normally follows the description of the job in a report or vocational assessment, (e.g., *Dictionary of Occupational Titles*:[8] Head Doffer (textile) 689.366-010.)

In a personal interview, practicing counselors usually ask their clients to name the jobs they have done in the past beginning with the most recent job. The Social Security Administration is concerned with what is termed a person's past relevant work (PRW). For their purposes, only the work the claimant has done in the past 15 years is considered relevant. The Social Security Administration considers the work skills learned in any work done earlier than 15 years to be obsolete and irrelevant. In addition, the Social Security Administration considers a job done in the past as relevant only if it has lasted long enough for the individual to learn the job skills and reach adequate performance in the job. On the other hand, rehabilitation counselors involved in job placement may be looking for any information that may lead them to possible work alternatives. This means they often consider work done beyond the 15 years and work performed for shorter periods.

To understand the past work of their clients, rehabilitation counselors will usually ask their clients to provide them with certain job information. This information will include:

- the title of the job,
- a description of the work processes,
- tools they used in performing the work,
- the length of time it took to learn the job duties and to reach full proficiency in the job,
- the time periods in which the jobs were performed,
- reasons why the worker left the job (e.g., fired, promoted, quit the job),
- the wage level at the time they left the job, and
- the physical demands for each job.

An accurate description of the physical demands of the job is very important for evaluating the past work and preparing for a job search. When considering work for persons with limitations, the physical demands must be compared with the doctor's residual functional capacity (RFC). The doctor's RFC is considered binding in determining the client's ability to do past work and or any other work. For instance, a job that has a lifting requirement of 50 pounds frequently and 100 pounds occasionally (heavy work) cannot be performed by a client with lifting restrictions from their treating physician of 20 pounds frequently and 50 pounds occasionally (medium work). Here again a comparison between the job as described in the client interview and the job as listed in the DOT provides verification of the verbal information.

The Social Security Administration, the *Dictionary of Occupational Titles*,[8] and the rehabilitation field all use essentially the same categories to describe the physical demands of occupations. (A discussion of the physical demands for work can be found on pages 1012 and 1013 of the *Dictionary of Occupational Titles*).[8] The following descriptions of the categories as applied in the federal regulations are taken from the *Vocational Expert Handbook*.[6]

- ***Sedentary***. Sedentary work involves lifting no more than 10 pounds at a time and occasionally lifting or carrying articles like docket files, ledgers, and small tools. Although sedentary jobs involve sitting, they also require a certain amount of walking and standing to carry out job duties. Jobs are sedentary if they require occasional walking or occasional walking and standing, provided other sedentary criteria are met. Because sedentary occupations may require occasional standing and walking, the actual periods of standing or walking should generally total no more than 2 hours of an 8-hour workday. Sedentary work entails no significant stooping, but most unskilled sedentary jobs require repetitive hand and/or finger movements.

- ***Light***. Light work involves lifting no more than 20 pounds at a time with frequent lifting and carrying of objects weighing up to 10 pounds. Since frequent lifting or carrying requires a claimant to be on his or her feet up to 2/3 of a workday, the full range of light work requires standing or walking for a total of approximately 6 hours in an 8-hour workday. Sitting may occur intermittently during the remaining time. Even though the weight the claimant lifts in a particular light job may be minimal, the regulations classify a job as "light" when it requires a significant amount of walking or standing. Some light jobs, like sewing machine operator, although performed while sitting, involve pushing or pulling of hand or foot controls. However, light jobs generally do not involve the use of the fingers for fine manipulation to the extent required in most sedentary jobs.

- ***Medium***. Medium work involves lifting no more than 50 pounds at a time with frequent lifting and carrying of objects up to 25 pounds. A full range of medium work requires standing and walking for a total of approximately 6 hours in an 8-hour workday. Medium work generally requires only use of the hands and arms to grasp, hold, or turn objects. Medium jobs require considerable lifting and frequent bending or stooping.

- ***Heavy***. Heavy work involves lifting no more than 100 pounds at a time with frequent lifting or carrying of objects weighing up to 50 pounds.

- ***Very Heavy***. Very heavy work involves frequently lifting objects weighing 150 pounds or more.

*Factor #4: Identification of work skills and their transferability.* An important part of analyzing the past work experience of a client is the recognition of work skills and making a determination of which skills can be transferred to other occupations to provide your client with a competitive advantage in the open job market. These are the work skills derived from past work experiences and skills a client has learned through education or vocational training that can be used in other occupations; that is, skills from past work, education, and training that can be transferred to new or alterative work.

In the professional practice of rehabilitation, the recognition of work skills; and, in particular, the transferable work skills becomes very important. So many times, persons injured on the job or elsewhere can still work but their physical capacity has been reduced to a lower level of exertion. This disabling condition may make it impossible to return to their past work, but if they have transferable work skills, they may be able to use the knowledge and training gained from their past work to meet the requirements of other occupations at a lower level of exertion. For example,

> *John Dutton was a patrol officer with the Kentucky Department of State Police. He incurred a back injury in an automobile accident while pursuing a drunk driver. He had an operation on his back, and following surgery and recovery, his treating orthopedic surgeon released him to return to work with restrictions of lifting 20 pounds occasionally and 10 pounds frequently. He is thus reduced to the performance of light work. The Kentucky Department of State Police, however, requires a police officer to be able to lift and carry 50 pounds frequently, placing the job requirements at a medium level of exertion.*

Can he do his past work? Probably not, unless the department provides him with a special accommodation, something most police departments are reluctant to do. Does he have work skills that can be done in another occupation at a lower level of exertion? Yes, most security work can be done at light and sedentary levels of exertion. With his experience as a state patrol officer, he would probably be in high demand in many security occupations. The compensation would likely not be as high, but his transferable skills would provide him with an opportunity to find work in an alternative occupation.

*Identification of Work Skills.* What do we mean by skills, and how can these skills be transferred to other occupations. The federal regulations governing the administration of the disability program for Social Security defines a skill as "knowledge of a work activity that requires:

1. the exercise of significant judgment that goes beyond the carrying out of simple job duties and,

2. is acquired through performance of an occupation which is above the unskilled level.

It is practical and familiar *knowledge* of the principles and processes of an art, science, or trade, combined with the *ability to apply them* in practice in a proper and approved manner. This includes activities like making precise measurements, reading blueprints, and setting up and operating complex machinery.

Skills are divided into three (3) categories:

1. ***Unskilled Work***. Unskilled occupations are the least complex types of work. Unskilled work needs little or no judgment to do simple duties that can be learned in less than 30 days, requires little specific vocational preparation, and little or no judgment. Jobs such as construction laborer are examples of unskilled work.

2. ***Semi-Skilled Work***. Semi-skilled occupations are more complex than unskilled work and distinctly simpler than the more highly skilled types of jobs. Semi-skilled work needs some skills but does not require doing the more complex job duties. Jobs in the semi-skilled range require learning (schooling and/or on-the-job training) from one month to six months in duration.

3. ***Skilled Work***. Skilled occupations are more complex and varied than unskilled and semi-skilled occupations. They require more training time and often a higher educational attainment. Abstract thinking in specialized fields may be required, (e.g., chemists and architects). Special artistic talents and mastery of a musical instrument may be involved, (e.g., school band instructors and understanding of charts and technical manuals may be needed by an automobile mechanic). The president or chief executive of a business organization may need exceptional ability to deal with people, organize various data, and make difficult decisions in several areas of knowledge.

The skill level of a particular job is determined by the amount of time it takes to learn the job and reach an adequate or satisfactory level of performance. The amount of time it takes to learn a job is called Specific Vocational Preparation (SVP). (The *Dictionary of Occupational Titles*[8] lists this information in nine (9) categories in Appendix C on p.1009) These categories are:

Level/Time

1 Short Duration Only,

2 Anything beyond Short Demonstration up to and including a month,

3 Over 1 month up to and including 3 months,

4 Over 3 months up to and including 6 months,

5 Over six months up to and including 1 year,

6 Over 1 year up and including 2 years,

7 Over 2 years up to and including 4 years,

8 Over 4 years up and to including 10 years,

9 Over 10 years.

Jobs at level 1 and 2 are considered unskilled; levels 3 and 4 are considered semi-skilled; and levels 5-9 are skilled jobs.

The *Dictionary of Occupational Titles*[8] provides an SVP for each of the 12, 841 jobs listed. The level of each job can be found below the job description following the General Educational Development designations. For instance, job listing Maintenance Supervisor is on page 282 of the DOT. The SVP for the Maintenance Supervisor is a level 6. In a survey of this position in 1988 (DUI), the job analyst for the Department of Labor found that for a worker to learn the job of Maintenance Supervisor and reach an adequate level of performance takes one to two years. This work, therefore, is considered a skilled occupation.

*Transferability of Work Skills.* Once work skills are identified, the rehabilitation counselor determines which, if any, work skills can be transferred to other occupations to give the worker a competitive advantage in the open job market. Obviously, there can be no transferability of work skills at levels 1 and 2 because the jobs at these levels are unskilled. For instance, a maid or a housekeeper in a motel has to clean rooms, make the beds, sweep the floors, and replace the toiletry items for new guests. These tasks are things the maid or house person has to know how to do and perform to the employer's standards. However, the Department of Labor has determined that the job tasks of a housekeeper can be learned in 30 days or less and is considered unskilled. As a result, a person who has performed only the duties of a maid and housekeeper would have no work skills to transfer to new work.

Work skills unique to a work process in a particular industry may not be readily applied to work in other occupations (e.g., the skills of a carpenter in a construction industry may be useful in like and similar work settings at the same or heavier levels of exertion. Yet, most of the work of a construction carpenter is done at medium to heavy levels of exertion, and seldom can this work be performed at a lighter level of exertion without considerable work accommodation by the employer). Without a significant vocational adjustment by way of tools, work processes, work settings, or industry, these work skills would not be transferable to other occupations.

Some work skills are so specialized or have been acquired in such an isolated vocational setting (e.g., many jobs in mining, agriculture, or fishing) that they are not readily usable in other industries, jobs, or work settings. The work skills of a placer miner, beekeeper, or spear angler, for example do not readily transfer to other industries to give the worker a competitive advantage. Work skills in occupations like these are considered "job specific."

The Social Security Administration has determined that transferability of work skills is found most often when:

1. The same or lesser degree of skill is required. That is, from a skilled occupation to another skilled occupation or a semi-skilled occupation. Such was the case, described earlier, of the injured State Police Officer. His position with the State Department of Police was a skilled position. The positions in the Field of Security are both skilled and semi-skilled.

2. the same or similar tools and machines are used, and

3. the same or similar raw materials, products, processes or services are involved.

Work skills in clerical, professional, administrative, and managerial jobs are examples. Some work skills have universal application across industry lines. In clerical, professional, administrative, or managerial types of jobs, transferability of skills to industries differing from past work experience can usually be accomplished with very little, if any, vocational adjustment. Of course, the jobs must be within the person's residual functional capacity

In considering transferable skills, work skills (things you learn to do at work) have been the main focus of our attention. Educational Skills (work skills you learn at school) and Adaptive Skills (personality traits: who you are) have received less attention. Both are important in identifying vocational assets for persons with disabilities. Educational skills and adaptive skills become equally important in giving the client a competitive edge in the open job market. In addition, educational and adaptive skills often need to be the centerpiece of a counselors job-seeking skills training format. (See Chapter 8 for additional discussion of educational and adaptive skills.)

Educational skills are important in considering transferable skills. Most architects are not even considered for jobs without formal education or vocational training in architectural design. Most employers will not consider an employee for the position of accounting clerk without the client having taken the principles of accounting, bookkeeping, and auditing practice. Certainly, vocational training taken in high school, (e.g., auto mechanic and drafting) is a necessary prerequisite for certain entry-level positions in those fields. Even the attainments gained from a high school program, such as reading, writing, and simple math are educational skills necessary in employment. Therefore, educational skills need to be part of any report on, or discussion of, transferable skills.

To avoid confusion, vocational literature for rehabilitation counselors in the past has made a careful separation between transferable work skills (things you learn to do at work) and adaptive work skills (human traits, or "who you are as a person," with qualities important to work, such as good attendance, reliability, hard work, honesty, sincerity, motivation). Recently, research has shown that adaptive skills are often more important to employers than work skills. Robert Half[2] records the results of a survey conducted among personnel directors from the 1000 largest U.S. Corporations. The results show that most people are fired from their jobs because of an inability to adapt to the work setting. Only 4% listed "not doing the job' as the most disturbing employee behavior.[pp. 49-52] Responses related to actual job performance totaled only 32%. The remaining responses related to poor adaptive or life skills. The researchers found that in their interviews, employers look for adaptive skills first and only when they are satisfied that the applicant can adapt to the work setting are they interested in job-related skills.

For example, persons having been honorably discharged from the military are perceived by employers to have a high level of adaptive work skills even when they may lack direct transferable skills from their experience in the armed services. In job placement of persons disabled in the military, employers believe they may have strong adaptive skills, such as self-discipline, the ability to get along with co-workers and supervisors, reliability, ability to handle stressful situations, perform tasks in a timely manner, and the ability to work independent of others. As a result, private rehabilitation firms have found that many employers are willing to provide these clients with personal interviews and offer jobs to these persons on the basis of their adaptive work skills

# CONCLUSION

This chapter began with the presentation of a case study involving Mary Gilmore, a 26-year-old nursing assistant who had received third degree burns when a truck overturned on a mountain road in West Virginia. The case study was followed by a series of vocational questions about her ability to function in the workplace. Before reading the following vocational analysis, review the details of that case. This chapter concludes with a presentation of her vocational profile and an analysis of the vocational issues in the case.

## DEVELOPING A VOCATIONAL PROFILE

The first step in developing a vocational profile is to summarize the vocational essentials in the case. Mary Gilmore is 26 years old. She is a high school graduate from Morgantown High School. She has had no other formal education. The records show that she has had vocational training to become certified as a nursing assistant. She has had no other vocational training. Mary Gilmore's past work was as a cashier, a waitress, and a certified nursing assistant.

> *In her personal interview, Mary Gilmore told the rehabilitation counselor that as a cashier she worked at a local Burger King Restaurant. Her job duties were to operate the cash register, take orders from customers, and serve food over the counter. To perform this work she had to stand and walk throughout her shift, sitting only for a half-hour lunch and two 15-minute breaks. She had very little lifting in this job.*

This job closely matches the job description of a Cashier II in the *Dictionary of Occupational Titles*[8] (211.462-010). As performed and as listed in the DOT, this job is unskilled, with an SVP of 2, taking less than 30 days to learn the job duties and reach an adequate level of work performance. This work was light in exertion.

> *In the personal interview, Ms. Gilmore says she worked as a waitress at West Virginia Wayside, a full-service restaurant on the outskirts of Morgantown. The restaurant is no longer in business. Her job duties were to hand menus to customers, take orders from customers, serve food to customers, calculate the costs of the meals, occasionally operate a cash register, occasionally clean tables, and occasionally serve as the hostess in seating customers at tables. Once or twice a day she had to carry out buckets of trash that weighed about 30 pounds. Her job duties required her to walk and stand most of the day, sitting only during fifteen-minute breaks with a half hour lunch period, and constantly lift trays of food that weighed less than 20 pounds.*

This work as performed by Ms. Gilmore was medium in exertion with lifting occasionally in the 30-pound range. Nevertheless, the *Dictionary of Occupational Titles*[8] (311.488-030) lists this work as normally performed at a light level of exertion. Her work as a waitress is semi-skilled, with an SVP of 3, taking one to three months to reach an adequate level of performance.

*She worked six years as a Certified Nursing Assistant at the Fairmont Nursing Home in Fairmont, West Virginia. Her job duties, as she described them, included bathing, dressing , and undressing elderly patients, serving and collecting food trays, transporting patients in wheel chairs, assisting them in walking with walkers, turning and repositioning patients in bed, draping patients for examinations and treatment, changing bed linens, running errands, directing patients to various locations in the home, answering calls for assistance, taking and recording temperature, blood pressure, respiration rates, and food and fluid intakes, and cleaning and dusting the room for her assigned patients. To perform the job duties of this job she had to walk and stand most of the day and lift patients without assistance, some of whom weighed over 100 pounds. This work as performed was very heavy in exertion.*

The position of Nursing Assistant as listed in the *Dictionary of Occupational Titles*[8] (355.684-014) is normally performed at a medium level of exertion and is semi-skilled, with an SVP of 4, taking three to six months to learn the job duties and reach an average level of performance.

## VOCATIONAL ANALYSIS AND TRANSFERABILITY OF WORK SKILLS

Mary Gilmore is 26 years old. There is no evidence in the case to suggest that, as a younger person, she would have difficulty making a vocational adjustment to her past work or any other work setting. She is a high school graduate. She has had vocational training to become certified as a Nursing Assistant. She has had no other formal education or vocational training. There is no information to suggest that she would not be able to function educationally at the level of a high school graduate. Therefore, she would be expected to be able to read, write, and perform mathematical functions at the level of a high school graduate.

Her past work was both unskilled and semi-skilled. She would be able to use her knowledge of operating a cash register and communicating with customers in a wide range of similar work settings. She would have no transferable skills from her work as a cashier. This work is unskilled. From her work as a waitress, she would have some skills, but these work skills are job specific and would not readily transfer to other occupations to give her a competitive advantage in the open job market. Finally, she would have transferable skills from her work as a nursing assistant to other semi-skilled jobs at a light level of exertion. Such jobs would be that of a Companion (309.688-010) and Personal Attendant (domestic service) 309.684-014).[8] Both of these positions have a Specific Vocational Preparation (SVP) at level 3.

Now that the rehabilitation counselor serving as a vocational expert has established a vocational profile for Mary Gilmore, they are ready to address the vocational questions in the case. Of course, the determination of employability and the amount of wages the injured person may have lost due to the injury is a determination of the court. The rehabilitation counselor called into the case as an expert witness is neutral; and vocational testimony of the vocational expert is based upon their understanding of the case. Compensation to the expert for professional services has nothing to do with the outcome of the case or any monetary award. Most of the time, the expert does not even know, and is not told, the outcome of the court decision in the case.

Each personal injury case is different and much more complex than the simple details given in the short explanation in this chapter. Moreover, the volume of information, medical reports, psychological reports, treatment notes, medical, and vocational evaluations contained in each of these cases makes the resolution of the case more difficult. Added to that, each vocational expert may see the facts differently, based upon what they see as the most important aspects of the case; and, therefore, each vocational expert who examines the case may have a different response.

The responses provided to the questions below are fairly typical. The analysis and reasoning of the expert are just as important as the conclusions reached by the expert.

*Can Mary return to her past work as a Certified Nursing Assistant*? Based upon the facts presented in the case, she could not return to her past work. Her past work as a Certified Nursing Assistant was performed at a very heavy level of exertion. Her treating physician, Dr. Nolan, has said that she could not stand or sit for prolonged periods. In the opinion of this expert, her residual functional capacity would be reduced to a sedentary level of exertion. At a sedentary level of exertion, she would not be able to perform the duties of a Certified Nursing Assistant as it is normally performed in the national economy. This work is normally performed at a medium level of exertion (according to the DOT).[8]

*Can she return to that kind of work with a limited amount of work accommodation*? Again, in the opinion of this expert, she would not be able to perform the duties of a Certified Nursing Assistant. Even with a work accommodation, she would need to stand for prolonged periods of time. The job of a Certified Nursing Assistant cannot be performed at a sedentary level of exertion.

*Can she do a similar job that the Company may make available to her*? Any work the company would offer her would need to be at a sedentary level of exertion. Any work provided would also need to be entry-level, unskilled work since she has no work skills that would transfer to jobs at a sedentary level of exertion. Moreover, the job would need flexibility in sitting and standing and provide her the opportunity to elevate her legs every 30 minutes.

The company would not likely have a similar position available since her work skills were in patient care with very little medical knowledge provided in her training as a CNA. There is still a possibility of another position with the company, however. Should the company consider her an exceptional employee, and have a sedentary position open, (e.g., a clerical worker with lower-level skills that she can learn on the job or through a local business college), they may be willing to make an accommodation for her to elevate her legs at a level below the waist. Most vocational experts find that employers are not willing to make accommodations in this sedentary job level if workers have to elevate their legs at waist level or above.

*Can she do any of the work she has done in the past*? She has been a cashier, a waitress, and a certified nursing assistant. All of her past work was done at a light level of exertion or above. If she were reduced to a sedentary level of exertion, she would not be able to perform any of the jobs as she has done them in the past.

*What residual abilities does she have to do any work*? Her vocational profile suggests that she would be able to perform only sedentary work. This work would need to have the flexibility that would allow her to sit and stand as needed and elevate her legs every 30 minutes while sitting. She has no transferable skills to sedentary work; therefore, the kinds of work for which she would be qualified would be unskilled, entry-level work.

*Does she have transferable skills from her past work*? The only transferable skills she has would come from her work as a Certified Nursing Assistant. These skills would transfer only to occupations at a light level of exertion (e.g., a Companion or Personal Attendant). In the opinion of this expert, these jobs could not be performed satisfactorily at a sedentary level of exertion.

*Is Mary a candidate for vocational training*? Mary is a very young person at age 26. In the opinion of this expert, she would be a candidate for vocational training. The vocational training would need to be for sedentary positions and those positions would need to have a sitting and standing option with the ability to elevate her legs every 30 minutes. For the right candidate, employers are usually willing to allow their employees a sitting and standing option as long as they can perform the work activity in either position. For the right candidate, employers are willing to make an accommodation for the elevation of a leg as long as the level of elevation is below the waist. Business college programs may provide her with a viable option because they would provide the training needed for many sedentary jobs; and, at the same time, advance her level of education.

*Is Mary disabled from any sustained work activity*? This would depend largely upon the level to which she would have to elevate her legs and the frequency with which she would need to rise from her sedentary position to stand. If she had to walk away from the workstation with any frequency, she would not be able, in all probability, to do even a sedentary job with a work accommodation. The time that she would be off-task would exceed the normal 2 to 3 percent of allowable time off-task normally provided in structured, unskilled, and entry-level positions.

The provision of a work accommodation is entirely up to the employer. Some employers will allow a worker to sit and stand, as long as they do not have to leave the workstation, and elevate their legs as long as it does not interfere with the work procedures. Jobs offering such an accommodation would be that of a telemarketer, a sedentary cashier, or a booth ticket taker. As far as the need to elevate her legs, the degree of elevation required would determine whether an accommodation allowing the worker to elevate the legs would be provided.

## TOPICS FOR GROUP DISCUSSION

The following is a real case study, only the names and the locations have been changed. Have each group develop a vocational profile from the case information.

> *Mary Jane Balsom is 42 years old. She was born December 18, 1962. She graduated from Mt. Seymore High School in Cantonville, Ohio in 1981. In high school, she had a vocational concentration in Child Care and Business Administration. Among other courses in her high school program, she took and passed classes in business math, accounting, and typing. Following graduation, she undertook an educational program with the Peace Corp that taught her general business, the use of the telephone, and filing. Her former husband had a small candle-making business working from the home. She kept books for his business.*
>
> *Mary Jane divorced her first husband. They had one child, a girl, born in 1985. She and her daughter lived for a while in Fairmont, a suburb of Cleveland, Ohio. In 1992, she met her second husband, Jim, on the Internet. He was in the military, stationed in Heidelberg, Germany. She and her daughter moved to Germany where she married Jim in 1993. They had no children from this marriage.*
>
> *She got a job at the Burger King on the military base in Heidelberg, Germany as a food service worker, operating the cash register, cooking burgers and other fast food, and serving customers. Occasionally she had to help load and unload 35-pound boxes of food from service trucks. While employed at the Burger King at the PX in Germany, she attended and completed a nine-week program in Basic*

*Management (BMT) in the operation of the Burger King Restaurant. The training involved supervising employees, managing work crews, learning each of the jobs in the restaurant, operating the restaurant computer program, and handling money in the restaurant.*

*Following her certification as a BMT manager, she was promoted to Junior Assistant Manager. Her job responsibilities required a variety of duties, including managing the work crews, stocking supplies, operating the drive-through window, washing dishes, cleaning, cooking, and filling in for other employees. She had the responsibility for counting the daily receipts of the business and maintaining the safety vault. She really did not have to do any lifting over 20 pounds.*

*Mary Jane was injured on the job when she fell from a chair while changing a light bulb. She went to the ER at the base hospital where she was diagnosed as having chronic back and right-leg pain, degenerative disc disease, obesity, and bilateral wrist pain. In spite of medical treatment, she continued to have chronic back pain. Her employer dismissed her after a year because she could no longer perform the job duties. She is currently under the treatment of a pain management doctor, Dr. Keeper, who has given her various medications and even epidural shots without good results. He says that she has not reached maximum medical recovery. He says that she can sit for 30 minutes at a time, then she needs to stand up to stretch. She can stand for two hours a day and lift less than 10 pounds. He has given her Prozac for depression. Since the accident, she has divorced her second husband and returned to the Fairmont area.*

*The insurance provider asked the opinion of another consulting doctor, Dr. Amwell. This doctor says, "She has no evidence of nerve root impingement, and I believe that her injury is a contusion of her lower back superimposed upon a de-conditioned individual with L4-5 degenerative disc disease." Dr. Amwell says that, "She cannot lift over 20 pounds. She should not do any repetitive bending, but she can sit, stand, and drive herself to and from a sedentary job or light duty environment." Following the IME by Dr. Amwell she underwent a Functional Capacities Evaluation at Cleveland Physical Therapy Associates which placed her at a sedentary level of exertion with restrictions including the need for a sitting and standing option, with limited walking, bending, and twisting.*

Have each group answer the vocational questions below:

1. Can Mary Jane return to her past relevant work?

2. Can she return to her past work with a limited amount of work accommodation?
3. Can she do any of the jobs she has done in the past?
4. What residual abilities does she have to do any work?
5. Does she have any transferable skills?
6. Is she a candidate for retraining?
7. What jobs can she now perform?

# INDIVIDUAL EXERCISES

1. The following terms have been used in many places throughout Chapter 5. Define in your own words the meaning of the terms listed:

   Vocational Profile
   Residual Functional Capacity
   Global Assessment of Functioning
   Vocational Terminology: Occasional/Frequent/Constant
   Mental Limitations: Moderate/Marked/Extreme
   Educational Categories: Marginal/Limited
   Past Relevant Work
   Physical Functioning: Sedentary/Light/Medium
   Work Skills: Semi-Skilled/Skilled

2. Using the *Dictionary of Occupational Titles*,[8] locate the DOT designation (nine digit number), the Physical Demands, SVP, and the GED for the following occupations:

   (a) Parking Lot Attendant
   (b) Desk Clerk (motel)
   (c) Library Assistant
   (d) Hand Packer

3. Review and prepare the case study above under the section "Group Discussion."

# REFERENCES

[1]Farr, J. M. (1990). *Job Finding Fast.* Peoria, IL: Macmillan/McGraw-Hill.

[2]Half, Robert (1949). *The Half Way to Get Hired In Today's Job Market.* New York: John Wiley & Sons, Inc.

[3]Havranek, J., Grimes, J. W., Field, T. & Sink, J. (1994). *Vocational Assessment: Evaluating Employment Potential.* Athens, GA: Elliott & Fitzpatrick, Inc.

[4]Luborsky, L. (1962). Clinician's Judgments of Mental Health. Archives of General Psychiatry.

[5]McCaffery, M and Pasero,C. (1999). *Pain Rating Scale.* Pain Clinical Manual, Mosby, Inc.

[6]Social Security Administration Office of Hearings and Appeals, Philadelphia Region (February 2003). *Vocational Expert Handbook*, 2nd Ed.

[8]Social Security Administration (Spring, 2012). *Occupational Outlook Quarterly*, Vol. 56, #1.

[8]United States Department of Labor, Employment and Training Administration. *Dictionary of Occupational Titles*, 4th Ed. (1991).

# CHAPTER SIX

# THE VOCATIONAL EXPERT IN DISABILITY HEARINGS WITH THE OFFICE OF DISABILITY, ADJUDICATION, & REVIEW OF THE SOCIAL SECURITY ADMINISTRATION

# PREFACE

*Because of their specialized knowledge and experience in serving persons having disabling conditions, their knowledge of the impact of disability upon a person's ability to work, and their knowledge and experience in job placement of persons with disabilities, the Social Security Administration has called upon rehabilitation counselors to serve as vocational experts in their Social Security Disability Insurance (SSDI) and Social Security Income (SSI) programs. Serving as a Vocational Expert is an expanding area of opportunity for rehabilitation counselors.*

The Authors

To the Reader:

Have you wondered what makes the practice of rehabilitation counseling different from other kinds of counseling practice? You may recall the definition of rehabilitation counseling posed by Paul Ellwood[5] in "To the Reader" in the opening chapter. A partial quotation from that statement follows. Paul Elwood says, "Rehabilitation is a profession of professions. From the start, rehabilitation has attempted to circumvent professionalized categories and to create a unified and synthesized program of management designed to integrate the skills of many professions.... The essential quality that differentiates the rehabilitation profession lies in the dynamics of its multi-disciplinary, total concept approach to client service."[5, pg. 21]

Essentially, as Paul Ellwood[5] indicates, rehabilitation counselors are generalists by profession, drawing knowledge for their own identity from a number of other specialties. For instance, like psychologists, rehabilitation counselors engage in one-to-one dialogue with their clients and deal with client concerns on an individual basis, but seldom do they have all the skills or the need to engage in psychotherapy. Moreover, the rehabilitation counselor is concerned with alcohol and drug abuse problems, particularly when these problems affect client goals, but unless they are substance abuse counselors, they do not engage in the treatment of these problems.

As a rehabilitation counselor, you are expected to have knowledge and expertise in certain specialized areas. Two of these areas of knowledge are disability and work. The clientele for rehabilitation counselors are exclusively persons with physical or mental disabilities. Unlike physicians, as we saw in Chapter 5, rehabilitation counselors are concerned mostly with the functioning of their clients: how the physical and mental limitations affect a person's ability to work. You do not have to be a medical doctor to practice rehabilitation counseling.

An equally important part of the professional identity of a rehabilitation counselor is knowledge of the world of work. In the field of rehabilitation, knowledge of work pervades about everything a counselor does:

- Rehabilitation counselors in state rehabilitation agencies provide vocational guidance and job placement, as well as supportive employment assistance, to eligible clients in the State/Federal program.

- Rehabilitation counselors serve as vocational experts for both plaintiff and defense lawyers in the courtroom during personal injury cases to evaluate work potential, to clarify vocational issues, and to provide the court with information about work-related concerns.

- Rehabilitation counselors manage client assistance programs in business and for government agencies.

- Rehabilitation counselors are called upon by insurance companies as part of the worker's compensation programs to conduct labor market surveys, manage their disability cases, and help injured clients reconnect to work in their community.

Because of their specialized knowledge and experience in dealing with persons having disabling conditions, their knowledge of the impact of disability upon a person's ability to work, and their knowledge and experience in job placement of persons with disabilities, the Social Security Administration has called upon rehabilitation counselors to serve as vocational experts in their Social Security Disability Insurance (SSDI) and Social Security Income (SSI) programs.

These are expanding areas of opportunity for rehabilitation counselors. As a vocational expert, rehabilitation counselors examine the past work of claimants, sit through disability hearings, and provide testimony about the claimant's ability to perform their past work or other jobs that may exist in the national and regional economy. While not all vocational experts are rehabilitation counselors, the knowledge components of the rehabilitation profession closely match the background requirements needed for a vocational expert witness in Social Security Administration disability hearings.

The vocational expert is not an employee of the Social Security Administration. Vocational experts are independent of the disability process and their testimony is expected to be impartial. Nor does the rehabilitation counselor have responsibility for deciding the outcome of the claimant's case; all determinations of the court are made by an administrative law judge (ALJ). During the hearings, rehabilitation counselors respond to hypothetical questions about vocational issues posed by the ALJ to help the judge make a decision about a claimant's ability to work. Finally, while the rehabilitation counselor is asked about jobs in the local and national economy, job placement is not the goal. The consideration of a disability hearing is a cash payment for persons unable to work.

On the other hand, the vocational expert plays an important part in the disability determination process. Based upon the medical records, and possibly the testimony of claimants and medical experts, ALJ's make a vocational assessment from the evidence provided to them. Usually, the vocational expert is asked to classify the claimant's past work in terms of the skills and level of exertion. In response to hypothetical questions from the judge, the VE provides testimony about a claimant's ability or inability to work under different situations. The vocational witness is considered by the court to be an expert based upon their knowledge of disability and work,

Chapter 6 is written from the viewpoint of the rehabilitation counselor. The content of the chapter is meant to provide an understanding of what it is like to be a vocational expert in Social Security hearings. In this chapter, you will be carried through the 5-step process the administrative law judge uses to determine disability:

- You will meet the persons who normally participate in the disability hearings, including the administrative law judge, the hearing reporter, the medical expert, the claimant representative, and, most important, the claimant.
- You will follow the hearing process used to evaluate a claimant's disability.
- You will see how the VE evaluates a claimant's past work, with examples taken from live situations.
- You will see ways VE's use the Dictionary of Occupational Titles[12] to evaluate the past work of claimants.
- You will examine the criteria that make up the hypothetical questions asked by the administrative law judge.
- You will see how vocational experts respond to questions from attorneys during cross-examination.

- You will be presented with selective hypothetical questions and the kinds of responses typically given by vocational experts.

# BACKGROUND: THE EMERGENCE OF THE VOCATIONAL EXPERT IN SOCIAL SECURITY HEARINGS

When Congress passed the original Social Security Act of 1935[7] creating retirement benefits for persons over 65 years of age, there was already discussion about expanding the program to provide wage-related cash benefits to workers who became totally and permanently disabled before the age of 65. At that time the proponents of a disability program argued that "the permanently disabled were the only major class of people needing protection that did not receive it under the Social Security Act and yet no other group was more completely dependent or in a more desperate economic situation."[pg. 1]

It would be another 20 years before a national disability program would become a reality. One of the main reasons for the delay was concern over the difficulty of making disability determinations; that is, the subjectivity of determining whether a person was truly disabled. Concerns about the subjectivity in disability determinations have continued to follow the program to this very day.

On August 1, 1956, President Dwight D. Eisenhower signed into law the Amendments to the Social Security Act establishing the Social Security Disability Insurance (SSDI) program. The Social Security Income (SSI) program was established by Congress in the 1967 Amendments and implemented in 1974, eighteen years after the creation of the SSDI program.

In the year before the passage of the 1956 Amendments, the Commissioner of Social Security had appointed a Medical Advisory Committee (MAC) to formulate a policy for evaluating disability. The panel set forth medical criteria for evaluating specific impairments with the level of severity for each. The panel also suggested that factors such as age, education, training, and experience were important in the evaluation of disability even though the new law did not specifically require consideration of these factors. One recorded statement from the Medical Advisory Committee said, "In determining whether an individual's impairments make him unable to engage in such activity (work), primary consideration is given to the severity of his impairment. Consideration is also given to such other factors as the individual's education, training, and work experience."[7, pg. 3]

Following passage of the 1956 Amendments to the Social Security Act, the new law experienced problems in the courts. Numerous court cases challenged the practice of making a determination of disability based upon medical evidence alone. In a sense, the way the guidelines were set up, adjudicators simply looked at the medical evidence and if, in their own judgment, the disability was total, that was that. The converse was also true. If a person's impairments did not meet the requirements of the medical evidence in the adjudicator's mind, the applicant was turned down for benefits.

As a consequence of court challenges, congressional committees during the Lyndon B. Johnson administration took notice of the trends in case law and in the Social Security Amendments of 1967 and made it clear that a claimant may be found disabled "only if his physical or mental impairment or impairments are of such severity that he is not only unable to do his previous work but cannot, considering his age, education, and work experience, engage in any other kind of substantial gainful work that exist in the national economy regardless of whether such work exist in the immediate area in which he lives, or whether a specific job vacancy exists for him, or whether he would be hired if he applies for work."[7, pg. 5]

The courts had made it clear that in order to deny a claim for disability, the adjudicator for the Social Security Administration had the burden of proof to address the vocational issues in each case and show there were jobs a claimant could perform in spite of their physical or mental limitations. Initially, the Social Security Administration attempted to address the vocational issues in disability cases by relying upon "selected government and industrial studies,"[8, pg. 2] but the courts rejected this approach because the reports were "speculative and theoretical in determining whether there were employment opportunities available to disability claimants."[8, pg. 2] As a result of these court challenges, the SSA determined that a more specific and reliable way to address whether or not a person can work was to employ independent vocational experts who could provide live testimony related to a claimant's "particular and highly individual situation."[8, pg. 2]

The Social Security Administration has used vocational experts in cases appealed to the Office of Disability, Adjudication, and Review (ODAR) for roughly the past 50 years. During that period of time, the Social Security Administration has withstood numerous legal challenges to the use of vocational experts; but the courts have been relatively uniform in recognizing vocational expert testimony as an acceptable way to address work-related issues in disability cases. Today, administrative law judges with the Office of Disability Adjudication and Review (ODAR) rely upon the testimony of vocational experts in most adult cases during disability hearings on appeal.

# THE 5-STEP PROCESS FOR DISABILITY DETERMINATION

Both for the Social Security Disability Insurance program (SSDI) and for the Social Security Income program (SSI), a person is awarded cash benefits if their disability is of such severity as to prevent them from working. The process for evaluating disability is identical for both programs.

Congress has defined disability as "the inability to engage in substantial gainful activity by reason of any medically determinable physical and mental impairment which can be expected to result in death or which has lasted or can be expected to last for a continuous period of not less than twelve months.[1, pg. 2] To make disability determinations based upon this definition, the Social Security Administration has adopted a five-step sequential process that considers the uniqueness of a claimant's impairment or impairments.

It is important to understand the word *sequential* as used in the process of defining disability. The term *sequential* means a claimant cannot proceed from one-step to the next until it is determined that they are disabled. The burden of proof rests upon the claimant to show that at each step from one through four during the sequential process, they meet all requirements for disability. At step five, the burden of proof shifts to the Commissioner of Social Security and requires that the adjudicator (ALJ) provide evidence that the applicant can or cannot work.

*The first step of the five-step sequential evaluation process is for the adjudicator to determine whether the individual is engaged in substantial gainful employment.* The term *substantial gainful employment* is defined in monetary terms. For instance, from 1980–1989 a claimant's gross income became substantial gainful employment when that person earned $3600 a year; in 2014 that amount was $10,000. If a claimant has earned more than the established amount during a given year, that person is not eligible for benefits.

At *the second step, the adjudicator has to determine whether or not the individual has an impairment or combination of impairments that is severe.* In its regulations, the Social Security Administration has defined *severe* as "a medically determinable impairment or combination of impairments that significantly limits a person's physical or mental ability to do basic work-related activity."[15, pg. 14] For an impairment to be *medically determinable* the condition must have been determined by clinical or laboratory diagnostic studies or by other acceptable medical means. According to federal regulations governing the program, "the standard for assessing severity at Step 2 is medical only. Vocational factors, such as age, education, and work experience are considered by the judge at this step, but they are more important at Step 5 of the sequential evaluation process."[15 pg. 13] The impairment must have lasted, or be expected to last, for 12 months.

At *Step 3, if a disability claimant has an impairment that meets the durational requirements of 12 months and meets, or equals, one or more of the list of medical impairments provided by the Social Security Administration,* the *claimant is found disabled without considering the claimant's age, education, and work experience*. The Listing of Impairments contains 14 separate body systems and the conditions the claimant must meet to be declared disabled under each listing. These listings include:

1.00 Musculoskeletal Systems;
2.00 Special Senses and Speech;
3.00 Respiratory System;
4.00 Cardiovascular System;
5.00 Digestive System;
6.00 Genitourinary Impairments;
7.00 Hematological Disorders;
8.00 Skin Disorders;
9.00 Endocrine System;
10.00 Impairments that affect multiple body systems;
11.00 Neurological;
12.00 Mental Disorders;
13.00 Malignant Neoplastic Diseases; and
14.00 Immune System.

The List of Impairments is provided by the Social Security Administration and the book titled *Code of Federal Regulations* (CFR) is used by the administrative law judge, medical advisors serving as medical experts in Social Security hearings, and by a claimant's representative.

If, on the other hand, a person has a severe, medically determinable impairment that, though not meeting or equaling the criteria in the listing of impairments, prevents the person from doing their past relevant work, the Administrative Law Judge must determine whether the person can or cannot do other work. At Steps 4 and 5 of the sequential process, the determination is made based upon a claimant's ability to perform past work and other work that exists in significant numbers in the national economy.

Making the disability determination at *Step 4 involves consideration of the person's residual functional capacity (RFC) and the vocational factors of age, education, and work experience*. As we discussed in Chapter 5, a claimant's RFC is formed by an initial assessment of a person's physical and mental abilities and limitations and the kinds of work that person can do within those limitations.

At Step 4, the administrative law judge looks at the claimant's ability to perform past work. If it is determined that the claimant is able to perform past relevant work (work within the past 15 years), then the process stops right there. In analyzing the past work of claimants at Step 4, the administrative law judge relies on the testimony of the vocational expert to only a limited extent. Under the sequential evaluation, if a claimant cannot perform his/her past relevant work, the evaluation process continues on to Step 5.

At *Step 5, SSA has to determine the existence of a significant number of jobs in the national economy that the claimant is able to perform.* SSA has said "for the purposes of determining a claimant's ability to engage in work other than past relevant work, work is considered to exist in the national economy when there exists a significant number of jobs in one or more occupations that have requirements the claimant is able to meet with his/her physical or mental abilities and vocational qualifications."[15, pg. 18] At Step 5, the ALJ relies heavily upon vocational expert testimony.

The opinions expressed by vocational experts are formed from a review of the records provided to them, by listening to the testimony of claimant's and others during the hearing, by using vocational information derived from a variety of sources, especially the *Dictionary of Occupational Titles*,[12] and from personal experience gained while working with injured and disabled clients in employment situations. The testimony of the VE is crucial to the proceedings because neither the administrative law judge nor the claimant possess the education or the experience to analyze the exertion and skill required by particular employment situations. According to one critic, the testimony of the vocational expert is the foundational block of the SSA disability determination process, because, without it, a complete, accurate, and reasonable decision would not be possible.

# BECOMING A VOCATIONAL EXPERT WITH THE SOCIAL SECURITY ADMINISTRATION

In the literature of disability law, a vocational expert, as opposed to a rehabilitation consultant, is defined as a person giving testimony in a disability hearing. That is not to say that rehabilitation consultants do not testify in court; most of them do from time to time. However, the practice of a vocational consultant involves a wider variety of duties and responsibilities, (e.g., counseling, case management, and job placement: all the things we talked about in Chapter 1 in defining the role of the rehabilitation counselor). Vocational consultants can be vocational experts. Many of them serve in that role as part of their professional practice. The designation of vocational expert is specific to the function served by the consultant with the Office of Disability and Adjudication with the Social Security Administration.

A Social Security vocational expert, on the other hand, is involved exclusively in providing information about vocational issues to an administrative law judge to help the judge make disability determinations. In the past VE's were used more sparingly than today; in fact, in some federal jurisdictions, they were not used at all. In the litigious environment we live in today, most ALJ's rely upon the advice of vocational experts to help them decide the majority of adult cases. Why is this? By profession, an ALJ is an attorney. While most of the judges have a keen knowledge about vocational matters, they are not prepared by education or training to address vocational issues in a court of law. They need the presence of an expert to classify work in terms of skill and exertion, to address vocational areas that need explanation, and to help the judge understand the impact of a claimant's disability upon their ability to work in both their past work and other work that may be available to a claimant.

Can you picture yourself as a vocational expert in a court room with an auspicious judge in a black robe, looking like Darth Vader, peering down upon you from a raised platform, while across the table sits a smug attorney waiting for you to make one slight mistake before eating your liver? So many rehabilitation counselors refuse to take advantage of becoming a vocational expert because they conjure up an image similar to this when considering becoming a VE. It is not like this at all–for a variety of reasons:

1. The courtroom is not what you see on television. Admitting evidence into the file for consideration and taking testimony under oath are about the only formal procedures. Federal Rules of Civil Procedure and Federal Rules of Evidence are not stringently applied. In fact, the ALJ makes a deliberate attempt to place everyone who will testify at ease at the beginning of the hearing.

2. The work is challenging and the growth you experience in learning to become a VE easily carries over to other work with injured and disabled people, even in job placement, making you a much better professional. As noted in many places earlier in this text, possibly the most professional activity a rehabilitation counselor does is to determine the impact of a disabling condition upon a person's ability to work.

3. This work places you on the cutting edge of professional practice. Not only is serving as a VE in itself lucrative; most VEs exceed the national average salary for rehabilitation counselors. There is no better preparation for expert consultation in other court settings than the experience VE's gain in a Social Security hearing.

4. If you have a degree or degrees in rehabilitation or a related field, your skills are uniquely shaped to this kind of work. Unlike the negative images you may entertain, most of the judges and the attorneys respect the testimony of vocational experts.

5. Don't rule out the personal prestige that goes along with being an expert! It does wonders for your self-esteem.

## PERSONS PARTICIPATING IN A SOCIAL SECURITY HEARING

If claimants live within 75 miles of the hearing site, disability hearings are held at the Office of Disability, Adjudication, and Review (ODAR). Alternate hearing sites are also provided in order to hold hearings for claimants who live in more remote locations. In the recent past, hearings were held in other temporary sites, including Social Security field offices, other federal buildings, and even motels and hotels. Administrative Law Judges would regularly travel to these alternate sites carrying recording equipment and boxes of cases for the hearing. Vocational experts and hearing reporters would also travel to these sites, however, not as often anymore.

Today, hearing sites have become more uniform and most hearing rooms are designed exclusively for Social Security hearings. Even alternate sites are more uniform; motels and hotel rooms are used sparingly. This uniformity has been made necessary because of teleconferencing. Normally, when hearings are held using teleconferencing, the ALJ and vocational experts are in the main ODAR location, while claimants and their representatives are at the remote site. This arrangement has removed much of the travel for both experts and the ALJ.

The typical courtrooms have a formal arrangement of the furniture, forming a "T", a setting very similar to the more formal rooms in the district court setting (without the jury box). The judge's desk and chair stand behind a wooden rail on a raised platform. The hearing reporter normally sits to one side of the judge. A long table forms the base of the "T." The claimant sits at the end of the "T" facing the judge. Usually, a large television screen for use in teleconference hearings is attached to the wall behind the claimant. The claimant's representative, if there is one, sits to the left of the claimant at the table and the vocational expert is seated on the right. Witnesses on behalf of the claimant are often sworn in and then sequestered while the claimant testifies. Occasionally, persons who are not testifying are allowed to remain in the hearing for moral support to the claimant.

An Administrative Law Judge presides over the hearing. The ALJ has a broader range of duties than a trial judge does. The ALJ protects both the government's interest and the interest of the claimant while rendering an impartial decision. The cases come to the ALJ on appeal from the processing bureau, the Disability Determination Section (DDS). The hearings are *de novo* meaning the ALJ is not bound by previous determinations. The ALJ makes a completely new decision based upon the medical and other evidence in the case, the testimony obtained at the hearing, and the application of the evidence to the Social Security Law.

A hearing reporter is also present. The hearing reporter is responsible for setting up and operating the recording equipment, taking notes, and making sure that the hearing runs smoothly. Normally, the hearing reporter will gather any new evidence the claimant or the claimant's representative present on the hearing day and deliver the new information to the judge for review. The hearing reporter usually ushers the claimant and others into the hearing room. At the beginning of the hearing, at the judge's direction, the reporter turns on the recording equipment and announces the opening of the hearing by saying "on the record." At the close of the hearing, at the judge's direction, the reporter announces that the hearing is "off the record" and turns off the recorder. At the request of the ALJ, the reporter may stop the recording at any time. The normal hearing length is 45 minutes to an hour.

Not all claimants are represented by counsel. Most are, but a claimant has the right to choose whether to have representation. Claimant representatives are mostly attorneys although some are non-attorneys. The non-attorneys are usually persons familiar with disability law and the disability determination process. If claimants are not represented by someone of their choice, at the beginning of the hearing the ALJ will advise them of their rights to representation and describe what a representative can do for them. Should the unrepresented claimant choose to have a representative, the hearing may be postponed until a later date. A representative can help claimants gather and present to the court the medical and other records needed for the judge to make the disability determination, counsel claimants on what to expect at the hearing, question claimants at the hearings, and cross-examine experts and others during the hearing process.

The main point of the hearing is for claimants to prove to the Administrative Law Judge that because of a disabling condition, they can no longer work. To help the ALJ make a favorable decision, claimants or their representatives submit medical evidence from a variety of treating sources. When vocational issues contribute to the disabling condition, claimants or their representatives may submit other records (e.g., school records or employer statements). Claimants may also choose to have family members, friends, medical professionals, and others appear at the hearings to testify about their disabling condition.

Medical experts may also appear at the hearing. Medical experts are either expert in the field of medicine or expert in the field of mental health. Experts from the field of medicine are physicians, usually retired physicians, but still with current medical credentials, such as a board certification in their medical specialty (internal medicine, orthopedics, etc.). The testimony of the physician concerns the physical aspects of a claimant's disability. Also appearing at the hearing may be a psychiatrist or psychologist to testify on the mental and emotional aspects of a claimant's disability. Experts in mental health are usually practicing professionals.

Medical experts examine evidence in the records and offer an opinion as to whether a claimant meets or equals the Listings of Impairments, a Step 3 determination. Therefore, the testimony of the medical expert will precede that of the vocational expert. Like a vocational expert, medical experts are paid by the government but are expected to offer impartial testimony. Should the testimony of the medical expert determine that the claimant meets or equals the Listing of Impairments; the testimony of the vocational expert may not be needed.

Finally, appearing last in the hearing are vocational experts. As noted earlier, the vocational expert testifies on the vocational issues in a case, including classification of a claimant's past work in terms of skills and exertion, transferability of work skills for persons over 50, and possible jobs a person with the same background and work experience as the claimant can perform given a series of hypothetical situations formulated by the ALJ.

Timothy Field and Jack M. Sink[6] describe the qualifications needed by vocational experts.

> *A vocational expert is expected to possess current and extensive experience in counseling and/or job placement of adult, handicapped people with a work history. The experience should include (1) the utilization of standardized occupational material, such as the Dictionary of Occupational Titles; (2) an understanding of the structure and function of work, and the concept of transferability of skills; and (3) the ability to evaluate age, education, and prior work experience in light of residual functional capacities, as specifically related to industrial and occupational trends and local labor market conditions is necessary.*[pg. 5]

As noted, the testimony of the vocational expert is impartial and based upon the expert's own education, professional experience, and understanding of the Social Security Law.

## THE HEARING PROCESS

A typical hearing begins with the ALJ and the attorney discussing any housekeeping issues, such as new, last-minute evidence the attorney would like entered into the file, or a request to the ALJ by the claimant's representative to keep the file open after the hearing to submit new evidence. Once on the record with the recording machine operating, the Administrative Law Judge usually begins with an introduction or opening statement explaining the hearing process and what is expected of the claimant.

The following is an actual opening used by an administrative law judge. The opening was chosen for inclusion in this text because the content contains most of the essentials needed in an opening statement. As observed, this particular opening statement has had the effect of making claimants feel more comfortable and at ease at the beginning of the hearing. The names of the persons in this excerpt are fictitious.

## ADMINISTRATION LAW JUDGE'S OPENING STATEMENT

> We are ready to proceed in the case of Matthew Higgins. I am Judge Henry Atkins. I have been assigned to hear your case. As you are probably aware, there have been prior decisions in your case. I am not bound by those prior decisions. Rather, I get the chance to take a whole, fresh look at your case. My decision will be based upon the evidence in the file, and testimony that comes before us today. If the record were held open for additional evidence, the decision would be based upon those records as well. After that, I will make a decision. It will be in writing, and it will be mailed to you and your representative.
>
> I would like to emphasize that this is your hearing. If you have any questions you wish to ask or recognize something that is not being brought to my attention, I ask that you not be bashful. Let me know before the end of the hearing because we want to make sure this is a full, fair hearing.
>
> As you may gather from the microphones before you, we are making an audio recording of the hearing. The microphones are sensitive. We do ask that you speak up so whatever you say is picked up and made a part of the record. I trust you will do that, because if we do not get a good recording, they may make us come back and do this all over again, which we would all like to avoid. Operating the equipment is our contract-hearing reporter. She takes notes and tries to keep me on track.
>
> As you may gather from the surroundings, this is not a formal hearing. The rules of evidence do not apply. We do not get to do these cases as you see on television–no Perry Mason, no Law and Order, no Boston Legal. Rather, we like to believe

> this is more like a conversation around the dinner table. Even though this is an informal proceeding, however, there are a few formalities. I am required to enter into evidence the exhibits in the file. I am also required to take evidence under oath. I will be swearing you in shortly. After we get done with these preliminary matters, I will let the representative make any opening statement he deems appropriate. After that, I will question you and your representative will question you. After that, we will discuss your medical situation with Dr. Haney. Then we will turn to the vocational expert, discuss with him your past work, and work background and I will also pose some questions to him about a hypothetical individual. That will bring our hearing to a close.
>
> We are here to determine whether you are disabled within the guidelines of the Social Security Act. Disability under the Act is defined as the inability to engage in any substantial gainful employment based on a physical or mental impairment that results in death or that has lasted or is expected to last 12 months. I will cover all material facts to determine if you are eligible for benefits under the Social Security Law. Material facts include any work you have done since your onset date, the severity of your impairments, and the effect of any impairment upon your ability to do your past work or any other work that exists in the national economy based upon your age, education, and work experience. That is a long-winded way of saying we are here to determine if you are disabled, but that is it in a nutshell. Do you have any questions how we will proceed today?

The introduction raises two technical points that may not be clear to most of us. The judge says that he is not bound by prior decisions. When a case comes before an Administrative Law Judge, the case has been reviewed twice by consulting physicians working for the Disability Determination Service (DDS) and a determination was made in those reviews that the claimant was not disabled. The hearing is, at a minimum, a third review. The ALJ is stating up front that he does not have to consider the results of those former decisions; his decision will be a wholly new decision. This is the only time in the disability process that a claimant will meet with the live person making the decision. At all other levels of appeal within the Social Security Administration the determinations are made by file review. If the claimant receives an unfavorable decision from the ALJ, there is another level of appeal within the Social Security Administration. That level of appeal is the Appeals Council, but that level of appeal is also a file review.

In the introduction, the ALJ says that the judge will make the decision based upon the testimony and the evidence in the file. You may remember our discussion in Chapter 5 concerning what types of evidence are considered important in making disability decisions. In hearings before an administrative law judge, the greatest weight toward making disability decisions is given to the opinions and medical evidence of the claimant's treating physician(s). Other evidence, such as the opinions of the vocational expert, receives a lesser weight in these decisions.

Following the opening statement, the ALJ admits the exhibits into the file and asks the representative if any of the claimant's impairments meets or equals a listing in the List of Impairments. The Judge may ask the representative for a summary of the case; that is, reasons why their client meets the requirements of the Social Security Law and is eligible for benefits under the Law.

Afterward, the ALJ introduces the persons participating in the case and defines their role in the hearing. The introductions usually go something like this:

> I am Joe Houser; I am the judge who has been assigned to hear and decide your case. Seated to my left is the hearing reporter. He takes notes and keeps the hearings running smoothly. On my right is a vocational expert. She is not employed by the Social Security Administration and has no interest in the outcome of the case. She will be classifying your past work and answering questions about other work that may exist within the national economy.

If there are other experts at the hearing, the ALJ will introduce them as well:

> We also have with us Dr. Applebee, a medical doctor, and Dr. Mullinax, a psychiatrist. Both have reviewed your medical records in reference to your case and may be asked to provide testimony based on their professional experience. These medical experts are not employees of the Social Security Administration and they have no interest in the outcome of our proceedings today.

After introducing the participants at the hearing, the ALJ administers the oath to those who will be testifying at the hearing.

He first addresses the claimant, saying,

> "Do you have any objection to taking an oath? (Presumably the claimant's answer is no). Then if you and our expert(s) Ms. Childress (VE), Dr. Applebee (ME), and Dr. Mullinax (ME) would please stand and raise your right hands. Do you swear to tell the truth, the whole truth, and nothing but the truth under penalty of perjury? (Everyone says, "I do").

The ALJ may elect to begin the questioning of the claimant or decide to allow the claimant's representative to begin asking the questions. In either scenario, the examination usually begins by asking the claimant personal information (e.g., height, weight, marital status, type of dwelling (house, apartment, mobile home), and whether they have performed any work since the onset of disability. The questions then begin with the medical issues in the case. Among the issues raised will likely concern, if appropriate, a claimant's past history of drug or alcohol use, or periods of incarcerations. Under Social Security Law, the ALJ cannot award benefits to a person while that person is incarcerated; nor will the ALJ award benefits to a person if drugs are material to the case.

At the conclusion of the questions from the judge and the claimant's presentation of the case, the administrative law judge usually turns first to the medical expert(s), if medical testimony is needed in the case. Whether or not to use a medical expert is a decision made by the administrative law judge. If medical experts are to appear, the first matter under consideration is for the judge to ask the claimant, and/or the claimant's representative, if they are willing to accept the opinions of the medical witness as that given by a medical expert. Unless the claimant or the claimant's attorney has reservations about the credentials of the medical expert, the ALJ declares the medical witness an expert in the case. This is a very important point. The judge will not accept the testimony of a witness appearing as an expert unless they are recognized by the court as an expert in their field.

Most often, the first question addressed to the medical expert is whether or not the claimant's medical impairments meet or equal the conditions provided in the Listings of Impairments (i.e., the ALJ is asking the medical expert if a favorable decision can be made at Step 3 of the sequential analysis). If the claimant's medical condition does not meet or equal the requirements of the listings in the Listings of Impairments, the ALJ may then ask for the medical expert's analysis of the case records. If the medical expert states that the claimant's conditions are not severe enough to preclude work, the judge will usually ask the expert to construct their own residual functional capacity (RFC) based on their examination of the evidence. Vocational experts need to take note of the medical expert's RFC because some of the judge's questions that will be asked of the vocational expert will likely be based upon those physical or mental restrictions the medical expert witnesses present in their RFC.

The analysis then moves into Step 4 and Step 5. In the order of progression, the testimony of the vocational expert logically follows the presentation by the medical experts. The judge begins the questioning of the vocational expert by asking the VE if the resume on file with the Social Security Administration is current and up-to-date. The ALJ will then ask the VE if there is any reason they cannot testify as an impartial witness. Following these procedural questions, the ALJ turns to the claimant's representative and asks if there is any objection to having the VE testify as an expert on vocational matters. With the up-to-date resume in the file and the acceptance of the claimant and/or the claimant's attorney, the judge then declares the vocational witness an expert witness on vocational matters.

Before actually questioning the vocational expert, the judge goes through the following list of prepared questions to establish the impartiality of the VE.

1. Have you and I had any discussion prior to the hearing concerning the merits of this case?

2. Do you know the claimant or have you had any personal or professional contact with the claimant, or the claimant's representative about the merits of this case?

3. Is there any reason you cannot testify as an impartial expert on vocational matters?

Given a negative response to each of these questions, the ALJ will likely conclude this line of questioning with an admonishment to the VE that if any of the responses to the questions about their past work or hypothetical questions about their other work differs from the information provided in the *Dictionary of Occupational Titles,*[12] they must alert the court to the differences so that the conflict can be resolved.

## CLASSIFYING THE PAST WORK

Normally, the first question the ALJ asks of the vocational expert is to classify each job the claimant has performed over the past 15 years in terms of the skills needed to perform the jobs and the exertion levels of the jobs. Jobs outside of the 15 years are not considered relevant by the Social Security Administration. Classification of past work provides the Administrative Law Judge with the vocational information needed to decide whether or not the claimant can perform their past work (this is Step 4 of the sequential analysis).

If the judge decides the claimant can perform any of the jobs done in the past 15 years at Step 4, the analysis may stop there and the request for benefits will most likely be denied.

When requesting the vocational expert to classify the past relevant work, the judge expects the vocational expert to describe the past work in the way the work is listed normally in the *Dictionary of Occupational Titles* and how that work was actually performed as indicated in the records of the case and the claimant's testimony.

Prior to the hearing, the vocational expert is provided with the vocational records in the case. Reports prepared earlier of an interview with the claimant by representatives in the local Social Security office are the most important vocational records in the case file (i.e., the *Disability Report–Adult* and the *Work History Report).* Each of these reports contains a place to list the jobs performed over the past 15 years. The *Work History Report* also contains a space to describe the job duties and the exertion level of each job the claimant has performed. The vocational expert is expected to review the information provided by the Social Security Administration before coming to the hearing and to listen to the testimony presented by all of the witnesses during the hearing.

From the information provided by SSA and the hearing testimony, the vocational expert makes an assessment of the claimants past work as reported, and compares that assessment with the descriptions of the jobs as they are listed in the *Dictionary of Occupational Titles.*[12] Few vocational experts have heard the testimony of their colleagues or had any formal training, so while the style of presentation may vary among different experts, the information provided is much the same.

For example, suppose the claimant, Matthew Higgins, performed the job of a fast food worker from 1999 to 2003 at an Arby's restaurant in Baton Rouge, Louisiana. During the testimony, the claimant says that he served customers, made money transactions, cooked burgers and fries, and, during slow times, cleaned the tables in the restaurant. Most of this work had lifting requirements of less than 20 pounds, but at the end of the day, Mr. Higgins took trash to the trash bin. The trash barrels weighed about 45 pounds. The *Work History Report* listed 45 pounds as a weight he lifted on an occasional basis. The vocational expert may classify this job in the following way:

> Mr. Higgins worked as a Fast Food Worker in an Arby's Restaurant between 1999 and 2003. The reference to this work in the *Dictionary of Occupational Titles* is 311.472-010. As normally performed in the national economy, this work is light in exertion and unskilled. However, as listed in the *Work History Report* and testified to at the hearing, Mr. Higgins had

> occasional lifting of 45 pounds. This would place the work as performed in the medium range. This is unskilled work with a Significant Vocational Preparation (SVP) of 2 taking less than 30 days to learn the job duties and perform the work adequately.

Let's take another example. From 2004 to 2005, Mr. Higgins worked as a Dietary Aide in St. Marks Nursing Home in Baton Rouge. In this job, he mostly carried trays of food to elderly patrons during mealtime, but in the off hours he cleaned and mopped the floors and collected trash that he says weighed about 35 pounds. He testified that once in a while, he had to empty bedpans and escort patients to the bathroom. He estimated that the patient care required him to lift over 75 pounds. This work may be classified in the following way by the vocational expert:

> Between 2004 and 2005, Mr. Higgins worked as a Dietary Aide in which he had to carry trays to patrons in their rooms and sometimes had to help lift and carry these patrons. This work as listed in the *Dictionary of Occupational Titles* is medium in exertion with frequent lifting of 25 pounds and occasional lifting of 50 pounds. The DOT reference to this job is 319.677-014; but, as testified, he occasionally had lifting requirements of 75 pounds, placing the lifting level for this job, as performed, in the heavy range. Lifting in the heavy range has frequent lifting of 50 pounds and occasional lifting of 100 pounds. This is also unskilled work with a Significant Vocational Preparation (SVP) of 2 taking less than 30 days to learn the job duties and perform the work adequately...

## QUESTIONS TO THE VE IN HYPOTHETICAL FORM

After classifying each of the past jobs the claimant has performed over the past 15 years, the vocational expert will then be asked several hypothetical questions. These hypothetical questions are circumstances that mirror the information in the file, the claimant's testimony, the testimony of the medical experts, the job classifications by the VE, and the arguments the claimant's attorney presented in the examination of the claimant. The purpose of these questions is to determine if the claimant can make a vocational adjustment to other jobs that exist in significant numbers in the national and local economy. The type of hypothetical questioning leaves the burden of interpreting the medical evidence to the Administrative Law Judge.

For most observers, the questions in hypothetical form are the most confusing part of the hearing. Hypothetical questions about the vocational issues in the case are formulated by the Administrative Law Judge and presented to the VE in several different scenarios. Usually, each succeeding scenario becomes more restrictive. Hypothetical questions create objectivity by allowing the judge to discuss a claimant's condition without specifically identifying the person sitting at the end of the table. Using a hypothetical format gives the judge choices for ultimately making the disability decision.

The examples below show the phrasing of hypothetical questions an ALJ may pose to the VE. These hypothetical questions are not comprehensive but are designed to provide a general understanding of the pattern delineated in the judge's inquiry. Hypothetical questions are typically arranged in this order:

1. Vocational Profile: age, education, and past relevant work,
2. Physical Restrictions: walking, standing, sitting, lifting, and pushing and pulling,
3. Postural Limitations: climbing, balancing, stooping, kneeling, crouching, crawling,
4. Manipulative Limitations: handling, feeling, and fingering,
5. Environmental Limitations,
6. Psychological Limitations, and
7. Visual Limitations (if any).

## SAMPLE HYPOTHETICAL QUESTIONS POSED DURING VOCATIONAL TESTIMONY

Consider a former construction laborer who is 53 years old with a high school education and complains of a chronic back problem. The hypothetical questions posed to the VE by the Administrative Law Judge may be as follows:

ALJ: Mr. Bradford, assume a person with the same work background as the claimant and that I find from the evidence that this hypothetical person can stand and/or walk for approximately 6 hours in an 8-hour day, and lift no more than 20 pounds at a time with frequent lifting or carrying of objects weighing up to 10 pounds. Would he be able to engage in his past work or, if not, could he engage in any other work?

VE: Under these limitations, the worker would not be able to perform his past work that was very heavy in exertion. This person would be reduced to a range of light work.

ALJ: Further assume, Mr. Bradford, I find from the evidence that the hypothetical person can sit for up to 6 hours in an 8-hour day, stand, and walk for no more than 3 hours in an 8-hour day, and lift up to 10 pounds. Can he engage in his past work? If not, can he transfer any skills to perform other skilled or semi-skilled work?

VE: The person would not be able to perform his past work. This person would be limited to sedentary work. Construction work is normally very heavy in exertion. The records and the testimony show that this person's past relevant work was performed at a heavy level of exertion. This work is unskilled and there are no transferable skills from unskilled work.

ALJ: Now, Mr. Bradford, assuming that I find the claimants testimony about his back impairment to be credible, and that he can only sit for up to 3 hours, stand and/or walk for no more than three hours before experiencing severe pain, and lift no more than 10 pounds, and that he must lie down for at least 2 hours in any 8-hour period to relieve pain. If I accept this description of his limitations, could the claimant engage in his past relevant work?

VE: This person is reduced to a less than a sedentary level of work. Under these limitations this person would not be able perform any full-time gainful employment. The need to lie down 2 hours in an 8-hour time period is not an accommodation employers are generally willing to make.

Following the questioning, the ALJ would address the claimant's representative and ask if the representative has any questions to ask of the vocational expert. (Cross-examination of the vocational expert is addressed in the concluding section of this chapter). The line of questioning, presented above, is similar to the format used in most Social Security hearings. Below are other, more complex examples of hypothetical questions with suggestions for breaking down and analyzing hypothetical situations.

## SITUATION # 1

ALJ: Please assume a hypothetical individual of the same age, education, and past work that the claimant has described and you have summarized. This person would be able to sit for six hours and stand for six hours. Lifting is limited to 20 pounds occasionally and ten pounds frequently. She could occasionally climb, balance, stoop, kneel, crouch, and crawl. She would be limited to frequent fingering and handling. She would need to avoid concentrated exposure to extreme heat, humidity, respiratory irritants, and no exposure to hazards and unprotected heights. Because of frequent anxiety and panic attacks, this person would need to have only occasional interaction with the public. Because of poor concentration and memory loss, this person would need routine, repetitive, unskilled work. Would a person be able to return to their past work given these limitations?

We will simplify this hypothetical by breaking it down according to the D.O.T. definitions.

1. You will already have been given the claimant's file to review so you know their age, level of education, and work history.
2. Sitting = 6 hours, standing = 6 hours, and lifting 20 pounds occasionally/10 pounds frequently. This is the definition of light work (You may wish to review the definitions given in Chapter 5). Under these limitations, this person would be able to perform light and sedentary work.
3. Frequent fingering and handling means that one could perform fine and gross manipulation up to 2/3 of the time spread throughout the workday but not at the constant level. (Frequent fingering and feeling would preclude many, but not all, production jobs).
4. Avoid extreme heat, humidity, and respiratory irritants means that you will probably be looking for jobs that are performed indoors instead of jobs such as an unarmed security guard who may need to walk regularly the perimeter of a building on hot days or a gate guard who may be exposed to diesel truck fumes.

5. Occasional interaction with the public means you want to avoid positions such as customer service, cashier, sales attendant, or ticket taker that have constant interaction with the public.

6. Routine, repetitive, unskilled work means that all the work that would fit into this hypothetical will be Significant Vocational Preparation (SVP) of 1 or 2, and the job tasks can be learned and performed adequately within 30 days or less.

Here is a hypothetical example with some different limitations.

ALJ: Please assume an individual with the claimant's age, educational level, and work history. Further, assume that this person can lift up to 50 pounds occasionally and 25 pounds frequently. This person can sit for six hours and stand/walk for six hours out of an eight-hour day. This person can stoop, crouch, crawl, kneel, balance, and climb occasionally. This person should avoid even moderate exposure to hazards and temperature extremes. Can this person return to his/her past work? If not, are there any transferable skills to other work that would fit within these restrictions?

This hypothetical is a bit different. The lifting and standing/walking restrictions are frequent which would suggest a wide range of medium work. Nevertheless, many jobs at the medium level of exertion require more frequent balancing, crouching, and stooping. Several, but not all, jobs at the medium level require some exposure to hazards such as moving machinery and temperature extremes that are consistent with working outdoors (e.g., carpentry and construction work). Even though this hypothetical is very restrictive, there are jobs in the medium range that can be performed within those limitations (Hand Packager (920.587-018), Motor Vehicle Assembler (806.684-010), or a Sandwich Maker (317.664-010). (Check each job with the D.O.T. to be sure that it falls within the limitations of each hypothetical.)

The next hypothetical is the most restrictive and contains limitations that have been a source of stress for many vocational experts.

ALJ: Please assume an individual of the claimant's age, education, and work history. Also, assume that this person can stand for 2 hours, sit for 6 hours, and can lift up to 10 pounds occasionally and 5 pounds frequently. He can occasionally stoop, crouch, crawl, kneel, balance, and climb with no exposure to hazards, dangerous machinery, heights, and respiratory irritants. This person can perform simple, routine, unskilled work with no public interaction. Would this person be able to return to the claimant's past work?

This hypothetical places the exertion at a sedentary level because of the standing and walking as well as the lifting restrictions. The positive aspects of this hypothetical are that postural limitations (stooping, crouching, crawling, kneeling, balancing, climbing) do not normally impact the sedentary occupational base nor do the environmental limitations. Most sedentary work is performed indoors. The difficult aspects of this hypothetical are, the work needs to be unskilled and he must have no public interaction. If the claimant does not have any past work that fits within the limitations of this hypothetical, the judge will ask the VE to find other work within the national economy. In this hypothetical, the judge has asked for sedentary, unskilled work. This requirement vastly erodes the sedentary occupational base.

Finally, the addition of no public interaction even further reduces your options. In an unskilled job, an employee is mainly restricted to either customer service (e.g., receptionist, appointment setter) or working with their hands (typically production work). If the limitations rule out interaction with the public, then you are only left with sedentary production work. At this point, it is important to remember that production work in the United States has been declining at a very rapid pace for several decades. (See Chapter 7, "A Counselors Introduction to Work in the New American Economy"). Most of the production work that has remained or has returned to the U.S. is skilled production work. So you are being asked to find unskilled production jobs that are becoming fewer by the year. In addition, this production work needs to be performed sitting down for at least six hours out of the workday. This hypothetical will exclude many of the available jobs. However, there are some (e.g., bench assembly work, grading, inspecting, and testing).

## IDENTIFYING JOBS IN THE NATIONAL ECONOMY:

In the illustration given earlier under "Sample Hypothetical Questions Posed during Vocational Testimony," the judge asked the VE to consider the profile of a former construction laborer who is 53 years old with a high school education and complaints of a chronic back problem. The hypothetical posed to the VE was:

ALJ: Mr. Bradford, assume a person with the same work background as the claimant and that I find from the evidence that this hypothetical person can stand and/or walk for approximately 6 hours in an 8-hour day, and lift no more than 20 pounds at a time with frequent lifting or carrying of objects weighing up to 10 pounds. Would he be able to engage in his past work or, if not, could he engage in any other work?

VE: Under these limitations, the worker would not be able to perform his past work that was very heavy in exertion. This person would be reduced to light work.

If the Administrative Law Judge considered light work to be a possible option for alternative work, the judge would likely ask the VE to name a representative number of jobs the expert believes this hypothetical person could perform within these limitations. A representative number of jobs provided by the VE usually range from three to six. Questioning would continue:

ALJ: Mr. Bradford, if the hypothetical person could not perform his past work under those limitations, are there other jobs this person could perform given the same vocational profile and limitations?

VE: In my opinion, there would be a range of light work a person with this vocational profile could perform. This person could work as a cafeteria attendant, a house cleaner or house person, and a hand packer. In the national economy, there are 380,000 thousand cafeteria attendants. Over 14,000 of these jobs have been identified in the State of New York. Nationally, there are over a million maids and house persons and over 46,000 of these jobs are in the State of New York. Nationally there are over 430,000 hand packers with 30,000 located in the State of New York. These jobs are light in exertion and unskilled.

These jobs are only representative of the light jobs in the national and regional economy this person could perform.

## COMMON HYPOTHETICAL QUESTIONS

As described earlier, the purpose of the hypothetical format is to present alternative work opportunities to help the administrative law judge make a determination whether or not the person seeking disability payments is able to make a vocational adjustment to other work that exists in the national and local economy. The hypothetical question leaves the burden of interpreting the medical evidence to the Administrative Law Judge. This type of questioning comes at Step 5 in the decision-making process. Presumably, the ALJ reached a decision at Step 4 in the 5-step process that the claimant cannot do their past work.

Each hypothetical situation begins by assuming that the "hypothetical" person has the same vocational profile—age, education, and work experience—as the claimant. The vocational profile is then followed by having the VE assume a set, maybe several sets, of medical limitations that are just possibilities and naming jobs the person can perform within each set of limitations. Only if the ALJ accepts a set of limitations as accurately portraying the vocational abilities of a claimant does the situation become part of the disability decision.

After presenting each set of limitations, the ALJ will ask if there are any jobs the expert can name that this person would be able to perform. The concluding statement of the hypothetical would be something like this: "Considering a person with this vocational profile and these functional limitations, are there jobs in the national economy you can name that this person can perform?"

If a vocational expert believes there are jobs this hypothetical person can perform within the limitations given by the ALJ, the VE will name the jobs in a statement as follows: "Your honor, given these limitations and considering this person's vocational profile presented earlier, it is my opinion that this person could perform the following jobs." The VE would then proceed to name the jobs. If, on the other hand, the VE believes that the person cannot perform any jobs under the limitations, the response to the hypothetical question is that there are no jobs and the response would be, "In my opinion there are no jobs that a person can perform within those limitations."

Dr. Amy Vercillos[13] posed questions similar to those below to a group of vocational experts and asked if, given those situations, they would be able to locate jobs. There is a surprising variation among the responses, showing how different various experts view work in the national economy. Some experts in attendance were able to find jobs under each set of limitations. Only one of the questions received a unanimous response from the experts.

1. If a hypothetical includes a person who requires a range of work at a light level of exertion with the need for a sit/stand option, meaning the employee would need to sit for several minutes during each hour of work, would there be jobs available?
   (a) Yes (94%)
   (b) No (5%)

2. If a hypothetical includes a person who requires a range of work at the sedentary level of exertion with the need for a sit/stand option, meaning the person would need to stand for a few minutes during each hour of work, would there be jobs available?
   (a) Yes (90%)
   (b) No (9%)

3. Are there jobs available if an employee can use their non-dominant hand only occasionally (1/3 of the day) if they are also required to work at a light level of exertion?
   (a) Yes (83%)
   (b) No (16%)

4. If an employee can use the non-dominant hand only occasionally and was required to work at a sedentary level of exertion, are there jobs that exist?
   (a) Yes (49%)
   (b) No (50%)

5. If an employee can perform work at the light level of exertion, but can only use their dominant hand occasionally, are there jobs?
   (a) Yes (61%)
   (b) No (38%)

6. Are there jobs at the sedentary work level if an employee only has the use of the dominant hand occasionally?
   (a) Yes (30%)
   (b) No (69%)

7. Are there jobs at a light level of exertion available for non-English speakers?
   (a) Yes (95%)
   (b) No (4%)

8. If a person is restricted to a light level of exertion but cannot work with the public, would there be any jobs they could perform?
   (a) Yes (95%)
   (b) No (5%)

9. If an employee working at the light exertion level found it necessary to elevate their legs to 12 inches occasionally (up to 1/3 of the day) would work be available?

(a) Yes (43%)
(b) No (56%)

10. If an employee is restricted to the sedentary level of exertion and needed to elevate their legs at a height of 12 inches occasionally (1/3 of the day) would work be available?
    (a) Yes (74%)
    (b) No (25%)

11. If an individual requires more than occasional supervision on a sustained basis, would he/she be able to engage in substantial gainful employment?
    (a) Yes (13%)
    (b) No (87%)

12. If a hypothetical person at any level of exertion is unable to work with co-workers in work-related tasks (no tandem work) but would be able to work in proximity to other workers, are jobs available?
    (a) Yes (77%)
    (b) No (23%)

Some vocational experts feel that that an ALJ expects them to find jobs and they become frustrated when the job base becomes so eroded that there are very few jobs located in the national or local economy in significant numbers. The vocational expert needs to remember several things in reference to presenting statistical information to the court, such as the numbers of jobs:

1. *The ALJ, not the vocational expert, determines whether or not jobs exist in significant numbers.* The expert needs to provide the numbers given in the source material and let the judge decide the relevance of the numbers,
2. *The vocational expert must present the information truthfully and accurately to the court.* The VE have been sworn to tell the truth and in presenting information to the court needs to be as accurate as possible and true to their source material, and
3. *Remember, the VE is the expert on vocational matters for this case.* Nevertheless, experts are expected to stay within their role, providing vocational guidance and information based upon their knowledge and experience to help improve the quality of the decision the ALJ has to make.

## SOURCES OF INFORMATION FOR VOCATIONAL EXPERTS

The most obvious questions that arise from the classification of the past work and the hypothetical questions in the previous sections are: Where does the information come from? What is the source of the information that the vocational expert provides to the court? We will look at this information as it relates to:

(a) the classification of jobs,

(b) characteristics of the jobs, and

(c) numbers for jobs in the national and regional economy that the VE believes a claimant can perform given the limitations provided in the judges hypothetical questions.

New vocational experts may feel overwhelmed by the vocational information needed to become a vocational expert, not to mention the ability to convert this information into vocational testimony. Nevertheless, the information is available to new vocational experts and others who have a commitment to learning. All of us became vocational experts through knowledge and skills learned on the job and in the courtroom. Moreover, recent computer technology now available to vocational experts makes the information even more accurate and precise. This information not only includes the sources on the numbers for jobs nationally and regionally, but also the components for analyzing jobs some of which are not included in the *Dictionary of Occupational Titles*.[12]

As we discussed in earlier chapters, rehabilitation counselors are well suited for VE work. This is the only profession that closely ties together the knowledge components of work and disability. Additionally, experience from learning about jobs and observing how jobs are performed is central to the things rehabilitation counselors do every day. With practice and after learning the methodology and the basic techniques of job analysis, rehabilitation counselors soon become more comfortable in the expert role. Nevertheless, counselors still have to be attuned to the continuous study and interpretations of the law and the ever-changing way experts practice.

The process for analyzing jobs and providing national and regional statistics is not an exact science. As previously discussed, you do not have to be a medical doctor to practice rehabilitation counseling. The same is true when it comes to information about jobs that is presented to the court. You do not have to be an economist to analyze jobs and provide accurate information about jobs to the court. Provided below are some of the basic sources of information vocational experts use during testimony to formulate their responses to hypothetical questions.

## CLASSIFICATION OF JOBS

The main source of information for the classification of jobs comes from the Department of Labor's *Dictionary of Occupational Titles*,[12] the DOT. The 1991 edition includes a description and analysis of 12,741 jobs in the United States. Below each of the jobs described in the DOT are some of the symbols needed to classify jobs, including the strengths (sedentary, light, medium, heavy, and very heavy), the Specific Vocational Preparation (SVP), and a number to represent the time it takes to learn a job and adequately perform the job tasks. These are the two most important components to the codes used to classify work during a disability hearing.

For example, let us suppose the claimant has listed a previous occupation of a Baker as a job he/she had performed. The description of the occupation of a Baker can be found on page 368 of the DOT under the reference code of 526.381-010. Beneath the job description, the DOT lists the Strength as "H" with an SVP of 7, meaning that the job is heavy in exertion requiring 50 pounds of lifting frequently and 100 pounds of lifting occasionally. To learn the job duties and perform the work adequately at an SVP 7 takes one to two years. For most jobs, the Strengths and SVP are all the components of a job analysis needed to analyze and classify the past work during a disability hearing.

There is one little wrinkle in currently describing the job in the courtroom. You will remember that the ALJ usually concludes the opening statement to the VE with an admonishment, (e.g., "If any of your responses to questions about the past work or hypothetical questions about other work differ from the information provided in the *Dictionary of Occupational Titles,*[12] please alert me to the differences so that the we can reconcile these differences.") For most testimony, there are no significant differences. The testimony is simply to provide for each job the Strength and the SVP classification as given in the DOT.

However, problems arise occasionally because the DOT was last published in 1991 and many of the jobs were last analyzed by a person viewing the job performance in the late 1970s. Based upon professional knowledge or experience, if VE's recognize differences between the DOT and the way they have observed a job performed, they just need to openly state these differences and go on.

The Dictionary of Occupational Titles (DOT) was first published by the Department of Labor in 1938 and updated periodically after that date until 1991. Although the DOT was not designed specifically for use by The Social Security Administration, SSA adapted its disability program to the DOT, incorporating many concepts and definitions from the DOT into its regulations and policies.

The Department of Labor stopped updating the DOT in 1991 and replaced the Dictionary of Occupational Titles with the Occupational Information Network (O'NET), a publication designed for training and career exploration. The O'NET did not include the quantifiable factors for analyzing jobs that we discussed in Chapter 5, nor did it reflect the existence or incidence of work in the national economy. As a result, SSA did not consider a presentation of job information in the O'NET format to be defensible in a court of law. To many, presentation of information in the O'NET format would have been "theoretical and speculative" which the courts had rejected earlier when the SSI and SSDI disability programs were first started. In 2012 the Social Security Administration signed an interagency contract with the Bureau of Labor Statistics and the two agencies are currently in the process of coming up with a new format to be titled the Occupational Information System (OIS).

## CHARACTERISTICS OF JOBS

Once again, the information for analyzing jobs comes from Department of Labor publications. In 1991, the Department of Labor published *The Revised Handbook for Analyzing Jobs*[3] that described the methodology job analysts with the United States Employment Service (USES) used to analyze jobs. *The Revised Handbook for Analyzing Jobs*[3] defines and breaks down many of the terms used in job analysis.

The job descriptions for most of the jobs the USES analyzed were later published in the DOT. Beneath the description of the job in the DOT are included some of the worker characteristics to assist vocational experts and others in analyzing jobs. In the section above, we discussed two of these (i.e., Physical Demands and the SVP). The symbols under each job description in the DOT includes information helpful to career counselors, such as a reference to the *Guide to Occupational Exploration* that allows job counselors to cross-reference occupations with similar characteristics, interests, and required job skills. The line beneath the job description in the DOT also notes the date the job was updated (DLU). The Baker position, discussed above, was last updated in 1980.

There are physical demands and environmental conditions analyzed by the United States Employment Service not included in the *Dictionary of Occupational Titles*[12] that vocational experts need to analyze jobs for the Office of Disability, Adjudication, and Review (ODAR). These worker trait characteristics include the *physical demand* (i.e., pushing and pulling (the only strength demand not included in the DOT); the *postural demands* (i.e., climbing, balancing, stooping, kneeling, crouching, crawling), *manipulative requirements* (i.e., handling, fingering, and feeling), and the many *environmental conditions* under which the work is performed. These come from another Department of Labor[4] publication titled *Selected Characteristics of Occupations, 1992*. This publication contains worker trait characteristics for each of the 12,741 DOT occupations.

In *Selected Characteristics of Occupations,* the Department of Labor[4] analysts rated the worker traits for each of the 12,741 jobs listed in the DOT by the frequency in which they appear during the normal workday. Each job listed is given one of four codes representing the frequency these factors normally appear during the workday as follows:

| CODE | FREQUENCY | DEFINITION |
|---|---|---|
| N | Not Present | Activity or condition does not exist |
| O | Occasionally | Activity or Condition exists up to 1/3 of the time |
| F | Frequently | Activity or Condition exists from 1/3 to 2/3 of the time |
| C | Constantly | Activity or Condition exists 2/3 or more of the time |

For example, we earlier considered the position of a Baker, and in the *Dictionary of Occupational Titles*[12] (526.381-010) we found this position was heavy in exertion and skilled with an SVP at level 7, taking one to two years to learn the job and adequately perform the work. In addition, the *Selected Characteristics of Occupations*[4] shows this position requiring the physical demands of frequent reaching, handling, fingering, and feeling, and occasional stooping.

Vocational experts are moving into the 21st Century with computerized programs to help locate and analyze data more accurately and effectively for help in their testimony. Perhaps the most popular programs are Job Browser Pro by SkillTRAN, LLC[11] and OccuBrowse by Vertek. SkillTRAN[11] appears to be the program of choice. These computerized programs contain all of the data we have discussed in an easy to use format with job summaries and the worker trait characteristics for all 12,741 DOT occupations.

## Numbers for the Jobs in the National and Regional Economy

In our earlier illustration, the VE was asked by the ALJ, "Mr. Bradford, if the hypothetical person could not perform his past work under those limitations, are there other jobs this person could perform given the same vocational profile and those same limitations?" To this question, the VE responded with the names of three occupations he thought the hypothetical person with the same vocational profile as the claimant could perform. These occupations were Cafeteria Attendant, Hand Packer, and Maid/House Person. After naming the jobs, the VE listed the approximate numbers for these jobs in the national and regional economy.

Where do these job numbers come from? In the past, vocational experts relied upon a number of data sources. There were businesses set up to analyze data, extrapolate information from a variety of government and private resources, and provide vocational experts with job numbers especially for the purpose of testifying in disability hearings. The primary resource for job information has always been research provided by the United States Department of Labor.

Today, most vocational experts use computerized programs as the main source of their information. These computer programs also rely heavily upon information from the Department of Labor. For instance, SkillTRAN[11] reports that its primary source for the job numbers it reports come from the Occupational Employment Survey (OES), (i.e., data collected directly from employer survey responses). OES statistics are widely recognized in the United States today as the best and most accurate source of job numbers because the Survey is taken from sources closest to the actual jobs.

## Qualifying the Vocational Expert in a Disability Hearing

Qualifying the vocational expert is an important moment in the hearing. In addressing the question to the claimant or the claimant's representative, "Do you accept the VE as an expert on vocational matters?" the ALJ is giving them the opportunity to ask questions regarding the credentials of the vocational expert. Once the claimant and the representative accept the VE as an expert in the hearing, judges do not usually allow questions about the background of the VE (i.e., inquires about the expert's academic education, professional experience, invited presentations, publications, memberships in national or local associations, or status in the professional field). Following qualification of the VE, they are accepted as an expert in the vocational field. Subsequent questions can only concern the testimony of the VE, including their classification of the past work, their responses to hypothetical questions about alternative work, and clarification of the testimony during cross-examination.

As noted earlier, disability hearings under Social Security do not adhere strictly to the rules of evidence. Once a professional is chosen by the Administration to serve as an expert, only the ALJ can decide otherwise. (This almost never happens). Most of us are familiar with what occurs in other courts where the rules of evidence are more strictly applied in establishing the expert's credentials in personal injury cases. After having been grilled about their professional credentials by opposing attorneys in civil cases, providing vocational testimony to the court on vocational issues often seems like a moment of relief. It is natural to feel a little uneasy while the ALJ is presenting the expert's credentials to the court. Yet, on a personal level, VEs need to remind themselves that once the judge accepts the VE as an expert, their credentials are no longer an issue. VEs can and should turn their attention away from themselves to the real purpose of the hearing and the role they are to assume in the hearing.

## CROSS EXAMINATION OF THE VOCATIONAL EXPERT

During the testimony of the vocational expert, the Administrative Law Judge examines several possible outcomes, and through hypothetical questions presented to the VE, the judge gains support for the option that is ultimately chosen. As one ALJ put it, "At Step 5, the testimony of the VE is critical to the information the ALJ needs to resolve the case."

At the conclusion of the VE testimony, the ALJ asks the claimant or the claimant's representative if they have any questions of the vocational expert. Subsequent questioning on behalf of the claimant is intended to strengthen the case for the claimant that they can no longer work. Some of the questions may reinforce statements made by the claimant during the testimony of the claimant; some may emphasize information in the medical records; some may draw attention to medical source statements from treating or non-treating sources (see Chapter 5); and some may concern the jobs the VE has named during the series of hypothetical questions.

Generally, the way a claimant or a claimant's representative raises issue with the jobs named by the VE is by adding additional limitations to the hypothetical questions the ALJ has already asked. Seldom are these questions meant to embarrass the expert or expose flaws in the sources of vocational information. Computerized programs have improved the quality of the information.

Presented below are typical questions addressed to vocational experts by claimants and claimant's representatives that provide additional limitations. These additional limitations have the effect of eroding job performance or eliminating the possibility of performing sustained work activity. Typical questions containing additional limitations include:

- How much time off-task is typically allowed by an employer?
- If an employee were off-task more than 20% of the day, would any full-time competitive work be available?

- How many unscheduled breaks are typically allowed in a workday?
- If an employee can only perform occasional fine or gross manipulation, how would that affect that person's ability to work?
- Do the sedentary positions you have named allow an employee to stand up and stretch as long as they remain at the workstation?
- If an employee can only stand for four hours in an 8-hour day, could they perform light work?
- If a person needed to elevate their legs, how would that impact the performance of sedentary work and what about light work?
- Would the use of an assistive device, such as a walker or cane, have any impact upon sedentary work?
- If an employee has occasional visual/far acuity or depth perception, could they perform the jobs you have described?
- If an employee could have only occasional contact with the public, co-workers, or supervisors, what effect would that have upon the jobs you have named?
- If an employee had no use of their non-dominant arm, how would that affect the ability to perform the jobs you have cited?
- If an employee needs more than occasional supervision, would substantial gainful employment be available to that person?
- Can this work be performed if a person has only a 6th grade education?

## SUGGESTIONS FOR RESPONDING TO HYPOTHETICAL QUESTIONS

From time to time vocational experts ask what advice we would give to rehabilitation counselors and others wishing to become vocational experts. We thought that a good way to end this chapter was to ask several persons we considered experts to list some of the pointers they considered important in responding to hypothetical questions from an Administrative Law Judge. Here, in no special order, are some tips a vocational expert will do well to remember:

- *The ALJ Makes the Decision.* The vocational expert is in the hearing to provide information on vocational issues requested by the judge. Most of this information is provided in response to hypothetical questions. Hypothetical questions are designed to provide input to help the judge make the disability decision. Understanding that the judge makes the decision prevents the expert from role confusion, (e.g., responding to medical questions, questions that lie outside of the vocational expert's professional field).

- *The Hearing is about the Claimant, Not about You.* With the tension of a disability hearing, listening to the testimony of others, and sorting through all of the information before you, there is the tendency to lose your perspective and think more of your role and the responses you will provide. One way to keep your focus and the right perspective is to say to yourself "this is the claimant's hearing."

- *Listen to Each Word of the Hypothetical and Respond Only to the Content of the Hypothetical Question.* It is natural, particularly at the beginning, for vocational experts to feel they are "under the gun," so to speak, and for either the VE to anticipate what they think the judge is going to say or, feeling pressure and missing some of the content within the hypothetical. Always ask the judge to repeat the hypothetical or any part of the hypothetical you think you may have missed.

- *Function is Everything.* Attorneys and claimants are not always well versed in how to phrase questions to vocational experts in functional terms. As a VE, you cannot provide a response unless the question is placed in terms of function, (i.e., what a person can or cannot do). When questions are asked calling for a subjective answer, it is all right to ask the person to rephrase the question in functional terms.

- *The Job is Not About Numbers, but the Numbers Need to be Accurate.* So much emphasis seems to be directed toward providing statistical information. There is the tendency to think that the whole job is giving numbers to the judge. Providing accurate statistics is important, but vocational experts cannot narrow their perspective and allow themselves to settle into such a reduced role. Most judges look upon vocational experts as experts in their professional field. Should we expect less of ourselves?

## TOPICS FOR GROUP DISCUSSION

1. Invite an Administrative Law Judge (ALJ) from the closest office of the Office of Disability and Adjudication and Review (ODAR) to speak to the group. Our suggestion is that they be asked to address the topic: "Decision making in the disability process with particular emphasis upon the place and importance of the role of the vocational expert in the 5-Step disability determination process."
2. Invite a vocational expert (particularly an expert with CRC credentials and a background in rehabilitation counseling) to speak to the class or group on the subjects of:
   - credentials needed to become a vocational expert,
   - an anecdotal impression of the courtroom experience, or
   - methods vocational experts use to obtain national and regional job statistics.

## INDIVIDUAL EXERCISES

Below are presented hypothetical questions addressed by an ALJ to a vocational expert. The past work and the hypothetical questions are taken from an actual case; only a few of the facts have been changed. Examine the content of Chapter 6 that concerns hypothetical questions and provide the best answers you can to these situations.

For this exercise, consider a claimant, Agnes Harper, who is 39 years of age with a 10th grade education. Her past work was as a waitress in a local restaurant from 2009 to 2011. She worked as a food assembler in the kitchen at the Outback Restaurant in 2008. She also worked as a fast food worker making biscuits at Hardies from 2006 to 2007; and she worked as a cleaner at St. Vincent's Hospital from 2004 to 2006. There is no work history report in this file to compare the exertion level of the past work as actually performed.

1. Develop a Vocational Profile for Agnes Harper.

2. Classify her past work according to the skills and exertion level for each of the jobs outlined above as they are normally performed in the national economy and listed in the *Dictionary of Occupational Titles*.[12] List the DOT reference number following each classification.

ALJ: Assume a hypothetical person who was born on April 21, 1969, has an education as provided in your vocational profile, and has past work experience as you have described in your classification. Assume further that this individual has the residual functional capacity (RFC) to perform work that requires lifting of 20 pounds occasionally and 10 pounds frequently. This person can sit for 8 hours in an 8-hour day. However, the individual can only occasionally climb, balance, stoop, kneel, crouch, and crawl, and should avoid concentrated exposure to cold, pulmonary irritants, chemicals, and hazards.

1. Could this person perform any of the claimant's past jobs as they are normally performed in the national economy?

2. If yes, identify the jobs the individual could perform and explain how the RFC can accommodate these limitations.

3. If no, explain how the RFC precludes the performance of any or all of the past jobs.

ALJ: Assume a hypothetical individual who was born April 21, 1969, has the educational level you have stated in your vocational profile, and has past work as you described in your classification. Assume further that this individual has the residual functional capacity (RFC) to perform work that requires lifting of 20 pounds occasionally and 10 pounds frequently. This person can sit up to 8 hours in an 8-hour workday. However, the individual can only occasionally climb, balance, stoop, kneel, crouch, and crawl, and should avoid concentrated exposure to cold, pulmonary irritants, chemicals, and hazards. This person requires a low-stress job (defined as having only occasional decision making or changes in the work setting) with only occasional interaction with the public.

1. Could the individual described perform any of the claimant's past work as normally performed in the national economy?

2. If yes, identify the jobs the individual could perform and explain how the RFC can accommodate these limitations.

3. If no, explain how the RFC precludes the performance of any or all of the past jobs.

4. Could the individual described above perform any unskilled occupations with jobs that exist in the national economy?

5. If yes, provide the DOT title, code, and SVP for three such jobs.

ALJ: Assume a hypothetical individual who was born April 21, 1969, has the education level you have stated in your vocational profile, and has past work as you described in your classification. Assume further that this individual has the residual functional capacity (RFC) to stand for 2 hours in an 8-hour workday, walk for 1 hour in an 8-hour workday, sit for 8-hours or more in an 8-hour workday, and frequently lift and carry 10 pounds. However, the individual can only occasionally climb, balance, stoop, kneel, crouch, and crawl, and should avoid concentrated exposure to cold and pulmonary irritants, chemicals, and hazards. This person requires a low-stress job (defined as having only occasional decision making or changes in the work setting) with only occasional interaction with the public or co-workers.

1. Could this individual perform any of the claimant's past jobs as normally performed in the national economy?

2. If yes, identify the jobs the individual could perform and explain how the RFC can accommodate these limitations.

3. If no, explain how the RFC precludes the performance of any or all of the past jobs.

4. Could the individual described above perform any unskilled occupations with jobs that exist in the national economy?

5. If yes, provide the DOT title, code, and SVP for three such jobs.

ALJ: Assume a hypothetical individual who was born April 21, 1969, has the educational level you have stated in your vocational profile, and has past work as you described in your classification. Assume further that this individual has the residual functional capacity to stand for 2 hours in an 8-hour workday, walk for one (1) hour in an 8-hour workday, sit for 8-hours or more in an 8-hour workday, and frequently lift and carry 10 pounds. However, the individual can only occasionally climb, balance, stoop, kneel, crouch, and crawl, and should avoid concentrated exposure to cold, pulmonary irritants, chemicals, and hazards. This person requires a low-stress job (defined as having only occasional decision making or changes in the work setting) with only occasional interaction with the public or co-workers, and will likely be distracted from work tasks at least 20% of an average workday and be absent from the workplace at least 2 days a month.

1. Could this individual perform any of the claimant's past jobs as normally performed in the national economy?

2. If yes, identify the jobs the individual could perform and explain how the RFC can accommodate these limitations.

3. If no, explain how the RFC precludes the performance of any or all of the past jobs.

4. Could the individual described above perform any unskilled occupations with jobs that exist in the national economy?

5. If yes, provide the DOT title, code, and SVP for three such jobs.

# BIBLIOGRAPHY

[1]Annual Statistical Report on the Social Security Disability Insurance Program, Office of Retirement and Disability Policy, Social Security Administration, 2008, September 23, 2009, pp. 1-11.

[2]Blackwell, Terry L., Field, Timothy, and Field, Janet (1992). *The Vocational Expert Under Social Security*, Athens, GA: Elliott & Fitzpatrick.

[3]Department of Labor, (1991). *Employment and Training Administration Revised Handbook for Analyzing Jobs.* Reprinted and distributed by Indianapolis, IN: Jist Works, Inc..

[4]Department of Labor, *Employment and Training Administration* (1992). *Selected Characteristics of Occupations* defined in the Dictionary of Occupational Titles.

[5]Ellwood, P.M., Jr. (1968). Can We Afford So Many Rehabilitation Professions. *Journal of Rehabilitation*, 34(3), pp. 21-22.

[6]Fields, Timothy F., and Sink, Jack M. (January 1981). The Vocational Expert. VBS, Inc.

[7]A History of the Social Security Disability Programs (1986). Disability History Report Social Security Administration, pg. 1-10.

[8]History of Social Security During the Johnson Administration, 1963-1968. Vocational Expert Program, Social Security Administration, pp. 1-7.

[9]Hubley, Nathaniel O. (Fall, 2008). The Untouchables: Why a Vocational Expert's Testimony in Social Security Disability Hearings Cannot be Touched. *Valparaiso University Law Review*, Number 1, Volume 43, 353-406.

[10]Kearsey, John R. (2006). Social Security and the "D" in OASDI: The History of a Federal Program Insuring Earners Against Disability.

[11]SkillTRAN Data Resources (2001-2005). A History of the Social Security Disability Programs, Social Security Administration.

[12]United States Department of Labor, Employment, and Training Administration, 4th Ed. (1991). *Dictionary of Occupational Titles*

[13]Vercillos, Amy, (2012). *Social Security Vocational Expert Most Common Hypotheticals*. A presentation at the International Association of Rehabilitation Professionals Conference in Puerto Rico.

[14]Vocational Expert Handbook, 2nd Ed. (2003). Office of the Chief Judge, Philadelphia Region, Social Security Administration.

[15]Vocational Expert Handbook, November (2010). Office of Disability Adjudication and Review, Office of the Chief Administrative Law Judge.

# PART 3

# JOB PLACEMENT FOR PERSONS WITH LIMITATIONS IN THE NEW AMERICAN ECONOMY

# CHAPTER SEVEN

# THE COUNSELOR'S INTRODUCTION TO THE WORLD OF WORK IN THE NEW AMERICAN ECONOMY

# PREFACE

*Ignorance of jobs and occupations in the national and local economy is no longer an option in rehabilitation, if it ever was. It is malpractice to train or educate clients in jobs or occupations they are unable to perform because of their limitations; and it is criminal to place clients in occupations for which there is no future.*

The Authors

To the Reader:

As of this writing, the national economy seems to be finally emerging from the worst recession since the Great Depression of the 1930's. Yet, parts of the nation are still experiencing unemployment rates higher than 8%, and in some places and for some groups the rate is much higher. Moreover, a recent McKinsey Global Institute report found that 71% of workers in the United States hold jobs for which there is decreasing demand, increasing supply, or both (*Newsweek*, December 21, 2009). We can only imagine the effects unemployment, job obsolescence, and decreasing demand for jobs in this country have, and will continue to have, upon the aspirations of persons with disabilities.

Your knowledge of jobs and the world of work may be the most important service you have to offer your client. Why, because rehabilitation counselors are the professionals best prepared to address the two main issues in rehabilitation: work and disability. This assumption (i.e., that a person with disabilities need rehabilitation counselors to help them with their employment goals) is confirmed by surveys showing that clients seek help from rehabilitation, not for therapy or to help them secure and retain benefits, but because they want to work. In fact, a major impetus of the Social Security Administration's "Ticket to Work" program has come from beneficiaries calling in and saying they think they could work if they had continued medical benefits and proper help in getting an appropriate job. Rehabilitation professionals are a client's best source for information and vocational counseling to help them achieve their employment goals.

The need for professionals to assist persons seeking rehabilitation service is expected to continue well into the next decade. Projections from the Department of Labor lists rehabilitation counseling as having the most job openings during the period 2012- 2020 among the 20 occupations requiring an advanced degree.[5, pg. 14] The opportunities for rehabilitation counselors are exciting. You will soon find that the more you know about jobs in the national and local economy and the world of work, the more opportunities will come your way.

Nevertheless, rehabilitation counselors need to do a better job in the vocational side of rehabilitation. Ignorance of jobs and occupations in the national and local economy is no longer an option in rehabilitation. It is malpractice to train or educate clients in jobs or occupations they are unable to perform because of their limitations; and it is criminal to place clients in occupations for which there is no future. Rehabilitation counselors must take it upon themselves to know at least the general principles under which the US economy operates and understand the kinds of jobs normally performed by their clientele.

This is the first of four chapters dealing exclusively with the process involved in finding jobs for persons with disabilities. Chapter 7 presents a broad picture of the American job market as we look back over the last 40 or so years of gut-wrenching changes that have taken place in the American economy, changes that have moved this Nation from a goods producing economy to a services economy. This chapter also looks at the supply and demand projections for select jobs in the near future. You will recall from Chapters 2 & 3 that we identified classes of Americans normally provided rehabilitation services. These were the working and the baseline classes. In Chapter 7, we identify many of the occupations normally performed by working class people and provide an outlook of the future supply and demand for these jobs.

# EMPLOYMENT TRENDS IN THE NATIONAL ECONOMY: 1970–2014 AND BEYOND

## AN OVERVIEW

In the past four decades, the national economy has undergone enormous change affecting every community in America. Practically everyone has felt the stress of changing times. Foreign competition, technological advances, and deregulation have swept away jobs in our major corporations; and funding cuts at all levels of government have cost thousands of jobs in the non-profit sector with a grim forecast for non-profit sector jobs in the present decade. According to a recent article in the *Washington Post*, there has been zero net job growth in this country since December 1999. No previous decade going back to the 1940's had job growth less than 20%. Economic output in this country rose at its slowest rate in any decade since the 1930's (*Washington Post*, January 1, 2010).

During the past four decades, as the national economy expanded with long periods of sustained growth, other parts of the economy have grown to compensate, in part, for some of the job losses. The newly created jobs are different from those lost, requiring additional preparation, new knowledge, and higher skill levels. An examination of these national trends over the past four decades follows.

## AMERICA LOSING JOBS: THE "DARKER SIDE" OF NATIONAL EMPLOYMENT TRENDS

So much of the success in employment of persons with disabilities in the middle to latter part of the 20th Century was centered in the primary market (i.e., the market that includes government, federal, state, and local, and large corporations with greater than 500 employees). Good-hearted officials and managers, with the help of affirmative action programs, gave newly rehabilitated workers job opportunities. Unfortunately, over the past twenty or so years during the sustained adjustments in the national economy, both government and large corporations have received many of the shock waves.

Changes in government employment have significantly affected young people and minorities, including disabled workers. Traditionally, a government growing at all levels provided well-paid, entry-level jobs for young people, minorities, and disabled workers. In the past, the "goods-producing" sector of the economy provided a high-proportion of our best jobs. These jobs included reasonable wages, job security, fringe benefits, opportunities for advancement with seniority, and opportunities to learn on the job and advance for those workers with relatively low levels of formal education.

Government employment peaked in 1975, under the Great Society programs, and then flattened out in successive years thereafter. Governments at all levels have become hard-pressed to support funding levels caused, in part, at the national level by our enormous national debt, and at the state level by future obligations to retirement programs for an aging population of workers. Even during the 1990s, with eight years of a Democratic Administration under President Clinton, government employment showed only minimal growth. Federal employment, both defense and non-defense is listed among the employment sectors projected by the Department of Labor to have the most job losses between 2012 and 2020. Expected losses in government jobs have sent the ominous message that many potential jobs for young people, minorities, and disabled workers would not be there in the future.

With fewer government jobs available, the competition has sharpened for the remaining, private sector jobs, but "downsizing" and "outsourcing" has resulted in job losses in most of the nations' largest corporations. *Fortune Magazine* provides data on the 500 largest corporations in America (i.e., the so-called Fortune 500). One-third of corporations that made up the Fortune 500 in 1970 had disappeared by 1983. From 1979 to 1990 the Fortune 500 companies reduced the number of people they employed by 3 million. During the same period, their percentage of the national work force dropped from 18% to 11%. By the end of the 20th Century, Fortune 500 companies represented a mere 9% of the US economy, causing some to refer to the Fortune 500 companies as the "Misfortune 500".[2, pg. 14]

Data indicate there has been little growth in the employment numbers in these large corporations in recent years. An article from *USA Today* reports there are currently about 17,000 of these large corporations in the United States and that the growth in the number of big employers–those with 500 or more workers–has been flat since the 2001 recession. (*USA Today*, September 21, 2009).

Most of the remaining jobs are different as well. Today, in large corporations, not only are there fewer management positions, but these positions do not pay, proportionally, the salaries they once did. To cut costs and maintain profitability, corporations have had to reduce staff at all levels. Among the casualties are white-collar, management jobs. Unfortunately, many of these middle and upper level managers are older and have difficulty finding similar positions with similar salary structures in other companies. For example, in an early study of unemployed middle-aged managers in Southern California, Lee Dyer[3] found that 53% of the managers they surveyed had previously been employed by corporations of 100 or more employees, but only 19% of them found employment with firms of that size. Significantly, almost three-quarters of those who supplied salary data reported a decrease in income in their new position.[3, pg. 26]

Current labor market projections for laid-off workers and other unemployed workers indicate that these downward trends will continue with alternative positions paying proportionately less in the future. *USA Today* forecasts that "millions of workers who've lost their hold on the labor market are seeing their incomes reset to a permanently lower level." (January 7, 2010) Research conducted by Bernard Condon and Paul Wiseman as reported by the Associated Press on January 23, 2013, found that "in the United States, half of the 7.5 million jobs lost during the Great Recession paid middle-class wages, ranging from $38,000 to $68,000. Conversely, only 2% of the 3.5 million jobs gained since the recession ended in June 2009 are mid-pay. Nearly 70% percent are low-paying jobs; 29 percent pay well. Experts warn that this "hollowing out" of the middle-class workforce is far from over." (*USA Today*, January 23, 2013)

Job opportunities in labor unions, moreover, do not offer much in the way of relief to American workers. Union membership plummeted in 2012 to the lowest level since the 1930s as cash strapped state and local governments shed workers. Unions had difficulty organizing new members in the private sector despite signs of an improving economy. As reported in the Associated Press on January 24, 2013, government figures showed union membership in recent years has declined from 11.8 percent to 11.3% of the workforce "another blow to a union movement already stretched thin by battles in states to curb bargaining rights and weakened union clout. Overall, union membership fell by about 400,000 workers to 14.4 million according to the Bureau of Labor Statistics. More than half the loss came from government workers including teachers, firefighters, and public administrators." (*The Staunton News Leader*, January 24, 2013)

Likewise, support positions within large corporations have undergone a reduction. There are few support positions that have not been touched by technological innovation of the computer microchip (e.g., word processing for the secretary, data storage and search for support positions with corporate lawyers and research specialist, and problem-solving positions for the manager, to mention a few). The ability of the computer to perform complex functions and to process and assimilate information at faster and faster speeds has both raised the skill level of support positions and reduced the need for many lower-level support positions, such as data entry keyers. How many positions are affected by computer innovation? In 1984 it was estimated that one worker in eight was using a computer; today virtually every business, large and small, relies upon the computer.

When compared with factory workers and other blue-collar positions in large corporations, white-collar staff has made an easier transition to the new demands of the marketplace. Adjustments within the white-collar workforce have been made possible by higher levels of education, greater transferability of work skills, and growth in white-collar jobs in other parts of the economy. Factory workers, on the other hand, have seen their jobs disappear to foreign competition, technological advancement, and deregulation with little or no hope of re-employment in those or similar positions. We will look at these three "agents of change" more closely.

*Foreign competitors* have eaten into the labor-intensive manufacturing industries, (e.g., apparel, motor vehicles and parts, furnaces and other steel products, motorcycles, and bicycles) to name only a few. With quality improvements, lower labor costs, and, in many cases, government subsidies; foreign manufacturers have gained a larger and larger foothold in the domestic market. Robert Wegmann[8] reports that in 1975 foreign goods provided only 13% of domestic sales and by 1985, their share had grown to 26%. Today, foreign manufacturers provide 57% of domestic sales.[pg. 15]

Foreign manufacturers have taken over much of the domestic market for automobiles. Between 1975 and 1985, foreign manufacturers captured over 30% of domestic automobile sales. *USA Today* reports that at the turn of the 20th Century, foreign manufacturers produced more than half of the pickups, minivans, and sport utility vehicles sold in America. At the beginning of 2006,

Toyota became the largest manufacturer of automobiles in the world, supplanting General Motors (*USA Today* January 22, 2001).

Then, in 2009, China replaced the United States as the largest auto market in the world (*The Staunton News leader*, January 11, 2010), and the outlook for growth in sales in this country is unlikely to change much in the near future. Government forecasters expect the sale of cars and light trucks will reach only 14.4 million by 2018, down from the 16 million level reached in the mid-2000s. (*USA Today*, January 8, 2010)

As American manufacturing firms have found cheaper labor in foreign countries, particularly in the Far East, jobs in the United States have continued to be "shipped overseas." Since the year 2000, more than 3 million manufacturing jobs–one in six–have been lost. In 2010 Mark Zandi, chief economist for Moody's Economy.com, a private consulting firm, says "U.S. manufacturing jobs have withered over the past five years and many of those jobs are never to return" (*USA Today*, January 8, 2010). According to the Bureau of Statistics, the government expects the nation's employers to cut 1.2 million manufacturing jobs by 2018.

Among the hardest hit industries in the United States has been the textile industry where the long-range outlook is dire: "If you work in a textile mill the days of your job are numbered," says Steven Cochrane, Managing Editor for Moody's Economy.com" (*USA Today*, January 8, 2010).

Unskilled and semi-skilled jobs in the manufacturing industries are not the only ones to have moved overseas. Higher-level positions, such as service worker positions have also been hurt by foreign competition. The ability to transmit massive amounts of information to far-away places has led companies in the United States to send overseas jobs in such high-tech areas as architecture, computer software, medical services, and engineering.

While global competition has helped hold down labor costs, the largest single cost item for American manufacturers, the influx of foreign goods has created massive trade deficits (*The Staunton News Leader*, November 28, 2005). China edged past Germany in 2009 to become the largest exporter in the world: "yet another sign of its rapid rise and the spread of economic power from West to East" says Joe McDonald of the Associated Press International (*The Staunton News Leader*, January 11, 2010). Trade deficits, resulting from the loss of market share, were anticipated to be over 100 billion by the end of the year 2000. In 2010 alone, the trade deficit was approximately $137 billion. With trade deficits, American businesses lose jobs in two ways:

- Jobs are lost at home as the American buyer chooses foreign instead of domestic products.

- Jobs are lost in exporting companies serving markets abroad as American goods fail to sell in competition with foreign manufacturers.

*Technological advances* in manufacturing industries have likewise cut into the job market for blue-collar workers. The much-publicized manufacturing robots have reduced the number of unskilled and semi-skilled jobs needed in the factories and drastically altered others. Bylinski reports that the Japanese have a factory, Yanazaku Machine Works, with 12 workers and a night watchman that produces the same volume of goods that formally required 215 workers and four times the machinery. Two examples closer to home: General Electric now builds locomotive frames in one day that used to take 16 days and 70 workers, with the frame untouched by human hands. Walgreen's has installed robots in its warehouses that can handle 900 less-than-case-load shipments per hour. Human packers formerly handled 110 shipments per hour.[8, pg.20-21]

Since 1982, the number of robots used in the manufacture of automobiles has increased while person-hours required to build an automobile have dropped steadily. In 1982, the Chrysler Corporation required 172 person-hours to build an automobile. In 1989, Robert Wegmann[8] reported that it was taking an average of 26 person-hours. By 1994, *USA Today* reported that General Motors had set a goal for its Eisenach plant in Germany at 20 person-hours, six hours below the American industry average, and 16 person-hours less than typical European plants require (*USA Today*, August 16, 1994).

*Deregulation* has had almost the identical effect as foreign competition upon lower-skilled positions in the transportation, communication, and finance industries (i.e., prior to deregulation, government agencies decided who could run a bus service between what cities, the interest rates banks could offer on savings accounts, and how much could be charged for an airline ticket). Firms in these industries are now much freer to compete, but to compete puts pressure on a company to lower costs to hold its market share. This has meant lowering people cost by slimming down the size of the organization, with loss of work for some, and for others, longer hours with less money. For example, more than 300 trucking companies failed following deregulation in the transportation industry, and many local teamster unions working with smaller trucking companies had to take sizable cuts in their contracts to save jobs. Compromises like these are still the order of the day in 2014.

Chart 1 shows a cross section of some of the occupations that, in all likelihood, will be adversely affected by changes in the national economy. The Bureau of Labor Statistics has published labor market projections every other year in the Occupational Outlook Handbook since the fall of 1957. The projections are now found online at Occupational Outlook Handbook online.

CHART 1

## OCCUPATIONS LOSING THE MOST JOBS PROJECTED 2010-2020

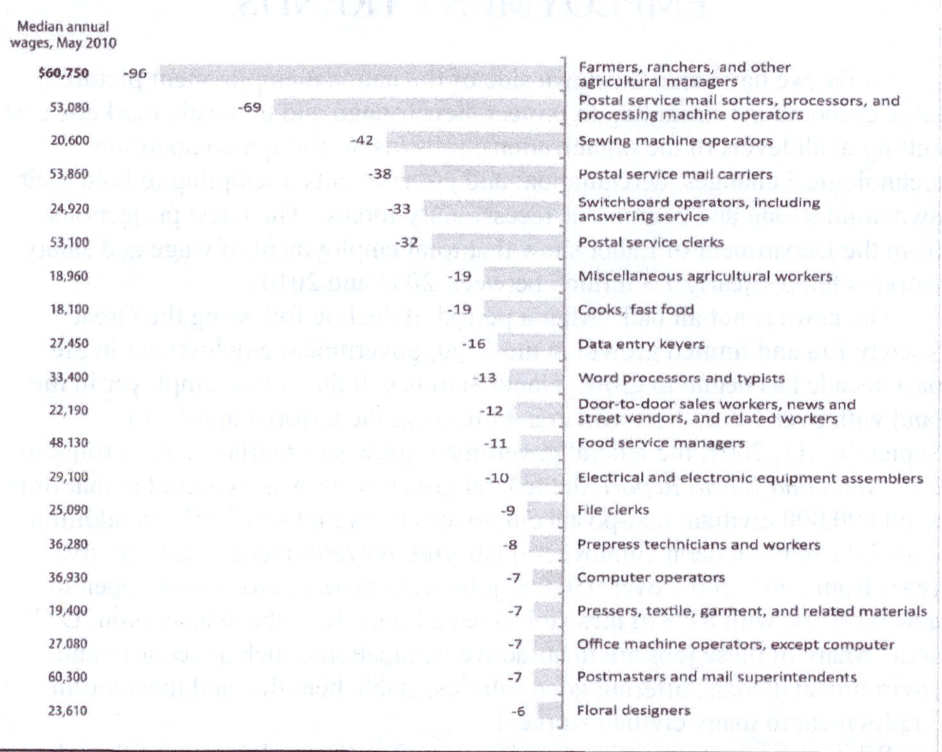


The statistics in this chart may be found in the Department of Labor publication 5, page 24.

Things have changed in the latest projections from the Department of Labor for occupations with the largest job losses. Once again, apparel knitting mill occupations stand close to the top in occupations with the largest job losses. This is no surprise as so many jobs in the textile industries have moved overseas. Surprisingly, for the first time, job losses in the Postal Service and job losses in government, both federal and state, stand out on the list of the occupations losing the most jobs. Printing of newspapers, periodicals, books, and directories, as well as printing and related support activities, occupy top spots on the new list among occupations losing the most jobs.

# AMERICA GAINING JOBS: THE "SUNNY SIDE" OF NATIONAL EMPLOYMENT TRENDS

So far, we have seen the down side of the national employment picture: large corporations struggling to protect their foreign and domestic markets; cost cutting at all levels of the organizations; jobs lost to foreign competition, technological changes, deregulation; and governments attempting to hold their own amid strong and continuous recessionary forces. The latest projections from the Department of Labor show that total employment of wage and salary workers fell by nearly 7.8 million between 2007 and 2010.

The news is not all bad. After a period of decline following the Great Society Era and limited growth in the 1990, government employment in the past decade has begun to grow. Uncle Sam is still the largest employer in the land with over 1.8 million workers. Following the terrorist attacks of September 11, 2001, the federal government grew substantially. According to *U.S. News and World Report*, the federal government was expected at that time to add 90,000 civilian, non-postal employees to its ranks in 2002. In addition, with 53% of the federal employees qualifying for retirement within the five years from 2002–2007, over 950,000 jobs were expected to become open to new workers, with 84% of these jobs located outside of the Washington, D.C. area. Many of these jobs are in attractive occupations, such as security and environmental areas, offering good salaries, stable benefits, and meaningful employment to many civilian workers.

While American manufacturers lost over 3 million jobs, most of the job losses among American manufacturing firms have been in unskilled and semi-skilled positions. The Associated Press reported that since 2001 U.S. textile and apparel manufacturers lost 350,000 jobs due to low-cost overseas competition. On the other hand, American industry is successfully competing among foreign competition in automated manufacturing of precision products with high-performance, skilled workers, such as machinists.

The National Association of Manufacturers (NAM) says the loss of jobs in the manufacturing sector does not mean the U.S. is moving toward a post-manufacturing economy. Explaining the results of their survey in 2005, the National Association of Manufacturers says the manufacturing sector is growing faster than the overall economy. Where we (The United States) are competitive is in the high value added, says the report. Of the over 800 firms included in the survey, 49% ranked the quality of their work force foremost among the three factors most important to their success over the next three years. Falling behind the "quality of the work force" in the survey were product innovation (49%) and low-cost product (45%).[6] Skilled manufacturing jobs are viewed by many experts as leading the national economy out of the 2008-2010 recession.

Most impressive is the number of jobs in America had been increasing, not decreasing, in the overall job market during the three and a half decades until 2000. Between 1970 and 1980, employment went up by over 20 million, an extraordinary increase, with an additional increase of 10 million jobs between 1980 and 1986. In the year 2000, the Clinton Administration reported that over 20 million jobs had been created between 1986 and 2000, with over a third taking place in the export industry. In the decade of the 1990s, the U.S. export industry grew from one-fifth, or 20%, to over 30% of economic activity. The United States Department of Labor projects that from 2010-2020 the total labor force in America will reach 164 million, reflecting the addition of about 20 million new jobs between 2010 and 2020.[5, pg. 2]

Job losses in the primary job market have been made up, in part, by substantial growth in other parts of the economy. The expansion in jobs has been accompanied by an even greater increase of the labor force. After 1975, the nation's labor force added to its numbers three large groups of workers:

1. immigrants, both legal and illegal,
2. the so-called "baby boomers," and
3. women seeking paid employment outside the home.

Legal immigration in this country has remained high. During the 1970s, legal immigration to the United States exceeded 4.4 million that, at that time, was the highest level in half a century. Legal immigration has continued at an unparalleled rate in recent years. About 6 million legal immigrants have arrived since 2000, 59% from Latin America and 23% from Asia. Legal immigration was expected to hit more than 14 million by 2010, up from the previous high of 12 million in the 90s. More than 34 million people in the USA or almost one in eight was born in another country, according to a government survey of 62,500 households in March 2004. (*USA Today*, February 22, 2005).

Along with legal immigration, estimates are that another 5.5 million *illegal aliens* came in during the 1980s. How many illegal aliens there are in this country is not known, and estimates vary widely. Richard Freeman in *Troubled Waters in the Labor market* (1980) suggests that about 10% of the work force may be illegal aliens; and Walter Fogel Fogel (1977) in *Illegal Aliens: Economics Aspects: and Public Policy Aspects* cites an estimate by the Immigration and Naturalization Service of eight to 12 million.[8, pg. 9-10] In the year 2005, the estimate of illegal immigrants presently working in the United States was about 14 million.

In October 1979, the 16 to 24 year olds commonly called *"the baby-boomers,"* reached working age. Baby-boomers include the roughly 79 million Americans born between 1946 and 1964. The last of this group were expected to finish high school in the 1980s. This meant that beginning in the 1980s the 'baby-boomers" swelled the numbers of people seeking employment, and then the numbers declined.

Meanwhile, the numbers of women seeking paid employment continued at an unparalleled rate. During the period 1970-1988, the labor force grew by 10.7 million men and 15.2 million women, roughly a ratio of two to three. The 1990 census showed that the ratio of men to women had remained relatively constant through the 80s.

The participation rate of women in the workforce and immigration has continued to add large numbers to those seeking employment. During the period 1986 to 2000, women made up 64% of the net additions to the workforce, with a net increase of over 11 million workers. In 2009, the number of women in the workforce surpassed men for the first time in any country in human history. Dennis Cauchon of *USA Today* writes that at of the end of 2009 "women were on the verge of outnumbering men in the workforce for the first time, a historic reversal caused by long-term changes in women's roles and massive job losses for men during the recession." In June, 2009 women held 49.83 percent of the nation's 132 million jobs and they're gaining the vast majority of jobs in the few sectors of the economy that are growing, according to the most recent numbers available from the Bureau of Statistics. That's a record high for a measure that's been growing for decades and accelerating during the recession." (*USA Today*, December 8, 2009) Women reached a majority in the work force in October or November 2009.

Following mid-1970, an expanded economy created millions of jobs to accommodate these three classes of workers: legal and illegal aliens, baby-boomers, and women seeking employment. The expanded job base held down the unemployment rate; only once, during the recession of the early 1980s, did our unemployment exceed 9%. In the recession of 1989-1990, the unemployment rate reached about 7%. Considering the number of jobs lost to the forces of change and the pressures placed upon national employment by these large groups of job seekers, those unemployment rates were pretty good. In 2010, mired in a recession of historic dimensions, the average jobless rate for the nation exceeded 10%. In 2014, the unemployment rate in most places in the U.S. stands at 6% to 7%. However, in some places, the unemployment rate is less than 6%.

There is cause for optimism. The conclusion of the chapter suggests some of the positive directions the American economy and the global economy may be taking in the next few years.

# JOB GROWTH IN THE NEW AMERICAN ECONOMY

Most of the job growth that has taken place in the national economy has been in the secondary job market, in small businesses, as defined by the Department of Labor, those employers with less than 250 employees. Today, about two-thirds or 66% of employed Americans work in these businesses. In 2002, American Express ran an advertisement saying that small businesses made up 99% of all businesses in America. Clearly, these businesses are the source of most of the new job growth in our economy.

A surprising statistic is that most of the nation's job growth has been in the smallest of these businesses, those with less than 20 employees. In an analysis of data from Dunn and Bradstreet, David Birch[1] discovered that, of the new jobs created between 1969 and 1976, businesses with less than 20 employees were responsible for creating 80% of the net new jobs, while large corporations accounted for only 13%. Moreover, between 1981 and 1985 the net new jobs created by these small businesses had increased to 88%. The "small businesses (2 to 20 employees) make up a universe of 41.3 million employed persons in the USA which was expected to grow to 51.6 million by 2002, over a third of the total employment of the country."[1, pg. 9]

Numbers can be deceiving and results often depend upon who is doing the research. While it is true that small business has grown steadily in size and numbers, many "small fish" have been swallowed up by the "big fish" in recent years. *USA Today* reports that much of the freedom of running a small business has eroded through buyouts and consolidation. The article goes on to say that consolidation has hit hardest in retail and manufacturing, where thousands of small firms fell to big corporations in the past decade. The number of independent drug store companies, for example, plummeted 28% from 1990 to 1998. As a result, according to this report, the majority of workers in this country currently work for big companies instead of small ones–a switch that occurred around 2000. *USA Today* (March 27, 2002). So it seems, once again, that what goes around comes around.

What gets lost in the overall numbers is that not all parts of the economy have experienced job growth, the government and large corporations notwithstanding. In fact, almost all of the growth has been in the Services Sector of the economy. Indeed, we seem to have become a services economy. Today, the Services Sector of the economy accounts for about 86% of the jobs in America. (*Newsweek*, December 21, 2009)

Now when we speak of growth in the Service Sector of the economy, most people consider this to mean most of the job growth has been in eating and drinking establishments and that the job growth has been in unskilled and semi-skilled, often minimum-wage jobs, (i.e., cashiers, counter clerks, food service workers such as bus persons and dishwashers, short-order cooks, etc.). To no one's surprise, there has been phenomenal growth of jobs in these establishments. Between 1973 and 1985, food stores and eating establishments grew 87 percent.

The wholesale and retail trades, however, make up only 18% of the jobs in the Services Sector. Business services–not fast foods–are the fastest growing division of this Services Sector and have been for many years. Business Services include temporary help agencies, computer and data processing services, medical services, forms mailing and reproduction services, and advertising and management consulting. Though somewhat dated, this glaring statistic illustrates the extraordinary growth of the Services Sector. The apparel industry was once the largest export industry of New York City. By the late 1980s, New York City's largest export industry had become legal services.

Chart 2 shows a select number of the jobs expected to grow by the year 2020. The *Occupational Outlook Quarterly*[5] says the 20 occupations shown below are projected to gain the most new jobs between 2010 and 2020 and account for almost 36% of the projected new job creation in all occupations during the period.

## CHART 2
### OCCUPATIONS WITH THE MOST JOB OPENINGS, 2010–2020

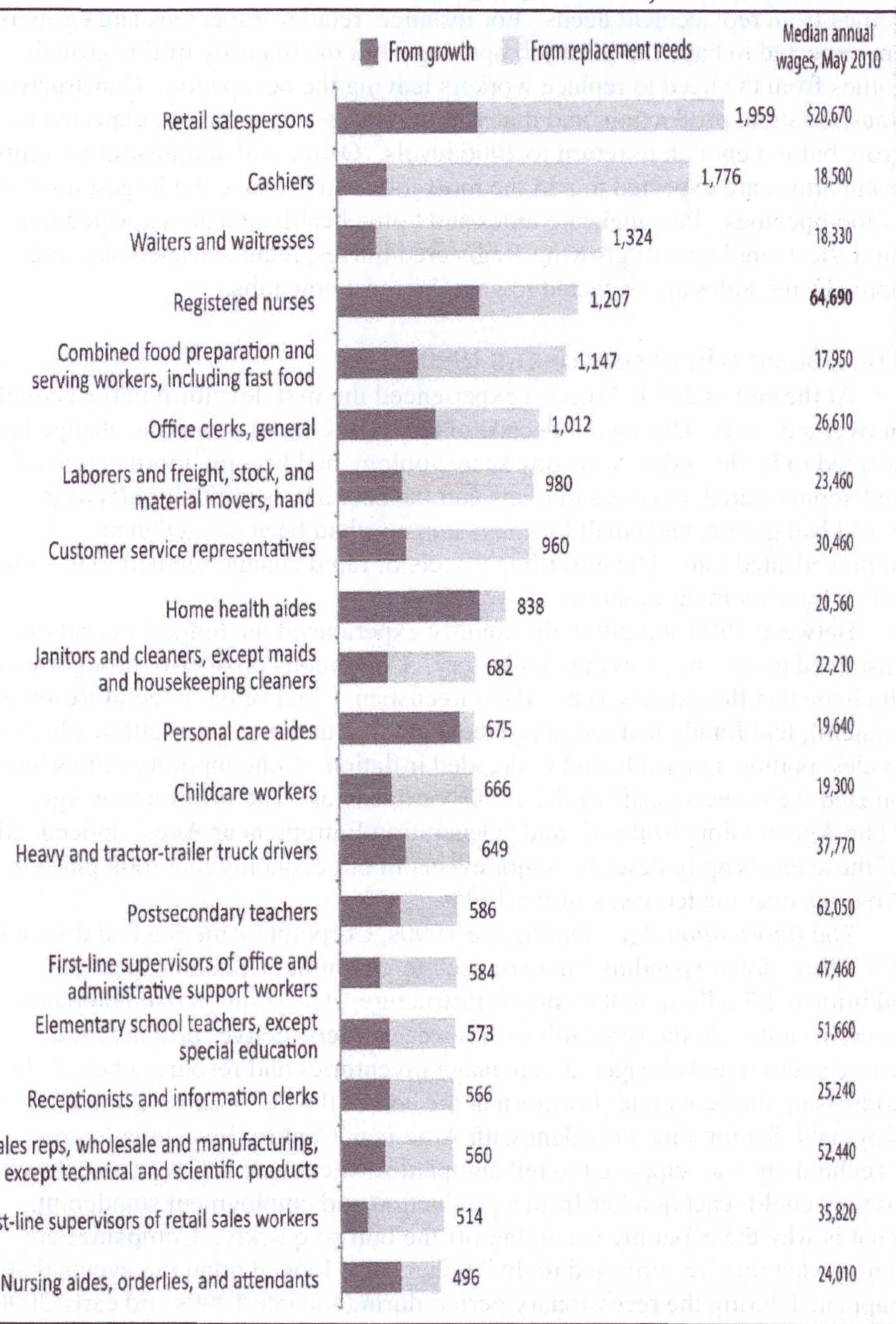


The statistics in this chart may be found in *Occupational Outlook Quarterly*, winter, 2011-2012.[5, pg.13]

All of the occupations represented on this list are projected to grow between 2010 and 2020, but the job growth in many of these occupations comes from replacement needs. For instance, retail salespersons and cashiers are expected to have the most job openings, but the majority of this growth comes from the need to replace workers leaving the occupation. Construction, transportation, production, and material moving occupations are expected to grow but not enough to return to 2006 levels. Office and administrative support occupations are expected to add the most jobs and produce the largest number of job openings. Personal care aides and home health aide are expected to have the fastest employment growth. Registered nurses, retail salespersons, and home health aides are expected to gain the most new jobs.

## THE BOOMING ECONOMY OF THE 1990S

At the end of 2000, America experienced the first downturn in the economy in over a decade. During the decade of the 1990s, rapid economic change had seemed to be the order of the day as technology had become more pervasive and sophisticated, overseas markets and the economies in other parts of the world had grown, and small business start-ups had been created at an unprecedented rate. The unsettling effects of rapid change seemed to have been offset by a booming economy.

Between 1990 and 2000, the country experienced the longest period of sustained economic growth in its history. Continuous prosperity brought with it the hope that the experts, (i.e., Alan Greenspan, Chief of the Federal Reserve System), had finally learned to reduce wide fluctuations in the nation's business cycles, putting a possible end to dreaded inflation. Contemporary critics have labeled the robust decade of the 1990s variously as "The Information Age," "The Age of Globalization," and "Generation Entrepreneur Age." Indeed, all of these labels aptly describe major events in our economy that took place in America over the ten years of the 1990s.

*The Information Age.* During the 1990s, Corporate America had driven the 2.8 billion dollar spending binge on technology in the USA and spent an additional 2.5 billion on telecom infrastructure. The result is that companies in America today do the same job with fewer workers, deliver products and services faster and cheaper, and manage inventories and resources better. In addressing the economic downturn at the end of the 20th Century, Mark Kopinski, Senior Vice President with American Century Investments says, "Technology was supposed to tell companies when their business was slowing so they could react quicker from a production and employment standpoint. That is why the economy is coming off the boil so quickly. Companies are doing what they're supposed to do." Others also looked upon the events that happened during the recessionary period during the late 1990s and early 2000, (what has come to be called the Dot.Com Recession) as positive evidence the technology is working. Tim Timkin, Chief Executive Officer of Timkin Co., a bearing and specialty steel products company based in Canton, Ohio, believed the downturn in the economy was nothing more than an "inventory curtailment." (*USA Today*, January 22, 2001)

It seems that new and improved technology has given American companies the ability to respond more quickly to economic changes, allowing them to reduce inventories and the work force to meet new conditions. However, improvements in business seldom come without corresponding costs, particularly where people are concerned. In recent years, the biggest challenge faced by managers has been finding, training, and keeping employees in a tight market for skilled labor. Employee reduction causes disruption to the families involved, additional recruitment and training costs to the company when business improves, and reduced employee loyalty and morale throughout the company, resulting in higher turnover and lost productivity. Surveys have shown that loyalty among employees in US companies has been on the wane since the downsizing of companies in the 1980s and 1990s.

*The Age of Globalization.* During this same period of time, the United States and economies in other parts of the world became more tightly interwoven than ever before. "But make no mistake," writes James Cox "the USA dominates. It accounts for 30% of the global growth over the past three years, even though its economy represents only 20% of the world's gross domestic product (GDP)." The 2500 largest US companies sold about 12% of their goods and services outside the USA in 1980. That figure has tripled in the past two decades, says Peter Pekar, a consultant with investment banking firm Houlihan, Lokey, Howard & Zukin. As a result, he says, "American multinationals should be better cushioned from contraction in the economy because they now have customers in more places and have spread their investments and production around the globe." (*USA Today*, January 22, 2001)

The multinationals are not the only business in the United States benefiting from globalization. A report from The Institute for the Future, a think tank located in Silicon Valley, California, projects that as the global economy grows, half of the U.S. small business will be involved by 2018. Just like corporate giants, small firms today can readily sell their goods and services worldwide because of new technology, quicker and cheaper manufacturing, and stronger shipping and banking networks. Steve Preston, Administrator for the Small Business Administration (SBA) says that exports are the under-recognized opportunity for many American small businesses; a lot of small businesses have very good products that are very competitive overseas.

The report goes on to say that the impetus for small businesses "leaping into the global marketplace" seems to be coming from entrepreneurial immigrants with strong ties between the USA and their cultural homelands in Asia, Latin America, Europe, and the Middle East. Twenty-five percent of new US technology and engineering companies that were launched from 1995 to 2005, says the report, have at least one founder who is foreign born. These firms hauled in $52 billion in sales in 2005, according to a study by Duke University and the University of California at Berkeley. (*USA Today*, April 8, 2008)

*Generation Entrepreneur.* Some thinkers believe that the long period of prosperity in the decade of the 1990s was brought about not by new technology or by globalization but by a spirit of free enterprise that has its roots in American individualism and dates back to the 1970s. William Sahlman of the Harvard Business School sees what he calls the "Bedrock of the American Renaissance" in the 1990s as the newfound entrepreneurial spirit. "The new economy is entrepreneur led rather than technological led. Technology is only as good as the uses found for it and the markets identified for its sale. The businesses that emerge as long-term successes from the technology gold rush will be those that are based on business principles of meeting consumer demand rather than those simply based on bright new technology."[2, pg. 91]

In 2001, William Sahlman believed that the current US economy is in good shape and would be that way for years to come "if the government just manages to stay out of the way." Its strength, he believed, is based upon a business model that works and one that continually ratchets up its efficiency. "The old American economy" he says "was characterized by bloated companies protected by carefully constructed entry barriers, which was fine until the 1970s when foreign competitors descended like locusts. The tough times of the 1970s though planted the seeds for the entrepreneurship of today. The new model was invented by people like Bill Gates and Michael Dell and is being continuously reinvented by new arrivals."[2, pg. 100]

The entrepreneurial revolution has seen the rapid expansion of small businesses, those businesses with 1 to 20 employees. Small businesses are still the fastest growing segment of the business community, making up 13 percent of *INC* magazine's 1998 Top 500 list. Dunn & Bradstreet describes the average small business as having three employees, generating between $150,000 and $200,000 in revenue each year, operating from one location, privately owned, with an owner who puts in 50.4 hours a week

Technology, and more recently the Internet, has been a main spring of the entrepreneur. The Internet provides a platform to the marketplace for original ideas, thus making it well suited for the entrepreneurial challenge. Since 2000, we have seen a purging of many of the Internet companies, many of which have never made a profit. Some believe the Internet is merely "ratcheting up inefficiency," a healthy state of affairs for the communications medium.

Historically, every major downturn in the national economy has come about as the result of excessive optimism and zealous over-speculation, a euphemism for greed, with investment in risky ventures. The dot.com crisis at the turn of the 21st Century, and now with the Wall Street debacle at the end of the first decade of the 21st century, illustrates some of the dangers of "get rich quick schemes" and other forms of human excess.

# THE OUTLOOK FOR THE NEW AMERICAN ECONOMY BEYOND 2010

At the time of this writing, the unemployment rate in this country is 5.9% with unemployment rates higher in some places in the country. Most prognosticators believe unemployment is likely to remain high for several years. The unemployment will remain flat and wage growth will continue to be flat, according to George Soros who predicted the coming crisis four months before the current recession began in 2007. He goes on to say, "The average American will not be better off in five years." (Newsweek, December 21, 2009, pg. 53) During this period of uncertainty, no statement of doom and gloom seems to have had more of an impact than the prediction of Simon Johnson, former chief economist of the International Monitory Fund. In an article printed in *The Atlantic* in May of 2009, Simon Johnson wrote, "the conventional wisdom among the elite is still that the current slump cannot be as bad as the Great Depression. This view is wrong. What we face now could, in fact, be worse than the Great Depression."

Seven years later, in 2014, we have not seen as much change as many of us expected. Unemployment is still high and little has changed in the future forecasts about employment. Overall, things look nothing like they did in the 30s. "The predictions of economic and political collapse have not materialized at all," says Fareed Zakaria in his article "The Secrets of Stability." (*Newsweek* December 21, 2009, pages 54-60) He goes on to say he believes there is a fundamental reason why we have not faced global collapse in the last year. "It is the same reason that we weathered the stock-market crash of 1987, the recession of 1992, the Asian crisis of 1997, the Russian default of 1998, and the tech-bubble collapse of 2000. The current global economic system is inherently more resilient than we think." (*Newsweek,* December 21, 2009, pg. 58)

In this article, Fareed Zakaria cites four (4) reasons for what he considers the resilience of the global system:

1. The spread of *peace*: "You would have to go back 175 years, if not 400 years to find any prolonged period like the one we are now living in." Peace allows for the possibility of a stable economic life and trade.

2. Although there are many variations, the world is left with a single workable economic model, *capitalism*. The consensus has enabled the expansion of the global economy in which almost all of the countries across the globe are participants. That means that everyone is invested in the same system.

3. The *victory over inflation.* Severe inflation can be far more disruptive than a recession because while recessions rob you of better jobs and wages that you might have had in the future, inflation robs you of what you have now by destroying your savings. Low inflation allows people, businesses, and governments to plan for the future, a key precondition for stability.

4. *Connectivity.* A force that has underpinned the resilience of the global system. (*Newsweek*, December 21, 2009, Pg. 58-60)

Globalization today is fundamentally about knowledge being dispersed across the world. The production of almost every complex manufactured product now involves input from a dozen countries in a tight global supply chain. Diffusion of knowledge may be the most important reason for the stability of the current system. The majority of the world's nations have learned some basic lessons about political well-being and wealth creation. They have taken advantage of the opportunities provided by peace, low inflation, and technology to plug into a global system and they have seen indisputable results.

## THE DEPARTMENT OF LABOR'S JOB PREDICTIONS, 2010 – 2020

In spite of the current disruption, the United States Department of Labor predicts a steady growth in employment over the next decade. Employment had been expected to increase by 21.3 million in the decade 2002-2012, adding about 600,000 more jobs than were added in the previous decade. Research from the Department of Labor, Bureau of Labor Statistics, projects that by 2020 the total number of jobs is expected to reach 164 million, reflecting the addition of nearly 20 million new jobs between 2010 and 2020.

Not all occupations are likely to benefit from this large new job expansion. Depending upon a number of factors, some occupations will grow and others will shrink. Here is the Bureau's analysis and predictions: Occupations that are expected to decline are those that have already been hit the hardest during the transformation to the new services economy. These include unskilled and semi-skilled factory jobs, like apparel workers, shoe and leather workers and repairers, packers, and textile machinery operators; and positions displaced by consolidation of services and new technology, such as bank tellers, computer operators, word processors, typists, file clerks, order clerks, telemarketers, and communication equipment operators. In the sweeping adjustments, the economy has made in recent years, factory jobs and jobs affected by developing technology have suffered the most severe cuts as American companies have changed their traditional way of doing business and placed the manufacturing of many products in facilities overseas.

For the period 2010 to 2020, the Department of Labor projects faster than average growth in a number of occupations. The anticipated growth is based upon assumptions about population changes and other factors that affect economic activity. For instance, occupations that serve the demands of our aging population are expected to experience faster than average growth. These include physical therapist assistants, pharmacy technicians, medical assistants, dental hygienists, health information technicians, human services workers and assistants, social workers, personal care aides, home health aides, and licensed practical nurses.

In some health care occupations and other professional fields, para-professionals are taking on additional job duties formerly performed by doctors and other treatment specialists that require higher levels of skill and greater responsibility. For instance, nurse practitioners now perform routine annual checkups for patients without the involvement of a physician. Health care occupations are expected to grow at a faster than the average rate by upgrading to include physicians assistants, counselors, dental assistants, medical assistants, nurses' aides, occupational therapy assistants, physical therapists assistants and aides, and home health and personal care aides. Medical practitioners have been among the fastest growing occupations for many years. In the 2005 edition of the *Occupational Outlook Quarterly,*[5] medical assistants were projected to be the fastest growing occupation in the national economy. The *Quarterly,*[5] projects home health care services to be the fastest growing occupation over the next 10 years.

In a like manner, other professional occupations are likely to experience faster than average growth through upgraded skills and responsibility. While the demand for lawyers and judicial workers is expected to grow at a normal rate, paralegal and legal assistants are projected to have among the fastest growth in the economy as these occupations assume greater responsibility in the legal field. The same is true in elementary and secondary education, as well as colleges, where teacher assistants are expected to assume the duties of the classroom teacher to help reduce the non-teaching burden upon teachers and reduce student classroom size.

To no one's surprise, occupations in the high-tech fields are anticipated to grow faster than average with the continuing expansion in the use of computers, new applications found for computerized technology, and increasing demands for technology in a variety of fields. Representative of these fast-growing occupations are electronic semiconductor processors, computer programmers, computer systems analysts, computer automated teller and office machine repairers. The 2007 edition of the *Occupational Outlook Quarterly* projected Network Systems and Data Communications Analysts to be the fastest growing occupation over the next decade.

The administrative and support personnel in the high-tech fields are expected to grow along with the technology occupations. These include receptionist and information clerks. Faster than average growth is also expected in a number of industries because of increased demand for their special services. Because of societies concerns about crime and security, occupations in the protective services field, such as correctional officers, guards, and investigators are expected to generate a large number of jobs in the years ahead. In addition, because of the large consumer debt, there is expected to be a greater than normal demand for adjusters, investigators, and collectors. Because of heightened interest in investing in the stock market, there is expected to be a growing need for additional sales representatives in the securities, commodities, and financial fields.

The overall growth rate in the economy, as measured by the gross domestic product (GDP), is projected to increase by 3% per year, on average, between 2010 and 2020. This is much faster than the 1.6% annual growth for 2000 to 2010, which was pulled down by two recessions during the decade including the severe 2007-2009 downturn. The 2010-2020 statistical projections from the Department of Labor reflect an anticipated increase in the GDP. Many of the new jobs are in occupations replacing workers who have left an occupation, rather than from occupations with the need to fill newly created jobs. In some ways, this is good for job placement in rehabilitation as a large number of the new jobs are in occupations normally held by working class individuals. These occupations include cashiers, personal care aides, retail sales persons, general office clerks, over the road truckers, childcare workers, housekeepers and janitors, gardeners and groundskeepers, construction laborers and material handlers.

Chart 3 shows the Department of Labor projections of occupations producing the most new jobs over the decade from 2010 to 2020. These occupations are expected to produce almost 36% of the new jobs projected over the next 10 years.

CHART 3

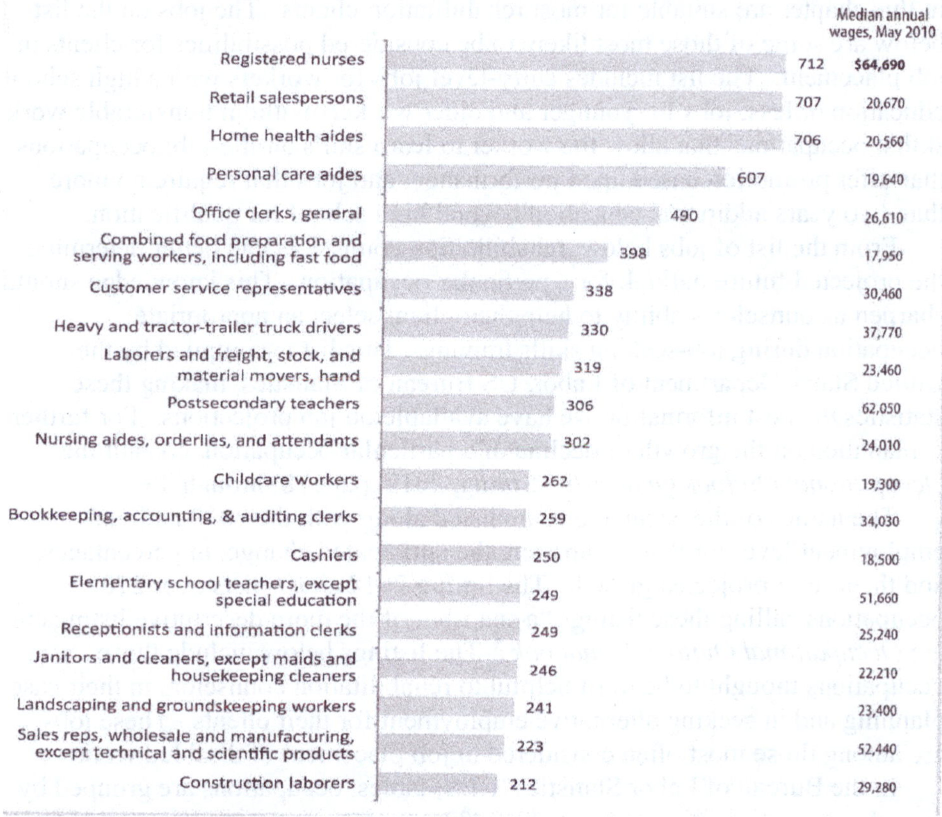


OCCUPATIONAL OUTLOOK HANDBOOK, WINTER 2011-12, PAGE12.

# CASE PLANNING FOR THE REHABILITATION COUNSELOR

Occupational projections appear in the *Occupational Outlook Quarterly*[5] (OOQ) about every two years. It is sometimes amazing how much change takes place in these statistics over a 2-year period. Interestingly, the 2010-2012 edition of the OOQ projects growth in many entry-level jobs, (i.e., jobs that require no work skills at entry or an acquaintance with the occupation or work place). Some of these jobs grow into semi-skilled positions after employment, as responsibilities increase, but there is no skill requirement for these entry-level jobs when new employees begin work. Rehabilitation counselors will find it helpful to consult the latest edition of the *Occupational Outlook*

*Quarterly*[5] for these projections in job placement before planning training for any client. Some of the new jobs may be well suited for clients seeking alternative work.

Only a select few of the occupations included in the charts presented earlier in this chapter are suitable for most rehabilitation clients. The jobs on the list below are some of those most likely to be considered possibilities for clients in job placement. The list includes entry-level jobs for workers with a high school education or less; jobs for younger and older workers without transferable work skills; occupations that allow the worker to learn skills on-the-job; occupations that offer promotion based upon performance; and jobs that require no more than two years additional education beyond high school for qualification.

From the list of jobs below, rehabilitation counselors can better determine the projected future outlook for a particular occupation. This knowledge should sharpen a counselor's ability to help their client select an appropriate occupation during job-seeking skills training. This list is compiled by the United States Department of Labor, US Bureau of Statistics, making these statistics the best information we have available on job projections. For further explanation on the growth or decline of a particular occupation, consult the *Occupational Outlook Quarterly,*[5] Spring, 2012, pages 8 through 43.

The names of the occupations are listed along with the 2010 national employment level for that occupation, the anticipated change, in percentages, and the size of projected growth. The Spring 2012 *OOQ*[5] lists over 270 occupations calling these listings "a snapshot of the more descriptive listings in the *Occupational Outlook Handbook.*[5] The listings below include those occupations thought to be most helpful to rehabilitation counselors in their case planning and in seeking alternative employment for their clients. These jobs are among those most often considered in job placement of disabled workers.

In the Bureau of Labor Statistics (BLS) tables, occupations are grouped by growth rate. Occupations expected by 2020 to:

- Increase 29% or more are labeled "Much Faster than Average,"
- Increase 20% to 28 % are labeled "Faster than Average,"
- Increase 10 to 19% are labeled "about as fast as average,"
- Increase 3% to 9% are labeled "Slower than Average,"
- Decreases or Increases of 2% are labeled "Little or No Change,"
- Decreases of 3 to 9% are labeled "Decline Moderately,"
- Decreases over 10% are labeled "Decline Rapidly."

CHART 4

## OCCUPATIONS WITH THE MOST NEW JOBS, PROJECTED 2008-2018

| OCCUPATION | EMPLOYMENT 2010 | % CHANGE (+ -) ANTICIPATED (PROJECTED) | REASON |
|---|---|---|---|
| **MANAGEMENT, BUSINESS & FINANCIAL OCCUPATIONS** | | | |
| FOOD SERVICE MANAGERS | 320,600 | -3% | DECLINE MODERATELY |
| LODGING MANAGERS | 51,400 | 8% | SLOWER THAN AVERAGE |
| SALES MANAGERS | 342,100 | 12% | ABOUT AS FAST AS AVERAGE GROWTH CAUSED BY CONTINUED LIBRARY AUTOMATION. BEST OPPORTUNITIES IN HOSPITALS, CORPORATE AND SPECIAL LIBRARIES. |
| SURVEYORS | 51,200 | 25% | FASTER THAN AVERAGE |
| **LEGAL & EDUCATION OCCUPATIONS** | | | |
| COURT REPORTERS | 22,000 | 14% | ABOUT AS FAST AS AVERAGE |
| PARALEGALS & LEGAL ASSISTANTS | 256,000 | 18% | ABOUT AS FAST AS AVERAGE |
| TEACHER ASSISTANTS | 1,288,300 | 15% | ABOUT AS FAST AS AVERAGE |
| **HEALTHCARE PRACTITIONERS AND TECHNICAL OCCUPATIONS** | | | |
| EMT & PARAMEDICS | 226,500 | 33% | MUCH FASTER THAN AVERAGE |
| PHYSICIAN'S ASSISTANT | 83,600 | 30% | MUCH FASTER THAN AVERAGE |
| PSYCHIATRIC AIDE | 142,500 | 15% | ABOUT AS FAST AS AVERAGE |
| REGISTERED NURSE | 2,737,400 | 26% | FASTER THAN AVERAGE |
| **HEALTHCARE SUPPORT OCCUPATIONS** | | | |
| DENTAL ASSISTANT | 297,200 | 31% | MUCH FASTER THAN AVERAGE |
| HOME HEALTH AIDES | 1,017,700 | 69% | MUCH FASTER THAN AVERAGE |

| OCCUPATION | EMPLOYMENT 2010 | % CHANGE (+ -) ANTICIPATED (PROJECTED) | REASON |
|---|---|---|---|
| **HEALTHCARE SUPPORT OCCUPATIONS (CONTINUED)** | | | |
| MASSAGE THERAPISTS | 153,700 | 20% | FASTER THAN AVERAGE |
| MEDICAL ASSISTANTS | 527,600 | 31% | MUCH FASTER THAN AVERAGE |
| MEDICAL TRANSCRIPTIONISTS | 95,100 | 6% | SLOWER THAN AVERAGE |
| NURSING AIDES, ORDERLIES, & ATTENDANTS | 1,505,300 | 20% | FASTER THAN AVERAGE |
| OCCUPATIONAL THERAPY, ASSISTANTS AND AIDES | 36,000 | 41% | MUCH FASTER THAN AVERAGE |
| VETERINARY ASSISTANTS & LABORATORY ANIMAL CARETAKERS | 73,300 | 14% | ABOUT AS FAST AS AVERAGE |

**PROTECTIVE SERVICE OCCUPATIONS**

| | | | |
|---|---|---|---|
| CORRECTIONAL OFFICERS | 493,100 | 5% | SLOWER THAN AVERAGE |
| POLICE & DETECTIVES | 794,300 | 7% | SLOWER THAN AVERAGE |
| SECURITY GUARDS & GAMING SURVEILLANCE OFFICERS | 1,090,600 | 18% | ABOUT AS FAST AS AVERAGE |

**FOOD PREPARATION & SERVING-RELATED OCCUPATIONS**

| | | | |
|---|---|---|---|
| BARTENDERS | 503,200 | 9% | SLOWER THAN AVERAGE |
| CHEFS & HEAD COOKS | 100,600 | -1% | LITTLE OR NO CHANGE |
| COOKS | 2,050,800 | 8% | SLOWER THAN AVERAGE |
| FOOD & BEVERAGE SERVING & RELATED WORKERS | 4,110,400 | 12% | ABOUT AS FAST AS AVERAGE |
| FOOD PREPARATION WORKERS | 813,700 | 10% | ABOUT AS FAST AS AVERAGE |
| WAITERS & WAITRESS | 2,260,300 | 9% | SLOWER THAN AVERAGE |

## BUILDING & GROUNDS CLEANING & MAINTENANCE OCCUPATIONS

| OCCUPATION | EMPLOYMENT 2010 | % CHANGE (+ -) ANTICIPATED (PROJECTED) | REASON |
|---|---|---|---|
| GROUND MAINTENANCE WORKERS | 1,249,700 | 20% | FASTER THAN AVERAGE |
| JANITORS & BUILDING CLEANERS | 2,310,400 | 11% | FASTER THAN AVERAGE |
| MAIDS & HOUSEKEEPING CLEANERS | 1,427,300 | 8% | SLOWER THAN AVERAGE |
| PEST CONTROL WORKERS | 68,400 | 26% | FASTER THAN AVERAGE |

## PERSONAL CARE & SERVICE OCCUPATIONS

| | | | |
|---|---|---|---|
| ANIMAL CARE & SERVICE WORKERS | 234,900 | 23% | FASTER THAN AVERAGE |
| BARBERS, HAIRDRESSERS & COSMETOLOGISTS | 712,200 | 14% | ABOUT AS FAST AS AVERAGE |
| CHILD CARE WORKERS | 1,282,300 | 20% | FASTER THAN AVERAGE |
| PERSONAL CARE AIDES | 861,000 | 70% | MUCH FASTER THAN AVERAGE |
| RECREATIONAL WORKERS | 339,100 | 19% | ABOUT AS FAST AS AVERAGE |

## SALES & SALES RELATED OCCUPATIONS

| | | | |
|---|---|---|---|
| CASHIERS | 3,362,600 | 7% | SLOWER THAN AVERAGE |
| RETAIL SALES WORKERS | 4,465,500 | 17% | ABOUT AS FAST AS AVERAGE |

## OFFICE & ADMINISTRATIVE SUPPORT OCCUPATIONS

| | | | |
|---|---|---|---|
| BILL & ACCOUNT COLLECTORS | 401,700 | 14% | ABOUT AS FAST AS AVERAGE |
| BOOKKEEPING, AUDITING & ACCOUNTING CLERKS | 1,898, 300 | 14% | ABOUT AS FAST AS AVERAGE |
| COURIERS & MESSENGERS | 116,200 | 13% | ABOUT AS FAST AS AVERAGE |
| CUSTOMER SERVICE REPRESENTATIVES | 2,187,300 | 15% | ABOUT AS FAST AS AVERAGE |
| GENERAL OFFICE | | | |

| OCCUPATION | EMPLOYMENT 2010 | % CHANGE (+ -) ANTICIPATED (PROJECTED) | REASON |
|---|---|---|---|
| CLERKS | 2,950,700 | 17% | ABOUT AS FAST AS AVERAGE |
| INFORMATION CLERKS | 1,605,300 | 7% | SLOWER THAN AVERAGE |

**OFFICE AND ADMINISTRATIVE SUPPORT (CONTINUED)**

| | | | |
|---|---|---|---|
| POSTAL SERVICE WORKERS | 524,200 | -26% | DECLINE RAPIDLY |
| RECEPTIONISTS | 1,048,500 | 24% | FASTER THAN AVERAGE |
| SECRETARIES/ADMINISTRATIVE ASSISTANTS | 4,010,200 | 12% | ABOUT AS FAST AS AVERAGE |
| BANK TELLERS | 560,000 | 1% | LITTLE OR NO CHANGE |

**CONSTRUCTION & EXTRACTION OCCUPATIONS**

| | | | |
|---|---|---|---|
| BRICK MASONS, ETC. | 104,800 | 40% | MUCH FASTER THAN AVERAGE |
| CARPENTERS | 1,100,700 | 20% | FASTER THAN AVERAGE |
| CONSTRUCTION LABORERS & HELPERS | 1,250,200 | 25% | FASTER THAN AVERAGE |
| ELECTRICIANS | 577,000 | 23% | FASTER THAN AVERAGE |
| PAINTERS, CONSTRUCTION, & MAINTENANCE | 390,500 | 18% | ABOUT AS FAST AS AVERAGE |
| PLUMBERS, PIPEFITTERS & STEAMFITTERS | 419,900 | 26% | FASTER THAN AVERAGE |
| ROOFERS | 136,700 | 18% | ABOUT AS FAST AS AVERAGE |

**INSTALLATION, MAINTENANCE, AND REPAIR OCCUPATIONS**

| | | | |
|---|---|---|---|
| AUTOMOTIVE SERVICE TECHNICIANS & MECHANICS | 734,400 | 6% | SLOWER THAN AVERAGE |
| ELECTRICAL & ELECTRONICS INSTALLERS & REPAIRERS | 141,100 | 3% | SLOWER THAN AVERAGE |
| MILLWRIGHTS | 36,500 | -5% | DECLINE MODERATELY |
| SMALL ENGINE MECHANICS | 8,800 | 21% | FASTER THAN AVERAGE |

| OCCUPATION | EMPLOYMENT 2010 | % CHANGE (+ -) ANTICIPATED (PROJECTED) | REASON |
|---|---|---|---|
| ASSEMBLERS/ FABRICATORS | 1,626,500 | 5% | SLOWER THAN AVERAGE |
| LAUNDRY & DRY CLEANING WORKERS | 225,200 | 1% | LITTLE OR NO CHANGE |
| QUALITY CONTROL INSPECTORS | 416,400 | 8% | SLOWER THAN AVERAGE |
| SEWERS/TAILORS | 57,500 | 1% | LITTLE OR NO CHANGE |
| PRINTING WORKERS | 304,600 | -4% | DECLINE MODERATELY |
| WELDERS/CUTTERS SOLDERES/BRAZERS | 337,300 | 15% | ABOUT AS FAST AS AVERAGE |

**TRANSPORTATION & MATERIAL MOVING OCCUPATIONS**

| | | | |
|---|---|---|---|
| HAND LABORERS & MATERIAL MOVERS | 3,315,400 | 14% | ABOUT AS FAST AS AVERAGE |
| HEAVY & TRACTOR-TRAILER DRIVERS | 1,604,800 | 21% | FASTER THAN AVERAGE |
| MATERIAL MOVING MACHINE OPERATORS | 669,000 | 12% | ABOUT AS FAST AS AVERAGE |
| TAXI DRIVERS & CHAUFFEURS | 239,900 | 20% | FASTER THAN AVERAGE |

Occupational Outlook Handbook, Spring, 2012, Vol.56, Number 1.

# CHANGING WORK ENVIRONMENTS: ISSUES AFFECTING EMPLOYMENT OF REHABILITATION CLIENTS

Rehabilitation counselors providing vocational guidance and counseling to persons with disabilities need to be aware of some of the subtle changes taking place in the American economy, changes that will affect their clients in the workplace. The following are two issues currently raging in employment literature:

1. educational level of the worker, and

2. mutual loyalty in the workplace.

Both of these issues affect the employability and job retention for disabled clients.

## EDUCATIONAL LEVEL OF THE AMERICAN WORKER

Now, more than ever before, higher levels of education mean job security and more money. A 1995 study by the National Center of Educational Quality of the Workforce looked at 3100 US workplaces. The research found that an average 10 percent increase in the workforce's educational level led to an 8.6 percent increase in productivity. In contrast, a 10% increase in plant and equipment increased productivity by only 3.4 percent. In other words, according to this study, education has had a greater impact upon productivity than other factors of production. Moreover, Thomas Stewart of *Fortune* magazine reports that the only group of American men to make gains in their real weekly earnings since 1979 is college graduates, who are paid an average of 80 percent more than are high school graduates. In the new American economy, the evidence suggests more than ever it pays to have a higher level of education.

Certainly, these and other studies come as no real surprise to professionals in the rehabilitation counseling field. Poor vocational choices, particularly in their education, often have relegated clients to the most poorly paying and undesirable jobs in the economy. As evidence of the importance of education, these recent studies show a close linkage between education and productivity. For whatever reason, more education means that the person can accomplish more.

These studies show the income gap between persons with a high school and college education has grown continuously over the years. This suggests that staying in school, attaining higher levels of education, or learning additional, marketable skills have paid dividends to American workers in the new American economy and will likely do so in the future. The authors of *Generation Entrepreneur* suggest that in the future "there will be a shift where, instead of your income level being determined by what country you are from, it will be determined by your education level."[2, pg. 41]

## LOYALTY IN THE WORKPLACE

There seems to be no end to the amount of organizational change taking place in the new American economy. Workers in the new American economy can expect more career start-ups and job displacement. We are told of a time in the 1950s and 1960s when there was a kind of psychological contract between the organization and the workers, particularly at the management levels, where loyalty and dependability were rewarded over productivity. "Once upon a time corporations were like ocean liners," writes Richard Pascale, formerly of the Stanford Business School, "anyone fortunate enough to secure a berth cruised through a career and disembarked at retirement age. A clear agreement charted the voyage; in return for loyalty, sacrifice, bureaucratic aggravation, and the occasional demanding boss, you receive job security for life."[2, pg. 188]

Downsizing in the 1980s and 1990s marked the end of the psychological contract. For many of our clients, the news may come like a breath of fresh air. The concept of jobs for life for the loyal foot soldier was largely a mirage. There never was true job security in the corporate structure, even though the concept of a job for life became welded in the mind of a whole generation of workers. The truth is that even in the most stable times, at the lower levels of the hierarchy, where most of our clients work; people were hired and fired with abandon. To these workers, loyalty on the part of their employer was largely a myth.

Loyalty is a major concern in the American workplace today. On the one hand, with advanced technology, companies can react more quickly to market changes, as seen in recent years. This means frequent disruption in the lives of the workers. With the ever-present threat of a pink slip, employees are not likely to hang on and ride out the bad times. New information shows that there has already been a huge reduction in the loyalty employees feel toward their employer. In the 1998 survey, highlighted in the publication *Broken Bonds*,[2] the authors found that over 90 percent of the employees surveyed said their loyalty toward their employer had decreased, with two-thirds of them reporting that their loyalty had decreased a lot. The strength of feeling was consistent across the board, at all levels in organizations and in all age brackets.

For both the worker and the organization, the new psychological contract is more likely to be built on developing skills, worker productivity, and marketability of work skills rather than blind loyalty. In one sense, workers are now free to be in charge of their own jobs and careers in a marketplace that will determine their worth, but is being a "free agent" what American workers really want? In spite of the volatility of the current work place, with noise about a decreased work ethic, some sort of a physical relationship to the workplace is important to people at work. "People want to feel part of a team and of something bigger. They want to be connected," says Gerry Griffin, author of *The Power Game*.[2, pg. 210]

To substantiate this finding a new Fidelity survey found that one in four workers ages 22 to 33, part of the new recession generation, now say they want to stay with the same employer for life, up from 14 percent in 2008. "It's a touching commitment," say the researcher of the survey. The question that comes to mind is how many employers are really looking to be hitched." (*Newsweek*, December 31, 2009)

The reality is that people are loyal to the environment they spend every day in and to their colleagues. Moreover, although the "days of a job for life" have gone, people need to have a feeling of safety, confidence in the leadership, and a sense of ownership in the business.

Increasingly, the values that a company holds, such as "green companies," are important to worker motivation and their loyalty. The worker today must somehow feel that what they are doing is important and worthwhile. (We consider the subject of corporate values and their effect upon worker motivation in Chapter 5). What the company believes, says, and does, helps replace the notions about lifelong work. "People want to hold their heads up when they are with their peers. They don't want an embarrassed silence when they announce who they work for."[2, pg. 225] Company values, it seems, are the new route to developing loyalty among employees.

# CONCLUSION
# REHABILITATION COUNSELING IN THE NEW AMERICAN ECONOMY

As we attempt to understand the changing work environment in America, the implications for rehabilitation counselors become rather clear. Professionals must pay more attention to global concerns, such as market trends, employment outlooks, and the close relationship between the rehabilitation process and work. No longer is it enough to look for a job; we have to know how that job fits into the bigger picture. For instance, if the new psychological contract is to be built upon "developing skills, worker productivity, and marketability of work skills," rehabilitation counselors will need to examine training sources to determine the future worth of the training and the likelihood that the learned skills will increase productivity for the employer.

Rehabilitation counselors will also need to keep in mind that their clients are looking for stability in employment. They need to belong and to feel that they are contributing to the productivity of the company and that the job will be there in the future. The rehabilitation counselor's knowledge of the economy and the meaning of work may need to become a central feature of the counseling session.

In addition, as we explored in Chapter 5 on motivation, counselors cannot ignore the mounting evidence that adaptive skills (i.e., those skills that help a person get along and meet the changes in the work environment), are equally, or more important than work skills, when looking for work. Finally, rehabilitation clients, like other workers in the new American economy, will likely be looking at the reputation of their employer and the employer's standing in the community. The "big picture" may become an important factor in client job satisfaction and work retention.

# STANDARD REFERENCES ON EMPLOYMENT IN THE AMERICAN ECONOMY (ANNOTATED)

UNITED STATES DEPARTMENT OF LABOR, *DICTIONARY OF OCCUPATIONAL TITLES (DOT)*, 1991

This classic reference provides job descriptions for over 12,000 occupations. The 1991 edition contains cross references to the Guide for Occupational Exploration (GOE) to allow counselors to locate occupations with similar characteristics. Like Dot's earlier publications, this edition contains information to help counselors classify jobs and job requirements, e.g.,

- a strength factor code, the physical strength required for an occupation (sedentary, light, medium, heavy, and very heavy);
- information of the relative levels of ability (reasoning, math, and language); and
- a specific vocational code to measure the education and training required for entry into the occupation.

The DOT is not scheduled for future revisions. At present, the DOT is expected to be replaced by an electronic database titled The O*Net Dictionary of Occupational Titles.

THE O*NET DICTIONARY OF OCCUPATIONAL TITLES, 1988-1998 EDITION.

This is the first printed form of the information contained in the Department of Labor's research database called the O*Net (for Occupational Information Network). This new reference includes job titles and job descriptions, the educational requirements, the knowledge, skills, and abilities required for entry into the job, the general work activities, job characteristics, and references to other publications, such as the GOE. For the first time average wage figures are given. The most obvious omissions are the strength factor codes (sedentary, light, medium, heavy, very heavy), the relative levels of ability (reasoning, math, and language), and the specific vocational code.

OCCUPATIONAL OUTLOOK HANDBOOK, United States Department of Labor, 2000-2010.

The Handbook describes changes in the workplace, working conditions, training and educational requirements, earnings, and job prospects in a wide range of occupations. The Handbook covers over 250 occupations that account for about six of every seven jobs in the economy. The OOH is revised every two years. The latest edition contains cross-references to the O*Net as well as references to other sources of information about the occupation, (e.g., professional associations), along with web sites. The Handbook is particularly helpful in providing the outlook for an occupation clients may be considering.

OCCUPATIONAL OUTLOOK QUARTERLY, 2000, United States Department of Labor, Office of Employment Projections, Bureau of Labor Statistics.

This publication projects the future of industries, occupations, and jobs in the national economy. Each year, the Office of Employment Projections lists categories of occupations and projects their growth or decline in the near future. For rehabilitation counselors serving as a vocational expert in the disability programs of the Social Security Administration, this publication lists the numbers of jobs presently in the national economy. This reference was used extensively in preparing this chapter on the new American economy.

# TOPICS FOR GROUP DISCUSSION

1. Do you believe that work is therapeutic? That is, do you believe it is possible that clients get better medically when they are engaged in work activity?

   This is an important concept because it calls into question a main objective of rehabilitation counseling: finding jobs for persons with disabilities. It may be helpful to divide into small groups, discuss the value of work openly, and assign group reporters to report their findings back to the larger group.

2. In what ways can an understanding of the American economy be useful to rehabilitation counselors? Several reasons rehabilitation counselors need to have an understanding of the history and the economy are provided in this chapter.

Compile a list of reasons an understanding of jobs and employment history is useful to rehabilitation counselors in professional practice.

3. Describe some of the changes you have noticed in the jobs and occupations in our economy over the past several years. In other words, what are people doing today that they were not doing a few years ago? What changes do you believe will occur in the US economy over your work life?

4. Research has shown a decline in employee loyalty in America. Do you believe this is true? What is the proper relationship between an employer and worker? How can you, as a rehabilitation counseling professional, prepare for changes that will take place in your profession?

5. Research has shown that higher levels of education will be needed to succeed in the new American economy. One of the obstacles persons with disabilities have is that many clients have lower levels of education. How can rehabilitation counselors encourage clients to seek higher levels of education, to stay in school, and advance their vocational skills through vocational training?

## INDIVIDUAL EXERCISES

1. Using the information from Chapter 7 and the references at the end of the chapter, list the five (5) fastest growing occupations and the five (5) fastest declining occupations in the national economy and provide reasons for the rise and decline of each.

2. Using the 1991 *Dictionary of Occupational Titles* (DOT), locate the references for each of the ten (10) occupations identified in Question #1. Where there are several categories, decide which one you feel most closely approximates your understanding of the occupation.

3. Locate the occupations *Rehabilitation Counselor* and *Licensed Professional Counselor* in the DOT and make a list of the job duties described there. Write a short paragraph telling how the job duties in the DOT compare with your

understanding of these occupations and list the things that have made you choose this occupation for your career.

4. Look up the O-Net Dictionary of Occupational Titles on the Internet and list the KSA's for the following occupations:
   a. file clerk,
   b. receptionist,
   c. library assistant of clerk, and
   d. nursing assistant.

5. Appendix C of the DOT discusses the specific vocational preparation (SVP), the general educational development (GED), and the strength ratings (sedentary, light, medium, and heavy) for the various jobs described. Locate the SVP, GED, and strength ratings for the following occupations:
   a. watch assembly instructor,
   b. maintenance carpenter,
   c. lock assembler (furniture), and
   d. service station attendant.

# REFERENCES

[1]Birch, David (Fall, 1981). "Who Creates Jobs," The Public Interest, Fall, 1981, pp. 3-14.

[2]Crainer, S. & Dearlove (2000). *Generation Entrepreneur*. Great Britain: Pearson Education, Ltd. London, England.

[3]Dyer, L. (April, 1973). "Job Search Success of Middle-Aged Managers and Engineers," *Industrial and Labor Relations* Review.

[4]Farr, J. M. (1991) *The Very Quick Job Search*. Indianapolis, IN. JIST Works, Inc., 1993.

[5]*Occupational Outlook Quarterly*, Winter, 2011-2012, Volume 55, Number 4

[6]*Occupational Outlook Handbook*, Spring 2012, Volume 56, Number 1.

[7]Skills Gap Report (2005). A Survey of the American Manufacturers Workforce, National Association of Manufacturers, 2005.

[8]Wegmann, Robert, Chapman, Robert, and Johnson, Miriam (1989). *Work in the New Economy: Careers and Job Seeking into the 21st Century* Indianapolis, IN: JIST Works, Inc.

# CHAPTER EIGHT

# THE JOB SEARCH: HOW JOBS ARE FOUND IN THE NEW AMERICAN ECONOMY

# PREFACE

*A recent McKinsey Global Institute report found that 71% of workers in the United States hold jobs for which there is decreasing demand, increasing supply, or both.*[6] *We can only imagine the effects unemployment, job obsolescence, and the decreasing demand for jobs in this country have, and will continue to have, upon the aspirations of persons with disabilities.*

*In case planning, professionals in rehabilitation counseling must pay attention to global concerns, such as market trends, employment outlooks, and the close relationship between the rehabilitation process and work. No longer is it enough to look for a job; we have to know how that job fits into the bigger picture. If the new psychological contract in American business is to be built upon "developing skills, worker productivity, and marketability of work skills," rehabilitation counselors will need to examine training sources to determine the future worth of the training and the likelihood that the learned skills will increase productivity for the employer. Moreover, rehabilitation counselors will need to keep in mind that their clients are looking for stability in employment. Their clients need to belong, to feel that they are contributing to the productivity of the company, and to know the job will be there in the future. The rehabilitation counselor's knowledge of the economy and the meaning of work may need to become a central feature in counseling sessions with their clients.*

The Authors

To the Reader:

In Chapter 1: "The Rehabilitation Counselor's Role in Case Management," we opened with a phrase coined by Paul Ellwood "Rehabilitation is a Profession of Professions" and went on to explain that the base of knowledge that makes up the rehabilitation profession is drawn from a number of other occupations and professions.

If nothing more, in trying to lay the foundations for job placement, the preceding chapters provide a taste for how the rehabilitation profession absorbs and uses the knowledge from other professions to form its own distinctive body of knowledge. For instance, Chapter 1, "The Rehabilitation Counselor's Role in Case Management" and Chapter 4, "Client Motivation and Empowerment" demonstrate how the rehabilitation profession absorbs knowledge from the fields of industrial psychology and management to give structure to professional practice in rehabilitation; Chapters 2 & 3 on the "American

Character" draw upon the field of sociology to show how individual and group behavior affect work in our society; Chapter 5, "Client Function" and Chapter 6, "The Vocational Expert in Social Security Hearings" take a page from the professions of law and medicine to give us an understanding of how client function becomes the basis of vocational testimony for personal injury consultations and disability hearings with the Social Security Administration. Chapter 7, "The Counselor's Introduction to the World of Work in the New American Economy," traces employment patterns in the United States over the past 40 or so years and shows how the rehabilitation profession uses essential knowledge gained from American Economic History and the field of business. Throughout all of these chapters, the fields of counseling and counseling psychology provide the unifying framework for the profession, tying together the many facets of professional practice in rehabilitation.

Thus, as Paul Ellwood has suggested, rehabilitation counselors may be considered "generalists," in one sense, culling select areas of knowledge from many other professions to form their own professional identity. Yet, we have as our own domain, something the other professions lack and look to us for guidance, and what is that? Considered a central theme in the book and stated throughout, the principal domain of rehabilitation counseling is the presence of a disabling condition and the effects of that condition upon a person's ability to work.

The last three chapters of this book are concerned exclusively with the world of work. From this point forward, from Chapter 8 through Chapter 10, the focus narrows as we look at specific ideas and techniques for finding employment for our clients. Chapter 8 "The Job Search" is divided into three sections. Section 1 provides an overview of the methods job seekers use to conduct a job search in the United States. Section 2 provides suggestions for developing community resources to uncover job leads in a community. Section 3 provides guidance to counselors on how to design specific tools for the job search–the resume, the cover letter, and complementary correspondence–documents that most clients will need to prepare properly and use effectively when undertaking a job search.

Chapter 9 "The Selective Approach to Job Placement" and Chapter 10 'Networking for Jobs in the Hidden Job Market: A Client-Centered Approach" explore two well-documented methods used in rehabilitation to find jobs for persons with disabilities and offer new job-search techniques based upon contemporary developments in the job market. Again, as is our habit in rehabilitation, we borrow from the body of knowledge in two related occupational fields: the Fields of Personnel Management and the Field of Contemporary Job Search literature.

# SECTION 1
# HOW PEOPLE FIND JOBS

In a Department of Labor survey taken in January 1973, a sample of the population was asked how they went about their search for employment and which job search method led to their present job. This survey has more or less become the main statistical reference experts in the employment field have adopted since that time to separate the various job-search methods. The following were the results of the survey:

| Method | Percent |
|---|---|
| Applied directly to employer | 34.9% |
| Asked Friends and Relatives | 26.2% |
| Answered Newspaper Ads: Local | 12.2% |
| Answered Newspaper Ads: Non-Local | 1.3% |
| Used Private Employment Agencies: | 5.6% |
| Used State Employment Services | 5.1% |
| Used School Placement Office | 3.0% |
| Other | 13.0% |

Source: U.S. Department of Labor, 1975

The Survey discovered that most people found their jobs by:

- exploring a variety of traditional community resources,
- working through their friends and acquaintances, and
- making application directly to the place of employment.

A year later, in the fall of 1974, the Department of Labor commissioned Camil Associates for a follow-up study. Unlike the population survey of the year before, based upon a nationwide sample of households, the Camil study was limited to a set of 20 medium-sized cities with populations between 100,000 and 250,000. These were the conclusions reached in the Camil study:

| Method | Percent |
|---|---|
| Applied Directly to Employer | 30.7% |
| Asked Friends and Acquaintances: | 29.8% |
| Answered Ads in Newspapers: | 16.6% |
| Used Private Agencies | 5.6% |

| | |
|---|---|
| Used Employment Services | 5.6% |
| Asked Business Associates | 3.3% |
| Used School Placement Offices | 3.0% |
| Other | 5.4% |

Source: Department of Labor, 1976

Essentially, the Camil study confirmed the results of the population survey: most workers found their jobs in one of three ways:

- exploring *traditional job sources*–classified advertising, state employment services, private employment services, placement offices, and other related services,

- *networking* through family members, relatives, friends, and acquaintances, and

- making *direct application* to employers.

The three job-search methods are not pathways into three separate and distinct job markets. They all lead to jobs that lie within the community as a whole, but the effect is essentially the same. Each of the methods uncovers new job possibilities that the others are unable to reach. Therefore, for a comprehensive job search to make sure they reach each of the job sources counselors have to understand each of the market divisions they are trying to reach and the job-search methods needed to reach them.

In the first section of this chapter, we examine traditional job search methods, which normally involve the use of formal lists. These include the newspaper, the state employment services, private agencies, and placement offices. A discussion of the job search method for making a direct application to employers, including how to prepare applications, follows the presentation of the traditional job search methods. Chapter 10 "Networking in the Hidden Job Market: A Client-Centered Approach," explores the final job-search method addressed in the two surveys under "asking friends and acquaintances."

**Note**: *The employers that took part in the Camil study have a profile similar to employers in smaller cities and small towns as discussed in Chapters 2 and 3. Eighty-two percent (82%) of the employers participating in the study owned small businesses with 25 or less employees; the owner or the manager personally did the hiring; and informal methods of hiring predominated in these small firms. Employers hired from a group of people recommended to them or they hired from among those who came on their own initiative. It is reasonable to conclude, therefore, that the way people successfully find jobs in* *the medium-sized cities is essentially the same way people succeed in finding jobs in smaller cities and towns.*

*Obviously, the Internet was not available when the original survey by the Department of Labor and the follow-up survey by Camil Associates were taken. In recent years, searching for jobs on the Internet has received much publicity and web sites such as Monster.com, have become household names. The pervasive Internet has made its impact upon all of these job-search methods. Employer web sites can yield valuable information for making direct application to employers and seeking information about job referrals; and formal job lists from newspapers and other media sources in virtually every city and town in America are contained on the Internet. The use of the Internet to support the job search is discussed in Chapter 9, "The Selective Approach to Job Placement."*

---

## TRADITIONAL JOB SOURCES: WHERE MOST PEOPLE GO FOR JOBS

Ask just about anyone where jobs are found in a given community and they, almost without exception, will identify one or several of the following sources:

1. the local newspaper,
2. the State Employment Service,
3. private employment services, or
4. placement services

These are the best-known traditional job sources–the established places we have come to think jobs can be found in this country. These sources contain advertised listings for local jobs, accessible to the public in almost every city and town across the country. These sources list employers immediately in need of people for their businesses. In fact, they are about the only places that accumulate sizable lists of job openings. To access these jobs you really do not need to have any connection to the community at all. They are ready-made for the canvassing job seeker. We will look at each of these traditional job sources in more detail.

*Classified Advertising.* The local newspaper provides the most immediate access to the local job market. Any counselor can pick up the local newspaper, open to the classified advertising, and there are several pages listing employers with job openings in the community. Local employers and businesses have paid for these listings and they expect responses to their listings from the public. Usually, the addresses or the phone numbers contained in the ads lead to additional information about these jobs. In recent years, local newspapers have begun placing their classified advertising on the Internet so job seekers do not even need to purchase the publications.

Studies on the content of these ads and their rate of success among job seekers, however, have revealed a number of limitations to this job source. Knowledge of these limitations can both improve the success rate with the local media and eliminate some of the frustration counselors have had in using classified advertising.

First, since classified ads are open to the public, just about every job seeker reads them. Research indicates that about 10% of the workforce read the classifieds on a daily basis. In a city of 200,000 approximately 130,000 would be in the work force and about 13,000 would read the job listings. The percentage of readers is likely greater in small towns and small cities where local newspapers have a higher percentage of subscribers. Obviously, there is fierce competition for these jobs.[4, pg. 23]

Second, the ads may not be what they appear to be. Robert Wegmann[9] indicates that only three in ten are of interest to most job seekers. Private employment agencies seeking individuals to market to employers represent about 20% of the total listing.[pg.163] (Sunday ads are more likely to be dominated by private employment agencies; the daily classified advertising is more likely to list local job openings from local advertisers). In these ads employers often list qualifications they do not require. Work experience or educational levels are often raised to limit the responses to the more highly qualified applicants and some ads require interpretation. For instance, ads saying, "No experience needed; we train," usually means sales jobs on commission.

Third, the positions listed are often not the jobs most people want. Jobs in the classifieds stand at extreme ends of the spectrum. At one end are the service jobs. Roughly, 25% of the listed ads are for janitors, food service workers, domestics, etc. These are high-turnover jobs and for most people these jobs are their last resort. At the other extreme are the highly skilled jobs, including inquiries from private employment agencies seeking skilled workers. People with these skills often find good jobs through the classified listings. However, surveys have found that very few of the middle jobs–good paying jobs with reasonable status and security–are listed. Noticeably absent are jobs in finance, insurance, and real estate.

Fourth, the jobs in the newspaper do not seem to stimulate a good job match. These surveys show that at the end of the year only 12% of the people who had obtained their jobs through the classified ads were still employed in these jobs.

Finally, the classified ads cover only a small part of the local job market. According to the National Center for Career Strategies, Inc., these ads represent only about 14% of the available jobs in the United States. A study of two large cities in the United States reveals that employers make limited use of classified advertising. In one survey, 85% of the employers in San Francisco and 75% of the employers in Salt Lake City reported that in a typical year they do not hire anyone through the classified ads. Only one of seven seeking employment, reports Robert Wegmann, are able to find work by this source; and, as we have seen, many of these jobs are the lowest paying, most competitive, and least desirable jobs in the economy.[9, pg. 164]

Then why use classified advertising as a job source? There is an upside to classified advertising. Richard Bolles[2] in his 2007 publication found a much higher rate of success using the local media for certain levels of jobs. He says answering local newspaper ads produce a 5 to 24 percent success rate. This is a higher success rate than earlier writers have indicated or the success rate recorded in the Department of Labor survey and the follow-up Camil study. Even more important, the percentage rate may reach the upper level for entry-level, unskilled work. Bolles[2] says, "the higher the salary that is being sought, the fewer job hunters who are able to find jobs."[pg. 12] Conversely, persons seeking lower salaries find more success with classified advertising. This may be good news. In most cases, rehabilitation counselors are working with persons seeking entry-level, unskilled, and semi-skilled work.

Obviously, some people do find work through these ads, or businesses purchasing advertising through the media seem to think so. In 2002, businesses in the United States spent over 4 billion dollars on classified advertising.

In summary, the local newspaper can be a reliable, current source for some available jobs. (Local newspapers are much more effective in listing local jobs than non-local newspapers). When used with caution and the knowledge of what they are really saying, the newspaper can produce results. Richard Bolles[2] writes that classified advertising is most effective when used in combination with other job identification methods. As we see later in this chapter, other sections of the local newspaper can become just as useful as the classified ads.

*State Employment Service*. The state employment service is a referral service. Local employers provide the employment office with job openings and the employment service seeks qualified persons to refer from among their registered pool of applicants. State employment systems fill about 5% of the jobs nationally.

State employment offices have many of the same limitations as the local newspaper. They list a disproportionate number of jobs at both ends of the spectrum. Their listings are dominated at one end by low paying, low status jobs–semi-skilled and unskilled service jobs–which are normally filled shortly after being received. Robert Wegmann[9] found that these jobs represented 40% of the listings, triple their proportion in the job market. At the other end of the spectrum, the employment service lists jobs with high skill demands. These jobs are rarely filled by the employment service. Employers seeking specialized skills typically list these jobs with several services, such as private employment agencies; and presumably, other, more aggressive sources match the skilled applicants with these jobs.

Many of the better job listings are placed with the employment service by firms with federal contracts to meet the federal contract requirements and may not be real job openings. Few of the jobs from the state employment service fall into the middle range (e.g., teachers and retail service workers). Only one in twenty people using the employment service find jobs through this source. Half of the people placed by this service hold their jobs less than 30 days, indicating many of the placements are for temporary employment. However, the greatest limitation of the state job service may be that the jobs they list are usually two weeks old. Considering that the average job opening remains unfilled for about 15 days, many job seekers have had the opportunity to pass over these jobs before clients have access to them. By the time the registry is published, many of these jobs are not still available.

Few placement counselors report much success using these statewide services. Changes in their policies and procedures in recent years have made the jobs these services have to offer more difficult for rehabilitation counselors. Job leads are given to registered applicants, but may not be available for review by a counselor assisting persons with a disability to find employment. Moreover, applicants often receive ratings, and points are awarded to special groups, such as veterans and minorities. Some counselors report difficulty having their clients registered with the state employment service if their clients are receiving worker's compensation.

Still, there are exceptions! During our "Finding a Job on Main Street" conference in Minneapolis, Minnesota in 1998,[7] counselors from the state agency reported having a close relationship with the state employment service and placed clients regularly through the service. Moreover, some clients do fit into the special groups and receive preferential treatment in job referrals; others are able to find suitable openings. In addition, the employment service listings contain more of certain types of jobs–accounting clerks, janitors and porters, clerk-typists and truck drivers–than the want ads in the newspapers. Finally, some of the researchers in the job-search field report a higher rate of success using the state employment service. For instance, Richard Bolles[2, pg.13] records a success rate of 14%.

Although the state employment service is a state-federal program, there are some differences in the way local offices operate. Some of the offices, particularly in smaller communities, have a greater penetration into the local economy; and, therefore, are more in touch with local employment needs. It is likely these offices register a greater percentage of job leads from local employers. Some employment offices serve part of the personnel function for select employers within the community, providing applicant screening, aptitude testing, and applicant referral. Other offices provide job search workshops, career counseling, and other helpful services. Obviously, offices with greater penetration and special ancillary services receive a larger number of job listings from the employers they serve. Michael Farr found that "in some areas as many as 30% of the job seekers find jobs with the service.[4, pg. 26]

Most counselors, even in the private sector, insist that their clients register with the local employment office. For the best results in using the state employment system, many counselors and job market specialists recommend:

1. Counselors find out how the office in their community operates and what services the office will make available to their clients.

2. After registering, clients learn the name of the employment specialists assigned to them and stay in touch with them regularly.

As a rule, employment specialists with the state service have large caseloads. Clients seeking employment must find a way to "stick out" if they expect to locate job opportunities with this referral service. The best news for counselors using the government employment service may be that now most of their job postings for any region in the country are on the Internet at www.ajb.dni

*Private Employment Agencies*. Most of the private employment agencies, including head hunters, are in the business of matching job applicants with specific skills to a select group of employers who need those skills. Generally, the professionals in these agencies work for the people who pay the bill; usually this means the employer, not the job seeker. Typically, the professional staff working in these agencies is salespeople not career counselors.

About 5%, or one in twenty of all the people nationally, secure jobs through private employment agencies. Some researchers record a higher rate of success using private employment services for select groups. In *What Color Is Your Parachute* Richard Bolles[2] says "the range of success for this method has risen slightly in recent years, in the case of women not men: in a comparative recent study, 27.8 percent of female job-hunters found a job within two months by going to a private employment agency."[pg.12]

With such a low success rate, does it seem feasible to approach this job source? That depends. Private employment agencies are most successful with experienced people who have sharply defined work and/or educational skills and a consistent work record of experience in the same occupational field. In their skill identification, counselors may discover that a particular client has specialized skills and a consistent work record–qualities these salespeople can really sell to their employer contacts. In such a case, the private employment agency stands an excellent chance of placing clients in a good-paying job. They know the employers to contact and they have knowledge of some job openings. Normally, these agents are skilled in the presentation of their clients' credentials to potential employers, but a word of caution! The private employment agencies work for fees–fees from either the employee or the employer. These fees are substantial, often in the range of 10% to 15% of the first year's salary. To protect clients, counselors must make sure the employer bears the cost of the job placement.

How do these agencies learn about local jobs? The answer is that they are in the main stream of the local employment market, have a select number of employers they serve regularly, and they aggressively seek out jobs in the community. They call businesses, network among employers and others in the community, anticipate the upcoming needs for workers, and they seek out applicants, often through public advertising. In other words, their access to local jobs is not much greater than anyone else. Most of the information they use is readily available to job placement counselors and their clients.

*Placement Services: Institutions of Higher Learning & Vocational Schools*. Most colleges and universities as well as vocational schools provide job placement and other vocational services for their students. Institutions of higher education and some vocational schools may provide optional job counseling. In addition, most colleges, universities, and vocational schools have annual career days and a select number of employers visit the campus to interview rising seniors. For the most part, placement offices in schools and colleges are just another referral service. Companies and institutions in need of specialized skills the graduates have learned at a particular institution send in a list of job openings to the placement offices and the placement offices post the job openings on their job boards. About one in ten graduates find their jobs using placement services.

The success of placement services in vocational schools depends upon supply and demand factors. Some vocational schools train graduates in skill areas both local and non-local employers regularly need, such as secretarial skills, computer science, and accounting skills. Vocational schools attempt to anticipate employer needs and train their graduates in high-demand vocational areas, such as computer programming and legal assistance. These placement offices are generally successful in placing their graduates; and, often, if their job surveys are on target, the graduates are placed before graduation. Remember, most of these job sources rely upon anticipated need; few have arrangements with or promises from employers to hire their graduates. When looking for vocational training for clients, read with caution those advertisements guaranteeing a job at the end of the training.

Vocational training is always an option–and a good option–for those without the work skills in current demand from employers. Clients need to learn marketable skills and vocational schools provide excellent alternatives to long-term, expensive degree programs at universities and colleges. As long as the national economy stays in a state of flux, schools have a bright future if they are able to anticipate employer needs for skilled workers and provide the graduates to meet those needs. For obvious reasons, the placement offices at these vocational schools reserve the job listings for their own students. Therefore, they provide limited options for job seekers outside of the vocational programs they offer, even if the job seeker has training and credentials in those occupational areas.

## A Direct Approach to Medium and Large Employers: "Pounding the Streets for Jobs"

The Department of Labor Survey and the follow-up survey by Camil Associates found that about a third of the job seekers locate their jobs by direct application to employers. One of the difficulties with these statistics is that the surveys do not reveal how many of the job-seekers making direct application to employers received their job leads from one of the other sources (e.g., a traditional job source, a recommendation provided by a family member, a relative, or an acquaintance of theirs, or job leads and job lists provided on the Internet).

Regardless of how the statistics may have been skewed by the presence of other job search methods, most experts consider a direct approach to employers (i.e., job seekers going directly to the business or corporation) one of the more viable ways to search for jobs.

Medium-sized organizations (250-999) make up about 16% of all businesses in America and large organizations (1000 employees or more) make up another 13%. The larger the organization the more formal they are likely to be in their hiring procedures. Within most communities, there are a few large employers that provide a substantial number of jobs to local people. To accommodate large numbers of applicants, many of these employers use a formal hiring process with a human resources or personnel department being the initial contact with job seekers.

Although only 15% of the employers in this country use a human resources department, they still represent the source for a substantial number of available jobs. Before attempting to approach medium and large employers, counselors are encouraged to make sure their clients have a resume of qualifications and are able to discuss the contents of the resume. Counselors also need to make sure their clients are prepared to fill out an application, possibly by having a generic application already filled out before approaching the employer. In their job-skills training, counselors need to teach clients how to address difficult questions about their education, their disability, and their work history. (Later in this chapter, the preparation, and use of the resume and other documents, and proper ways to prepare applications and to address difficult questions are discussed).

*Approaching the Human Resources Department.* The point of contact for most job-hunters seeking work in medium and large organizations is the human resources (HR) department. (Some companies still use the more dated name, personnel departments). What most job seekers do not realize is that, typically, human resources departments do not hire new employees. They meet applicants, have them fill out an application, and provide an initial screening. If the applicant remains in consideration for employment after that, the human resources department refers the application to a hiring official in the department with a job opening. In some companies, the human resources department official conducts the initial hiring interview. Through the years, these departments have gained a less-than-attractive reputation. With tongue in cheek, Richard Bolles[1] records his impression of the kinds of people job-hunters are likely to encounter in the human resources departments. He says,

> *There are actually two kinds of personnel departments in those organizations that have them. Some personnel departments harbor the kindest and warmest souls in the entire building, who will move heaven and earth to help you find a job there. But other personnel departments harbor souls who either (a) are overzealous about protecting the people 'upstairs' or (b) get some perverse delight out of screening people out, or (c) are frightened about losing their own job. If you fall into their hands you can get screened out and never get to see the person who actually has the power to hire you–even though in fact you might be exactly the person the company is looking for.*[pg. 155]

Personnel departments have gained a reputation among job-hunters. They also have gained a reputation among professionals for their unsuccessful track record in choosing employees. Richard Bolles in, *What Color is your Parachute,*[2] records the results of a survey taken among a dozen top employers in the United Kingdom some years ago. Ironically, it was discovered that the chances of an employer finding a good employee from an interview conducted by a so-called human resources expert was 10% below the success rate of picking a name out of a hat.

Things seem to be changing in recruitment and hiring practices among medium to larger American organizations. First, more and more companies are taking over their own recruiting and hiring function, relying less upon outside recruiters and consultants. Joseph McCool, Editor-in-Chief of Kennedy Information Incorporated, says in the world of recruiting "things have changed. Today, job seekers will most likely have less contact with the middleman, job boards, executive recruiters, and human resource professionals. Instead, applicants will have more one-on-one contact with the hiring organization and the hiring manager directly."[3, pg. 95]

More and more companies are holding their human resource department managers accountable for the success of the hiring function. Joseph McCool says,

> *The people who hire are forced to demonstrate the impact their hires have on the company. Before, HR professionals and recruiters were thought of as non-strategic to the organization–serving functions that did not have an impact upon the bottom line. That is changing rapidly, and the hiring of human capital is now considered part of the overall corporate strategy and critical to the bottom line. In essence, HR professionals and recruiters are being held accountable for who they bring in and the retention of the best employees.*[3, pg. 93]

More and more companies are looking to their current employees to find and bring in top-quality talent. Joseph McCool says, "People want to work with people who hold the same values as they do, and current employees are an organization's best spokesperson to find and bring in that talent."[3, pg. 96]

Finally, more and more companies are showing a preference for hiring local talent. By hiring local talent companies avoid last-minute cancellations, the cost and stress of moving, and difficulties that sometime arise in the retention of non-local hires. There is clearly a perception that hiring locally results in more loyal employees. Joseph Cabral, Director of Corporate Human Resources for New York Presbyterian Hospital says, "Employers clearly look for and prefer candidates who are local. There are no two ways about it. In fact, many times when companies post openings on job boards, they state that only local candidates should apply. There is a definite preference for local talent."[3, pg. 110]

The patterns of tightening up the human resources programs by assuming greater authority of the HR function, holding HR departments responsible for their hiring decisions, using current employees to seek out talent, and focusing more on local hiring seems consistent with current trends in American industry. A relatively small talent pool and sharp competition both domestic and abroad leaves companies in the United States with little room for errors in hiring. Each individual counts! There is little "wiggle room" anymore! Mistakes count mightily! Therefore, it seems that the current rage about "corporate fit" and "organizational integration" may have a very practical, economic foundation.

The Internet seems to be the moving force behind these changes. The Internet has provided many creative options for companies desiring to assume more control over their own recruiting and hiring function. New buzzwords have appeared such as "electronic keyword screening," and "application tracking systems," all of which relate to ways companies are using the computer and the Internet for locating and retaining the right employees. Naray Viswanathan, Ph.D, President of Interview Exchange in Shrewsbury, Maine says, "Ten years ago a job search was a paper process. Today, the entire market has changed and many, many companies use Web-based applicant screening software and tools to facilitate the evaluation and selection of candidates to interview."[3, pg. 97]

Now, companies can place ads on the Internet for new employees and expect responses from candidates at all levels. Jim Oddo, Staffing Manager for Oxford Health Plan, Inc. writes,

> *The Internet has emerged as an amazing tool for companies and candidates. Three years ago, the Internet was not a good source to recruit nurses and other health care professionals. Today, about 50 to 60 percent of health care professionals are putting their resumes on line. As such, companies like Oxford now place their ads online in anticipation of finding the right candidate without having to pay a 20 to 25 percent fee to a recruiter.*[3, pp. 102-103]

Moreover, companies can design their Web sites to show not only what products the company makes and their general philosophy but also to display their corporate personality and show the kinds of people who will likely fit into their corporate culture. Jo Bredwell, Senior Partner for JWT Specialized Communications says about web sites:

> *Companies describe themselves both verbally and geographically when discussing the types of people who work there. Many times organizational advertisements will show photographs of people working. These photos are carefully chosen to depict the types of work being done and create a specific image and feeling.... Is the feeling formal or conservative? Is the photo electrifying, with a sense of energy and power? Does the company project a willingness to do new things? Companies express their personality just like people do.* [3, pg. 104]

## WHAT RECENT TRENDS IN EMPLOYMENT MAY MEAN TO PERSONS WITH DISABILITIES SEEKING JOBS

How do these new trends in the human resource systems in large companies affect rehabilitation clients seeking jobs in these companies? These trends will probably have a positive effect upon the hiring of persons with disabilities. If employers prefer hiring new employees locally, this is good news for injured workers and rehabilitation clients. Some of the reasons for hope:

- Persons receiving rehabilitation services seem to have less mobility than the general population. Part of this has something to do with class distinction, as most of the clients in rehabilitation come from groups labeled in this book as the working people and baseline people. Persons from these groups tend to be reluctant to move from their local neighborhoods to find work in other communities. As a rule, working class people have not been part of the "exodus from the village" described in such standards of American literature as Thomas Wolfe's *You Can't Go Home Again*.

- In these large companies, referrals are being received and processed by persons in departments closer to where the job is being performed. If company employees help in the recruiting process and these companies are truly committed to a cultural fit, this is more good news for injured workers and rehabilitation clients, particularly those with vocational skills. Historically, human resource departments tend to be sensitive toward special need program initiatives and make exception for persons with limitations. Affirmative action programs have often been housed in these human resource departments.

More good news, particularly for well-qualified applicants: most of the larger companies have web pages in place on the Internet. These web pages are a rich source of information for applicants about these larger companies. As described above, many web pages attempt to present an image of the company that helps the applicant gain a feel for what it is like to work in that business environment. Many of these web pages contain names of persons and their positions that allow an applicant to go directly to the person doing the hiring and by-pass some of the red tape and unrelated layers of management. The job-search literature is relatively uniform in recommending that prior to making application to organizations, large and small, applicants study the contents of the web page for each company.

Finally, if larger American companies are expecting their own employees to seek out and recruit local talent, and if the hiring is done by company personnel close to where the job is to be performed, more of the jobs will be found in the "hidden job market." In fact, in local hiring the odds increase that a person in the client's network will know the person or know of the person in charge of the hiring. In order to access these "hidden job market" jobs, rehabilitation counselors will need to have their clients more involved in the job search, making contact with these companies through family, friends, and acquaintances. The job-search strategy suggested in Chapter 10 "Networking in the Hidden Job Market: A Client-Centered Approach" and in the companion booklet, the "Job-Search Organizer," take the counselor and their clients step-by-step through some of the ways clients and counselors can penetrate the "hidden job market" and locate at least some of these jobs.

## THE EMPLOYMENT APPLICATION

Within the corporation, the employment application is seen as a measure for reducing the number of applicants to the most qualified persons for the job. Typically, the human resources department receives the applications, and someone from the department reviews them, reduces the number of applicants to the most qualified, and sends a few applications to the hiring official in the designated department. The person doing the hiring, in many cases the job supervisor, reviews applications of the highest-rated candidates and invites the finalists to come for a personal interview. From these finalists a selection is made.

That is the way the process is supposed to work, but seldom does the process that begins with the application reach its ideal objective. As indicated, the person doing the screening may not know the job to be performed. As a result, that person may use faulty criteria for eliminating candidates. In fact, they may not base their decisions upon job skills at all. Appearance of the applicant or the application, responses that reflect negatively upon a candidate or personal bias often come into play. Moreover, the application on average receives the attention of the reviewer for less than 60 seconds; rarely are they reviewed again. It thus becomes obvious that the application takes longer to prepare than the reviewer takes to process the application.

There are ways to improve a client's chances for having their application get beyond the initial review. Here is some advice from the experts:

- *Take the application home.* If possible, have clients take the application with them and return it later rather than try to fill out the form amid the stress and pressure of the human resource department. In this way, a counselor has the opportunity to review the form with a client to make sure they have read the directions, filled out the form neatly and completely, and answered the difficult questions appropriately. (It is often wise to run off a copy of the application form before trying to fill in the information. Corrections can be made and still have a clean copy to submit).

- *Attach a cover letter to the application.* Cover letters (described later in this chapter) are a powerful influence for getting clients to the interview. Cover letters are frequently used with resumes; but many job seekers do not know that cover letters can also be used with an application. If the human resources office will allow the use of a cover letter, and most do, a client has the opportunity to state boldly how their skills relate to the job and remove the possibility that inexperienced reviewers, unfamiliar with the job, will exclude the application based upon the lack of work-related experience. The cover letter allows a client to assume some of the initiative in an otherwise passive process. Cover letters almost always get read.

- *Attach a resume to the application.* The more care that is taken with the preparation of the application, the greater the chance clients will be among the finalists. One of the most important parts of the application is the work history. Seldom is the space on the application sufficient to cover the work history as it is presented on the resume. The worst the reviewer can do is disallow the resume. Try placing the resume in with the application. This may be a case where it is easier to beg forgiveness, "sorry, I didn't know" than to ask permission, "may I include my resume with the application."

## HOW TO ANSWER PROBLEM QUESTIONS ON AN APPLICATION

Applications provide an employer with a snapshot of the job seeker, but when the applications are reviewed, the person narrowing the list of applicants may have never seen the person. As a result, the judgments they make are based upon what they see in the writing before them. In preparing the application unless care is taken in answering these questions, much of that information can yield a negative impression of the client. The screening process designed to answer the question: "how can I locate the best-qualified person for the job" often becomes "what information can I find out from this application to eliminate this person from consideration."

The following suggestions are to help clients avoid elimination based upon the responses contained in the application. In all instances, honesty must prevail. Fraudulent statements on the application may result in dismissal later, but clients may avoid elimination during the screening process by knowing how to deal with difficult questions. The following are some suggestions.

*Questions about Race, Religion, Age, Disability, and National Origin.* It is illegal to omit persons from consideration for a job based upon their race, their personal beliefs, their age, or their nationality. Most corporations have eliminated these questions from their applications; some smaller employers may still use a form that includes some of these questions. If questions are asked on the application that have no relevance to performing the job, but may stereotype the client, the best advice seems to be to leave the space blank, even though blank spaces on an application draw attention to themselves. Another alternative may be to write in the space "will discuss in the interview." If the questions relate to a client's ability to perform the job, like being of driving age, then by all means, answer the question honestly.

*Questions about Disability and Physical Limitations*. The Americans with Disabilities Act (ADA) implemented in July 1992 prohibits discrimination in all employment practices including job application procedures, hiring, firing, advancement, compensation, training, and other terms, conditions, and privileges of employment. This act covers all employers with 15 or more employees.

Under the Americans with Disabilities Act, an employer cannot deny employment to a qualified individual based upon disability. ADA prohibits employers from making inquiries about any disability an applicant may have, or the nature or severity of a disability. Conversely, an employer may ask questions about the ability of an applicant to perform the duties required of the position, either with or without accommodation. A client may find questions on the application, such as "is there any reason why you would not be able to perform any function in the job description for the position you have applied."

Although not required by law, an employer may provide a job description along with the application. If such a description is not available, clients with disabilities need to know how the job they seek is normally performed in the work force. (Counselors can be helpful to clients in determining the functional requirements of a position). Once satisfied that the client can perform all the required job functions, the answer to the question is *no*.

On the other hand, if the client cannot perform the full duties required of the job, both the rehabilitation counselor and the client may need to examine the vocational objective; but not all may be lost! The client may be capable of performing the essential job duties and simply needs an accommodation that the potential employer may be willing to provide. In such instances, rehabilitation counselors can be helpful as an intermediary to help the employer make this vital decision. Another possibility is if the client believes duties of the job may be performed with a simple work accommodation provided by the employer, a client may choose to leave the space on the application blank or state "will discuss in the interview."

Further discussion of ADA is beyond the scope of this text, but counselors working in job placement or career counseling with a person with physical or mental limitations need to familiarize themselves with the basic tenets of the law. ADA is a comprehensive Act and there are many books and resources available to counselors.

*Questions about Workers' Compensation.* Worker's compensation is payment a client may have received for a job-related injury or illness. Employers have insurance to cover work-related injuries and illnesses; but the rates are based upon employers having to pay compensation. Many employers will not knowingly hire persons who have previously received worker's compensation because of their fear of a rate increase or fear that the applicant will have another illness or accident, even though laws in most states provide protection to the employer for prior work-related injuries.

Under ADA, an employer may not make inquiries about an applicant's worker's compensation history before making a conditional offer of employment. After the conditional offer of employment has been made, however, an employer may inquire about a person's worker's compensation history in a medical inquiry or examination, as long as the inquiry is made of all applicants in the same job category.

*How many job-search methods are enough?* We have examined in detail five different job-search methods. Four of these–classified advertising, the state employment service, private agencies, and placement offices in schools and colleges–were in what we called the traditional job market. The fifth job search method, just completed, explored the pros and cons of approaching large employers directly. In Chapter 10: "Networking for Jobs in the Hidden Job Market: A Client-Centered Approach" we will explore yet another job-search method, bringing the number to six. How many is enough? Are some better than others? Let's look at what some of the research in the job-hunting field has to say.

For readers unfamiliar with job-search literature, the most widely known text in the job-search field is *What Color Is Your Parachute* by Richard Bolles,[1] first copyrighted in 1970. A revised edition, under the same title, has been written and published almost every year since that time. The research and job-search methodology are updated in each year's edition. In his 2007 edition, Richard Bolles[2] provides an answer to the question of how many job-search methods to use in finding jobs for our clients. He says:

> *Investigators discovered some years back that one-third of all job-hunters give up by the second month of their job hunt. They stop job hunting. (Of course, they have to resume their job search, somewhere further down the road, when things get really desperate). But why do they give up so soon? Well, it was found that giving up was related to how many job-hunting methods a job-hunter was using. In a study of 100 job-hunters who were using only one job method, typically 51 abandoned their search after the second month. That's more than one-half of them. On the other hand, of the 100 job-hunters who were using several different ways of hunting for jobs, typically only 31 abandoned their search by the second month. ...further research revealed that your chances of uncovering a job does indeed increase with each additional method that you use–but only up to four, in*

*number. If you use more than four methods of job hunting, your likelihood of success begins to decrease, and continues to decrease with each additional method that you add to your job search.*[pg. 8-9]

The four (4) job-search methods we recommend for use by rehabilitation counselors are:

- classified ads,
- state employment services,
- approaching employers directly, and
- locating jobs in the hidden job market.

These job-search methods seem most compatible with the ways jobs are found in our field of rehabilitation. As you have read earlier in this chapter, the use of the Internet to find jobs for rehabilitation clients supplements each of these methods rather than offers a different job-search alternative.

# SECTION # 2 DEVELOPING AND MARKETING COMMUNITY RESOURCES

National estimates show that close to seventy percent (70%) of the jobs in a given community pass through the informal network. Before a job reaches the stage where advertising becomes necessary, someone takes the job with whom the employer feels meets at least the minimum qualifications; or an employee knows a family member or friend looking for work and recommends the friend for the job; or an acquaintance knows a person with the work skills the employer needs; or other employers refer someone they have met to the employer with the job. Thus, most jobs, filled through an informal network, never reach the traditional job sources. These jobs are in what has come to be known as the "hidden job market."

If clients are to enter the "hidden job market," their counselors have to find ways into this informal stream of communication where the decisions are made, and in some way influence the hiring process on behalf of their client. Counselors have to set the table, so to speak, make themselves visible in the community (i.e., let other people know what they do for a living, namely, reconnect disabled people or injured workers to the community, and market the informal network for job leads). The following are at least some of the places to go and some of the people counselors can talk with along the way while they make use of community resources. We will explore informal ways to identify job leads using community resources that are readily available in most communities. (Chapter 10: "Networking in the Hidden Job Market: A Client-Centered Approach" and "The Job-Search Organizer" provide additional ways to identify and surface job leads using family, friends and acquaintances).

## STUDY THE LOCAL NEWSPAPER

The local newspaper is clearly the place to begin marketing the community. The classified section of the newspaper, as noted earlier, identifies many of the most immediate job openings and the locations of these job openings, and this source of information is easy to use. You do not have to get involved with anyone. There is a larger picture of the community that emerges from other sections of the local newspaper that often goes unnoticed in our haste to undertake the job search and show results for our time. A study of these other sections almost always provides insight to many of the best jobs and introduces the counselor to potential openings in the "hidden job market."

Unlike national newspapers, (i.e., *The Washington Post, The New York Times*, and *USA Today*), local newspapers are devoted almost exclusively to local events. Local people purchase these newspapers and they expect an abundance of space devoted to activities in their community. William Allen White[10] spent most of his work life as editor-in-chief of the Gazette in Emporia, Kansas. Listen to what he has to say about how the local papers in most communities are organized. He says, "On the first page, 'the parlor of the paper' the *Gazette* features news of national and international significance with formal headings in bold print. Beginning with the second page, 'they and we go around in our shirt sleeves, calling people by their first name; and letting out the family secrets of the community without much regard for the feelings of the supercilious."[pg. 6]

The editorial policy of the *Emporia Gazette* reveals the mission of the local newspaper: to give all the space possible to local news, name as many community residents as possible, and describe the activities of local citizens. William Allen White[10] says that the *Gazette* is like "hundreds of other newspapers across the country."[pg. 6]

Here are some of the things the local papers disclose about business and employment in the community. The local newspaper announces business openings; prints editorials concerning local developments and local problems; names employers in the community; scatters bits of information about local people, particularly employers; and identifies plans for business and community expansion, plans that can lead to predictable jobs.

Most newspapers have reading rooms for counselors to examine current and back issues of the newspapers. By taking the time to review past issues, counselors gain a better understanding of the ways the paper is organized and see continuity among community events. For instance, the reader can keep up with the progress of an incoming business or gain an understanding of how national trends over time are affecting the local economy. In addition, in these reading rooms a counselor can make contact with staff people who follow community events regularly. These staff people are very often wonderful sources of information about local jobs and employment trends. Finally, today most newspapers not only place their classified advertising on the internet, but whole newspapers can be found online. But a word of caution: don't let the impersonal use of the computer cause you to overlook the personal touch of personal contacts and the newspaper reading rooms, particularly in small towns and cities.

## VISIT THE CHAMBER OF COMMERCE

The Chamber of Commerce is a primary resource for published material about the business community and about business and industrial developments in the community. Their publications typically include a list of businesses that are members of the Chamber of Commerce, a list of local manufacturers, the location of open housing, and street maps of the community.

Moreover, the state division of the Chamber of Commerce in many states publishes an industrial directory that references manufacturing and mining firms by county throughout the state. The listings include the address and phone number of the firm, the corporate officers, and the products produced by the company. The products are the counselor's clue to the kinds of jobs in these firms and the job skills needed by these employers. Used in conjunction with individual company web sites, the industrial directory is an excellent reference for directly approaching medium to large businesses. Except for the industrial directories, most of these publications, including the maps, are either free or at a small cost.

The Chamber of Commerce has much more to offer than the "freebies" at the front desk. Did you know that the Director of the Chamber of Commerce in most communities attends the opening of almost every new business or corporation? In the business section of the local newspaper, you will often see the Director standing with new business owners. The Chamber sets up this publicity for new businesses with the local media, providing free advertising for the business and the Chamber. If you want to know what businesses have opened recently, or those that are coming into the community in the near future, the Chamber is the place to find out this information.

Did you know that the Director of the Chamber of Commerce attends the monthly meetings of the city council and/or the board of supervisors where all of the proposals planned for the community are considered? Most of us would not readily attend these meetings, but by getting to know the Director of the

Chamber of Commerce, a counselor will have access to this information, some of which may prove valuable in placement planning. When you know the right questions to ask, the Chamber will probably have the right answers. Go into the Chamber office and introduce yourself; tell them what you do–find jobs for persons with disabilities–and you will likely meet a helpful friend.

## ASK PEOPLE WITHIN THE COMMUNITY

Almost everyone in the community knows what is going on locally. They know the way the community conducts its business; they know the people you need to contact; and they know the location of the main centers of employment. Regardless of their position in the community, anyone may have the potential for surfacing a job lead.

In Chapters 2 and 3, we discussed community organizations in America, broke down society into groups and classes, and listed several characteristics for each. The research shows that some of the most prominent people in the community hold jobs that deal with the public; these are "acceptable jobs." Many of the small shops in the community are owned by wives and families of prominent lawyers, bankers, and public officials. Their lofty position and their regular interaction with all groups of people give them insight into the inner workings of society. They know just about everybody. They are excellent contacts; and as they often hold views that are more liberal, they may show a willingness to provide information about jobs and job leads for those people doing "meaningful work" like finding work for persons with disabilities.

As presented in Chapter 3, those among the working people know where work is being performed. What they may lack in influence over the direct hiring process, they make up for in the daily contact with the people doing the work. In locations where employment strategies have become more local, and employers are actively seeking to hire people in the community, the recommendations of working people often carry a great deal of weight in hiring decisions.

One counselor reports how the influence of the client's family–all working people–presented a unique opportunity in job placement. Her client was a 35-year-old former grocery clerk living in a coal mining area where the local jobs in the production industries were on the decline and most of the remaining jobs required heavy physical labor. Jesse had been injured on-the-job and could no longer do heavy work, but Jesse's family have a reputation as hard-working, honest people, well thought of in the community. In fact, there were six children in this family of miners and all of them had excellent work records.

The counseling approach used with Jesse was to gather the family together for an informal conference. The counselor then related to them the planning efforts that had gone into finding work for Jesse, the obstacles encountered so far, and the kinds of jobs Jesse would likely be able to do given his physical limitations. Then, she simply asked them to help her locate job leads for her and Jesse. This is a simple kind of networking, but one that seems to work well in job placement for injured workers. The number added up to nine job seekers, including his mother and father. Needless to say, that was enough.

In addition to the more prominent people, who know just about everybody, and the working people who know the people doing the work, you can include even the most casual acquaintance in the community. One of the best-kept secrets, that every business owner knows, is that people you do business with like to do business with you. Restaurant owners, motel and hotel proprietors, and service stations–places you will likely patronize–understand the practice of reciprocity; and helping you uncover job leads in the "hidden job market" is just one way of saying "thank you for your business."

The grass root network is an excellent strategy for locating job leads, particularly at the beginning of the job search: desk clerks at the motels where you stay, waiters in the restaurants where you dine, clerks in stores where you purchase personal goods, and salespeople in stores you visit to survey jobs and observe work being performed. Once you explain what you do–assist persons with physical or mental limitations to find new work–these casual contacts cannot resist becoming interested in your work and show a willingness to become at least minimally involved.

You see, most people know from experience the feelings of emptiness and quiet desperation that accompanies disability and unemployment. The satisfaction you receive from your job–seeing renewal and hope in the lives of your clients–is the same satisfaction they receive in knowing they have made a difference in the lives of their neighbors. Most people identify with their community and even if they do not know your client, they recognize the human need you serve.

The people counselors meet in the community cannot be involved, however, unless counselors allow them to be. Marketing the abilities of a client can be as easy as telling a story–a story about someone leading a healthy life who had their independence taken away by an accident or illness, suffered through a long recovery, and now want a new start in life. Each story is different, and each story is the same. People easily relate to accounts of persons with disabilities. Most of the time, they listen with interest and empathy. Moreover, your willingness to talk with them signals your openness and interest in them and their community. As often happens, the next time you meet them, they are bubbling over with information and suggestions to guide you in your job search. In your self-disclosure, you have made a friend and a contact for all time.

## VISIT A SERVICE CLUB AND ATTEND THE MEETING

Over a hundred years ago, Alexis de Tocqueville, the French observer of the national scene, recognized the tendency to join groups for a variety of purposes as a salient characteristic of the American people. Today, that tendency has continued in spite of the rise of American individualism and the mask of self-sufficiency that has characterized the latter part of the 20th century to the present. In most communities, special interest organizations still exist and continue to flourish.

The most prominent and accessible among these special-purpose organizations is community service clubs: for men, the Kiwanis, the Lions, the Rotary, the Elks, and for women, the Soroptomist Club. Community Service Clubs have as their purpose:

- to bring together people with similar interests,
- to sponsor community service projects, such as youth sports leagues and projects for the disabled, and
- to strengthen business and professional relationships.

In the past, the Lions, Rotary, and Kiwanis clubs excluded women. Today each of these clubs actively recruit women into membership, (Soroptomist clubs, however, remain a community service club for professional women). These clubs provide members a way to become involved in improvements within the community and associate with persons of like interests.

Most of these clubs meet once a week for a meal and a program. (What a great way to learn about the community while getting to know its people!). As a member, you will be given the chance to tell others about your business and to enlist the assistance you need to get your job done. You need not feel like a mercenary by associating with a club for the purpose of improving your business. That very purpose is the reason for the establishment of the clubs cited above and why they continue to exist. All of the members are there because being involved in the community is good business and good for business.

While most service clubs may have a similar purpose, all clubs are not the same. Within a particular club, class differences are unimportant; everyone associates on a first-name basis, but clubs are often formed along class lines or, at least, lines of similar interest. Counselors building a network within their community will need to choose a club where employers congregate. In most communities, the choices are the Kiwanis, the Rotary, and the Lions clubs. Some organizations, such as the Masons are ritual-bound lodges, exclusively for men; the Elks, the Moose, the Eagles, and the Odd Fellows clubs are social lodges typically for working people. Whereas the latter clubs offer social outlets, they are limited in their ability to help counselors surface job leads as most of the members are working people, not employers.

An additional benefit of the service clubs is that each will have similar clubs located in other communities. As a member of one club, counselors are welcomed, even encouraged, to attend meetings of that club when visiting other towns and cities. One counselor gives this example of how his membership in the Kiwanis club helped him in a job placement assignment. After a particularly frustrating experience in placing an injured worker outside his native community, the counselor contacted the local club in that community and attended the next meeting. He was known to some of the members from having attended their meeting with an inter-club group. When he was introduced as a guest, he told them about his profession and the difficulty he was having in placing his client. From this brief encounter, he was able to connect with the community and gain job leads, one of which took him closer to the eventual placement.

Service clubs are a ready-made way for counselors to gain access into the informal network where most local jobs pass. The clubs are established for business networking and for getting community business done. The possibilities for business and professional contacts are endless.

## MARKETING AMONG THE DECISION-MAKERS

Earlier we talked about ways for approaching large to medium businesses. Yet, in a given community, over 70% of the jobs are in small businesses, businesses with 1 to 29 employees. The owners of these businesses are not hard to reach. Likely, they work long hours in their places of business and are readily accessible. They know that everyone entering their places of business represent new business opportunities. Most of the time these owners will take time from their busy schedules to interview people entering their business. Typically, these owners are involved in community activities. They respect people willing to work, and they are seeking to know about people looking to better themselves even when they do not have a hiring situation.

The approach counselor's use will likely determine whether or not the first introduction to the owner is the last meeting or the beginning of an on-going relationship. To illustrate the way counselors can approach these small business owners, we will take a few useful ideas from successful sales representatives who for years have called upon these kinds of business.

Sales representatives fall into two groups: order takers and professionals. The order-takers have a passive approach to the market. They enter a business with the idea that if they hit the owner at the right time, use the right methods of persuasion, or just "get lucky," the owner may bless them with an order. Hope, chance, and circumstance prevail in the life of the order-taker. Success depends upon the reaction on the part of the owner rather than upon the order-takers own action. The philosophical basis for the order-taker is the old adage that if you make so many calls a day, the magic number seems to be around 12, you will make enough sales for a marginal living. Remarkably, some salespersons canvass this way day after day, year after year.

Unfortunately, many job-placement counselors operate like order-takers. Those using the "canvas method" are good examples. These counselors take the approach that employers hire their clients because of their concern for disabled people or out of empathy for people out of work. These counselors weave their way through the business community hoping to find a few bleeding hearts, or get a few lucky breaks in what is otherwise an ulcer-producing experience. If their timing is right, the owner is in a receptive mood, and employees are desperately needed, management and labor can come to terms. Sometimes placements are made in this way; like the order-taking sales representative, with enough "cold calls" sometimes counselors press the right button.

Here is the way the real professionals approach the marketplace. Professional salespersons know that in order to market their products and develop a long-term relationship with a particular business, they must ask themselves "how does my product fit into the plans of the buyer? What needs of the business will my product satisfy?" They see themselves as a resource to the business. Before they try to sell their products, they take the time to research the business–learn the owner's name, observe the competing products carried by the business, and design a plan to present to the owner demonstrating ways the features and benefits of their product can increase the productivity of the business. In the past, gathering this type of information on businesses may have taken years; today, so much of this information, even about some of the smallest businesses, is readily available on the Internet. (Chapter 9 "The Selective Approach to Job Placement for Persons with Disabilities" explores additional uses of Web sites for locating jobs in the local community).

Effective placement professionals go through a similar process. They know that a job-match and a long-term job for their client can only come about when their clients are seen as contributors to the future of the business. Their first step is to determine "how can my client be a contributor to the business?" Likewise, before entering the business, they learn the owner's name, if for no other reason than knowing the name of the owner is a common courtesy. It is also important to learn something about the business–the products the business makes and/or sells, the number of employees in the business, the kinds of jobs they perform, the job skills required to do the work, whether or not the business provides appropriate work for injured or rehabilitated workers, and something about the general economic outlook for that kind of business.

## A FINAL NOTE

Marketing within the community and developing community resources opens on a regular basis the "hidden job market" that produces job leads for persons with limitations. If rehabilitation counselors become involved in their community and acquire a reputation as a market and employment resource to business, placements come as a by-product of their involvement and expertise. Think this can't be done? John Haas worked for the Virginia Department of Rehabilitation in Winchester, Virginia, a community with a population of about 40 thousand people. He became known as the "rehabilitation man" in the community. When employers had a job opening, they called John. In the worse days of the recessions (e.g., the recession of 1980-1981, when counselors were crying about bad markets and the need for smaller caseloads), John placed over 200 people each year in local jobs from his caseload. He had made himself indispensable to the community and the community responded with jobs for John's clients.

# SECTION # 3
# TOOLS OF THE JOB SEARCH

Choosing the right market strategies is an important step before conducting a job search. We have looked at six different ways for locating jobs within a community and the way to develop community resources that are readily available in almost every community, large and small. Prior to beginning the job search, rehabilitation counselors need to help their clients prepare to meet employers.

We cannot assume that clients are ready to undertake a job search. Be cautious when clients tell you they have a resume already prepared and that they know how to conduct a job search. Mounting evidence, from both now and in the past, shows that clients lack basic job-seeking skills. As we have seen in the research in the rehabilitation field, clients are seldom prepared to conduct a job search without help from a specialist in the field. Recall the results from the Minnesota Rehabilitation Center study[7] that showed serious deficiencies in their clients' job-seeking skills. Eighty percent (80%) of the clients did not look for work frequently enough, eighty-five (85%) could not explain their skills to employers, and ninety percent (90%) could not explain their handicapping condition. Much of the blame for these poor survey results can only be attributed to improper preparation of clients for the job search.

So much attention has been given in our field to the job search and so little attention has been given to job search preparation. In fact, most professionals have experienced conflict with insurance adjusters unwilling to pay for counseling or basic job-seeking skills training. Some preparation is usually necessary. At the very least, counselors must prepare documents (e.g., the resume), for their clients and show them how the documents are used effectively in the job search. The following discussion of the "Tools of the Job Search" seeks to help rehabilitation counselors accomplish both of these tasks:

1. How to prepare a professional resume, the cover letter, and complimentary correspondence to employers.

2. How to use the resume, the cover letter, and the thank you notes to improve the chances of employment for their clients.

## THE PROFESSIONAL RESUME

Recent years have given rise to the professional resume. Pick up the telephone directory yellow pages in almost any community and you will find advertisements by job counselors who will write you "the winning resume." No doubt, a good many inexperienced job seekers have benefitted by having their credentials organized and presented in a polished format.

The professional resume has created some new problems. It seems just about everybody has a different idea about how to write a resume. (We are no exception). This lack of consensus has brought about a wide variation in the format of the resume. Unfortunately, many employers and human resource intermediaries who screen applications are unaware of some of the latest trends in resume writing. This is particularly true in some of the more conservative areas and in businesses with lower-level jobs, often the very kind of jobs we seek for our clients. Normally, these people take a brief look at the resume (research suggests about 60 seconds) and when they are unable to locate the information they expect, they often pass over the applicant. In addition, employers and others tend to become suspicious of non-traditional resumes, believing applicants seek to hide deficits by revising the resume form. For these reasons, the client may lose with a "winning resume."

An even greater problem is that a client may believe that the resume is the primary stepping-stone to a good job. Placing too much emphasis upon the resume may cause a client to deal casually with other parts of the job search and rely upon the resume to do the work. For the most part, the resume has been oversold. The resume is not as important in the job search as the advertisements would have you believe. Richard Bolles,[1] records the results of a survey that showed "only one job offer is tendered and accepted in the whole world for every 1470 resumes floating around."[pg. 13]

Seldom does the resume, detached from the person featured in the resume, find fertile ground and grow into a job offer. Except in high-level, skilled positions, mailing out resumes blindly will seldom succeed in getting an interview. Richard Bolles[1] goes on to say "for every person you know who did get an interview by sending out a resume, I know ninety-nine who didn't."[pg. 158]

Lower your expectations of what a resume can do for your client, but do not lose sight of the fact that the resume has its place in the job search. You will need to provide one for your client. If nothing else, the resume demonstrates that applicants know their background and work experience. The resume should include what they hope to achieve in a new job or occupation. The process clients go through in developing the resume prepares them to present their skills and abilities to employers and talk about their employment assets. In addition, as discussed in Chapter 9, the resume becomes the textbook for training in job-seeking skills. Finally, if your client learns how to use the resume effectively, the resume will assume a much greater level of importance in the job search. Knowing how to use the resume–not the document itself–is what makes "a winning resume."

Most clients need some instruction in how to use the resume. Once again, the counselor is placed in a teaching role. Here are two (2) suggestions based upon personal experience in the field of rehabilitation and the best research available for instructing clients in the use of a resume.

*Use the Resume As An Extended Calling Card.* Once your client has made contact with a potential employer or employer representative, leaving this person with a resume provides reference to the personal contact. In this way, the resume is there if the employer wants to review the conversation or contact the client. An even better way is to have the client take down the name of the employer contact and mail the resume prefaced with a cover letter that:

- highlights the main points of their conversation,
- points out the skills the client brings to the job, and
- expresses continued interest in the job.

Do not expect too much from the extended calling card. If no reply comes in a few days, nothing will likely come from the contact. Once a resume reaches the files, the final resting place for resumes, the end is close at hand. Seldom are resumes resurrected from the files when new jobs open. After a week or two, your client will need to contact this employer again.

*Use the Resume For Reference During An Interview.* Normally, employers (interviewers) have examined your client's resume before the interview and have the document before them in the interview. You may consider instructing your client to do the same and have the resume close at hand during the interview. The answers to most of the difficult questions and some of the special concerns the employer may have are contained in the resume. Additionally, having a resume in hand may give clients a source of comfort by knowing most of the facts their counselor has discussed with them earlier are right before them.

## THE RESUME FORMAT

There are many self-help books on the market today to help you prepare a resume for your clients. Most experienced counselors have already settled upon a form they like best, but for those counselors with a mind for thoroughness who seek that one best reference, we add our view to the many experts, most of whom far exceed our expertise. Perhaps the one reference that has been the most helpful in forming our opinions on resume writing is *Resume Solution* by David Swanson.[8] David Swanson[8] has prepared a step-by-step workbook on the preparation of resumes.

Keep in mind the resume will have only a limited impact upon the job search. Many actions taken on the part of the client will exceed what they are able to do with a resume. For instance, a network person who knows an employer and is willing to refer your client exceeds in importance anything you can hope to accomplish with a resume. Moreover, the resume seldom does well standing alone. Handed directly to an employer contact or used with a cover letter increases the effectiveness of a resume. This personal approach also takes some of the pressure off the counselor creating the resume. You need not worry whether or not you have the "right" form. If in creating the resume, you have given thought to the format, your finished product will probably do the job.

Our practice has been only to use the simple chronological resume and create variations off of that format. The reasons for this are:

- Most employers, particularly the small business owners, tend to be more conservative in their hiring practices. Our belief is that these employers look for information in certain places on the resume and we want them to find what they are looking for.

- The format of the chronological resume does not attract attention to itself. While other forms, such as the skill or functional resume forms, allow the person to hide some of the weaknesses, variant formats can become self-defeating. Some employers become more suspicious of unfamiliar resume forms.

- The resume is a vehicle to convey certain information; it is unlikely to dazzle anyone. The chronological resume keeps it simple.
- It is important to keep in mind the clients we serve are mostly working people and, what we called earlier, baseline people. Variant forms seem to be the most useful among skilled, sophisticated candidates.

Robert Half[5] says in *The Robert Half Way to Get Hired in Today's Job Market,* a well-designed resume should tell prospective employers,

- that you expect to contribute to the job you take,
- that you are well-organized, ambitious, and goal-oriented, and
- that you are a person worth a second look.[pg. 93]

None of these points has much to do with format; each can be achieved within the traditional, chronological form.

## CONTENT OF THE RESUME

Remember, as you read, the single most important concept in resume writing is that there are no rules, and that is precisely what makes resume preparation most difficult; here are some simple tips for resume writing selected from recent publications in the job-search field that seem most appropriate for our purposes here.

*Confine the resume to one, no more than, two pages, (maybe a back and a front).* Begin the resume with the client's name, address, e-mail, and all contact phone numbers with type enhancements, such as bold (preferred), italics, or underlining.

*Beginning with a vocational objective is optional.* One of the contributors to Enelow & Goldman's, *The Insiders Guide to Finding a Job*[3] says if you are going to use a vocational objective, be succinct and to the point, (e.g., "Seeking a Position as a Sales Representative" not "Seeking a Position Offering Challenge and Opportunity for Advancement." Vague statements like the latter are "me-oriented" and draw attention to the candidate. What the observer in human resources wants to see is what the candidate can do for the company.

One contributor of a chapter to Enelaw & Goldman's[3] book offers the suggestion of starting with a "Summary of Qualifications" rather than an objective. This makes good sense, but if you choose to use a Summary of Qualifications, the writer says, first "go to the web page, research the company, learn about the people and the organization, understand its products and services, and then write your summary to reflect the desired skills and experiences."[pg. 53] Always use the active voice in your grammatical presentations.

*The main content of the resume is the past work.* Here it is important to highlight achievements rather than responsibilities. Enelow and Goldman[3] say, "resume writing is not about listing responsibilities. Instead, you want to highlight your achievements in handling those responsibilities. Don't tell your reader, 'This is what I did.' Rather, tell the reader "This is what I did and this is how well I did it."pg. 57 Highlighting achievements includes showcasing the breadth of the responsibilities, major projects in which the client was involved, quantifiable achievements, certifications, and letters of commendation or professional recognition earned. The best advice is to concentrate on the last 10 to 12 years and personal accomplishments during that time frame.

*The section on Education should be comprehensive and include college degrees (or college attendance if no degree was obtained, certifications, and professional licenses).* One chapter contributor to *Insider's Guide to Finding a Job*[3] suggests, "If the person has had a lot of professional training programs, highlight those that are most relevant to the position to which the person is applying. If the candidate is 50+ years of age, do not include dates of attendance for degrees obtained, information that might be used to immediately exclude the candidate from consideration."pg. 151

*Please refer to the Appendix at the end of this chapter. The Appendix contains two sample chronological resumes counselors or their clients may model in creating their resumes. Both of these were prepared for actual persons seeking jobs.*

From the two sample resumes, you can see that working within the chronological format allows flexibility without changing to a variant form. For instance, education and work experience can be switched in the format, giving emphasis to the stronger of the two. You can leave out dates in your chronology if age is a factor or there are gaps in employment. Our belief is that counselors will find greater success in using their ingenuity by working within a familiar format than trying to solve problems, such as an inconsistent work record, with a resume format they are not used to using.

Most of the changes in resume writing have arisen from some basic changes in the way a company views hiring and recruiting of new personnel. We are seeing in the literature new buzzwords (e.g., "Organization and Cultural Fit," "Cultural Integration," and "Chemistry Issues.)" Weldon Rougeau,[3] president of Congressional Black Caucus Foundation, Inc., Washington, D.C. explains reasons for the prominence of these new terms: "Never before in the history of the industrialized world have the concepts of organizational and cultural fit been so critical. As companies worldwide have streamlined their work forces to reduce expenses and improve profitability, organizational and cultural fit have emerged as two critical factors in hiring and retaining the right talent."pg. 53 He gives this advice to job seekers, "Consider your values and principles carefully to determine whether you will be comfortable working for a particular organization and whether you fit into their culture."[3, pg. 53]

Chemistry issues and concerns about cultural fit have caused some companies to not only view the selection process differently but also to do things differently in interviewing and hiring. The literature suggests that:

- Companies are now doing more of their own recruiting and hiring and have reduced their dependence upon staffing companies.

- More weight in hiring is being placed upon recommendations from staff within the organization with less emphasis upon traditional and non-traditional resources.

Internal recommendations for hiring and recruitment by recommendation would be the logical result of concerns about organizational fit and cultural integration. As companies have reduced their staff, the ones that remain are more vital to the life of the business. (If the literature were correct about hiring upon recommendations from persons known within the company, networking through family, friends, and acquaintances, as presented in Chapter 10, would seem to be the new job placement method of choice).

*Some companies are placing more emphasis upon adaptive skills than work record and work skills: getting the right person as opposed to simply getting a person who can do the job.* Douglas Hardin, Senior Vice President for the Federal Systems says,

> *It is extremely difficult to evaluate a candidate's technical capabilities in an interview. I won't know that until the candidate is hired. Much of the evaluation during an interview is based upon character, integrity, and attitude." In the job interview his advice to job seekers is: "Be ready to talk about values, character, culture, and more. We want to know what culture means to them and what values they hold dear.*[3, pg. 151]

## THE COVER LETTER

The resume is a necessary tool of the job search. The poor response rate comes mainly from the way clients use the resume once the document is in their hands. They mail them out indiscriminately, they give them to the most casual contacts (who promptly trash them), and they leave them at every job contact regardless of whom they talk with. The apparent assumption is that the resume will find its way to a potential employer who will read the resume with care, find some magical hidden quality they like, and call the individual for an interview. It is just not going to happen this way very often–if ever!

The effectiveness of the resume improves with the way your client uses it. We have seen how placing the resume in the right hands can increase the response rate, but nothing makes the resume go forward like a cover letter. Almost always, the cover letter gets read. As an employer, I can remember bypassing a lot of resumes; but I cannot remember a cover letter that I did not read in its entirety. The cover letter provides a client:

- A personal entrée to the employer
  The cover letter says the applicant has looked up or researched (it does not matter which) the name of the employer, the title, and the address and has paid close attention, at least enough to remember the employer's name from their brief encounter. Seldom will this effort go unnoticed. Most employers will remember any special effort on the part of an applicant that sets them apart from other persons they interview. A cover letter suggests that, once employed, this applicant will conduct the company's business in the same careful manner.

- A tie between the qualifications and the job
  Survey evidence shows that employers handle each resume for a minute or less. This length of exposure may not allow an employer time to make a linkage between the client's qualifications for the job and the job itself. In a cover letter, the client has the opportunity to show the employer how he or she can do the job. If there is not a close match, the cover letter can ease this concern in a sentence by tying the applicant's qualifications to the job requirements.

- Expresses a personal interest in working for the employer
  Enthusiasm is contagious. A brief sentence or two expressing a desire for the job can go a long way toward making a lasting impression. Employers do not just want to know you are qualified to do the job; they want to know if you are interested and willing to perform the job. In other words, employers are just as interested, or maybe more so, in an applicant's adaptive skills as their work skills. Remember, job skills are only one of the criteria employers look for in the candidates they interview.
  Just as important are the personal qualities, and, in particular, how the candidate will fit into the work setting or corporate culture. The cover letter is an opportunity to say the personal things that will help the employer decide whether the candidate has the human qualities necessary to succeed in the work place. (Chapter 10 "Networking for Jobs in the Hidden Job Market: A Client-Centered Approach" contains an expanded discussion of work skills and adaptive skills).

*Format of the Cover Letter.* There may be many ways to write a cover letter. Our belief is that the format for the cover letter needs to be as simplistic as possible so that it can be easily taught to clients. Our suggestion is to limit the cover letter to three (3) short paragraphs, each paragraph having a designed purpose.

Paragraph #1: The opening paragraph makes a connection between the candidate and the person the letter addresses.

If you met that person in an interview, the opening would read something like this: "Thank you for taking the time to talk with me about the position of Accounting Clerk with the Acme Staffing Company last Monday, November, 23, 2007."

If you have been referred by a relative, friend, or acquaintance, the opening may sound something like this: "I have received notice from May Bradley, your Administrative Assistant, that the position of Accounting Clerk is now open. I am interested in making application for that position. My resume is enclosed with this letter."

Paragraph # 2: In a short, to-the-point statement, make a connection between the job requirements and the client's qualifications for the position.

What this means is that the job seeker must obtain the employer's list of qualifications for the job prior to the application. This may require contacting the employer and requesting the job requirements if the notice is insufficient. (Newspaper ads and notices in such publications as CareerBuilder are typically too brief and often filled with irrelevant promotional information, such as inflated job requirements).

The best support information may be found on the Internet. The World Wide Web has revolutionized the job seekers ability to connect with a business or corporation. Most companies now have a web page that tells the job-seeker about the company, the products the company has to offer, and the image the company wants to project to the public. Currently, revised web sites, in many cases, contain statements and other hints about cultural fit and the kinds of people they seek to hire. A review of the web site enables the job seeker to pinpoint key words for insertion in the cover letter to help make the connection between the job requirements and personal qualifications. This review also can help the clients envision what it would be like to be a part of that organization's culture.

Paragraph # 3: The closing of the cover letter gives clients the opportunity to say something about their personal qualities, adaptive skills, such as their work habits, the ability to get along with co-workers and supervisors, the personal values they hold, and how they see themselves fitting into the corporate or business culture. A review of the web site is a good source for framing this statement. (Exhibit 3 in the Appendix provides a sample of the cover letter).

## THE THANK-YOU NOTE (FOLLOW-UP COMMUNICATION)

With recent trends in employment practices (e.g., employers

1. looking for more than job skills, or warm bodies who can perform the job,

2. examining human qualities in the people they hire such as values and cultural fit, and

3. giving preference to referrals from employees, and to people they have come to know.

A Thank-You note would should be commonplace in every job search. This, however, does not seem to be the case. With this level of importance, job seekers would routinely write Thank-You notes, but that does not seem to be the case. The author of *What Color is Your Parachute*, Robert Bolles[2] writes "Every expert in interviews will tell you two things: (1) Thank-You notes must be sent after every interview, by every job hunter (preferably two, an e-mail and a hand-written note) and (2) most job hunters ignore the advice."[pg. 102]

Writing a thank-you note gives clients seeking employment several important advantages:

1. *The note is simply a matter of common courtesy.*
   A thank-you letter or note (preferably a hand-written thank you note) saying you enjoyed the interview shows you respect the time the interviewer spent with you. In addition, the note lets the interviewer know you are still interested in the job.
2. *The note can correct a wrong impression.*
   The thank-you note gives applicants an opportunity to correct any wrong impression they may have left behind. So

many times, after leaving an interview, statements a person has made continue to weigh on their minds and lingering feelings of regret remain long after the contact. The thank-you letter can eliminate this concern and instead of regret, produce a feeling of being in charge of the job hunt and your life.

3. *The note can address special issues brought up in the interview.*
   As in the cover letter, the thank-you note provides the opportunity to address key points or elaborate on important issues, thus allowing the job seeker to demonstrate the value he/she may bring to the company.

4. *A thank-you note may make a lasting impression.*
   Even if the applicant did not get the job, a letter saying, "I enjoyed the interview and would definitely like to be considered for future openings" may extend the life of the application. It is all about cultural fit! The authors of *The Insiders Guide to Finding A Job*[3] say, "if you have remained in touch with someone in the company, chances are they will immediately be in touch with you. Just think! How much easier it would be for them to hire you, who they already know and are impressed with, instead of having to start all over again."[pg.175]

Exhibit 4 of the Appendix provides a typical example of a thank-you note.

# CONCLUSION

The following Appendix contains samples of two resumes, a sample cover letter, and a thank you note. Each of these samples is based upon real cases that have helped clients find jobs.

# APPENDIX

The sample resumes on the next two pages present some of the features to include in the resume. The first sample is a standard, chronological form most employers recognize. The second is a variation of the chronological resume that actually won a highly competitive job for this young golf professional.

EXHIBIT 1

## SAMPLE RESUME OF QUALIFICATIONS

Sharon L. Tate
114 High Street
Harrisonburg, Virginia 22801

E-mail: Shatate@ gmail.com
(703) 248-5862 (home)
(703) 248-3711 (cell)

POSITION DESIRED:

Seeking a management or sales position in retail sales of quality home furnishings. Job duties may include carpet sales, interior decorating, use of computer design, and supervision of sales personnel.

### EDUCATION AND TRAINING

Blue Ridge Community College, Weyers Cave, Virginia.
Associates Degree Received: June, 2002

Completed two-year program in Interior Decorating and Design.
Courses included retail sales, furniture construction, interior design, color coordination, art history, with a six-week practicum at Shenandoah Interiors Ltd. in Staunton, Virginia. Grades in top 15% of my class.

Spottswood High School, Harrisonburg, Virginia.
Diploma Received: June 1990
College Preparatory Program with emphasis in art and business.

### WORK EXPERIENCE

2003–2007 Sales Manager, Sears Roebuck & Co. Charlottesville, Virginia
Managed bedding department, providing sales and customer service. Kept employee records, placed orders for goods, assisted in the selection of floor samples, placed special orders for customers, and managed inventory levels. Supervised assistant manager and two salespersons. Sales volume increased in my four years by 20 %. Received regular merit raises for performance.

2003–2004 Sales & Customer Service, women's apparel.
Leggetts, Harrisonburg, Virginia
Made demonstrations of a variety of clothing fashions and completed sales to customers. Learned to understand customer needs in clothing, explain the features and benefits of clothing products to my customers, dealt with customers and took care of customer problems to their satisfaction. I had many customers who came to me for repeat business.

PERSONAL

I have excellent references, I learn quickly, and I am willing to relocate for the right position.

EXHIBIT 2

SAMPLE RESUME OF QUALIFICATIONS

PROFESSIONAL QUALIFICATIONS

| | |
|---|---|
| John L. Clayton | e-mail: lclayton@ gmail.com |
| 813 Clark Court # 316 | (703) 886-4037 (home) |
| Leesburg, Virginia 22075 | (703) 886-7744 (cell) |

CAREER OBJECTIVE: Obtain PGA membership and become head golf professional

WORK EXPERIENCE

May, 2005 to Present: First Assistant Golf Professional for a large public golf course in Northern Virginia providing over 65,000 rounds per year, Reston Golf Course, Reston, Virginia

- Provided daily supervision to four (4) shop assistants and twenty-five volunteers in the Starter-Ranger program.
- Taught over 400 individual golf lessons per year.
- Instructed golf car personnel in day-to-day maintenance and minor repair of 55-golf car fleet.
- Prepared displays, ordered merchandise, sold golf supplies and equipment, and assisted in the management of golf pro shop with annual sales of over $250,000.
- Instructed and assisted in organizing the Paul Berry Clinic for needy children.
- Organized tournaments and outings in the junior golf program of Northern Virginia.

February, 2003 to May, 2005 Assistant Golf Professional for a private country club serving the Eastern Shore of Maryland and the Baltimore-Washington area. Caroline Country Club, Denton, Maryland.

- Assisted head professional in all phases of the golf course operation, including individual golf lessons for members, fleet maintenance, golf shop merchandizing, and daily supervision of golf cart personnel and helpers.
- Assisted in the operation of the Maryland Interstate Seniors Golf Association.
- Held weekly instructional clinics for members.

## EDUCATION

High School and College
Lee High School, Staunton, Virginia    Diploma Received: June 2000
Blue Ridge Community College (1) year
Concentration: Business
Piedmont Community College (1) year
Concentration: Liberal Arts

Professional Golf Association
Play Ability Test (passed on first attempt)
Business School 1 (Charleston, South Carolina)
Certificate of Completion, 2002

Professional Seminars
Financial Planning, Golf Instruction, How to Buy/Lease Gold Courses, and the Art of Selling

## PERSONAL INFORMATION

I am self-motivated, a hard worker, and in every position I have held I have been willing to make the necessary sacrifices to get results for my employers.

EXHIBIT 3

## SAMPLE COVER LETTER

4015 N. Peach Street
Frederick, Maryland 20016

September 27, 2012

Ms. Gloria B. Hampton
Chief Administrator
Home Health Care of Maryland
Box 7243
Glen Burnie, Maryland 20123
Dear Ms. Hampton,

I was delighted to see your advertisement for Supervisor of Nursing Assistants in the News Gazette yesterday, Monday, September 26, 2012. I have recently moved to the area and this position offers the career opportunity I am seeking.

I served as a Nursing Assistant and Nursing Assistant Supervisor in the Huntington, West Virginia Retirement Home for seven (7) years prior to moving to the area several months ago. Before that, I was a home health aide for two years in the Morgantown area. I have my certification as a Nursing Assistant in both Maryland and West Virginia, and continuing education in home health care and basic computer science from Morgantown Community College.

I am enclosing my resume that more completely describes my education and experience. I look forward to meeting you in the near future.

Sincerely,

Veronica Chattam

EXHIBIT 4

## SAMPLE THANK YOU NOTE

Sally K. Obenchain
216 Strait Street
Staunton, Virginia 24401
January 15, 2014

Ms. Katherine Simmons
Director of Personnel
Memorial Gift Shops, Inc.
Kingsport, Tennessee 35004

Dear Ms. Simmons,

Thank you for taking the time from your busy schedule to interview me on Monday, September 23, 2002 concerning the open position as Manager of the Memorial Gift Shop in Charlottesville, Virginia.

As we discussed in the interview, I have nine years' experience as manager of a Pennsylvania House Gallery store in Staunton, Virginia. As owner and operator, my responsibilities included purchasing merchandise, maintaining inventory, making sales to customers, handling customer concerns, and supervising the activities of seven (7) warehouse and sales employees. In the last eight years of employment, I was the main purchasing agent for our firm at the High Point market. Two of my sales staff sold over a million dollars annually.

I believe myself to be a self-starting manager who works well with people, both customers and employees. I am looking forward to exploring with you the job duties of the Memorial Gift Shop in more detail.

Sincerely,

Sally Obenchain

# TOPICS FOR GROUP DISCUSSION

1. Chapter 8 presents several community resources that are available to rehabilitation counselors when searching for job leads. Are there others? The instructor may choose to list the resources suggested in the chapter and explore other job sources that may be available.

2. Chapter 8 makes the point that in filling out an application, if a client is able to perform all of the job duties of a particular job, then there is no disability present and the client does not have to disclose a past disability. This is important and should be the subject for class discussion. The subject of how to fill out an application for persons with a disability is valuable in class discussions about seeking work.

3. The chapter goes through several of the formal job sources, newspapers, state employment office, etc., and discusses their value to persons looking for jobs. The instructor may choose to make each of these a subject of discussion. Then ask the group to suggest other sources of jobs where job lists are available.

4. In the case study below, have the group divide into sub-groups and prepare a resume, a cover letter, and a thank you note.

# INDIVIDUAL EXERCISES

In the case study below, prepare a resume for Warren Potter and a cover letter.

## THE CASE OF WARREN POTTER

*Warren Potter is 28 years old. He attended Fulton High School in Martinsburg, West Virginia, but left in the11th grade in 2001. He lives at 116 Clover Lane in Martinsburg. He has not returned to school or obtained his GED. While he was in high school, he was in automobile mechanics in the vocational program. A year after leaving high school he attended a twelve-week vocational course to become a truck driver.*

*Warren has worked in his father's shop for the past 11 years. He has learned to perform most of the job duties needed in the shop, with the exception of the more "exotic" cars like BMWs and Mercedes Bends: "but we don't get many of these kinds of cars in our shop anyway."*

*In 2011, he was injured in an automobile accident and since the accident has had trouble with neck pain and dizziness when he looks up and down for more than 10 to 15 minutes at a time. Most of the automobiles and trucks that come into the shop are placed on hydraulic lifts requiring Warren to work on these vehicles while constantly looking up. He has tried to keep working in his father's shop but is unable to sustain a whole day and must be absent for several days each month.*

*Warren has applied for a job as a counter sales clerk at Auto Zone in nearby Winchester, Virginia.*

Please provide Warren with a 1-2 page resume. Also, prepare a cover letter for Warren that shows his qualifications for the job. (Don't forget to look up the Auto Zone web page and to stress his adaptive skills in the cover letter).

*On November 14, 2012, he received a letter from William Spooner, the manager at Auto Zone, at 116 High Street in Winchester, Virginia 24301 asking Warren to come in for an interview.*

Do you think that Warren needs to mention his work limitations in the interview? Write a few sentences stating your opinion about his limitations and the need to discuss the limitations in an interview (review the statement in Chapter 8 about what the ADA says concerning work limitations).

*Following the interview, Warren thought it was a good idea to write and thank Mr. Spooner for considering him for the job opportunity at Auto Zone. Also, Warren wanted to reiterate some things about his qualifications he mentioned in the interview that he felt were important. In addition, Warren felt that his work limitations would not affect his performance in that job and wanted Mr. Spooner to know that.*

Write a thank you note to Mr. Spooner.

# REFERENCES


[1]Bolles, R. N. (1991). *What Color Is Your Parachute?* Berkeley, CA: Ten Speed Press.

[2]Bolles, R. N. (2007). *What Color Is Your Parachute?* Berkeley, CA: Ten Speed Press.

[3]Enelow, W. S. & Goldman, S. (2005). *Insider's Guide to Finding a Job*. Indianapolis, IN: JIST Publishing, Inc.

[4]Farr, J. M. (1991). *The Very Quick Job Search.* Indianapolis, IN: JIST Works, Inc., 1993.

[5]Half, Robert (1949). *The Robert Half Way to Get Hired In Today's Job Market*. New York: John Wiley & Sons, Inc.

[6]Newsweek, December 21, 2009

[7]Roessler, R. W. (1985). "Self-Starting in the Job Market: The Continuing Need for Job-Seeking Skills in Rehabilitation." *Journal of Applied Rehabilitation Counseling*, 16, p. 2.

[8]Swanson, David (1991). *Resume Solution. Indianapolis, In. Jist Works, Inc.*

[9]Wegmann, R. (1989). Work *in the New Economy: Careers and Job Seeking into the 21st Century*. Indianapolis, IN: JIST Works, Inc.

[10]White, W. A. (1937). *Forty Years on Main Street.* New York, NY: Farrar and Rinehart.

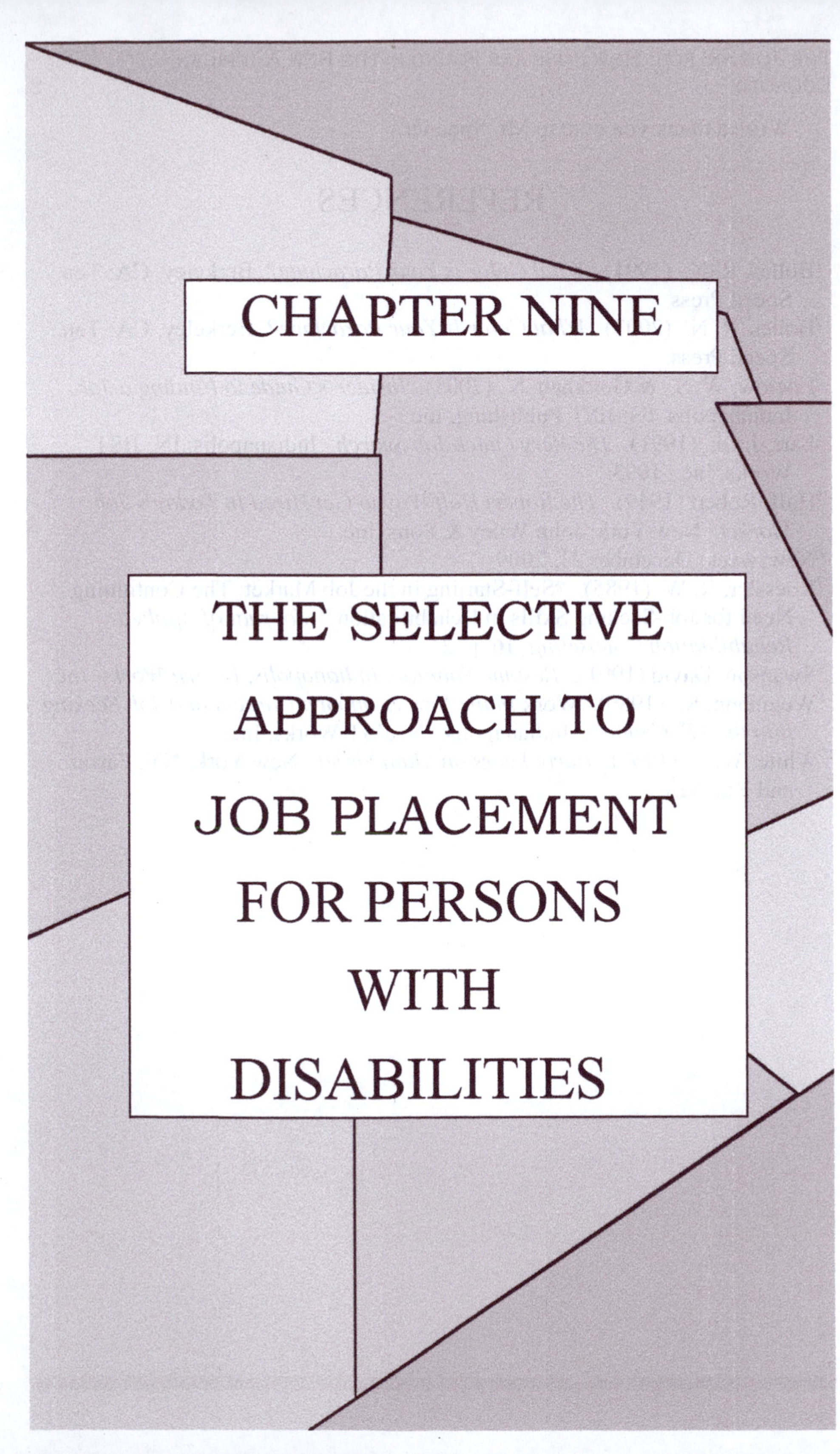

# CHAPTER NINE

# THE SELECTIVE APPROACH TO JOB PLACEMENT FOR PERSONS WITH DISABILITIES

To the Reader:

In Chapter 1, we began our discussion of the rehabilitation counselor's management role in job placement. We presented the argument that a counselor's responsibilities changed dramatically as the counseling relationship moved from the planning, coordinating, and organizing stages to the job hunt, with much of the control over the case shifting from the counselor to the client during the final stages of job placement.

Three different approaches were presented as alternative ways to deal with the issues of control in job placement. Under the Laissez-Faire approach, the client has almost complete freedom and assumes most of the control over all phases of the job hunt. Under the Selective approach, the counselor maintains almost complete control over the case from beginning to the end; and under the Client-Centered approach, the activities of job placement become shared responsibilities. Arguments were presented with each approach to show that there are choices in the management of most cases for both the counselor and the client.

The Client-Centered approach, the focus of Chapter 10, seems to present a more ideal situation for assisting persons with disabilities to find jobs in our present economy. In a democratic society like ours, it is hard to argue against shared responsibility as the most acceptable way for doing business. However, current practices in the market place today are mostly variations of the Selective approach. This is particularly true in private-practice rehabilitation. Most of the time, counselors in private practice locate the jobs and refer jobs to their clients. Clients are expected to set the appointments, attend the interviews, and report back the results. In some cases, the counselor will set up the appointments and even attend the interviews. After a job interview, to assure their clients are making a sincere effort to secure the position, counselors often contact the employers directly for responses to the client's application and to learn how well their clients performed in the interview. These pragmatic job placement practices seem to have won out over approaches emphasizing client involvement and vocational counseling. As expected, the pitfalls of the Selective Approach are commonplace, with extended periods of waiting for contacts from the counselor, resulting in long gaps of inactivity.

The widespread use of the Selective approach for clients seeking alternative work under worker's compensation would suggest counselors find success using the method. To be certain, the techniques used in this method are necessary for counselors with responsibilities for conducting labor market surveys. Moreover, the internet has made selective methods more precise than in the past. The Internet today provides new ways to penetrate the local job market and to locate local job offerings that typically lie within the hidden job market.

This chapter on the Selective approach shows counselors how to prepare themselves and their clients for the job search, how to prepare a case prior to making employer contacts, how to use the Internet for locating job leads, how to address disability issues in conversations with employers, and how to project a positive image of the client during telephone conversations.

# THE CASE PROCESS: INTRODUCTION

To this point, if nothing more, this book should raise serious questions about haphazard, unplanned methods for job placement of persons with disabilities. Changed conditions in the current job market–and conditions anticipated in the job market of the future (see Chapter 7) have increasingly doomed to failure several of these antiquated job-placement methods. For illustration, the *random method* is used. In this method, the rehabilitation counselor wanders into a community, gathers up the local newspaper, and over a cup of coffee examines the daily-classified listings. Once the survey of want ads is complete, the counselor begins to make "cold calls" upon the places of business listing the openings. How stressful those days were! Another of the antiquated job placement techniques may be called the *canvas method.* By this method, a rehabilitation counselor starts at one end of the business section, often fast food row, and contacts every business along the way. You make a lot of contacts this way and log in a lot of time, and if you are particularly good at self-deception, you gain some sense of movement in the case. After all, you need to show something for your time! Who knows, in the right economy, you may get lucky, but getting lucky in the new American economy today has become increasingly difficult.

Even though job placement continues to be more of an art than a science, experience has taught us some things. Most experienced rehabilitation counselors today know that much of the guesswork can be taken out of job placement with careful planning and preparation.

> *Job placement is not a separate activity from case planning and case development; it is the outgrowth of an overall design that begins the moment the case is assigned to the counselor. Thereafter, a thoughtful examination of the records, paying close attention to the medical limitations, and asking the right questions early on, refines the case, narrows the job options, and points the rehabilitation counselor to the right places in the job market.* The Authors

## CASE ASSIGNMENT

For counselors in private practice, the case process usually begins with a phone call from an insurance company adjuster, a case management firm, or from a practicing attorney outlining the case they would like to assign to the rehabilitation counselor. The information received over the phone will likely be a short, verbal statement about the vocational profile of the individual in question (age, education, and work experience), a brief summary of the case, including how disability occurred (an automobile, recreational, or industrial accident), and a verbal request stating what the person assigning the case would like the counselor to do.

The assignment usually includes one of the following:

1. case management, which involves following the case until the injured person returns to work,
2. job placement for alternative work,
3. a labor market survey of the local job market, or
4. a vocational evaluation of the injured person's employability and possible wage loss.

If the counselor is not known to them, adjusters, case managers, and attorneys may request a resume of professional qualifications, professional insurance coverage, a fee schedule, and a summary of court appearances.

This initial phone call is usually followed some days later by the arrival of a case folder, a letter of assignment, and other assorted records. In some cases, if the assignment is from an attorney, medical records can be huge, sometimes a foot high. If the counselor is lucky, the medical and vocational records are in a notebook prepared by a paralegal and presented chronologically. (Records organized in this way show a sure sign of professional respect).

Acquiring a case will be different for counselors in public agencies. These rehabilitation counselors may receive calls and case folders from a variety of governmental sources, most of which are agencies (e.g., the Disability Determination Services (DDS) with the Social Security Administration).

## CONTENTS OF THE CASE FOLDER

Regardless of where the case folders come from, the information will be much the same for both private and public rehabilitation counselors. The case folder can contain, among other things, the assignment letter, an employment application, hospital records, and treatment notes from a variety of treating sources. It is important that the counselor receive a complete record. As we discussed in Chapter 5 "Determining Client Function: the Diagnostics of Rehabilitation," a complete record will contain statements from treating doctors that the individual has reached maximum medical improvement (MMI), functional restrictions from medical sources limiting the kind of work activity the person is likely to be able to perform satisfactorily (RFC), and a statement from a treating doctor or doctors saying that the person is released to return to work (RTW).

After sorting through the records and placing them in the order of events, counselors examine the case folder. The word *examine* is an important principle in looking through the file. While most of the information is important in forming a mental picture of the events that have led to the disabling condition, the focus of the file review is always upon client function as described earlier in Chapter 5. What is most important from the file review is that counselors gain an initial impression of the abilities and limitations of the injured or disabled individual in order to begin the process of defining a person's ability to function in the work place.

## COMPARING THE MEDICAL PROFILE WITH THE VOCATIONAL PROFILE

Chapter 5 explored the subject matter of a Medical Profile and a Vocational Profile. We will just highlight the main points of that discussion. From the Medical Profile a rehabilitation counselor gains an understanding of the functional restrictions as stated by the doctors treating the rehabilitation client. These functional restrictions lay out the limitations a rehabilitation counselor *must consider* when returning that person to work, whether that rehabilitation client is returning to the same job, a new job with the same employer, or alternative work. In order for the restrictions to be useful, treating doctors must place these restrictions in functional terms.

Functional restrictions usually eliminate jobs and define job limits. For instance, the doctor may say that a person is limited to lifting 20 pounds. That means the only jobs under consideration are light and sedentary jobs. Let us suppose the client is a forklift driver in a warehouse. The exertion level for that job is usually medium to heavy, depending on other job duties. In all probability, these restrictions mean the client will not be able to return to the work in the warehouse that was done in the past unless the employer permits certain accommodations for the worker. Functional restrictions, therefore, dictate the exertion level of jobs counselors will have to consider when looking for alternative work. In the job search for this client, all jobs at a medium and heavy level are beyond consideration.

Likewise, if the rehabilitation client was a production inspector in a poultry plant, and the treating doctor says that a person is restricted from using the hands for repetitive movement, that person will likely not be able to return to that kind of work since most production inspecting jobs in a poultry plant require constant and repetitive use of the hands and arms. As evident in both of these examples, on the one hand, functional restrictions refine and limit the job placement activity by telling the rehabilitation counselor where not to go; and, on the other hand, functional restrictions point the direction to different types of jobs, jobs that the client may be able to perform satisfactorily.

The vocational profile also has a refining effect upon the job placement activity. The *age* of the rehabilitation client may place limits upon the types of jobs available. It is unlikely that a person over 55 years of age will have a successful placement in production work if that person has not done that kind of work in the past. Usually, production work has quotas or production norms causing higher levels of stress and making adjustment to these kinds of jobs more difficult.

Likewise, a person's *education level* has to be considered. Unless the work experience dictates otherwise, a client with a limited education (below high school) is usually not going to be acceptable for many desk jobs requiring higher levels of math and language. (*The Dictionary of Occupational Titles* lists the math and language requirements for each job description. See Chapter 6).

Finally, a rehabilitation client's *past work* limits available jobs and points the direction for job placement. Unless additional training is indicated, the usual practice is to seek work alternatives as closely related as possible to work done in the past. The possession of transferable work skills, educational skills, and adaptive skills go a long way toward dictating the direction of the job search.

A careful integration of the medical and vocational profiles sets the direction of the job placement. Once the rehabilitation counselor has analyzed the contents of the medical records, determined the functional limitations, and developed the vocational profile from the vocational material in the case folder, job placement should be well under way. The rehabilitation counselor is now ready to meet the client.

## CONDUCTING A PERSONAL INTERVIEW

Examination of the case records provides the counselor with a history of the diagnosed condition, treatment outcomes, and the residual abilities and limitations of the client. The personal interview gives the counselor an understanding of the client's personal and work history and provides an idea of how their health problems affect them on a day-to-day basis. The interview centers upon the three main vocational factors of age, education, and work experience and sets the stage for job placement activity.

We have provided a sample format for obtaining interview information. There is no standard form counselors follow in their interview format. Every counselor, and each counseling firm, or counseling organization seems to have its own interview format. The interview format chosen for this text is very typical of most interview formats and covers the information very thoroughly.

# SAMPLE INTERVIEW FORMAT

You may begin the interview with a **statement of purpose** (e.g., *"Do you understand the reason why I am having this interview with you today?"*) Wait for an answer. *"You understand that I am an independent vocational counselor; I do not work for the insurance company that is paying for this service. I am in business for myself."* You can give the client or attorney your business card.

*"I am going to begin slowly because I have to write this down. If at any time you need to get up and walk around, please feel free to do so. We are not in any hurry here. I am a vocational counselor so the information I ask you will be about work and any problems that affect your ability to work. Any information I receive from you will be held confidential.*

*I will begin with simple questions about some personal data. If there are any questions you do not want to answer, just tell me."*

List:

1. all persons present at the interview,
2. the relationship of these people to the client,
3. the location of the interview, and
4. the date of the interview.

Background and History:

- *The position of employment at the time of the accident,*
- *A brief description of the accident (or medical condition)*

Personal Data:

- *Age*
- *Date of Birth (DOB)*
- *Address and Phone Number*
- *Last four digits of the Social Security Number*
- *Height and Weight*
- *Marital Status*
- *Children and others living in the home*
- *Sources of Income to the household*
- *Valid driver's license (any restrictions)*
- *Vehicle (automatic or manual)*
- *Living arrangements (home, mobile home, renting, buying)*
- *Military service*
- *Citizen of the United States*
- *Criminal record*
- *Status of disability (SSDI or SSI)*
- *Vocational Interest (hobbies, exercise)*

Education:

Academic:

*"What is the highest level of education completed, the dates of completion, the names and location of the school(s), type of program, vocational or college preparation, year graduated, and the type of diploma received, colleges attended, degree program, and classifications."*

Vocational Training:

*"The name of school(s) attended, their locations, the nature of the training, and the certifications, or DL classifications."*

Literacy:

*"Can you read, write, and do simple math? Can you complete an employment application, or read a note from a friend?"*

Academic Skills:

*"Can you use of a computer? Do you have a Face Book or Twitter account? Do you have office skills (typing, filing, use of office machines)?"*

Work History:

List the past jobs the client has performed beginning with the last position held. For each job ask these (5) questions:

1. the name of the job;
2. The average weekly, monthly, or annual earnings;
3. the job duties;
4. the exertion required to perform the job; and
5. the reason for leaving.

Medical History:

Summary of Primary Medical Treatment to Date, including:

1. the treatment,
2. the location of the treatment,
3. the doctors involved,
4. the diagnosis and outcomes,
5. the current treating doctor, and
6. current medications.

Secondary Medical Conditions:

Discuss any secondary medical conditions, such as treatment for mental or emotional problems, psychological treatment for related or unrelated problems, such as obesity, heart problems, diabetes, epilepsy, pulmonary problems, or other complications that should be considered when addressing employment options.

Functional Capacity:

Ask clients what it is that is preventing them from working. You may ask this question in this way: *"What is the # 1 reason you are not working?"*

If pain is the issue, ask about the kind of pain:

1. burning, sharp, throbbing, etc.
2. On a 10-point scale with one (1) being "no significant pain" and 10 being "excruciating pain" how would you rate your pain?
3. What makes the pain better? What makes the pain worse?
4. Do you have to lie down during the day?
5. Do you have to use an assistive device to ambulate?

Client's ability to perform certain work-related physical functions:

1. How far or long can you walk at one time?
2. How long can you stand at one time?
3. How long can you stand or walk in an 8-hour day?
4. How long can you sit at one time? How long can you sit in an 8-hour day?
5. How much can you lift frequently (2/3 of a workday), occasionally (1/3 of a workday)?
6. Non-exertion limitations: Can you bend, stoop, reach, and reach overhead, twist, crouch, crawl, balance.
7. Do you have any problems with the use of your hands?
8. Do you have any problems working outdoors or around moving machinery?

*"How do you get to the doctor's appointments? Do you drive yourself or do others take you? Have you been involved with the state vocational rehabilitation agency?"*

Behavioral Observations:

These are the things the interviewer has observed during the interview:

1. Punctuality
2. Appearance
3. Dress
4. Demeanor
5. Mannerisms
6. Physical features
7. Signs of pain and discomfort: changing positions, standing up, grimaces.

8. Attention and concentration: active listening; consistency of information, vagueness, body language, eye contact, cooperation.

Legal Involvement:

Pending litigation, attorney involved, time in jail or prison.

Activities of Daily Living and Personal Interests:

1. What do you do on a typical day?
2. Do you help with the chores around the house: vacuuming, cutting the grass, washing dishes?
3. Do you have any hobbies or special interests?
4. Are there things you used to do for fun or recreation that you no longer do?
5. Have you considered some other kinds of work

Conclusion of Interview:

At the end of the interview, you may close with a statement (e.g., *"Is there anything else you wish to tell me that we have not already gone over about your disability and how it affects your ability to work?"*

Be sure to thank the client for the time he/she has spent with you.

## INTERVIEW SUGGESTIONS

It is very important at the outset of the interview to make the client feel as comfortable as possible. This means making good use of your non-verbal skills learned in other counseling courses. Some of these include:

- removing any obstacles from between you and those interviewed, such as desks and other objects which may become barriers to communication,
- use good eye contact,
- seating yourself in a position facing your client with open arms and open palms when demonstrating a point, and
- speaking slowly, making each point clear and receiving a complete answer before moving forward.

Creating a counseling environment that is calm and relaxed makes the words of the introductory statement (the opening lines of the sample) seem more comforting and sincere.

Write slowly and make sure all recorded statements are complete. You see, the client is not the only person in an uncomfortable position at the beginning of an interview. When first meeting new clients, most counselors are somewhat anxious because, if nothing else, they have so much information going through their heads and so many objectives they hope to achieve in the interview. Meeting new people and new situations is never comfortable for any professional, no matter how much experience they may have. Most people–counselors and clients–take time to settle into an interview.

## INTERVIEW QUESTIONS ABOUT A CLIENT'S WORK HISTORY

Look at the questions under work history in the sample interview format. The suggested line of questioning gives a sense of order to gathering the work history and the results normally present a clear picture of the vocational choices made in the past. In inquiring about the past work, experienced counselors usually begin their questioning with the most recent job and working backwards, followed by the next most recent job and so on. Notice there are five (5) questions you need to ask about past work:

1. the title of the job,
2. the job duties,
3. the required exertion level,
4. the wage or salary, and
5. the reason for leaving.

We will consider separately how each of these points is developed in the interview.

*The title of the job and the approximate dates the job was performed.* Depending upon the age of the individual, this inquiry may go back in time well beyond the 15 years considered relevant by the Social Security Administration. Jobs done in the remote past may be useful in a number of ways. After all, any job done in the past shows an interest and familiarity with that kind of work even if the skills learned are too remote to be useful today. If clients cannot return to their past work, some of these other jobs may suggest avenues to alternative employment.

T*he job duties involved in each of the past jobs*. While the title may be the same as that found in the *Dictionary of Occupational Titles* (DOT), the job duties may vary widely among employers, making the work performed different from the textbook definition. Just as the job duties among various employment situations may vary, so too, the skills it takes to do the jobs may be different. A discussion of the job duties for each job often reveals hidden skills that may well transfer to other occupations that may be useful in identifying alternative jobs.

*The exertion levels* of the job need to be considered. As the job duties vary widely, there may also be variation in the exertion needed to do the job. Increased job duties usually make the jobs heavier in exertion than the way they are described in the DOT. For proper documentation in the initial and subsequent reports, counselors may need to provide a comparison between the job as performed and the job as normally performed in the national economy or as listed in the DOT.

*The wage level* of the job. The wage an employer pays usually suggests the skill level of the job and may provide an indication of how close the job title is to the way the job was actually performed. For instance, if the pay for a cook is a minimum wage job, the client was, in all likelihood, a short-order cook or a fast food worker rather than a cook in a full-service restaurant. You will also need wage information if determining wage loss is part of the assignment.

*The reason for leaving the job.* These questions may be more important when considered all together than individually. For instance, if the reason for leaving a job after a lengthy employment is for higher wages or because of a disabling accident, the question may have little importance to your job placement efforts. If there are many jobs of short duration, the question raises concerns about work stability and reliability.

## EXPANDING THE PERSONAL INTERVIEW

If the main objective of the interview is to complete a vocational evaluation and write a report for an insurance adjuster or others, following the sample format above should provide the information needed. If job placement is expected to follow the interview, a few additional steps may jump-start the placement activities and move the process to another level. The following job-search techniques start the client moving forward toward those goals and avoiding lengthy delays that often follow the initial interview.

Often at the end of the interview, the counselor and the client part ways with little or no preparation for the job search which follows. Nevertheless, an insightful counselor can put a positive face on the interview and direct the personal interview toward future vocational choices. Here are three (3) widely used techniques for expanding a personal interview and making preliminary vocational choices. At the end of the interview:

1. *Ask clients what they want to do with their life/work.*

This sounds simple enough, but there is no better way to go about selecting a vocational objective than simply asking clients what work they want to do. Note this statement made by John Holland and quoted in *What Color Is Your Parachute*,[1] the best-known book on career development and predicting the success of a vocational objective. John Holland says, "Despite several decades of research, the most efficient way to predict vocational choice is simply to ask a person what he/she wants to be (do). Our best devices do not exceed the predictive value of that method."[pg. 95] Your client may not give you an astute answer to this question, but the response will likely provide some idea of what the client is thinking that will help you in planning for job placement.

2. *Ask about family, friends, and acquaintances*.

At some point in the interview, you will be concerned about activities of daily living, often called ADL's. These activities might be what time clients get up in the morning, what they do around the house during the day, their hobbies, what they do for fun, and what persons make up the family complex. This is the opportunity for you to expand upon your client's family support system to include questions about what they do for a living (their occupations), their employers, and their places of work and where family members live. In this way you become acquainted with Aunt Thelma and Uncle Joe, begin to get a picture of the family complex and its values (see Chapter 3), develop a source for finding jobs, and gain a feel for the client's work ethic and the kinds of work acceptable to your client and other persons within the family complex. Most importantly, you begin to develop a network of family, friends, and acquaintances who may be used later by your client to find jobs in the elusive "hidden job market" (See Chapter 10: "Networking for Jobs in the Hidden Job Market: A Client-Centered Approach").

3. Prepare for the next interview by *making a homework assignment, such as a list of jobs clients would consider*.

If alternative work seems to be the direction, there is no reason to delay the inevitable. Why wait to open the discussion of jobs possibilities. A way to begin is, at the end of the interview, simply ask the client to make a list of ten jobs they may be considering now or have considered while recuperating from the medical condition.

Developing this list may also be an assignment (homework) that ends the interview and anticipates the next counseling session. The assignment to have clients make a list may also establish behavioral counseling as the counseling method of choice. When using the selective method for job placement, assignments are usually a regular part of an employment counseling session. At this point, do not expect earthshaking insight! Even vague answers will give the counselor an idea of what has been happening during the long hours in convalescence and provide some indication of how much the client has been considering work in the future.

## THE INITIAL EVALUATION

Once the counselor has reviewed and analyzed the case and held a personal interview, the time has come to make some preliminary decisions and communicate with the persons assigning the case. The reason for an initial evaluation is that decisions beyond this point will need the advice and consent of others to go forward. Normally, the initial evaluation comes in the form of a report that reviews the medical information, presents a vocational and medical profile of the injured or disabled worker, analyzes the vocational information, identifies transferable work skills, and makes recommendations for future actions.

For personal injury cases, the initial evaluation may be the only report prior to testifying in court. When the case is assigned, the attorney is seeking the professional opinions of a vocational expert. The content of the report addresses the questions very similar to those presented in "To the Reader" at the beginning of Chapter 5. (The reader might wish to review these questions before moving forward). To make an initial evaluation for a personal injury case, the counselor reviews the information in the record provided by the attorney, conducts a personal interview, engages in extensive labor market research, and, based upon this information, offers opinions to the court, mainly about employability and wage loss. If the attorneys in the case are unable to resolve their differences beforehand, the trial testimony of the expert will likely center around the opinions offered in the report.

In worker compensation cases, the rehabilitation counselor may need to take additional steps before preparing the initial evaluation report. If the vocational goal is returning to the worker's customary work, the counselor usually needs to contact the employer. From the employer the counselor needs to know:

First, if returning to work for the same employer following MMI (maximum medical improvement) is a possibility.
The employer may have filled the position or, for whatever reason, may not want the worker back.

Second, if the worker can do the work but is unable to perform the job the way it has been done in the past, the counselor, with the concurrence of the employer, may need to analyze the job duties to see if the work, or workstation, can be modified to allow the worker to return to the job.

Third, if the worker cannot do the past work, there may be other jobs available with the same employer that the worker can perform. Unless there are other circumstances involved, most employers know their business and make a conscious effort to accommodate their injured workers.

For worker's compensation cases, the report of the initial evaluation is normally addressed to the case adjuster at the insurance company. If the case involves medical case management during recovery, the case adjuster wants an update on the medical condition and to know, if possible, when the worker has reached maximum medical improvement (MMI) and can return to work (RTW). In these cases, the initial evaluation is followed by monthly progress reports until the worker returns to work.

If returning to work with the same employer in not an option, the adjuster will want to know the counselor's recommendations for alternative employment (i.e., what jobs the client can perform and what can be done to prepare the worker for a new job). Recommendations usually include counseling and teaching of job-seeking skills, retraining, the preparation of a resume, and possible suggestions on the kinds of employment the injured workers might pursue given their vocational profile and medical restrictions and other limitations.

Appendix 2 at the end of this chapter contains an actual report prepared for an insurance adjuster with the name and location changed. In this case, the injured worker was able to return to work following an injury to her thumb and subsequent surgery.

In the event a worker cannot return to the work performed in the past, the adjuster will likely request that the rehabilitation counselor proceed with job placement in alternative employment. The question then becomes, what work? In most cases, the selection of other work has already begun by the time the counselor gets approval to proceed in finding alternative work. To some extent, the medical profile and the functional restrictions provided by treating physicians will have eroded the base for potential jobs. There will be jobs the injured worker can no longer do. For instance, an over-the-road truck driver having undergone back surgery may not be able to resume driving an 18-wheeler because of restrictions in lifting, pushing, and pulling.

The creation of a vocational profile, along with identification of job skills, will have further refined the potential job options. For instance, if the injured worker is a younger person with a high school education and, prior to injury, has been a construction carpenter, the likely first step will be to search for jobs that have something to do with the trades. Thus, when job placement begins, earlier planning and analysis will have pointed the direction for the job search.

Yet, much remains to be done to ready the injured worker for re-entry into the job market. Four (4) main tasks that lie ahead in preparing clients for the job search include:

1. preparing the tools for the job search,
   See Chapter 8 for a sample resume and discussion about how to prepare cover letters, and thank-you notes including samples.

2. selection of the vocational objective,

3. communication of a marketing approach to the client, and

4. counseling in job-seeking skills.

## CHOOSING A VOCATIONAL OBJECTIVE

In vocational counseling, we ask our clients to make a career choice or a career decision. Underlying the word *career* is a mental picture of a one-time decision leading to specialized training and then a lifetime sequence of jobs (or self-employment) centered around a particular vocation or profession: law, medicine, accounting, management, marketing, journalism, counseling, to name a few. Underlying our concept of a career, and deeply ingrained in our consciousness, is a "one-time, one-occupational model." This is a picture we usually have in mind when we ask, "What do you want to do with your life?" Upward mobility following this model usually means formal education followed by a life-long program of continuing education to update knowledge and skills periodically.

In considering a vocational choice for our clientele, it is important to remember that most of our clients come from Class IV: "working people" and Class V: "baseline people," as discussed in Chapters 2 and 3. The jobs these workers perform often require higher levels of physical exertion and/or carry greater risk of injury. In vocational training or at work, these workers learn the skills of their trade. Their expectation is that they will perform these skills throughout their work life. They may have several job changes with different employers, but they will likely work in the same or a similar capacity with each employer.

A work-related injury or long illness can alter their aspirations and their life. Frequently, when these workers are ready to return to work, they can no longer do the job or jobs they have done in the past; and are unable to use the skills of their occupation. When alternative work becomes the vocational goal, the interest of these clients is normally in job placement; (e.g., finding a particular job, hopefully one that will use their work skills to some degree, rather than in engaging in educational programs required in most career development).

Rehabilitation counselors provide the bridge to help their clients move from disability to independence in work. Routinely, the counselor or case manager will follow the medical treatment as the case develops to the point that the individual is ready to return to work. When alternative work is indicated, counselors assist their clients in making vocational decisions by:

- Studying their client's work history to understand jobs in the way they were performed and to identify work skills.
- Researching vocational material to locate similar occupations or occupations that use like or similar work skills.
- Possibly, giving interest testing to help identify vocational possibilities, particularly if the clients are younger workers.
- Making sure that all vocational opportunities considered are within the client's functional limitations.

Most of the time, the counseling provided is directed toward locating a particular job or series of jobs, not upon a long educational process. As a result, job placement rather than career development often becomes the focal point of the dialogue between the client and the rehabilitation counselor. The selection of the job or jobs to pursue is based upon personal preference and acquired skills.

Few of us make an occupational choice without regard to personal preference and acquired skills. To make a vocational choice without considering these factors leaves the rehabilitation counselor and the client operating in the dark, seeking only low-pay, entry-level work or starting all over in occupations in which our clients may have little skill and aptitude and little, if any, interest. (Recall the canvas methods and the random method introduced at the beginning of this chapter)

Unfortunately, some vocational decisions are made without regard to work skills and client preference. Fears, both realistic and unrealistic, can overcome reason. Irrational decisions are often made out of desperation, leading to unwise vocational choices. An example that comes immediately to mind is of a history professor and a friend who was caught up in the market glut of liberal arts teachers in the early 70's. We will call him Bill. Fearing he lacked transferable skills to any other professional-level employment, Bill began looking into the possibility of becoming a bricklayer. At age 40, this was not a viable alternative for him. Not only are the physical demands different, but also masonry has its own career path. Today, I am pleased to say this professor is president of a small, mid-western liberal arts college. His academic skills served him well as a foundation for college administration.

A successful vocational adjustment leading to a new vocational choice needs to consider all the resources: life experiences (adaptive skills), educational resources (educational skills), and skills acquired from previous work (work skills). Weighing these factors and designing a plan of work for our clients is certainly one of the most important steps we take in the job placement process, requiring skill and intuition, experience and foresight, hard work, timing, and some luck.

## COMMUNICATION OF THE MANAGERIAL APPROACH

By now, the options available to the counselor for selecting a management approach to job placement should be relatively clear. Counselors must decide how much authority can be appropriately assigned to the client and the amount of authority counselors must keep for themselves. (*See* Chapter 1, "The Rehabilitation Counselor's Management Role in Job Placement.") Once this decision is made, counselors must then decide whether to use the Selective Approach, the main substance of this chapter, the Client Centered-Approach (*see* Introduction to Chapter 10), or some variation of the two, based upon their client's ability and willingness to accept authority.

What now becomes important is for counselors to decide specific activities they can expect of their client during the job search. High-functioning clients and highly motivated clients may be asked to locate and identify jobs in the community, fill out applications for these jobs, set up their own interviews, and meet employers without a lot of assistance from the counselor. What these clients can be expected to do largely depends upon their knowledge of and integration into the community.

On the other hand, for less motivated or lower functioning clients, clients without community connections, and clients who are perceived to have poor job-seeking skills, counselors may decide to do pretty much all of the essential activities of the job search, as outlined in the Selective Approach. In this scenario, the counselor would probably decide on the kind of jobs that are appropriate, given the client's functional abilities and limitations, locate the jobs, notify the client of the availability of the jobs, set up appointments, and even attend the interviews where appropriate. Just because counselors choose to do most of the placement chores, however, does not mean that their clients are not involved in the job search. It does mean that most of the decisions are made by the counselor and work-related activities are determined by their counselors.

Finally, the counselor may decide some form of a client-centered strategy with shared responsibilities based upon individual strengths. For instance, a counselor may have a better understanding of the kinds of jobs their clients can perform, given their abilities and limitations, while the client may have greater insight into the life and work of the community. In this case, counselors may rely upon job-seeking skills counseling sessions to teach the ins and outs of locating jobs in the "hidden job market" and expect their client to conduct the actual job search.

Whatever approach the counselor decides to use must be communicated to the client directly. This is so important! A counselor cannot expect their clients to do anything that the two of them have not discussed beforehand. Each action step must be communicated and negotiated carefully and clearly.

A typical negotiation between counselor and client might go as follows:

*Bill, I expect you to register with the Minnesota Employment Commission, to conduct your own job search, tell your friends and acquaintances the kinds of jobs you are seeking, and to spend at least two hours a day on the job search. Moreover, I expect you to take careful notes of the jobs you locate, the employers you talk with, and the people you contact about work. I expect for you to record clearly and accurately these contacts in your "Job Search Organizer." We will discuss your job contacts in our planning sessions. Finally, I will expect you to contact me before making appointments for interviews, then make the appointments for interviews, attend the interviews, and follow up on each interview with a resume and a thank-you note.*

*I will help you. I will prepare for you a professional resume, and do my part by looking over job lists, contacting employers, and reviewing job sources. I will give you job leads I uncover. During our next counseling session, I will begin to share with you some of the things I have learned about how to find jobs in the market today.*

## COUNSELING IN JOB-SEEKING SKILLS

From the example above, re-read the last sentence. The counselor says to the client "During our next session I will begin to share with you some of the things I have learned about how to find jobs in the market today." This statement is the counselor's announcement of the direction subsequent counseling sessions will take: in other words, the counselor will begin to teach the client job-seeking skills.

Never conclude that clients know how to find jobs no matter how knowledgeable they may seem. You know that to be successful in the job search, clients have to stay active and carry on the job search continuously despite discouragements and failures. Moreover, in the employment interview, clients must be able to explain their work skills in a positive manner and discuss their medical problems in a way that does not sabotage the job prospect. Do you think most clients can do that without help? As stated earlier, a 1985 study at a Minnesota Rehabilitation Center showed serious deficiencies in their client's job-seeking skills: eighty percent (80%) of the clients did not look for work frequently enough, 85% could not explain their skills to employers, and 90% could not explain their handicapping condition.

There is little or no evidence to suggest the abilities of rehabilitation clients today have changed significantly since that study. The current widespread use of the selective approaches in the marketplace provides sufficient evidence of deficiencies in the job-seeking skills of our clients. Therefore, it is imperative that counselors take time, formally or informally, to teach their clients job-seeking skills.

Rehabilitation counselors may, at times, feel inadequate when it comes to teaching others about finding jobs, but trust your instincts! You are the expert in this field (you know, all experts are self-appointed). Never doubt your own abilities. No matter how inadequate you may feel inside, you are probably light-years ahead of your clients in your knowledge of work and disability. Do not worry about your knowledge of the current trends in the workplace. Most rehabilitation counselors who do this work all the time have a hard time keeping up with developments in the job-search field.

At the beginning of the job search, you have to set the pace for future actions by getting the client started without delay. What better way to start the job search with a bang than teaching them how to prepare for a job search. (If you have read this book, our hope is that you are loaded with new ideas). Even though this chapter deals mainly with a job search conducted by the counselor, counselors still need to prepare their clients to meet employers and discuss their ability to perform the jobs presented to them.

Here are some of the areas that need to be addressed in a presentation of job-seeking skills. This list is not exhaustive. Each client will have different needs as identified in earlier counseling sessions. An effective job-seeking presentation will shape the skills set to the unique needs of each client. The list below includes the basic essentials of any job-seeking skills format.

1. Research has shown inactivity and long periods of disability among our clients result in a degree of situational depression with loss of confidence in their abilities. Motivational techniques, as presented in Chapter 4, help clients regain their self-confidence, and learn to re-connect with work, the community, and sources of support. Helping clients reconnect with work, the community, and sources of support is at the top of almost every list for job-seeking skills.

2. Most rehabilitation clients have difficulty explaining in an interview what happened to them and why there may be a gap in their employment records. As a general rule, openness with

employers goes a long way toward placing an interviewer at ease regarding disability. In fact, the right approach is to have clients learn to place emphasis upon their abilities and all the positive things they have done to overcome their medical problems. With this approach, disability becomes the asset of the client in the interview.

3. This transition to accenting abilities in an interview as opposed to limitations is not automatic, however. Clients have to learn that negative statements (e.g., "I can't do the things I used to do" and "I still have a lot of pain") are deadly in an interview. When negative statements like these are made in an interview, the focus then centers upon *dis*-ability and on what the client cannot do rather upon their assets and abilities, the things the client can do. One major principle to teach in the presentation of job-seeking skills is that medical limitations do not need to be brought up or expanded upon in an interview unless there are job tasks the client cannot do without accommodation from the employer.

4. Clients need to know how to use a resume to highlight their abilities. So often, counselors spend a lot of time putting together the resume for the client and spend so little time discussing ways the resume can be used to make an effective presentation to employers (see Chapter 8: "How Jobs are found in the New American Economy"). The resume outlines the abilities of the client. During strategy sessions, counselors can use the resume as a format for teaching clients how to talk about these abilities and other work assets.

5. Clients have to know how to use networking in the community, among family, friends, and acquaintances in order to find the jobs best suited to their abilities and to find jobs that pay the most money. If left to their own devices, without training, clients will invariably rely upon traditional job sources, principally the local newspaper. In this chapter the emphasis is upon counselors locating job sources, job leads, and to the extent possible, involving their clients in the job search. (See Chapter 10: "Networking for Jobs in the Hidden Job Market: A Client-Centered Approach" and "*Job-Search Organizer*," a step-by-step interactive strategy for finding the best jobs in the community).

# THE SELECTIVE APPROACH TO JOB PLACEMENT

Under the Selective Approach rehabilitation counselors are the central figures in locating jobs and matching their clients to available jobs, making employer contacts, and even, on occasion, accompanying clients to an interview. As we shall see later in this chapter, the Internet with its ability to locate employers and present information on community and employer web sites has improved the quality of a job search using selective methods.

The remainder of this chapter focuses upon counselor-directed ways to conduct a job search and improve the results using the Selective Approach. Most often, the job search is conducted over the phone. Rehabilitation counselors contact employers directly about advertised jobs and explore the community for job leads. Rehabilitation counselors are not just looking randomly for open and available jobs in the community, however. The jobs located and referred to clients must be suited to a client's vocational profile and must be within the physical or mental limitations as set by the client's treating doctors. A determination of the suitability of jobs, based upon the client's vocational profile and medical limitations, must be made prior to searching for jobs.

To demonstrate the Selective Approach we first discuss preparing a case summary and materials rehabilitation counselors need to have before them when contacting employers by phone. Then, using a highly personal approach in real time, we take the counselor through an informal job search using the Internet in a large city, Austin, Texas and in a small town, Mount Pocono, Pennsylvania to show the ins and outs of a telephonic job search. We also show some of the pitfalls that typically take place during a job search for persons with disabilities. Finally, we look at ways a counselor can present disability issues to employers in a truthful way while still advocating for their clients.

## DEVELOPING A CASE SUMMARY

The place to begin the job search using the Selective Approach is with preparing a case summary. A case summary involves a one to two page summary of the information gathered from the case records and the personal interview. Usually, a case summary will include:

1. A summary of the vocational and medical information in the case, concluding with the medical restrictions that need to be followed in exploring job sources and searching for job leads.

2. An analysis of the record and information gathered from personal contacts with the client to locate educational degrees and achievements, licenses and certifications, and work and adaptive skills to present to employer contacts.

3. A list of possible jobs the counselor believes the client can perform based upon the records and the personal interview, taking into account the work restrictions set by medical sources.

*A summary of the medical information* condenses the main points in the medical profile to a single sheet of paper so that the counselor does not have to go back through the file each time they work a particular client's case. Most counselors have other cases needing attention. A normal job search will take anywhere from 15 to 45 hours, requiring the counselor to review the medical information over a long period of time. The case summary allows the counselor to resurface quickly the information needed to continue the job search. The summary of medical information need not be drawn out, but it should detail the events of the accident or injury, treatment modalities, treatment outcomes, some personal information, and, of great importance, the medical restrictions *highlighted.*

A list of *adaptive skills, educational degrees and achievements, licenses and certifications, and instances of personal recognition*, such as promotions, gives the counselor points of interest to present to possible employers. Of course, when counselors are talking to employers, they will normally use the work skills learned and performed at past jobs to demonstrate their client's vocational abilities. As we have talked about so often in other chapters, most clients have personal qualities that if presented to employers, make them stand out from among other candidates for a job. Some of these are certifications and degrees, past promotions and achievements, a lengthy work record with a single employer, or skills they have learned along the way that may not be part of the formal work history. Research has shown that adaptive skills, achievements, and personal qualities may be more persuasive to employers than work skills. When talking with employers, counselors need to have a list of these qualities or personal traits close at hand. The case summary is an ideal place to list these qualities.

A *tentative list of possible jobs* the client can perform is normally part of the case summary. As counselors review the file and conduct interviews with their clients, the job possibilities narrow: medical restrictions eliminate some jobs; education and lack of experience eliminate others; and personal preferences reduce still other possible options. Before the job search begins, counselors generally make assumptions about certain jobs they believe fall within the medical restrictions and can be performed adequately by their client.

For instance, if a client is an automobile mechanic with a back problem, possible job options at a lighter level of exertion may include sales of auto parts, a service estimator at a car dealership, or service station attendant. Such a list allows the counselor to focus upon real possibilities when reviewing job listings and to identify proper sources of employment more quickly.

The sample case summary below was developed for an actual case. Only the names and location have been changed. The summary is brief, as it is supposed to be, but provides some of the main points the counselor working the case needed to review before contacting employers.

## SAMPLE CASE SUMMARY

Name: Valerie Stensen SSN: ... .. 9626
4735 Albany Drive
Centerville, Arkansas 72201

Date of Birth: September 31, 1964 Age: 48

Employer: Continental Suppliers

Date of Injury: December 16, 2009

Date of Assignment: December 9, 2011

Insurance Adjuster: Mary Boggus

Valerie Stensen lives in Fort Smith, Arkansas. Her husband, Walter, was stationed at Fort Chaffey. She is a high school graduate from Pine Bluff High School. Her husband is a Sergeant First Class and was deployed overseas sometime after the accident. He is now stationed at Fort Lee, Virginia. She visits him on holidays. Currently, her daughter lives with her in a nice, one-story house in Centerville.

In 1993, she took training as a Certified Nursing Assistant (CNA), but did not use her vocational training. She last worked as a Sales Associate in a furniture store on the military base at Fort Chaffey. She resigned her position because of her medical problems. From 1992 to 1995, she worked as a housemother for Sunrise, a program for mentally impaired children located on another military base. (She had 15 years working in youth centers on bases where her husband was stationed). She had a lot of lifting of patrons as part of her job duties; she also carried children on school field trips. From 1989 to 1992, she worked for the Regis Company and did fiscal inventory for a variety of stores, Wal-Mart and Home Depot. She took inventory in stores in several other states in the Southwest.

On December 16, 2009, she was kicked in the right knee by another employee wearing steel-toed boots. She was treated at the Western Army Community Hospital at Fort Smith and diagnosed with a right knee sprain. She was not hospitalized and returned to work. She later had arthroscopic surgery on the right knee. She got better and returned to work.

She was evaluated by Dr. H. Clark Winston, Orthopedic Surgeon, on May 25, 2011 and given the following restrictions: **"I think that she should be able to return to work without restrictions although I would not recommend any prolonged running or jumping from heights with her arthritic knee**."

Her treating physician has given her permanent restrictions to avoid aggravating activities that include prolonged standing or walking, repetitive knee bending or lifting, and cold temperatures. Based upon these work restrictions, she can do a wide range of light and sedentary work. Her problem is her right knee, but she is under treatment. She is very pleasant and seems to be interested in starting a new job that is within her limitations.

It would seem to me that she would be able to do sales work in a retail setting, companion work (her CNA has expired but she has had training in patient care), and inventory clerk or anything to do with counting inventory. She would have experience in the use of a computer program. She has a continuous work history and most of the jobs she had lasted three or more years.

## MOVING OUT
## THE SEARCH BEGINS FOR JOB LEADS

(Presented in first person)

When I first began these worker's compensation cases, it was part-time work in my undergraduate studies for extra cash. I did not know what types of questions I needed to ask of the employers and neither did my boss. In fact, he intensely disliked this portion of the job. I believe he was looking to shirk this responsibility. I soon found out why.

Apparently, a job search involves more than just sifting through classified employment advertisements, ducking my boss's emails for a completed assignment, and asking for extensions. Albeit searching for jobs is part of the process, but using only that method I kept coming up short for leads. The job-search process without training was chaotic. I understood the basics: I was to take the claimant's functional limitations and search for suitable employment that fit within those functional parameters. However, I soon found out there was much more to it than simply understanding the basics.

JOBS ARE NOT ALWAYS THE WAY THEY SEEM.

Several jobs at face value would ostensibly fall within the functional restrictions. However, I soon found out the environment in which these jobs were performed could vary widely. For instance, a job as a cashier in a convenience store is very different from a cashier working in a large corporate retail store, such as Wal-Mart or Target. A cashier position at Wal-Mart is similar to jobs within a production environment. Wal-Mart cashiers are fixed at their stations continuously operating the register to accommodate a very high volume of customers. If there are periods throughout the day when the typical influx of customers is not as rapid (e.g., Tuesday mornings), then cash registers may be closed and the cashiers are assigned other responsibilities, such as stocking shelves. These cashiers are usually required to lift heavier weight than their counterparts do at a convenience store. Stores such as Target may require lifting of fifty-pound bags of dog food and moving heavy appliances on a frequent basis.

In many convenience stores, cashiers are familiar with a much slower pace of work. The volume of customers will also vary upon the location of the convenience store. For instance, a convenience store in the city will more than likely generate an abundance of consumer traffic, whereas a rural or suburban convenience store will have frequent periods free of clientele. The cashier is usually given other responsibilities, such as cleaning the soda dispensers or tidying the store so that it is more presentable. These extra responsibilities can be performed at leisure as long as the work is completed by the end of the cashier's shift. A small store in a gas station is stocked with easy to grab, light items, such as drinks, packaged foods, and engine oils and filters. Rarely do these small markets carry heavy items that their cashiers would need to lift to the register. These cashiers may have stocking responsibilities, but the pace is much slower. They have more freedom to stand and move around. Some convenience stores even allow the cashiers to sit behind the counter during their slower hours.

A position as a front desk receptionist may vary depending upon the size of company being represented. A larger company will have a much more hurried pace. There may be more than one receptionist to accommodate the high volume of clientele and to support a larger number of staff members within the office requiring coordination and cooperation. Busy offices may require the receptionist to spend more time answering and redirecting incoming calls, thus frequently putting aside tasks that will need to be completed before the end of the workday. This kind of work would require a great deal of multi-tasking and would not be ideal for someone with an Attention Deficit Disorder, problems with concentration, or with significant memory loss as a result of their medical conditions.

Conversely, a receptionist in a small office setting may have less frequent phone calls and walk-in clients. These receptionists may be assigned more data entry and record keeping with less task coordination. A receptionist in a small office will enjoy a quieter work setting, without quite as much multi-tasking, and more of a sedentary position. This may better accommodate a client who uses an assistive device like a cane or who has another type of ambulatory disability.

## An Internet Job Search

I now believe that the most efficient way to manage each case is using a more holistic approach and better research methods. The Internet has made a holistic approach possible. In the examples that follow, I have used real time to show not only the path to follow in the job search, as I weave in and out of web sites, but also to give the reader a sense of movement, a feel for what the experience is like as I walk you through two actual job searches.

*Where to begin?* Regardless of the location of the local job market, the place to start is with the town or city in which the claimant resides. There will be a lot of variation depending upon the size of the area. I begin the job search by researching the size and population of the town and the economic history. The easiest web site to start with is Wikipedia; but, with this web site, you have to verify your information. Wikipedia is a great source of information; however, the website is updated and modified by its users and may contain errors. Next, go to the town or city website. If the claimant's town is too small for its own web page, find the website for the county in which it is located. Search engines are your friend at the beginning of a job search

While it is important to understand the full economic history of your client's location, much of the early history may be of little value. For instance, you will not find a job with Atlanta's street car magnate or with the Scranton (Pennsylvania) Button Company pressing phonograph records. Nevertheless, some city's predominant industries may still be in operation, such as Altria, the tobacco company, formerly Philip Morris, in Richmond, Virginia. In your exploration of the local job market, try to focus on industry growth within the last 30 years.

Because a job search can vary greatly between small towns and large cities, I will use one of each as an example. For a large city job market, I have chosen Austin, Texas; for a small city job market, I have chosen Pocono City, Pennsylvania.

## Cities with a Large Job Market: Austin, Texas

In a large city, employment opportunities are much more plentiful.

Sometimes you could even find enough jobs just by sifting through national employment websites and selecting a particular area. Web Sites such as *Career Builder*, *Indeed.com*, and *Snagajob.com* provide job lists for every section of the country. Still, I do not recommend limiting the job search to these or other national web sites. By taking the time to research more local web sites in the area, you will be able to find many more occupations that are appropriate for your client. You may consider an expanded job search of the local area that matches your requirements.

Let us start with a city like Austin, Texas. The easiest thing to do is to start with a broad scope and narrow your focus by eliminating the irrelevant. Enter Austin, TX into your search engine. Large cities will have several websites dedicated to its travel, entertainment, and industry. Find the official municipal website first (it usually ends in .gov). Try to locate the phone number for the Chamber of Commerce. Call and ask them to send you as much information about local employment as they are willing to give you. You may have to pay a nominal fee if the information is extensive. Contacting the Chamber of Commerce may seem somewhat of an antiquated method but it is important to gather as much research material as possible. All municipal websites will vary, but the core information is usually very similar. These websites will not only provide information on local private industry but will typically have government jobs posted as well. On the Austin website, there is a link to city jobs where job seekers can view all the current open positions.

Many municipal websites will feature a link to the local employment offices. The Austin, TX site offers three. Providing information about and addresses for these offices may be helpful to leave with the client after your interview. A startling realization I had when I first stepped into the rehabilitation profession was the lack of knowledge many of the clients had in relation to resources in their local community. Since every employment office is different, you may need to inform your client which services each office provides. This reduces confusion.

Whether your research area is an independent city or incorporated within a county, it is important to expand your research beyond the city proper. For instance, Austin, TX is the seat of Travis County and is the economic center of the Austin-Round Rock-San Marcos metropolitan area. Larger cities have several counties that are grouped within a metropolitan area. Find where these are located and include this within your research of the community.

Keep in mind the location of your client. If the client lives in the southwest part of the city and you find a suitable job that is located in a northeast suburb, the company may be more than an hour away. When you finally get to the actual job search, you will want to use the client's physical address as a starting point and then radiate outward, trying to keep most of the jobs within 25 miles. It is not realistic to locate entry-level job with a long commute.

From just looking at various websites about Austin, I can see that much of the city's growth emerged around technology and business in the 1980's. Wikipedia (to which some of you may even have contributed to complete your undergraduate degree) is usually a good starting source for the understanding of a city's industrial development. One caveat, which I am sure your former professors have expounded upon in detail, is to always find corroborating sources. From this site, I can discern that several headquarters and regional offices are located in this area, such as Texas Instruments, Dell, Whole Foods, and IBM.

At this point, you should be making a list of the major employers. The Austin municipal website contains an A-Z list of companies/employers that attended the 2012 Job Expo. Find the websites for as many of the local employers as possible. Open employment positions are often listed on their sites. Many companies do not bother posting jobs on other websites because of the community's familiarity, their desire to find employees locally, or because there are too many positions to list.

From a tourism website, I learned that Austin is well known for its music scene and festivals. Find out what is particularly notable about the tourism industry in each city you research. Is the city known for its casinos (Las Vegas, Atlantic City)? Is the scenery of the city the most salient feature (The Grand Canyon, The Smokey Mountains, The Ozarks, and Yellowstone National Park)? Is the colonial history a central feature (Yorktown, Virginia, Salem, Massachusetts)? From this information, you can learn about certain industries that are indigenous to the area.

Keep in mind the vocational history of your clients as well as their stated vocational goal since there is no point in spending extensive amounts of time researching the fashion industry if your client has always worked and wants to continue working in the healthcare industry. If your client has worked in retail, tourism websites often list the major shopping districts and the best stores.

Other industries to keep in mind are the ones that employ an array of disparate positions. For instance, McDonald's is not going to hire a receptionist and Staples will not have a human resource assistant (unless it is a corporate office). Hospitals and hotels will have these positions, along with jobs in housekeeping, food service, retail, bookkeeping, and transportation. The wider the variety of offered jobs, the easier job seekers will be able to find a job in their chosen field. Corporate offices and headquarters will hire many clerical and human resources workers as well as sales representatives, couriers, and mail clerks. Of course, if your client has a highly skilled work background, then your job-search will be narrower and more focused. Still, most job searches you will be conducting will be for clients from a working background who cannot return to their former work and have few to no transferable job skills.

## TOWNS AND RURAL AREAS WITH A SMALL JOB MARKET: MOUNT POCONO, PENNSYLVANIA

A small town or rural location can be a more daunting search because of the relative scarcity of the number of existing jobs and employment resources in the area. It may take longer but do not worry. Jobs can be found there (e.g., Mount Pocono, Pennsylvania, which has a population under 3,000). Like Mount Pocono, small towns may not have a website of their own. With a search engine, I was able to find the location, the population, the local schools, and a transit system.

You will also want to find any useful information from any town within a 25 to 30 mile radius starting from the inside out. It is important to map a 25 to 30 mile radius for your job search because it is difficult to argue that a claimant can reasonably be expected to commute farther than this. I used *Google Maps* to locate nearby towns because at the writing of this book, it is one of the most accurate. Things change quickly and another program may be more prevalent at the time of your reading this text. Stay current with these changes.

Looking at a map and the population density, I can see that Stroudsburg and Scranton are the nearest towns. Both are small but are more densely populated than Mount Pocono. The best of all, they are both within commuting distance. Mapping the distance, Stroudsburg is 17 miles southeast and Scranton is 30 miles to the northeast. Although Stroudsburg is closer, Scranton has a larger population and will have more job opportunities. In most cases, local people seeking employment are likely to commute regularly to these larger population centers. It is a good idea to start with the closest town despite the relative ease of finding jobs farther away.

At this point, it is advantageous to find a local newspaper. For this town I found the Pocono *Record*. Reading through the online paper will help you to familiarize yourself with the area and businesses. Before I even look for the classified ads, I already see a story on the front page stating that grant money has been allocated to a cosmetic manufacturing plant in Stroudsburg. This information indicates that the company is growing and will likely expand its employment.

From past experience, I know that that this type of plant may have sedentary assembler and hand packaging positions available. If not sedentary, certainly the lifting would be nominal. Sedentary work may be suitable for a client with standing and walking restrictions. If the assembly position is light (i.e. performed while standing but the lifting is nominal), this may be a good fit for a client with lifting restrictions. Entry-level jobs on an assembly line are generally unskilled positions that can be learned quickly, within 30 days. Unskilled work fits well with a client profile whose limitations include mild intellectual disability, cognitive deficits, or those suffering from short-term memory loss. This position would not be ideal for a client with manipulative limitations because of the constant fine and gross manipulation required to perform this job. A client with carpal tunnel syndrome would not be able to perform the repetitive hand motions necessary to assemble manufacturing products.

The Pocono *Record* only provides the company's name. I entered the name of the business into a search engine and immediately found the company website. This website did not have a list of job openings so I found their phone number, called the company, and asked to speak with a person in the human resources department. The personnel manager told me that they do have unskilled production jobs and gave me an email for application submission. I also asked her for details about the available jobs. This particular factory does not have sedentary assembler positions but the lifting requirements for their assembly jobs were less than 10 pounds.

Returning to the Pocono *Record,* I see many available pages on the community web site referencing schools, a visitor's guide, new resident information, and entertainment as well as the classified ads. Since our theoretical client lives in this area, I decide to open up the resident information. As I scroll down this page, I see an article about a local community college offering courses in the field of hospitality because, as they explain, it is a growing industry in the area. If you were not already aware, the Pocono Mountains are a major travel and resort destination. If your claimant has customer service in their work history, hospitality may be an area to explore in your job search.

Always keep in mind your client's work history, adaptive skills, and possible transferable work skills. If your client performed work in education but needs a job with a lower skill level because of a traumatic brain injury, maybe a teacher's aide would be an option. Then you may want to begin searching for all the schools within the area. If your client has past work as a housekeeper, search for hotels, inns, and hospitals. If your client has a clerical work background and can still perform that type of work, you will have a wide variety of places to search. Clerical workers can be found in almost every type of employment industry.

Returning to the Pocono *Record,* I am opening up the visitors' guide page. In the Lackawanna county area, I see that there are vineyards, antiques shops, a NASCAR raceway, and a new hotel that will soon open. The new hotel will need staff. Depending upon your client's work history, the hotel may offer a variety of jobs, such as a front desk clerk, servers and bartenders, gift shop cashiers, kitchen helpers, dishwashers, maintenance workers, cooks, laundry workers or valet. Many of these jobs are unskilled and may be suitable for a client with an unskilled work history or no post-secondary education.

Next, I am looking at the events calendar. This calendar lists the events for each month and their locations. I see that bus tours to New York City are offered to attend Broadway plays. Does your client have a background in taxi, commercial, or chauffeur driving? How about dispatching, if not, call and ask if the company is willing to train for these positions. This events calendar also lists a bowling alley that may hire cashiers; floor maintenance workers, concession stand attendants, or shoe rentals. These positions are unskilled and may fit the profile for a client with an unskilled work background or a client needing to transfer into a new job.

Searching the classified ads in the Pocono *Record*, I do not find a lot of choices because many listed jobs are at a higher skill level than most of the clients with whom you will be working. That is why it is important to research the community while keeping in mind your client's limitations and work history. Usually labor market surveys are completed over several days or weeks. It is helpful to remember to return to the newspaper every time you resume your job search for any new information that may be useful. In most cases, I try to complete the job search within 20 days since most jobs are open and available for only about 15 to 20 days.

After exhausting the local newspaper, I return to searching for any useful information about the town. Like Austin, I use Wikipedia to learn some of the economic and cultural history. Since the town is so small, there is very little information provided. I do see the Monroe County Transit Authority (another possible source of jobs) listed with service to Tobyhanna. What is Tobyhanna? Entering that into a search engine, I find that it is a nearby army depot. Army depots have a variety of jobs for civilians from sales attendants, cashiers, and food service workers to warehouse workers, maintenance workers, mechanics, and clerical workers.

The search engine immediately generates the prime webpage for Tobyhanna. At first glance, I do not see a link to employment opportunities. Many websites will not make it easy for you. With a little patience I find the career opportunities under the "about" link at the top of the page. Finding this website's employment opportunities was a very convoluted process, but I try not to be discouraged. The more you play around with each company's website, the more quickly you will be able to find the jobs offered. It can be frustrating at times, but with each difficult website, you learn to better navigate sites that seem to be ostensibly set up by moonlighting chimpanzees. After about half an hour of routing around this site, it finally takes me to *usajobs.gov*. This is very annoying because I could have typed *usajobs.gov* into the browser without wasting any of my time.

Many jobs at the Tobyhanna Exchange (also known as the PX) will be under the website *applymyexchange.com*. If you are working with a client who has an unskilled work background, the link to "hourly jobs" will be the most useful for your purposes. If you are working in an area near a military base, many of the jobs will be found here, especially if the town has grown up around the base. Most civilian jobs with the military do require a high school education or its equivalent.

After exhausting this avenue, I look to the nearest town. That, in this case would be Stroudsburg. There is no independent newspaper for this town so I will use the search engine to find relevant information. Wikipedia states that Stroudsburg is the seat of Monroe County. This information should broaden your search to the entire county. Reading straight from the site, I can see that Stroudsburg has 30 specialty shops, about 30 restaurants, 10 banks and financial centers, 9 art galleries, and 8 churches and 1 theater. Does your client's work history include working as a teller, in food service, or retail sales? This Wikipedia web site provides several options. As a side note: the position of bank teller is listed in the *Dictionary of Occupational Titles* as L-5. This technically counts as a skilled position. From experience, I know that this is an entry-level position in which the skills are learned on the job and the new employee is paid while they learn the job skills. Paid training is provided by the employer for an employee who is willing to learn. This may be an option for a client with a clerical background with no banking experience who is willing to learn the necessary job skills.

Since Wikipedia did not detail Stroudsburg as well as it would a larger city, I return to the search engine. Fortunately, Stroudsburg does have its own website: *Stroudsburg.com*. I start with the link to the town history. It contains no useful information unless you would like to know how to fortify your town from "Indian attacks." Moving on to the business directory: Let us start with "shopping." You can find a variety of work in retail, including cashiers, sales attendants, warehouse workers, floor maintenance, clean-up workers, and delivery drivers. If your client has a skilled retail work background, you can find managers, assistant managers, and shift supervisors.

Occasionally, you will have clients who have returned to school after performing years of unskilled work. They are looking for a higher salary, more job-flexibility, and more prestige. I have worked with students with an Associate's or Bachelor's degree in business management. Often, they were veterans and used grant money from the Post 9-11 GI bill or other government appropriations. These programs are relatively easy for veterans to enroll in and they likely have numerous returning veterans attending these programs.

Without proper guidance, many of these students have been led to believe that their degree equates to direct placement into management positions even with no knowledge of the types of products, information, or services these companies distribute. Your counseling skills will be useful in these types of situations. Employers are more likely to hire an applicant with years of experience in the field and train them in a management position rather than hire recent graduates who have little or no personal familiarity with that industry. It is important for your client to accept that they may have to apply for a lower-salaried position at first so that they can obtain the relevant skills necessary to gain an understanding of the trade and work their way into a management position at a later time.

Returning to the Stroudsburg website, I have exhausted the short list of retailers. There is a link from the business directory to dining. If a client has a background in the food service industry, this may be pertinent to your job search. If not, move on. Do not waste time if your client has never worked nor has any desire to work in the types of jobs offered in this industry. The next link in the business directory is arts and entertainment. At first glance, these do not seem to offer many job prospects. Yet, depending upon your client's work background, theaters and museums may offer jobs as ticket takers, clean-up workers, ushers, security guards, and concession workers.

If your client has not performed work in these areas but wishes to obtain a job as a docent, curator, museum attendant, registrar, or director while attending school or working their way up the ladder, volunteer positions may be a good way to get a foot in the door. This is also true of hospitals, libraries, youth education centers, environmental conservancy advocates, Veterans Affairs, Goodwill Industries, and so many more! There are several volunteer websites that match the desired industry with the volunteer. I frequently advocate volunteering a day or two a week to gain some experience in a desired work field.

Are you beginning to understand that all these links contain more than their stated purpose? I call this the breadcrumb method. Using your job-search skills, always look for another clue that might lead you to a congruent exploration of work options. If you view the job search at face value, the whole project may seem overwhelming. Try to perceive this as an investigative search. You are like Sherlock Holmes. When you are reading through the town website or similar websites, look for clues that might lead you to an employer. Call and chat with that employer. You will not always receive intelligence that leads you to a job from each source but then again, neither does a detective. Follow up on anything that looks like a legitimate lead.

It is important that you do not take the mindset that no jobs exist in whichever area you are searching. The most debilitating thing you can do for your career and advocating for your client is to believe that there is nothing out there. That will be the death knell of your career and an injustice to your client. Smaller town labor market surveys may take more time to locate appropriate jobs within your client's physical or psychological limitations, but no one expects you to find seven appropriate jobs in one day.

Now that we have depleted our resources in Mount Pocono and Stroudsburg, let us go to the next nearest city, which is Scranton. (You probably know about the small city of Scranton from the television series, "The Office," which is fictionally located in Scranton, Pennsylvania). Although Scranton is a comparatively small town, it is much larger than Stroudsburg and Mount Pocono put together. We may even be able to find enough jobs from the local classified ads. It looks like the *Times-Tribune* is the local newspaper. Try the town website, the local newspaper, or Wikipedia first. All roads lead to

Rome. You will notice that Scranton and Wilkes-Barre are sister towns. Normally, it would be fine to scour both towns, but remember to stay within a 25-30 mile radius. If you map the distance, you will notice that Wilkes-Barre is just outside of that radius. So in this case, stick with Scranton.

The first headline I see is that Lackawanna college faculty members are pursuing a new contract. Further searching Scranton colleges, I find that there are several colleges and universities in the area, including Marywood University, Johnson College, and the University of Scranton. That is an unusual number of higher learning institutions within a small vicinity. Make use of that information. Besides faculty, colleges also hire a wide variety of employees such as mail clerks, administrative clerks, secretaries, library clerks, admissions clerks, maintenance workers, groundskeepers, housekeepers, and registrars. Most of these jobs require only a high school education. Does your client have skills that would transfer into one of these positions or a work background suitable to these positions? If your client has a clerical background, colleges have many entry-level jobs. Working in a college setting may be considered relatively low-stress employment. If you have clients currently enrolled in that particular college, counsel them to ask about a work-study program. If the website indicates no vacancies are open, call the human resources department. They will be able to better direct you to imminent job vacancies.

Since Scranton is a larger city, compared to your client's home in Pocono City or the small city of Stroudsburg, I begin my search with the classified ads in the Scranton *Times-Tribune*. Typically, newspapers scrap their own classified section and now link you to larger commercial job-classified websites, such as *Careerbuilder.com, Indeed.com*, and *Snagajob.com*. Unfortunately, these websites quickly fall out of favor and may be obsolete by the time you read this. Again, stay current with the changes.

Clearly, the Scranton *Times-Tribune* web site is in its nascence. It is a beta site and it is not producing the results I would like; I am as surprised as you are. The US sent a man to the moon 45 years before the publishing of this text and I cannot obtain a relevant classified ad job search. Take a breath and understand that this is not unusual. Therefore, for my purposes I am going to search the job websites I listed earlier in the paragraph (e.g., *Indeed.com* is a web-crawler, and will search other job search websites). This is the one I typically search first. If this is not the case at the time of your reading, then make it a point to find those websites.

Searching through this site, I see several entry-level positions: front office assistant, store administrative assistant, customer service associate, greeter, warehouse worker, teller, production worker, restaurant host, desk clerk, and hospital patient representative. Remember that jobs listed on an employment search website are open to the public and the personnel or human resources department will be inundated with applications. These can be difficult jobs to catch for your client. That does not mean you should abandon this side of the job search, but keep in mind the networking skills referenced earlier. There are many jobs offered but only a few job-searchers can obtain these jobs because of the high demand. This is why teaching the skill of networking becomes so important for your client's wellness as well as for their independence.

## WORKING THROUGH DISCOURAGING SITUATIONS

Over the last ten years, I have learned something about how to expedite the process by exercising and improving upon my adaptive or interpersonal skills, organizational strategies, and the careful search of resources. In other words, I have been through seemingly endless periods of frustration, following bridges that led to nowhere, while on the way, learning a few things about finding jobs for persons with disabilities. My goal in this section is to help you avoid my early mistakes and possibly restore some of your faith in humanity.

When I first began a job search using the Internet, the task before me seemed simple enough: calling an employer and providing them with information about persons with disabilities; how hard could this job be? I certainly thought this would be much easier than the job of telemarketing selling vinyl siding that I used to perform a few years before; I would not be trying to sell them a product they did not need. In finding jobs for persons with disabilities I considered that I was helping people in need; and, at the same time, I was offering employers what I hoped were well-qualified and motivated employees. Nevertheless, I was still coming up short on job leads. I soon found out that I needed a more holistic approach and to use better research methods.

Businesses frequently receive unwanted solicitations from telemarketers. If you do not know how to put persons answering the phone at ease with your introduction, they often assume you are trying to sell them some sort of products or services. If you cannot get past the receptionist, you will not even get through to personnel or the hiring manager, the persons central to the hiring process. As a former receptionist for several different companies, I learned that part of the job entails screening these types of phone calls because the manager is busy and does not have time to handle a sales pitch from some company selling stegosaurus protection insurance.

When the person at the other end of the line answers, the best response, I have found is to state your name and that you are a rehabilitation counselor. Most companies are usually vigilant to follow the rules of the American Disability Act (ADA) lest they incur steep penalties from the government. If you are lucky, some companies actually seek to hire persons with disabilities for various reasons, including tax breaks. In talking to an employer's staff about a job they have available and are interested in filling, the dialogue needs to be kept brief; otherwise, the receptionist will not remember most of the message you would like conveyed to the hiring manager. After giving my name and my professional identity, I continue with a statement such as, "I just have a quick question about a position I saw advertised." That way the manager or human resources assistant will understand that you are responding to their advertisement. This method does not always work. Sometimes the conversation tends to go similar to the following:

Receptionist: "Conglomo Incorporated, how may I help you?"
You: "Human Resources, please"
Receptionist: "May I ask who's calling?"
You: "This is (your name here) from Whatever and Associates. I'm a rehabilitation counselor and I am calling to inquire about a position that is currently open as a collections specialist."
Receptionist: "Okay, you need to apply online."
You: "I understand. The information I am seeking is for my client. I'm inquiring about the requirements for this position."
Receptionist: "Okay, we do not use staffing agencies. We hire directly."
You: "I am not with a staffing agency. I am a rehabilitation counselor. I just need to speak briefly with a manager or someone in personnel so that I can better understand the necessary requirements for this position."
Receptionist: "Okay, that information will be in the job description on our Website."
You: "Yes, I did read that but the information I am seeking is not listed within the job description. I just need to speak with someone very briefly about this position."
Receptionist: "*sigh* Okay, just a moment." (on hold)
"Hello? Yes, Ms. Jenkins is not in her office right now. Would you like me to put you through to voicemail?"
You: "Yes, please."

The hiring manager is not likely to return your phone call because she is busy and your phone call is not relevant to any of the myriad responsibilities she needs to perform in any given day. If the job lead is promising, continue to call the company until you reach the hiring manager directly.

Remember, in talking with employers about persons with disabilities, you do not need to present a client's medical restrictions unless the position has requirements that a client can no longer perform without accommodation. There may be other limitations a client has that do not meet the requirements of the position as advertised. If, when examining the job listing, you discover your client does not have all the job requirements an employer is requesting, you may ask if the employer would be willing to train a motivated applicant.

Frequently, I will see requirements that state 1+ years of experience or an associate's degree. Instead of discarding that lead, I call and ask the hiring manager if they would be willing to interview an applicant that did not meet that criteria directly but has adaptive skills, such as a good work history, learns quickly, is eager to learn, or has some familiarity with the type of work for which the client will be applying. Often employers are agreeable. Remember, employers in today's job market are often more concerned with a person's ability to fit into the culture of their business than an applicant's job skills. Advertised requirements are sometimes placed at a higher skill level to weed out those applicants who are not serious or are just looking to fulfill unemployment requisites.

Do not be easily discouraged when reading through the job ads and do not be afraid to call and ask. The worst thing they can tell you is "no." You may expect to have a series of rejections within a short period. Learn from those experiences and possibly modify your approach. Sometimes, even when your approach is spot on, it may be just the luck of the draw. Letting negative experiences interfere with your productivity belies the job seeking methods you are trying to instill within your client.

## ADVOCATING FOR CLIENTS: ADAPTIVE SKILLS OFTEN MAKE THE DIFFERENCE

Now that you have a basic idea how to gather job leads over the phone, let us figure out what can be done to advance the chances of our client being considered for a position. Seldom does a client's credentials, or the credentials of any job seeker for that matter, exactly match the requirements of an open and available position. So often it becomes your job to place the vocational assets of your client before the hiring manager and hope to persuade that person that other qualities may be just as important as the listed job tasks in the advertisement. This may mean reexamining the qualities you listed on your summary sheet and advocating for your client in a phone conversation to a prospective employer.

For example, let us suppose we have a client with a clerical work background and you find a promising lead as a bank teller that fits within the residual functioning capacity (RFC). Your client has never worked as a teller but has several years of clerical and customer service experience in her background. The job advertisement explicitly states that the bank requires minimum six months cash handling experience. Your client has previously worked as a front desk receptionist and is familiar with customer care but has no direct cash handling experience.

There may be many ways to handle such a situation. This is the method I used in this situation to advocate for my client. When I spoke with the hiring manager, I explained that I am a rehabilitation counselor and that I help provide employment services for persons with disabilities (do not forget to use person-first language used in polite conversation). I explained that I was reading an advertisement for a position as a teller and I noticed the ad stated a minimum requirement of six months cash handling experience. I further explained that I have a client who has several years of experience as a front desk clerk and customer care representative but no direct cash handling experience. Then I asked if she would be willing to consider an applicant who learns quickly and is eager to assimilate new information. (I never ask a hiring official if they would be willing to *hire* an applicant with those qualifications. The hiring manager cannot guarantee the job even if the applicant is interviewed for the position). What I need to have her tell me is that she would be willing to give someone fitting that description a fair shot at the job (i.e., an interview). (You will notice that I framed my description in hypothetical terms in describing my client's vocational assets. I find it best to provide them with hypothetical situations).

In this situation, I was successful, at least for the moment. I was told that my client should apply for the position and that during the interview she and the client could talk further about the other attributes that might qualify her for the job. I was further told that the bank might be willing to train the right person. She went on to say my client's customer service skills might supersede her lack of direct cash handling experience. I consider that a win: Yes! (I find it is important to compliment myself where possible in this tough business).

Next, we will look at an advertisement for a cashier at a home improvement warehouse retailer. For this example, my client has cash handling experience, but the RFC states that he would need to sit for at least four hours of the workday. A home improvement retailer is well suited for him because much of his experience has been in the trades. By the time I was able to reach the manager at the Home Depot, I had called almost every building supply in the local job market. In my conversation with the manager of Home Depot, I was told that sitting and standing options can be discussed in the interview and that in the past, the Home Depot has made accommodations for the employees they wish to hire. Another win!

For the last example, my client had worked as a dietary aide in a nursing home (D.O.T. 319.677-014) and his restrictions prohibit him from lifting more than 20 pounds. A dietary aide position, as it is typically performed within the national economy, is performed at the medium exertion level, meaning that the lifting requirements are 50 pounds occasionally and 25 pounds frequently. My client had job experience as a nursing assistant, giving him experience in a health care organization. The accommodation I would need to ask for included having other coworkers assist with lifting that would be beyond my client's functional capacity. This accommodation would be a bit more difficult for an employer to make.

Since I knew what I was looking for, I went straight to a search engine. In this case, the online *Yellow Pages.com* was a helpful beginning. The Yellow

Pages listed several nursing homes in the area. I phoned four nursing homes and they told me they were not able to make the accommodations my client would need. They stated that their nursing home did not employ enough food-service staff to help an employee with the lifting required for this position. Finally, I reached a nursing home with ample staff members capable of providing this kind of an accommodation. I described the attributes of my client's work history to the hiring manager and explained that my client would like to return to this type of work if only other employees could assist with the heavier lifting. The manager said that for a qualified applicant with experience, accommodations could be made where an employee could trade lifting responsibilities with other employees for their work tasks requiring a lighter level of exertion. Another win!

These are but a few examples for rehabilitation counselors to use as a guide in job placement of persons with disabilities. It is unusual to find a client's vocational assets that easily match the advertised job. Most of the time, the counselor needs to provide the prospective employer with a clients' adaptive skills to fill the gap in the employer's job qualifications. Know your clients vocational assets, particularly those assets that might make them stand out in an employer's mind. The above examples provide evidence of how rehabilitation counselors can find ways, using the client's adaptive skills, to get their client to the interview.

# APPENDIX 1

# USEFUL WEBSITES FOR BEGINNING A JOB SEARCH

*Indeed.com*

This website is simple to use and it searches through other job/employment search websites for precise results. There is no confusion; just two boxes: *what & where*. One box is for the job type and the other box is for the location of the job. You can leave the "what" box empty to cast a wider net over a particular location. The results are pertinent to your search and without the clutter of "work from home" opportunities and online-education advertisements. *Indeed.com* also lists a variety of both full and part-time jobs. This website is simple to use and it searches through other job/employment search websites for precise work or particular educational requirements. The site features advanced searches if you want to concentrate on salary, location, a particular company, or how many hours in one week your client would like to work.

*Career Builder.com*

In 2002, I used this site more than any other employment search engine. I cannot understand why it is still listed in so many counselors' top ten search sites because, today, *Career Builder.com* primarily lists advertisements, scams, hiring events, and staffing agencies. If you are lucky enough to find a company with a particular job opening, it is likely to list the same job several times in different locations in the same city. Also, it seems as though *Career Builder.com* puts out general advertisements for jobs with certain businesses that may or may not currently be hiring but have high staff turnover.

*Snagajob.com*

This website targets hourly workers. This site also has an array of semi-skilled and entry-level jobs. If you are looking for a position as a cashier, you are in business! *Snagajob* lists many different companies from retail home improvement to grocery stores.

*Simplyhired.com*

This site has many different jobs and companies listed. For example, my search for a housekeeping job produced employment ads for everything from "housekeeping aide" to "executive housekeeper." At the end of the search page, you will be given several options from similar work fields like hospitality, janitor, and other cleaning positions.

*Job.com & Beyond.com*

Both sites are similar, versatile, and easy to use. The job openings offered on these websites range all the way from high-level positions, such as surgeons to entry-level positions, such as security guards. There is an option to search for a position by the name of the company, which can be helpful in particular situations. The websites show a good variety of businesses and types of employment. *Beyond.com* does have some clutter from out of the mainstream advertisers (e.g., those selling kitchen cutlery and home-based data entry), but the site's usefulness outweighs this nuisance.

*Bright.com*

This site can be very helpful. The results are numerous, but just like *Snagajob, Simplyhired, Job.com,* and *Beyond.com* a lot of entries are repeated in other places. They mainly advertise for well-known chain businesses but not so much from local business owners. There is an option to select an industry category that can help narrow your search under a broad job title (e.g., *cashier*).

*Ziprecruiter.com*

*Ziprecruiter* brings you results from other online job boards (most of the ones listed above) so it does show numerous job entries and job openings.

Most of the results I have found were also represented on *Bright.com*. The site is straightforward and easy to use without having to wade through a clutter of irrelevant advertisements.

*Craigslist.com*

*Craigslist* will have a better selection of smaller, more localized businesses that can be difficult to find on other employment search websites. From a counselor's perspective, jobs listed on *Craigslist.com* can be frustrating because many of the job ads are anonymous and do not provide any information about the company, making it virtually impossible to contact the employer about restrictions and accommodations. In addition, not all of the listings are for legitimate job openings, although it is easy to decipher which ones are the real jobs. Job headlines like "make money now!" and anything with an abundance of exclamation points usually do not provide information helpful to the job search.

*Google*

While is not a job-search website, it will help clarify the information found on other web sites. Since *Google* is universal, it is much less restrictive. You can easily narrow your search by job title, company, specific part of town or street name.

# APPENDIX 2

# AN INITIAL REPORT TO AN ADJUSTER

Ms. Alma Johnson
Senior Adjuster
Holiday Insurance
Box 26363
Seattle, Washington 75060
June 30, 2009

RE: Claimant: Peggy Reynolds
Date of Injury: 5/23/08
Claim #: 654758

## INITIAL REPORT

Introduction:

To prepare this report I have examined the medical and other records provided to me for a history of the accident and other diagnosed conditions, treatment outcomes, and residual abilities and limitations. Moreover, I have conducted a personal interview with Peggy Reynolds in her home in Marion, Virginia to gain an understanding of her personal and work history, to discuss her treatment program, and to learn how her industrial accident has limited her activities. Finally, I have visited her employer, Telemont, Inc., including taking a tour of the work site and an interview with the Human Resources Coordinator, Rachel Smith.

Medical Problems and Limitations:

Peggy Reynolds was injured in her workplace when a flux chemical substance entered a hole in her work glove and seeped underneath her thumbnail on her right, dominant hand. She had surgery on May 25, 2009 removing tissue on the thumb. Stitches were removed on June 5, 2009 and she began a home exercise program. To this point, she has not been able to touch her little finger with her thumb, a hand motion she must be able to perform in her job.

Peggy Reynolds says she loves her job at Telemont, Inc., and wants to return to that work. She has not considered any other job at this point. She feels she will be able to return to that job after the completion of her therapy program. Her employer has also expressed the desire for her to return and is holding the job open for her.

Vocational Profile:

Peggy Reynolds was born February 4, 1943 in Marion, Smythe County, Virginia. She is now 66 years old. She is a high school graduate from Marion High School in Marion, Virginia, completing the requirements for her high school diploma in 1960. She has taken vocational training as a nursing assistant. In 1990, she attended the Cox Center for Nursing and in 1992, she received her license and certification as a Certified Nursing Assistant (CNA).

From 1962 to 1965, Ms. Reynolds worked as a sewing machine operator in the Heygood Sewing Factory primarily sewing collars on shirts. In this work, she says that she lifted bundles of clothing weighing approximately 30 pounds. This work as performed was medium in exertion with occasional lifting in the 50 pound range and semi-skilled. As normally performed in the national economy this work is light in exertion, with lifting of 20 pounds occasionally and 10 pounds frequently, and semi-skilled, taking one to three months to learn the job duties and perform the work adequately (*Dictionary of Occupational Titles*: Sewing Machine Operator: 787.682-066). Even though a sewing machine operator sits most of the workday, this work is considered light in exertion because of the use of foot pedals in this kind of work.

Her son was born in 1967 and her daughter was born in 1971. She did not work in these years. She returned to work in 1972 and worked as a sewing machine operator for the next 27 years for Buster Brown, making children's clothing. This work as normally performed is also semi-skilled and light in exertion. This job has the same DOT designation as the position above

In 1993, she received her nursing certification and in 1994, went to work in the office of the Valley Health Care Center in Wytheville, Virginia doing mainly clerical work: typing, filing, and operating the company computer program. This work is normally performed at a light level of exertion and semi-skilled (*Dictionary of Occupational Titles*: Office Clerk: 209.562-010).

From 1996 to 2004, she was in private nursing as a home health aide and companion for a patient with a high cervical injury: he could not move his head. She fed her patient, taught him language and math, and the use of computers. She even attended the community college with him at Virginia Highlands Community College in Abington, Virginia. Her patient died in 2004. This work as normally performed is light in exertion and semi-skilled (*Dictionary of Occupational Titles*: Home Health Aide (Elderly):309.677-010).

For six or seven months in 2005, before starting her work at Telemont, Inc., she worked as a cashier at Food City in Marion. This is unskilled work and light in exertion (*Dictionary of Occupational Titles*: Cashier II: 211.462-010).

Peggy Reynolds started to work at Telemont, Inc. on June 5, 2006. Telemont, Inc. is a maker of drill bits for the mining industry. They recondition used bits and make new ones. Some, but not all, of these bits require a shim (a sharp edge on a bit). The accident occurred when one of these shims cut into her glove and allowed the acid to penetrate her finger. Her job is titled a Roofbit Brazer that involves assembling parts to go into the drill. She also is a floater on the assembly line. She has to know how to fill in for each position, such as a worker on the paint line, the de-tipping machine, and the position of inspector. To perform her work she sits most of the day but has to stand, needing a sitting and standing option. There is almost no lifting in this job. The job of Brazer Assembler is normally medium in exertion and semi-skilled taking three to six months to learn the job and perform the job tasks adequately (*Dictionary of Occupational Titles*: Brazer, Assembler: 813.864-010).

Transferable Skills Analysis:

Peggy Reynolds has worked as a sewing machine operator, a nursing assistant, a companion, a cashier, and a brazer. She would not have any transferable skills from her job as a cashier since that work is unskilled. Moreover, she would not have transferable work skills from her work as a sewing machine operator and as a brazer, assembler. These skills are all job-specific and would not be transferable to other occupations to give her a competitive advantage in the open job market. Since she no longer holds her CNA certification her ability to work as a CNA is not possible. However, the skills she has learned in patient care and home health are much in demand and she might see jobs as a companion or home health aide as a job option should she not be able to return to her job with Telemont, Inc.

Conclusions:

In my opinion, Peggy Reynolds will be able to return to her job at Telemont, Inc. as a roofbit brazer. She believes that she will be able to meet the demands of the job once the therapy program is complete. The Human Resources Coordinator speaks highly of her performance and she is holding the job open for her return.

However, Telemont, Inc. is a union company and will not be able to accommodate workers who are unable to perform the normal job duties. The clear message from the company is that if she does not recover sufficiently to perform her past work, she will not have a job with them.

Ms. Masters is a pleasant woman who has a long and continuous work record. I have no reason to doubt that she has found success in every job she has held over the years. If she must have alternative work, I believe the best source of jobs would be in personal care, such as a private sitter with a disabled person, a home health aide, a private household worker, or a companion for the elderly. Even without her certification, she would appear qualified.

Beyond this point, she would have a vocational profile as a person of advanced age with no transferable skills to other occupations. However, because of her personal attractiveness, she may be considered for a number of unskilled, entry-level occupations. Friends and acquaintances may be helpful to her in locating other work. She has lived in the area all her life and seems to be a person who would know a lot of people. The place where she lives is very rural with a small number of people.

Rachel L. Welsh, CRC
Vocational Consultant

# TOPICS FOR GROUP DISCUSSION

The questions below are for classroom or workshop use. Our suggestion is to divide the group into three or four sections, depending upon the size of the group, and select a group leader and a reporter for each group. In small discussion groups, address one of the statements below and have the group leader present their group findings to the class at the end of the session.

1. Chapter 1 " The Rehabilitation Counselor's Management Role in Job Placement" and the "Introduction" to Chapter 9 identify and describe the two approaches to job placement of persons with disabilities most often addressed in rehabilitation literature. These are the Selective Approach and the Client-Centered Approach.

   Have each group:

   a. list the advantages and disadvantages of the Selective Approach,

   b. suggest ways the disadvantages of this approach can be overcome by the use of the Internet,

   c. Are there still problems with the Selective Approach that would be obstacles to placing persons with disabilities in employment?

   d. Why do you believe that the Selective Approach is still the most prevalent way to locate job leads and employment for persons with a disability? Support your answers.

2. In small groups, conduct an Internet job search for the large city of Lexington, KY and Harrisonburg, Virginia. Identify the population size, the main features of the community, the principal industries, and the main sources of jobs. Go to the web site for one of the main employers in either of these cities and try to identify the qualities they are looking for in their employees and the kinds of jobs they have to offer.

3. Using the interview format presented in this chapter, conduct a job interview using the brief description presented in the

case study below. Select volunteers from the group to serve as the rehabilitation counselor and the client Josh Turner. Encourage the participants to be creative and provide the information lacking in the description of Josh Turner during the interview.

# INDIVIDUAL EXERCISES

# CASE STUDY

*Josh Turner is a 38-year-old male with a high school education. He is married with one child. His wife works as a cashier at Food City in nearby Peabody. On June 8, 2009, he injured his back lifting an elderly patient and subsequently had to have back surgery. The surgery was partly successful, but he is limited to lifting of only 20 pounds occasionally with no prolonged walking or standing. Before his accident, Josh was employed for three years as a certified nursing assistant at the Safe Manner Nursing Home in Salem, Massachusetts.*

- Can Josh likely do his past job without accommodation? Why not?
- Does he have work skills that would transfer to other work? Discuss.
- What kinds of jobs will he be able to perform given his limitations? Name four jobs he would likely be able to perform within his medical restrictions.
- Conduct a job search of the community on the internet. What towns and cities are within commuting distance? What is the size of their population? Identify five (5) employers on the Internet who have jobs that Josh could perform within his limitations.

# REFERENCE

[1]Bolles, R.N. (1991). *What Color Is Your Parachute?* Berkeley, CA: Ten Speed Press, p. 95.

# NETWORKING FOR JOBS IN THE HIDDEN JOB MARKET: A CLIENT-CENTERED APPROACH

# PREFACE

*In a given community, researchers estimate that anywhere from 75% to 90% of the jobs, and most of the better jobs, lie in what has been called the Hidden Job Market. The only way to reach the hidden job market is by networking. The person looking for a job is the only person strategically located to network in the Hidden Job Market.*

The Authors

To The Reader:

The central theme of Chapter 9 was to show ways to get the most out of the Selective Approach to the job market. In the Selective Approach, rehabilitation counselors are the central figures, matching their clients to available jobs, making employer contacts, and even, on occasion, accompanying clients to an interview. As we have seen, use of the Internet and experience in organizing information for the job search can certainly improve the quality, as well as the results, in using the Selective Approach for job placement of persons with disabilities. Under the Selective Approach the client remains, for the most part, a passive figure in the job search.

Although widely in use in private practice, literature from the field of rehabilitation has pretty much dismissed as ineffective, the Selective Approach for job placement of persons with disabilities. For instance, Olney and Salomone[9] designated "selective placement as unsuccessful and resulting in poor job satisfaction, due to the controlling role of the rehabilitation professional and the non-participatory role of the job seeker."[pg.43] Olney and Salomone[9] believe that people with disabilities may be more inclined to leave their jobs when they have been uninvolved in the placement process. Furthermore, Marrone, et al.[6] believe the lack of involvement on the part of the client has something to do with job retention. They say an "essential element of helping people keep jobs is having the job seeker direct the job search."[pg. 39]

In Chapter One we discussed some of the limitations of the Selective Approach. We noted that in the practice of rehabilitation counseling, problems arise with a client's non-participation in the job search. As a passive partner in the job search, the client learns little or nothing about finding and securing a job. The lack of involvement in the job search becomes a likely obstacle to current and future employment. Furthermore, the Selective Approach builds dependencies. Client's cease to act independently, thinking the counselor is responsible for the job search. When the counselor assumes all of the authority, job opportunities are missed that clients could uncover for themselves if they were more involved. Much time is lost in the job search as clients await counselor job searches and assignments.

On the other hand, the same researchers uniformly recommend a Client-Centered Approach in which clients assume responsibility, secure job leads, contact employers, and make employment decisions: "personal involvement on the part of the job seeker makes finding the job an individual's success, and contributes to his/her self-esteem and confidence."[6, p. 43] In the literature, there is general agreement that having clients closely involved in the job search will lead to positive results in job placement.

There is an even more important reason for having the client involved in the job search. In a given community researchers estimate that anywhere from 75% to 90% of the jobs, and most of the better jobs, lie in what has been called the hidden job market. The only way to reach the hidden job market is by networking. The only person strategically located to network in the hidden job market is the person looking for a job. On a grass-roots level, counselors are not able to penetrate this job market or network without the involvement of the client.

Then why do we even consider an alternative to a client-centered approach? The reason is that, in practice, too often when clients conduct a job search independent of their rehabilitation counselor, they are unable to find appropriate work or any work at all, for that matter. Recall in the Minnesota study, cited earlier, where 40% of the clients had poor personal appearance or inappropriate mannerisms and 85% of the clients seeking work could not explain their skills to employers.[10, pg. 22] The study of older rural workers showed that 85% of the participants needed help to locate a suitable job, 52% needed to learn what employers look for in older workers, and 44% needed to improve their self-confidence.[7, pg. 22] On their own, clients often find jobs that are not appropriate for their vocational abilities or not within their functional limitations, situations that soon lead to frustration and failure. We believe there are ways of overcoming the limitations of the Client-Centered Approach. Chapter 10 explores two issues that in the past have been obstacles to the Client-Centered Approach.

*How can counselors have their client involved in the case, to take advantage of the networking possibilities, and still manage the case?*

This chapter addresses this issue in the presentation of the *Job Search Organizer*, a management tool for following the progress of the case, for teaching job-seeking skills, and for tracking job opportunities. (The *Organizer* is available in a separate inexpensive booklet). First presented in *Finding Jobs on Main Street,*[13] the *Job Search Organizer* has been revised after further research and through training seminars from counselor input.

*How can clients become involved in networking for jobs in their community?*

The annual report in 2004 from The National Organization on Disability expressed skepticism about networking among persons with disabilities. Their concern was that persons in the disabled community had what they called "high redundancy" because most of the people know each other and they have "weak ties" or contacts outside of the disability community. Networks with high redundancy, they pointed out, have been shown to be less useful in finding employment because everybody in the network has access to the same information and resources.

Frequently, persons with disabilities do have a more narrow range of contacts. Statistics on the use of networking come from surveys among well-educated professionals in more highly skilled positions than most of our clients. Many of our clients, on the other hand, have members in the family complex, friends, and acquaintances who not only provide support through covenant groups but also represent a relatively untapped source for job contacts. Chapter 10 shows ways networking among family, friends, and acquaintances can work among rehabilitation clients who are not well connected to the community and have limited contacts outside their own covenant groups.

# INTRODUCTION
# THE CLIENT-CENTERED APPROACH

The main thrust of the Client-Centered Approach is to find ways to involve the client in the job-seeking process. Chapter 10 provides two ways to achieve this end. First, through the use of the *Job Search Organizer* counselors have a format to share information with their client, to surface and identify the skills their clients can use in other work, and to track a client's progress during the job search. Second, through a step-by step process, clients are shown ways to use grass roots networking in the community to find jobs in the hidden job market.

Part 1: The *Job Search Organizer* places the information gained from the records and the personal interview into a usable format. The first step is to develop a personal inventory of the vital information so that clients have that information before them when they fill out applications, prepare for interviews, and talk to employers about their vocational assets. The process of getting this information on paper is as important as the information itself. In the dialogue, counselors have the opportunity to point out what is important to the client, share values and viewpoints, and pinpoint information employers need to hear.

Then, the *Job Search Organizer* takes the counselor and the client through skill-identification, helping the client to understand their vocational assets and to relate these assets to prospective employers. Here again, the counselor has the opportunity to emphasize adaptive, educational, and work skills the client will need to discuss in interviews. Done properly, a discussion of vocational assets can be uplifting and help the client feel better about themselves and their work possibilities.

Part 2: "*Grass Roots Networking in the Hidden Job Market*" takes counselors and their clients through the process for building networks (social capital) among covenant groups made up of family, friends, and acquaintances and for enlisting their help in finding job leads. The network a client builds can spell the difference between success and failure in job placement. Through networking, clients are able to identify jobs not normally found on any job list. These jobs represent anywhere from 75% to 90% of the open, available jobs, and most of the better jobs, in a given community. As one group of scholars explain: "Very few programs look at social capital as key to employment, yet we are learning that social capital plays a critical role in helping individuals find and sustain employment."[3, pg. 136]

## PART 1: THE "*JOB-SEARCH ORGANIZER*"

The "*Job-Search Organizer*" is simply a management tool for organizing job search information. The "*Job-Search Organizer*" was first created and presented in *Finding Jobs on Main Street* and in 1994 as a separate booklet entitled The "*Job-Seeker's Portfolio.*" The "*Job Seeker's Portfolio*" met with some success, but revisions were needed in order to make the strategy more useful to rehabilitation counselors. The presentation as The "*Job-Search Organizer*" contains those revisions. The "*Job-Search Organizer*" presents:

- *A way for clients to share in the activities and responsibilities of the job search.*

Using a step-by-step strategy, clients become involved in their own job search. Clients tap the traditional job sources and network through family members, friends, and acquaintances to surface job leads. Counselors manage and orchestrate the job search, determine the right directions for the client actions, interpret information, make intuitive suggestions, teach job-seeking skills to their clients, and help clients see for themselves where the job search is leading them.

- *A way to manage the job search that is consistent with established motivational principles.*

The "*Job-Search Organizer*" keeps clients involved in continuous action "doing things." Rather than having counselors devise elaborate plans and await the right moment for markets and job opportunities to open up, this strategy directs clients to consider alternatives on their own and make contact with other people continuously. New opportunities and new strategies arise with their activity. As they take action, no matter what the reason, they gain a stronger sense of control over their lives and begin to feel better about both themselves and their work potential.

➢ *A way to have an ongoing record and a permanent record of the job search.*

Record keeping is always a problem in the job search. Bits and pieces of information get scattered all over the place; oral information gets lost, leading to misunderstandings and assigned blame; and almost everything that happened beyond in the immediate past is lost or forgotten. The "*Job-Search Organizer*" records the events of the job search, becomes a case record for job leads and assignments, and serves as a format for conducting counseling sessions. The orderly procedures they have followed with success now will be a guide to them later. The *Organizer* gives a client the security of knowing that they have learned valuable skills they can use in the future.

➢ *A way for counselors to manage the job search.*

So often, the job search that clients undertake is disorganized; randomly, they go about the job search without really knowing what they are trying to achieve. Monitoring their progress is next to impossible. They do not understand the significance of much of the information they are gathering; and therefore, they cannot accurately relate important parts of that information to their counselor. The *Organizer* serves as a counselor's tool for managing progress in the job search. The format organizes the job search into logical sequences. If clients follow the steps outlined, they are assured of covering most of the places where job leads are found. This management tool forces clients to record actions they have taken in the job search. Documentation, if you will! The counselor can open the record to any page, review what actions were taken, and determine the direction in which the job search is headed. The *Organizer* serves as a road map for the job search.

In summary, the purpose of the *Job Search Organizer* is to help clients become more involved in the job exploration and reach better job opportunities in their communities, but, just as important for the counselor, the *Job Search Organizer* helps:

➢ enhance the dialogue with clients,

➢ organize counseling sessions, and

➢ serve as a format for teaching job-seeking skills.

Our discussion of the *Job Search Organizer* begins with the case study of Alison Benson. The case study asks counselors to apply the case events to the various sections of the *Organizer*. Except for minor changes, the basic essentials of the case study are real. Some of the facts and all of the names have been altered. Each section asks the reader to apply the principles of the *Job Search Organizer* to the case study toward building a vocational profile of Alison Benson.

## THE CASE OF ALISON BENSON

*Alison Benson is 47 years old. She had been employed as a salesperson by the Grand Alliance Furniture chain based in Hershey, Pennsylvania for the past nine years. The chain has 62 stores in Pennsylvania and New Jersey. Most of the Grand Alliance stores sell appliances, electronics, and medium to high-end furniture. Three of the stores in the chain are gallery stores serving high-end customers with name-brand home furnishings. The gallery stores are located in Pittsburgh and Philadelphia, Pennsylvania and Camden, New Jersey.*

*The chain was started by the Elrod family in the 1930s and it grew steadily through the years. Kenneth Elrod, Sr. at 83 still serves as chair of the board of directors. Kenneth Elrod, Jr. is the president and several of his children occupy lower positions in the chain. Most of the policies and procedures were set down by the original founders and have not changed significantly over the many years of operation. Basically, all policy changes have to be reviewed by upper management.*

*All new personnel, when they are first employed, come to the home office in Hershey for a two-week orientation and training program. There they meet the "brass" and learn about the "illustrious beginnings" of the chain operation. Each year the management has in-store training for salespeople to increase the product knowledge. All salespeople have had formal training selling Sealy bedding, their main line, and training for selling Pennsylvania House furniture. Once a year the top salespeople go to the furniture market in High Point, North Carolina for a three-day training session on selling retail and select other subjects (e.g., "How to Handle Customer Complaints," "How to Handle the Angry Customer," and "Employee Motivation.") All of the top salespeople have had these short training courses.*

*The gallery store at 215 Elm Street in Philadelphia is a typical high-end furniture store with 7500 sq. feet of retail space located on two floors. A stairway leads from the first floor to the* *second floor. The store is open every day (including Sundays) from 9:30 am to 5:00 pm and on Friday evenings until 9:00 pm. Each of the sales staff works 43 hours a week with two days off. They work every 4th Sunday. The store has nine (9) full-time commission sales persons, two clerical positions paid an hourly wage starting at $8.50 an hour, and three delivery persons on an hourly wage starting at $7.50 an hour. For the sales staff, "the backbone of the business," there is a draw against commission. The normal pay range for sales positions is from $13,000 a year to $32,000 a year. Grand Alliance provides health coverage and disability for salespeople after they have been with the company for six months. The Company pays half the premium and the employee pays the other half. All of the salespeople are covered under the health plan. The health benefits package carries a $200.00 deductible.*

*Selling to customers involves standing and walking continuously throughout the workday, bending "once in a while to wipe off a seat" or "work the handle on a recliner." The salespeople do not have to lift furniture: "we have warehouse people to do that"; but sometimes the salesperson is expected to take small items customers are carrying with them to the front of the store "not over 10 to 15 pounds." The salespeople carry with them a clipboard on which to write sales invoices and a tape measure. The invoices must be right; in fact, the clerical staff checks every invoice, and if there are mistakes, "the management comes down hard on them."*

*When a salesperson is not working with customers, they are expected to write notes to customers letting them know about upcoming sales events and thanking them for their patronage. These notes are written standing up since it is the policy of the Chain that salespeople must stand at all times. No office space or desks are provided for salespeople. The store manager, Thomas Hardy says these notes are very important because the store depends upon repeat business. Traditionally, all female employees have worn dresses and that is still the policy.*

*Salespeople also have to help set up displays in the store and the display windows. Mr. Hardy decides what goes on the displays: "I get a lot of advice from headquarters" and the salespeople and warehouse people set up the displays. While the salespeople do not have to do the lifting, they sometimes get involved: "sometimes it's easier to do it yourself than get them to do it." Setting up sales displays involves bending "and sometimes we have to get down on our knees, twisting, and turning." The display of furniture is very important "because customers need to go right to the things they have seen advertised." Helping with displays takes 4-6 hours in the normal week. The only other job duties salespeople routinely have are light dusting of the items on the sale floor.*

*Grand Alliance has always required a high school education or the equivalent. "It is desirable to have an acquaintance with interior decorating" but that is not required. In hiring, weight is given to new employees with experience in the furniture industry. New employees get some training in the two-week orientation; and, "except what they learn at annual market," the rest of the job they learn from other sales staff. Almost no one has a college degree. In fact, promotions to management come from success on the sales floor and loyalty to the company.*

*The Human Resources Manager, Jeffrey King, became alarmed with the turnover of experienced sales staff in the stores. In the past two years, several of the experienced salespeople have left employment because they could no longer withstand the exertion rigors of the job. This has left the business with new, inexperienced people whom Mr. King feels do not have the commitment of the former employees. He is also concerned that the new salespeople do not have the product knowledge to serve the customers effectively and the stores have lost customers to new, more aggressive competitors.*

*The issue came to a head last year when Alison Benson told her store manager that she was having problems with her knees. Alison Benson had 10 years' experience in sales with the Chain. She had been a top producer in the Pittsburg store for the past five years and had over $500,000 in sales per year. Alison Benson made $37,000 in the past year. Mr. Hardy had relied upon Alison when setting up displays because she had an associate's degree in interior design and "had a good sense of color."*

*Alison Benson is 47 years old. She was born June 6, 1960 in Norristown, Pennsylvania a suburb of Philadelphia. She graduated from Great Falls High School in 1977 in a general business program. Among others, she took courses in basis accounting, secretarial science, typing, and shorthand. She began her work-life after high school as a server in local restaurants and did this work for about 5 years. Then, in 1982, an opportunity arose for a courier traveling from town to town in Pennsylvania delivering package and correspondence to area businesses. She drove a courier van for eight years until she married in 1990. She quit this job to reduce being on the road so much; and in 1990, she took a position as a bank teller at the Community Bank in Norristown and worked there for about 8 years.*

*In 1996, she began a program at the Quaker Community College in Norristown and in 1998 received an Associate's Degree in Interior Design. Her course work included, among others, courses in Art, Introduction to Design, the World of Color, Room Scaling and Layout, Mechanical Drawing, and Advanced Interior Design. She did not take the State ASID examination and she is not certified in her field since that was not a job requirement. Soon after she completed her degree requirements, an opportunity arose at the Grand Alliance Furniture Gallery. She quit her job at the bank in 1998 for what she hoped would be a higher-paying job with the Gallery.*

*Allison married in 1990. She was divorced from her husband in 2002. She now resides with their 6-year old son, Raymond, at 127 Maple Street in the hamlet of Norristown, about 16 miles outside of Philadelphia. She and her son are members of the First Presbyterian Church in Norristown where they attend regularly. In fact, Alison teaches in the youth department of the Sunday school and holds a special arts and crafts program for the pre-teen youth in the Vacation Bible School at the Church. She is the original founder of the Soroptomist Club for professional women in Norristown.*

*Alison had expressed the desire to stay with the Philadelphia store, but she told Mr. Hardy "sometimes" she needed to sit down during the day. Mr. Hardy tried to get the "top brass" to allow her an accommodation, but the management of the chain would not make exceptions: "if we let one do it, then everybody will want to." Mr. Hardy sent her to the company doctor, Horace McCutchin, M.D., for an examination. He ex-rayed her knees and diagnosed "some degenerative changes in the knees with spurring." Dr. McCutchin did not believe that surgery would relieve her pain significantly. He agreed that she would need to sit for about one to one-half hours in the 8-hour workday and could not lift and carry over 10 to 15 pounds.*

*Management at the Grand Alliance Gallery reviewed the work restrictions and felt that they could not accommodate the restrictions. The Company retired her on long-term disability. The insurance adjuster felt that she could still work and hired the private rehabilitation firm of Williams & Williams for job placement. At the firm of Williams & Williams, the case was received by the rehabilitation counselor, David Asbury.*

MEDICAL AND FUNCTIONAL INFORMATION

As we have seen in earlier chapters, particularly Chapter 5, the medical community sets the medical residual functional capacity (RFC) for their patients and provides rehabilitation counselors with medical information about:

1. the diagnosis and treatment of their patients and the outcome of the treatment,
2. the patient's functional abilities to perform work activity, if any,
3. the date the patient has reached Maximum Medical Improvement (MMI), and
4. the date the patient can return to work (RTW).

The "*Job-Search Organizer*" does not provide a section for the medical profile. By design, the "*Job-Search Organizer*" is meant to be in the possession of the client. Rehabilitation counselors know the observations and treatment modalities of the medical community determine the client's mental and physical ability to work; and, to some extent, the kinds of jobs the person can perform given their limitations. The client must know their mental and physical assets and limitations. It is the duty of counselors to communicate the functional abilities and limitations to their clients before the job search begins and to monitor the job search–and job leads they uncover–to make sure that the jobs are within their clients' functional abilities.

# MEDICAL PROFILE OF ALISON BENSON

Dr. Horace McCutchin has provided a diagnosis for his patient Alison Benson. The treating doctor did not take Alison off work, but provided work restrictions. Complete the following based upon the information contained in the case study.

What is her diagnosis?

________________________________________________

What are her work restrictions?

______________________________________________

Based upon her work restrictions, what is her RFC?

______________________________________________

Can she do light work? Yes ____ No _____.

Can she do sedentary work? Yes____ No _____

Does she need work accommodations? Yes ____ No ____
Explain_________________________________________

______________________________________________

## CHANGING OF THE GUARD

The initial sections of the *Organizer* involve identifying personal and vocational assets that give clients a competitive edge as they approach the open job market. This process involves taking a personal inventory of past experiences in school and at work and identifying skills and accomplishments from the past that may be useful in narrowing the range of job options and in making a vocational choice. The source for this information can usually be found in the case file and recorded responses of the client in the personal interview. Likely, the counselor already has most of the information. The *Organizer* is the property of the client and clients need to list this information in their *Organizer. The activity of listing this information in their booklet has the effect, symbolically, of transferring authority for conducting the job search to the client.* It is helpful for counselors to remind their clients that preparing their *Organizer* raises the expectation that they will participate actively in the job search.

## THE PERSONAL INVENTORY

While filling in the sections of the personal inventory, counselors need to help their clients see the importance of the information. Verbal reinforcement from their counselor helps clients understand that having a thumbnail sketch of their development and their work life will enable them to see themselves more objectively and identify the parts of their life and work history that are of most interest to employers. In addition, while preparing the personal inventory, counselors need to let their clients know that they will refer to this information continuously in preparing applications and in responding to questions during interviews. The information will be right there at their fingertips. Although instruction on how to complete a personal inventory is contained in their booklet, verbal reinforcement from their counselor serves as a much stronger stimulant than the printed word.

Instructions counselors give to their clients prior to filling in the personal inventory should stress:

- the need for neatness and completeness, and
- the necessity to take the "*Job-Search Organizer*" with them to all face-to-face sessions with their counselor, to all businesses where they are making application, and to all interviews with employers.

The Personal Inventory section of the "*Job-Search Organizer*" begins with a statement addressed to the client:

> *Where does the job search begin? What is the first step? Most people start their job search by looking to the outside: picking up the newspaper to scan the classified advertisements or visiting the local employment office. To get to the whole job market–where the really good jobs are to be found–begins by looking inside you to:*
>
> 1. *inventory the assets you bring to the job search,*
> 2. *examine the skills you have acquired,*
> 3. *decide what you really want to do in your next job, and*
> 4. *prepare yourself to meet employers.*
>
> *If your personal inventory is done right, you will get to know yourself well; and knowing yourself well will give you a sizeable competitive edge in the job market.*
>
> *Your personal inventory is "The story of your life." The inventory details not only your vital statistics needed for this job search but the information you will need for any job search. If you take care in working through the information, you will have much of the basic information you need for jobs later in your career. Your "Job-Search Organizer" is your permanent record of the job search.*
>
> *In preparing your personal inventory, be neat and complete. This information will help you define the skills you need to progress toward the job you really want. Moreover, the information will be right in front of you while you fill out applications and answer questions from employers. In addition, the information will help you design the "tools*

*of the job search"–your resume, your cover letters, and your follow-up messages. This important information becomes a permanent part of your "Job-Search Organizer" and goes everywhere with you. As the credit card people say, from this point forward "don't leave home without it."*

# PERSONAL INVENTORY
# ALISON BENSON

Fill in the general information about Alison Benson from the case study.

Name:________________________________ Age: __________
Address: ____________________________________________
____________________________________________
DOB: ____________
Marital Status: ____________________ Dependents: _________
Age of Dependents: _______________
Member: Church? Yes ___ No ___
Name of Church ___________________________
Member: Community Organization: Yes ___ No ___
Offices held: ______________________________________

**Education**:
High School (name) ________________________________________
Years Attended: ____________
Course of Study: ___________________________
Diploma: Yes ___ No ___ Date: _______________
College (name) __________________________________________
Years Attended: _____________
Course of Study ______________________ Degree: Yes ___ No ____
Type of Degree: __________________________________________
Post Graduate: ____________________ Years Attended: ________
Advanced Degree: ______

**Vocational Training Attended: Seminars/Workshops**:
1. Course Title: _________________________ Course Content:
   (a) ______________________ (b) __________________________
   (c) ______________________
2. Course Title: _________________________ Course Content:
   (a) ______________________ (b) __________________________

(c) ____________________

3. Course Title: ______________________ Course Content:

(a) ____________________ (b) ______________________

(c) ____________________

**Work Experience**:

# 1 Job Title: ____________________

Place of Employment: ______________________________

Dates of Employment: __________ Position Held: ____________

# 2 Job Title: ____________________

Place of Employment: ______________________________

Dates of Employment: __________ Position Held: ____________

# 3 Job Title: ____________________

Place of Employment: ______________________________

Dates of Employment: __________ Position Held: ____________

# 4 Job Title: ____________________

Place of Employment: ______________________________

Dates of Employment: __________ Position Held: ____________

## SKILLS ANALYSIS & TRANSFERABLE WORK SKILLS

In rehabilitation counseling, we learn to focus upon the past work and look for and identify work skills that clients can use to give them a competitive edge in the open job market. For instance, a person applying for a job as a first-line supervisor has a better chance if that person has had experience supervising workers in the past. These skills, learned at work, are called transferable work skills. We also learn to make a careful separation between human traits like "appearance" or "alertness" and other things that help the worker adapt to a work environment but are not work skills learned in the work setting. These skills are called adaptive skills. Counselors often struggle to make this distinction between the two types of skills. Now, it seems in job placement, at least, the separation is very artificial. In fact, from what some employers are saying, adaptive skills may be more important in the hiring process than work skills. The "*Job-Search Organizer*" examines four types of skills: Work Skills, Educational Skills, Skills Learned in Seminars and Workshops, and Adaptive Skills.

*Work skills.* The "*Job-Search Organizer"* makes a brief statement about when work skills are important and then draws a distinction between work skills that relate to a certain job and work skills that can be transferred to other work to give the client an advantage in the open job market. About skills learned on the job, the Organizer says:

*Work-related skills are important, and when interviewers are satisfied that you can make the vocational adjustment to their work setting, these skills receive the most attention. Often you will know when an interviewer has "passed" you into the next stage. Questions become more specific about your work-related job skills. At this point, the job may be yours–if you can talk confidently about your work skills.*

*Work-related skills come in two types:*

1. *job-specific skills, and*

2. *transferable skills.*

*Job-specific skills relate to a specific kind of employment. A cook has to know how to prepare food, to select and use the proper seasonings, and determine the size of the portions to be served to customers. A landscape gardener must know plants, fertilizers, and planting technique. These are work skills related to these kinds of employment. Employers looking for cooks, gardeners, or grounds-keepers are looking for these specific skills. It is unlikely they will hire you for these positions without job-specific skills.*

*Transferable skills, on the other hand, are skills that transfer from one job to another or one occupation to another. Secretarial skills, such as typing or using a word processor, understanding the organization of a filing system, or communicating accurately in correspondence with the company's clientele are performed in a secretary's job with great proficiency; but these skills are important in other jobs as well. Sales clerks use word processors; library assistants and clerks use filing systems, and just about any job that has direct contact with the public uses communication skills. Thus, transferable skills are work skills that can be used in multiple occupations.*

*If you are changing jobs, changing careers, or just looking for work, the transferable skills are most important to you. But, sometimes these skills are difficult to locate and define. Even the experts become confused with the categories. However, finding the right slot to put the skills into is not the issue here. What is important is that you identify skills learned from your past work, recognize that these skills are important in other work, and become confident in talking about your work-related skills. The key word is confidence. Confidence is compelling when talking with employers.*

When it comes to locating and defining transferable work skills, the knowledge and skills rehabilitation counselors possess are about as good as it gets, but to clients the process may seem foreign. They do not understand how to look inside of a job to, like Little Jack Horner, "stick in their thumb and pull out a plumb." Counselors need to help them with identifying their work skills. As they help clients in surfacing these skills, counselors are actually teaching their clients to highlight these skills so that they can talk about them with employers. That is important!

# WORK SKILLS
# ALISON BENSON

Review the jobs from Alison Benson's past work and identify the work skills she would likely have learned from her past work. Be creative and read between the lines in the case study. If you are involved in a work group analyzing the case, be willing to suggest other skills that may not be readily evident. The discussion about work skills is as important as the particular skills you or your group may identify. Make a discussion of work skills a part of the class or group discussion.

JOB TITLE /WORK SKILLS

# 1: ______________________ ______________________
______________________
______________________ ______________________
______________________
______________________ ______________________
______________________
______________________ ______________________
______________________

# 2: ______________________ ______________________
______________________
______________________ ______________________
______________________
______________________ ______________________
______________________

# 3: ______________________________

______________________________

______________________________

______________________________ ______________________________

______________________________

______________________________ ______________________________

______________________________

# 4: ______________________________

______________________________ ______________________________

______________________________

______________________________ ______________________________

______________________________

**Are any of these work skills transferable to other occupations? Name these skills and list the occupations in which you feel these skills can be used. There is no set answer to this question. First, consider the skill and then ask yourself how the skill can be used in other occupations.**

| Transferable Work Skill | Other Occupations |
|---|---|
| ______________________ | ______________________ |
| ______________________ | |
| ______________________ | ______________________ |
| ______________________ | |
| ______________________ | ______________________ |
| ______________________ | |
| ______________________ | ______________________ |
| ______________________ | |

## EDUCATIONAL SKILLS

About educational skills, the "*Job-Search Organizer*" says:

*Every employer you meet will want to know about your educational skills. Your achievements in education almost always receive a lot of weight in any employment decision. Employers want to know, generally, how well you did in school. In vocational training? In community college? In higher education? In addition, they want to know about the courses you took: which courses you chose and which courses were of the greatest interest and benefit to you. You must be able to answer their questions about your education; and, in particular, talk freely about your educational achievements.*

*Most of all, employers want to know how your educational program relates to the job you are now seeking. These are general questions and most applicants will provide general answers. If you really want your educational skills to work for you in your discussions with employers, you need to identify the skills you learned in your course work. For example, suppose you are interviewing for the position of accounts manager with a retail store. You could simple tell the interviewer that you took a course in general business. If you are able to tell the interviewer that you had courses in basic accounting where you learned double-entry bookkeeping, or courses in communications where you learned to handle customer complaints–the skills needed to do the job–you greatly increase your chances of getting the job. Knowing your educational skills and how to talk about them, something most applicants do not do well, gives you a competitive advantage in the job market.*

The "*Job-Search-Organizer*" asks the reader to give some thought to the programs and courses taken in high school, vocational training, community college, colleges and universities, and professional training, (e.g., seminars and workshops.) The objective of this section is to identify the course work, to sift out the skills from these programs, to understand how these skills can be applied to jobs the client may be seeking now and in the future, and be able to talk about these skills both informally in general conversation and formally in interviews. A course taken at the high school level in basic computer skills may not have been important in the most recent job, for instance, a maintenance worker; but when looking for new work, the skills learned will at least be a pre-requisite for learning a company's computer program. The exercise–going back over what was done in the past, considering what they have learned from these programs, and thinking about how the skills learned may be helpful to them as they assume a job hunt–may be as important to clients as the answers they come up with while resurfacing past educational experiences.

Simply listing the programs and content is not enough. Clients need to look at the content of the course work to see if any of this knowledge will likely be helpful in the job search. The simple exercise of recall is valuable in preparing for the job search. Clients learn to look back at the educational experiences, try to determine what skills, if any, were learned in these experiences, and see how these educational skills are likely useful in future work activity. Once recorded in the "*Job-Search Organizer*" clients can examine their education, when needed, in light of new discoveries in the job search. Here is what the "*Job-Search Organizer*" says about educational skills:

*Some of your high school courses and courses taken later provided you with a general fund of knowledge and basic skills like reading, writing, and math that you use to get around in the world in which you live. Other courses taught you skills that you may now draw upon to strengthen your vocational objectives. These include, for example, skills like typing or mechanical drawing. The same is true of other educational experiences after high school, including both academic and vocational training.*

# EDUCATIONAL SKILLS
# ALISON BENSON

Review the Case of Alison Benson and list the courses you feel would have been a part of her normal educational experience. Then individually or in group sessions decide what skills she would have likely learned from the course work during her educational experiences. As a group or individually, decide how helpful these skills would be in Ms. Benson's pursuit of future work; that is, are these educational skills transferable to a work setting?

This is an important exercise. The discussion or thought process you are now going through will not be very different when you meet real clients. Almost every client in the real world has had some formal education; and, as a counselor, you will need to analyze the formal education your client has received for educational skills that person can use in other alternative work. Your ability to examine past educational experiences and suggest how skills learned from these experiences can be used in other work will go a long way toward determining a vocational objective and narrowing the range of the job search.

## 1. HIGH SCHOOL EDUCATION

Do not limit your exploration for educational skills learned in high school to those suggested in the case study. Go beyond the box. All of us have been through high school and taken courses in similar programs. Remember, the discussion is just as important as the conclusions you reach about her educational benefits. Assume that reading, writing, and math are a given and limit the identification of educational skills to specialized courses. Begin by asking what courses Alison Benson would have taken and what skills would she probably have learned in these courses that have helped her in her work experiences.

| Course Title | Vocational Skills |
|---|---|
| ____________ | ____________ |
| ____________ | |
| ____________ | ____________ |
| ____________ | |
| ____________ | ____________ |
| ____________ | |
| ____________ | ____________ |
| ____________ | |
| ____________ | ____________ |
| ____________ | |

Were the vocational skills Alison learned from these courses useful in any of her past jobs? Yes___ No ____

Which skills were used in past jobs? ____________________________________________

Will these skills be useful in jobs she will likely seek? That is, will these educational skills be transferable to other occupations within her work limitations? If so, explain:

____________________________________________

2. COMMUNITY COLLEGE, UNIVERSITY, COLLEGE, BUSINESS SCHOOL

Alison Benson took a two-year program at a local community college in interior design. Consider now if any of the educational skills she learned in her interior design program would be helpful in identifying vocational interests or in making a vocational objective about her future. Suggest other possible courses she may have taken as part of her design major. Expand your thinking about ways her higher education major may give her a leg up in another vocation or career concentration.

| Course Title | Vocational Skills |
|---|---|
| ____________ | ____________ |
| ____________ | ____________ |
| ____________ | ____________ |
| ____________ | ____________ |

Were the vocational skills she learned in her undergraduate or graduate courses helpful in her past occupations? If so, Explain:

Do her educational experiences in community college tell you anything about her general interests? When looking at her high school education, her community college education, and her past work, does it tell you anything about her as a person?

Do you anticipate these skills being useful in achieving her vocational goals? List the educational skills from her degree work that you feel will be useful in other occupations. Which, if any, skills do you think would be transferable to other occupations:

## 3. SEMINARS & WORKSHOPS

Seminars and workshops may be the most useful for identifying work skills as they focus upon specific learning experiences. The *Job Search Organizer* says about these short, compact educational experiences:

> *The content of these educational experiences contains subject matter that has a direct application to other work activities; (i.e., the subject matter may become immediately transferable to other work). As a rule, participants learn skills through practice. Also, many of*

*these workshops contain several skill areas. For instance, participants may take a course titled "office management systems" and in the course of several days learn the skills of "Time Management" and "Motivational Techniques" while learning how to run an office.*

*You may feel that even though you have some training, you are not competent to use these skills. Or, you may feel the training was in the remote past and may not have relevance to work today. List them anyway. No one is asking you to be an expert. All employers want to know is if you have had exposure to the ideas and concepts. They are betting the learning curve to update these skills will be significantly shorter. By being able to talk about these and other educational experiences, you improve your position and chances of getting the job you really want.*

In preparing for the job search clients recall these experiences and list them in their "*Organizer*." These educational experiences were likely taken over a few days or weeks. At the end of the session the participant likely received a certificate of recognition, a certificate of completion, or even certification. Both the title of the seminar and the statement of completion are important. The vocational skills learned in these educational experiences, in all likelihood, relate directly to the job they were performing at the time. In most cases, these skills can become great resume items!

## WORKSHOPS & SEMINARS
## ALISON BENSON

List the seminars she has taken in the past while she was working with Grand Alliance.

______________________________________________

______________________________________________

Do any of these seminars have work skills that would be useful in other job settings and, therefore, would be transferable to other work? Again, your discussion about education and skills gained from these educational experiences are just as important as the results you reach. When you meet your first clients, you will need to look at all education taken to determine if there are skills that can be used in alternative work.

______________________________________________

______________________________________________

______________________________________________

______________________________________________

## 4. ADAPTIVE SKILLS

The "*Job-Search Organizer*" says about adaptive skills:

> *What are employers looking for in the people they hire? Most of us would say the skills to do the job. And, you would be right. Skills acquired from work in the past are very important, and you would be right if you said that in many jobs you would not be hired without them. Employers are looking for other things as well; in fact, intangible qualities–things you cannot put your finger on–may play a major role in the employment decision. A survey of employers found the three most important criteria employers use to screen out applicants were: (1) appearance: the way you look and the way you dress; (2) dependability: can the employer count on you; and (3) acquired work skills. Notice work skills followed appearance and dependability–both adaptive or life skills.*

Michael Farr[4] in *Job Search Basics* lists basic adaptive skills as, "good attendance," "honesty," "arriving on time," "following instructions," "meeting deadlines," "hard working," and "getting along with others." Other adaptive skills he lists are: "ambition," "patience," "flexibility," "maturity," "assertiveness," "dependability," "learn quickly," "complete assignments," "sincerity," "motivation," "problem solving, " "friendliness," "sense of humor," "leadership," "physical stamina," "enthusiasm," "good sense of direction," "persistence," "self-motivation," "accept responsibility," "results oriented," "willingness to answer questions," "pride in doing a good job," "willingness to learn," and "creativity."[pg. 23-26]

Adaptive skills may not appear on a resume, but they are important evidence of successful work behavior. *An essential goal of behavioral counseling in any job search is identifying these adaptive skills and, in counseling sessions, reinforcing adaptive skills as success behaviors.*

Recognizing these behaviors and pointing them out to clients becomes

1. motivational and leads clients toward learning success behaviors.

   They receive recognition for what they have done when counselors say to them, "I was impressed with the way you set up that appointment and contacted the employer on your own." (ambition, assertiveness, self-motivation). Moreover, recognizing these behaviors and pointing them out to clients becomes important in

2. helping clients make an attitudinal adjustment.
   Simply saying, "Your work record shows that you have always been a hard worker and worked well with others," (hard working, getting along with others) can go a long way toward changing the negative images clients often have of themselves following disability. It also reinforces adaptive behavior that can help reduce their preoccupation with their limitations, and enable them to move toward positive expressions of hope. Clients need to see these adaptive skills as a way of self-promotion. Finally, recognizing these behaviors and pointing them out to clients

3. teaches clients to reach out to the employers they interview.
   When clients say to employers, "I believe I learn things quickly and you can depend on me," (dependability, learn quickly) interviewers understand the candidate believes they can fit into the business culture, get the job done, and work harmoniously with others. These adaptive or life skills are learned responses; clients do not recognize or say these things to employers and others unless their counselors demonstrate the importance of these skills to them.

# ADAPTIVE SKILLS
# ALISON BENSON

Take a look at the case study of Alison Benson and try to determine the adaptive skills she has learned along the way. Identify at least ten (10) adaptive skills you think she has learned and provide evidence from the case to defend your selection. There are no set answers to this question. As you can see from the earlier discussion, always being on target in identifying adaptive skills is not what is important. What is important is that counselors recognize the role adaptive skills play in changing behavior, constantly look for these traits in their clients, and learn to say to their clients "these are success behaviors; you must learn them to be successful."

1. List at least ten (10) adaptive skills you feel Alison Benson would have demonstrated in her work with Grand Alliance.

2. In your own analysis of the case, or in discussions with other classmates or seminar participants, express how you think these adaptive skills demonstrate behavior that leads to success at work and in life.

3. If you were aiding in a job search for Alison, how would you relate these adaptive skills to potential employers?

| Adaptive Skills | Success Behavior |
|---|---|
| | |
| | |
| | |
| | |
| | |
| | |
| | |

## SELECTING A VOCATIONAL CHOICE

Part I on vocational preparation ends with a momentary stop in the action to ask of yourself and your clients some essential questions. The first step in making a vocational choice is to ask the question: Can a vocational decision be made from the information you have already uncovered in the personal inventory or in the skills analysis? In rehabilitation, simply making a vocational choice is not enough. Rehabilitation counselors have to examine any vocational choice closely to address additional questions such as, "Is this vocational decision appropriate for a person with my client's limitations? Are the jobs in this occupation within my client's RFC?" If the vocational choice fits the limitations, the job search is well on the way.

If the vocational choice is beyond the physical or mental capabilities of the client, the next question to ask is: "do the skills identified–the adaptive skills, the educational skills, the skills learned in seminars or workshops, or the transferable work skills–lead to other occupations that are within the client's capabilities?" Rehabilitation counselors can really be helpful in showing their clients how their vocational skills can apply to other work settings.

Here is what the "*Job-Search Organizer*" has to say to clients about selecting a vocational objective:

> *You may have decided upon a vocational objective on your own. You may have known for a long time the kind of work you want to do, have the skills necessary to do the work, and have an idea where these jobs exist in the community. Excellent! Experts have yet to devise a system more predictable than simply asking what it is you want to do. Note the statement from What Color is Your Parachute, the best-known book on career development, about predicting success of a vocational objective. The author quotes from his friend and vocational expert, John Holland: "Despite several decades of research, the most efficient way to predict vocational choice is simply to ask the person what he*

*(or she) wants to be; our best devices do not exceed the predictive value of that method.* "[1, pg. 95]

The counseling session concerning making a vocational choice may not lead to hoped-for conclusions. Seldom do clients have definitive answers when asked questions such as, "What do you want to do?" Nevertheless, there are exceptions. The counselor's life can be greatly simplified if their client can identify areas of interest. Going through the process of making a vocational choice based upon a client's background experience and skill analysis allows counselors:

1. to see how much attention their clients have given work options to that point in the discovery, and

2. to offer suggestions of occupations that may be able to use their background and skills.

At any rate, the process of making a vocational choice should narrow the options in searching for alternative work.

## SELECTING A VOCATIONAL OBJECTIVE FOR ALISON BENSON

Return to the case study and the skills analysis you have just done. This time consider only the content included in the case study. Look at what she has done in the past. Look at what she and the company identify as success behavior. Look at skills gained from past jobs. Look at her educational achievements. Look at her sure-fire adaptive skills, and, of course, look at her RFC.

Individually, or as a group, *prepare a short essay*. Set the table by listing her age, education, and work experience. Assuming she will not be rehired by Grand Alliance, address the following questions:

1. What is her current Residual Functional Capacity?

2. With this RFC, can she do any of her past jobs without some accommodation?

3. What skills does she have from her past work to transfer to other work within her RFC?

4. What skills has she gained from her education?

5. What adaptive skills does she have?

6. Without additional education or training, using her current RFC, what is her best vocational objective(s)?

## PART 2: GRASS ROOTS NETWORKING IN THE HIDDEN JOB MARKET

There is hardly a book on the market today that does not identify networking as the most important of the job-search methods, and the statistics seem to bear out the level of importance given to networking as a job-search method. Chapter 8 presented the results of a survey conducted by the Department of Labor in 1973 that shows that almost 70% of all jobs were secured through direct application to employers and networking through relatives, friends, and acquaintances. A 26% success rate was attributed to networking alone. The results from networking were probably higher as many job applicants had received their job leads from family, friends, and acquaintances. The survey conducted by Camil and Associates completed two years later placed the results of networking at close to 30%.

The statistics from writers in the job-search field today give networking much higher marks. Enlaw and Goldman's,[4] *The Insiders Guide to Finding a Job,* determined that 85% of all jobs are filled through networking. The authors say about this method:

> *Everyone agrees that the single most important activity in your job search is networking. In the average market, 85% of your job search should be focused on networking. In a more difficult job search market, 90% to 95% of opportunities will be uncovered through networking.*[pg. 98]

Most other authors are more conservative in their estimates. For instance, Michael Farr,[5] author of *Job Search Basics,* says that about 40% of all people find their jobs through someone else. Regardless of who is right on this statistical roller coaster, the opinions of those studying employment patterns in the Unites States are uniform in recommending networking as the single most important job-search method.

The networks are generally made up of family, friends, and acquaintances. While the support of persons within the family complex and close relationships have been tied to better health, acquaintances or "weak ties" have been shown to be vital in finding job opportunities. "These weak ties are especially useful for employment because these people have additional contacts outside of one's own social network and thus access to a diverse amount of information, resource, and possible job opportunities."[3, pg. 135]

What is networking anyway, and how does it work? The answer seems all too obvious, and maybe it is. Enlaw and Goldman[4] define networking as "a collection of personal and professional contacts with whom you establish and maintain a relationship on an ongoing basis."[pg. 128] These authors say that the "collection of personal and professional contacts" should be made up of persons whose opinions you respect and who are positive, accessible, and straightforward. They should have insight, knowledge, or expertise that is in line with your career goals."[pg. 19] The key to making the network produce results for the job seeker is to ask for help and not for a job. You look to the network for ideas, recommendations, and referrals, and that is precisely what you want from them.

Look more closely at the participants Enlaw and Goldman[4] consider in their networking statistics. First, the authors refer to the network as "a collection of personal and professional contacts." Possibly the level of the persons within an organization accounts for the high success rate given to networking. The authors' experience in finding jobs for people is mainly among highly skilled workers, managers, and corporate executives with far-reaching professional contacts where networking is more prevalent.

The demographics of persons in the Enlaw and Goldman[4] network do not seem to fit the demographics of those normally referred to rehabilitation for job placement. Generally, rehabilitation clients are not high-level managers or corporate executives; most do not have work backgrounds that would be considered highly skilled; nor do they have far-reaching contacts. The contacts for our clients are generally much closer to home. The demographics Enlaw and Goldman[4] describe would apply more to Class II individuals rather than working or baseline people.

The lack of far-reaching contacts possibly explains the conclusions reached in published data from the National Office on Disability, data that would suggest that using the techniques of networking for employment among persons with disabilities would have serious limitations. These data say,

> *Many people with disabilities have small social networks with high redundancy, as most of the people in the network know each other. Many people with disabilities lack the weak ties (friends and acquaintances) or contacts that are not connected to other people in the network. While this is good in some instances, it is a barrier when it comes to employment. Networks with high redundancy have been shown to be less useful to finding employment because everyone in the network has access to the same information and resources.*"[3, pg.136]

It is true that "weak ties" within our clientele's social networks may limit the networking possibilities, but their social network has special advantages that do not readily appear. First, when we consider working people, or people in the trades, the range of jobs are smaller, work activities are more familiar to persons in the network, and those jobs are generally closer to home. The job seeker will likely know about the kinds of jobs in the community and have knowledge of the places of employment. Moreover, people in the network are likely to be employed in like or similar jobs to the ones our clientele desire. These contacts may not be in a hiring position, but they likely are in situations where they can influence the supervisors, managers, and employer who do have hiring responsibilities.

If indeed employers are now looking to their own employees for local referrals, choosing not to use outside resources in hiring, as recent research would suggest, friends, relatives, and acquaintances close to home present many possible opportunities. These advantages are in line with what the authors of "Social Capital: A View from the Field"[3] have concluded as keys to employment of persons with disabilities. While noting that few programs offering assistance in job placement look at what these authors call "social capital", namely, friends, relatives, and acquaintances "yet we are learning that social capital plays a critical role in helping individuals find and sustain employment."[pp. 133-139]

There is no doubt that factored into their statistics these authors present is the new research in business and industry that says that companies are looking to their employees for help in recruiting new talent. One of the contributors to *The Insiders Guide to Finding a Job*[4] speaks to persons seeking jobs, saying,

> *As a candidate for jobs, you will in all likelihood find your next job through reference, a referral, or recommendation from someone whom you know. Companies are viewing their employees as their very best recruiters. They talk up the company and its benefits, the great career tracks that are available, and overall advantages of working for the organization. Current employees are a company's best resource for finding and bringing in top-quality talent.* [pg. 95]

If companies are asserting more control over their human resource programs and looking to current employers to represent their companies in recruitment, the success rate for networking will doubtless be much higher than the more conservative estimates show.

## NETWORKING FOR JOBS

Here is what the "*Job-Search Organizer*" says about networking:

*While the value of networking is widely known, most people have little knowledge about how networking is done. Therefore, they go about networking in the same haphazard way and fail to get the full benefits from their networking experience.... The procedures you are about to use will show you how to get the most out of your networking plan and help you to keep organized while following the plan. But remember, there is no set way for networking. Each job search has its own pathway. You are like Sherlock Holmes uncovering clues at each juncture along the way. In fact, the more you look upon the job search as a game of investigating, the less likely you will view the unpleasant experiences in the job search as a life and death struggle. Let your basic instincts and your networking people become reliable guides.*

The networking procedure begins with having clients identify six (6) people from among their family, friends, and closest acquaintances ("their primary social capital"). We call these people the covenant group. These are the people the client relies upon for both moral and physical support. When things go bad, these are the people who have to step in and provide comfort and understanding, but these people are important in the job search as well. They are the ones who are most likely to reach out to others and expand the networking group. This group is so important that we ask the client to meet with each one individually, gather information about their occupations and their positions in these occupations, explain to them the vocational goals and objectives, and actually sign a covenant agreement that they are willing to help.

Then, we ask the client to identify six (6) other people they know from among their acquaintances to form a secondary group. These are people the client may not come in contact with more than several times a year. The job-search literature shows that they may be among the hardest working and most successful in locating job leads and referring the client to employers.

Making a list of people willing to help provide a job lead and refer clients to employers becomes a meaningless procedure without the guidance of the rehabilitation counselor. Clients will not carry out a network plan on their own. For the counselor, the formation of the network becomes nothing more than a platform for applying the basic principles of behavioral counseling. The counselor explains the purpose for forming the network; the counselor makes sure that all covenants are signed and included in the "Organizer;" the counselor makes sure the information on each person is recorded and complete; and, at each counseling session, the counselor reviews the list and makes recommendations and assignments. Counselor reinforcement makes the process work and, while managing the networking process, counselors learn to work smarter not harder. Following is a look at each of these phases of the networking process.

*The Covenant Group.* Clients are asked to identify six (6) persons close to them, gather from this group information about their occupations and their positions in these occupations, explain to them the vocational goals and objectives, and actually sign a covenant agreement that they are willing to help. The "*Job-Search Organizer*" says about the covenant agreement:

> *The agreement is between you and those you trust to help you. Choose carefully. Select a chosen few from among those who care about you and are willing to share this experience with you; and those you respect for their advice and judgment. As part of the covenant you pledge to (1) relate honestly to them your feelings (anxieties and aspirations), and (2) share with them the progress you are making toward finding new work opportunities. They cannot help you unless you keep them informed. Their part of the covenant is that they pledge (1) to be good listeners, (2) to provide you with the best thinking to help you make the right decisions, and (3) to seek out and let you know about appropriate job opportunities.*
>
> *Do not concern yourself that you may be placing your burdens at the feet of those you care for most. People helping people is the way the world works. Few of us have gotten where we are today without plenty of support from others. What you are saying to them is "I am asking you to help me now. But in your time of need, I will be there for you also. This is my covenant to you."*

What can the rehabilitation counselor learn from the list of persons selected for this group? Most of these people will come from the family complex and those closely related. The information clients gather about this group will likely reveal a great deal about the family complex, such as their education and skill level, the kinds of jobs this group normally hold, their work ethic, and the kinds of jobs most acceptable to them and the client. In your counseling and job-seeking skill sessions, examine everyone one on this list with great care. Note particularly how each of these people are connected within the community. Their recommendations are almost always valuable if the job openings are within the client's functional limitations.

Having the persons from the covenant group sign the agreement is important. The counselor can expect from the signed agreements that the client has:

1. met with each person individually and explained the circumstances,
2. been assertive enough to talk about work and their work goals, and
3. enlisted their help in the job search.

At least, based upon these individual conferences, there is some assurance that if persons from the covenant group locate job leads, in all probability they will refer this job lead to the client. Most of all, the signatures from the covenant group can be taken as a client's commitment to the job search.

*The Secondary Group.* More distant friends and acquaintances are an important part of the network. Clients often feel that those closest to them provide the best chance for surfacing job leads; and, as a result, give less attention to the outer fringe of the network. Research has found that a distant acquaintance may be more valuable than a close friend. Robert Wegmann[12] in *Work in the New Economy* describes a study by Mark Granovetter, a sociologist, whose research studied professional, managerial, and technical workers who had changed jobs within the past year. The subjects of his study were residents of Newton, Massachusetts, a Boston suburb. Participants were asked if they had obtained their new jobs with the help of a friend of relative. Surprisingly, many replied that they had heard about the opening from an acquaintance of theirs. Robert Wegmann[12] goes on to say:

> *Further questioning revealed that in more than a fourth of the cases, the information that led to the new position came from someone who was normally seen once a year or less. Yet more than 80% of these contacts did more than simply inform the unemployed individual about a possible job. They also 'put in a good word' to the employer, recommending the applicant be hired. Granovetter found that acquaintances were more likely to do this than were close friends.* pp. 136-137

The study found that acquaintances often have a more objective view of a job-seekers abilities and work harder to get them a job than close friends do. More distant friends and acquaintances help expand the network. You will recall from the "Introduction" to this chapter that the Annual Report from the National Organization on Disability[8] considered the networking technique ineffective among persons with disabilities because of "high redundancy" and "weak ties." Enlisting more distant friends and acquaintances expands the network and addresses a major concern about using networking for job placement.

Clients will most likely overlook their distant friends and acquaintances without their counselor's assistance. Counselors need to work with them. Prod them to come up with more names of persons they know but seldom see. Suggest to them people they may know like local ministers, former work associates, or old school pals. The more attention the counselor gives to developing the secondary list, the more important the client will consider the task. As can be seen from the research above, the list of acquaintances, no matter how distant, is very important.

Recall, we asked the client to have the members of the primary group sign a covenant showing that each person had been contacted and agreed to help in the job search. Contacts with this secondary, more distant, group have to be handled differently. Signatures would not only be hard to get; but, in many cases, would be inappropriate. You will notice that the "*Job-Search Organizer*" asks for a response to contacts with each member of the secondary group. Here, the client records a summary of their conversation with secondary group members. Counselors need to study these responses! What has occurred between the client and people in the network not only reveals a level of commitment but also gives the counselor some assurance a sincere effort has been made to enlist secondary group members.

*Conclusion: Maintaining the network.* Networking is often referred to as if there is some magical formula that opens up a whole new world of work possibilities. Unfortunately, there is no magic in networking. The process of networking is, pure and simple, forming groups of people who have an interest in helping other people, asking them for help in finding job information and locating job leads, and following up on these leads in the hope the leads will produce interviews that will take the client to the eventual job. Simple as the process may seem, it does work and it does surface a group of job possibilities your client would not otherwise know about. When the networking process is organized and the clients keep in touch with people in the network, chances of success in networking improve dramatically.

One final point, networking is very different from simply making initial contacts. Making contacts is the beginning step, and an important one. After the client has listed the people in the network, they need to contact them, let them know they are seeking work and the kind of work they desire, and enlist them as part of the primary or secondary network. Generally, very little happens at this point, however. Most of the people in the network will not have job possibilities immediately in mind. They may provide hints and vague ideas where the job seeker may go, but seldom do these suggestions blossom into concrete possibilities. Do not get me wrong. These suggestions are important. The client must make the initial contact, record these responses in their *Organizer*, and follow them up with phone calls and other communications, particularly if there are any changes in the vocational plan, but expect no miracles.

Results do come over time if clients maintain the network by regular contact with the networking people and keep them actively looking for job possibilities. This is not an easy task. The trouble most clients have with networking is that they contact their network a first time and become uncomfortable calling these people thereafter. This leaves the network contacts out in the cold; they do not know if the job seeker has found a job or anything about the present condition of the job search.

Therefore, counselors must help their clients manage the networking by:

1. Reviewing their progress at each counseling session, going over each contact with them, and determining the actions to be taken. Do not bypass any name until you have a satisfactory answer from the client about when people in the network were last contacted and what was the content of their conversation. The client must periodically have an action step for each contact.

2. Encouraging their client regularly by reminding them that the best job opportunities will come from these contacts. To get the kind of commitment you need, both you and the client must be convinced that networking is the most effective strategy. Your reinforcement makes all the difference.

# CASE STUDY
# ALISON BENSON (Cont'd.)

*When the rehabilitation counselor, David Asbury, received the assignment requesting him to locate alternative work for Alison Benson, he contacted her former employer about the possibility of accepting her back into employment. It was always his habit to contact the former employer first to see if the employer was willing,*

- *to make an accommodation for disabled workers,*
- *to modify the job to allow a disabled worker to perform the job within the limitation, or*
- *to locate other jobs in the company she could perform.*

1. Was David just wasting his time or could he build a case for making an exception in Ms. Benson's case?

2. Build a persuasive case why Grand Alliance should make an accommodation for Alison Benson.

3. Then, assume you are the employer and make a case for not hiring her. List your reasons below.

*Alison was devastated when she found out that the company was not going to hire her back and had no other jobs for her. She was also experiencing constant pain in her knees and had begun to feel that maybe she could no longer work. When Mr. Asbury talked with her, he had the feeling that she was experiencing situational depression. Her treating family doctor has prescribed depression medication for her and that seems to help.*

1. How would you suggest Mr. Asbury deal with her present condition?

2. Should he approach her on the subject of her depressive state?

3. Should he suggest disability income from Social Security (SSDI) as an option?

4. What might he say or do to prepare her to make the transition to alternative work?

5. List some of the ways you as a counselor might intervene.

*After reading the case file and gathering the information, David Asbury asked Alison to make a list of ten (10) jobs she thought she would be able to perform. She was concerned that none of the jobs she knew about would pay her the kind of money she had been making in the past. After some prodding, she came up with the following nine (9) suggestions:*

1. *Delivery person for UPS or Federal Express*
2. *Counter Clerk at a local Auto Zone store*
3. *Waitress with Cracker Barrel or Appleby's*
4. *Desk Clerk with Howard Johnson's Motel*
5. *Customer Service with Lowe's Appliance store*
6. *Accounting Clerk/Bookkeeper*
7. *Sales person with a privately owned Furniture business*
8. *Truck Driving*

9. *Manager, shoe store*

1. What does this list tell David about Alison's understanding of the job market?

2. Which of these jobs are realistic possibilities for Alison? Why?

3. Which of these suggestions would not be appropriate for her? Why?

4. Knowing her vocational profile, what other jobs might you list as possibilities she may pursue in the job search? List three: (1) ________________ (2) ______________ (3) ________________

## FORMING A COVENANT GROUP

*David Asbury explained to Alison about where she might find job leads. He asked her to follow the want ads in the newspapers and to register with the local employment service. He advised her to contact the largest companies in the area and see if they had job openings she might consider. Then, he told her that networking among family, friends, and acquaintances was recommended in most of the job-search literature, and if she followed the procedures he recommended, she stood the best chance of getting the job she really wanted. After all, she was only looking for a single job, and even if jobs were not as plentiful in the current recessive economy, there were jobs out there that she could do. Networking, he explained, would likely produce job leads for the better-paying jobs. This discussion aroused her interest in the possibilities of networking.*

*He continued to make his case for the idea that networking was the most likely job strategy to locate job leads. He asked her to make a list of six (6) persons to form her primary group from among those closest to her and those whom she respected and relied upon for advice in many areas of her life. He asked her to meet with them individually, explain to them her understanding of networking, tell them what she needed from them–emotional support during the job search, their ideas and recommendations, and referral of any job they thought she might pursue. She was a little uneasy about asking them to sign the covenant agreement, but after the first few times, the signing of the agreement came a lot easier. Later, she found out that signing the agreement produced a greater commitment from the persons in her primary group than just asking them for help. She came up with the following names:*

- *Her oldest brother John lived in Norristown and was a produce manager at Food City grocery store. He had been a truck driver before taking that job, but he hurt his back and could no longer do over-the-road truck driving. He had taken the job as cashier at the store and worked his way up to produce manager. He had not finished high school, but had obtained his GED.*

- *Her father Norman was still working at 66 years of age. He was a route salesperson with the Wonder Bread distributor in Norristown. The family had lived in the community for over 50 years and had a sterling reputation. Norman was a high school graduate.*

- *Her sister Sally had married Fred and they had two children, Orville and Cindy. The family lived in Pittsburgh. Fred was a sales representative for Litten Pharmaceutical based in New York and called upon physicians in the City of Pittsburgh. He had done this work for 30 years. The Company had a local distribution center in Pittsburgh where they packaged medical supplies for distribution.*

- *Alison's closest friend, Mary Hines, had always been a support to her. The two had gone to high school together and remained close ever since. Mary was an inbound telemarketer with Victoria Secret in Pittsburgh. She took orders over the phone and addressed customer complaints. She has been with the firm for three years. Earlier in her career, she had been a receptionist with a local dentist office in Norristown.*

- *Her mother Doris does not work, but is active in her church and several local garden clubs. She has won many awards for her flower arrangements in garden club contests. She had been the AVON representative in the Norriston community for many years.*

- *Charles, Alison's former husband, is vice-president at the ACME Corporation in Wierton, West Virginia. The two were married about 10 years and had their only son. The two talk regularly and the relationship now is better than it ever was before. He has not remarried.*

1. What does this list tell David Asbury about the family complex?

2. Do these family members have the personal resources and possible contacts to be helpful in the job search?

3. Give a brief profile of the family, their class position, the kinds of possible connections they may have, and the job sources they may be able to uncover.

*Once her primary group was in place, David Asbury advised her that the network of family and friends would not likely produce immediate results. She would have to update them with information about her progress regularly. It was his feeling that keeping Alison actively talking with network people would take her mind off her physical problems, improve her mental state as well, and give her a lot of hope in the job search.*

## FORMING A SECONDARY GROUP

*David also asked her to make a list of people to form a secondary network. These people would come from acquaintances, many of whom she did not see more than one time a year. He told her the job-search literature has shown that persons in the secondary network often work harder and produce better results than those in the primary network. Secondary network people, he said, would greatly broaden her possibilities.*

*He told her she may have some uneasiness about calling these people since she did not see them that often; but, in most cases, they would welcome her calls. He reminded her that she was not asking them to find her a job; that was her responsibility. They would be much more receptive if she asked them for advice about work and asked them to refer job leads to her if anything came up. She was relieved that David did not ask her to have the secondary network people sign the covenant. Signing the covenant was often difficult, he explained, in dealing with more distant people; but, in place of the agreement, she would need to place more emphasis upon contacting them regularly.*

*Alison compiled her list of six (6) secondary people and discussed each one with David Asbury. They included:*

1. *Natalie Slocombe had worked with Alison when she first came to Grand Alliance Furniture Gallery. She had been asked to quit after an altercation with Mr. Hardy about excessive overtime. Alison felt that Natalie had gotten a raw deal, and called her occasionally just to talk shop. Natalie had gone back to school and gotten her associate's degree to become a paralegal and now works in the law firm of Scalem and Guttom in Pittsburgh.*

2. *Alison is very close to her minister Robert Goodfellow and sees him every week, but she has not talked to him about her problems at work. She felt that although he did not work in the private sector he might be able to help her. The Reverend Goodfellow has been with the congregation at First Presbyterian Church in Norristown for 18 years.*

3. *Years ago, Alice Severs had been a waiter with Alison at the Richlands Café in Norristown. The two do not talk more than a couple times a year. Alice had held a number of jobs in the community, (i.e., waiter, food manager at the Food City Deli, and hostess at the Provincial Night Club). She was rich with stories about the rise and fall of the pretenders in local society, and could always make the worst of times seem better.*

4. *Alison's attorney Allen Farnsworth in Norristown had helped Alison and her husband through their difficult but amicable divorce. When it was all over, Alison and Charles both felt that Allen had taken great care to make sure both parties were treated fairly. He had also written a will for both. Mr. Farnsworth was greatly respected in the small city and he was well known for helping people such as Alison and Charles in difficult situations.*

5. *Martha Haggard lived next door to the Bensons for four years in the 1990s. Martha is an administrative secretary to the vice-president at the Perdue poultry processing plant in*

*Pittsburgh. She had begun her career in retail sales with Woolworth's Department Store, but when Woolworth went out of business, she returned to college and got her Associates Degree in Computer Science. From there she went to work at Perdue where she has been employed for the past 7 years.*

6. *Hanna Goldstein has retired now. For years, she was the manager of the pet store where all the locals purchased their animals. Alison loved cats and the two would talk for hours about the habits of cats and other animals. Alison has one house cat she loves dearly and misses her conversation with Hanna badly.*

Experience tells us that not all of the persons from either group will contribute to the job search. It does not happen. Ask yourself, from what you know about these people in her secondary group, what kind of contribution each is capable of making to Alison's job search.

Are there other people left off the list who may make a better contribution to a secondary group?

List what each of these people can bring to the table for Alison.

1. Natalie Slocombe

2. Robert Goodfellow

3. Alice Severs

4. Allen Farnsworth

5. Martha Haggard

6. Hanna Goldstein

# CONCLUSION

We have asked what contribution each of the network people are likely to make to the job search of Alison Benson. Of course, there is no way of telling until information begins to flow in from the primary and secondary networks.

When counselors do discuss the list with their clients, going over each one with them, clients begin to see the value of preparing the list of contacts and begin to recognize that their friends, relatives, and acquaintances have a wide range of personal resources and contacts to help them.

As we have seen, there is no magic in networking. What networking does require, and something clients often seem to have trouble doing, is maintaining contact with the groups. Unless the client does keep in touch with the people in their networks, these people have no way of knowing the status of the job search. This is where the counselor comes in. Our recommendation is that at every counseling session the main agenda will be to go over each person on the list and set forth action steps that need to be taken in the network. Making the assignments is a natural part of behavioral counseling.

## TOPICS FOR GROUP DISCUSSION

1. The Case of Alison Benson is designed to walk students and professionals through the *Job Search Organizer* and the networking process for job placement. Our suggestion is to divide the class or work group into study groups and have them go through the case, answer the questions requested, and have them make decisions asked for in the Chapter. The instructor may choose then to have each group appoint a leader and recorder. The recorder would have the responsibility to take notes and compile the suggestions for presentation. The leader would assign parts of the project to each member and, if instructed, make a presentation on the group findings to the main body in the class or workshop. This assignment could serve as a final examination.

2. *The Job Search Organizer* has been designed as a tool to help rehabilitation counselors manage the case in job placement. Throughout the text, the authors have spoken about the difficulty of management in job placement. Do you feel that this is a viable way to manage a case? Can you suggest other strategies for managing cases in job placement?

3. Chapter 10 discusses the pros and cons of networking in job placement among persons with disabilities. Is networking a strategy worth considering? As a rehabilitation counselor, is this a strategy you would use? Do you have other suggestions for having clients involved in their own job search?

# INDIVIDUAL EXERCISES

Following instruction in the procedures, and the features and benefits of using the *Job Search Organizer* and networking among friends, family, and acquaintances as a strategy for job placement, the instructor may choose to make an assignment of the case of Alison Benson to each member of the class or group for independent study. Each person would answer the questions in the chapter, make the necessary decisions, and prepare a paper on the value of networking for jobs as a job-search strategy for persons with disabilities.

# REFERENCES

[1]Bolles, R.N. (1991). What *Color Is Your Parachute?* Berkeley, CA: Ten Speed Press.

[2]Bolles, R.N. (2007). What *Color Is Your Parachute?* Berkeley, CA: Ten Speed Press.

[3]Condeluci, Al, Ledbetter, Melva Gooden, Ortman, Dori, Fromknecht, Jeff, and Defries, Megan (2008). "Social Capital: A View from the Field," *Journal of Vocational Rehabilitation, 29*, pp.133-139.

[4]Enelow, W. S. & Goldman, S. (2005). *Insider's Guide to Finding a Job*. JIST Wirks, Inc., Indianapolis, Indiana.

[5]Farr, J. M. (1991). *The Very Quick Job Search.* JIST Wirks, Inc., Indianapolis, Indiana.

[6]Marrone, J. Gandolfo, C. Gold, M. & Hoff, Gandolfo, Gold, and Hoff, D. (1998). "Just Doing It: Helping People with Mental Illness Get Good Jobs," *Journal of Applied Rehabilitation Counseling, 29*(1), pp. 37-47.

[7]Myers, John W., et al., (June, 1983). Counseling the Older Rural Worker: A Report, *Journal of Employment Counseling,*

[8]National Organization on Disability (NOD) (2004). NOD/Harris Survey of Americans with Disabilities.

[9]Olney, M. F. & Salomone, P. R. (1992) Empowerment and Choice in Supported Employment: Helping People to Help Themselves. *Journal of Applied Rehabilitation Counseling, 23*(3), pp. 41-44.

[10]Roessler, R. W. (1985). "Self-Starting in the Job Market: The Continuing Need for Job-Seeking Skills in Rehabilitation," *Journal of Applied Rehabilitation Counseling, 16*(2), p. 22.

[11]Tew-Washburn, Suzannem (2000). Job Placement Methods and Models, pp.133-139.

[12]Wegmann, Robert, Robert Chapman, and Miriam Johnson (1989). *Work in the New Economy.* Jist Wirks, Inc., Indianapolis, Indiana.

[13]Wells, Gerald (1994). *Finding Jobs on Main Street*. Elliott & Fitzpartick, Athens, GA.

# BIBLIOGRAPHY


Andrew, J. & Faubion, C. W. (2014). *Vocational Rehabilitation: An Introduction for the Human Services Professional 3rd. Edition.* Linn Creek, MO: Aspen Professional Services.

Blackwell, T. L., Field, T. F., & Field, J. E. (1992). *The Vocational Expert Under Social Security.* Athens, GA: Elliott & Fitzpatrick, Inc.

Bolles, R. N. (1991). *The 1991 What Color Is Your Parachute?* Berkeley, CA: Ten Speed Press.

Bolles, R. N. (2007). *The 2007 What Color Is Your Parachute?* Berkeley, CA: Ten Speed Press.

Brown, D. L. & Beale, C. L. (1981). "Diversity in Post–1970 Trends" *in Non-Metropolitan America in Transition*, ed. By Hawley, A. E. & Mazie, S. M. Chapel Hill, NC: The University of North Carolina Press.

Bylinski, G. (1983). "The Race to the Automatic Factory," Fortune, 107, February 21, 1983.

Condeluci, A., Ledbetter, M. G., Ortman, D., Fromknecht, J., Defries, M. (2008). "Social Capital: A View from the Field" *Journal of Vocational Rehabilitation*, Vol *29*(3), pp. 133-139.

Conference on Postwar Changes in the American Economy (1980). Cambridge, MA: National Bureau of Economic Research.

Crainer, S. & Dearlove (2000). *Generation Entrepreneur.* Great Britain: Pearson Education, Ltd.

Cull, John G. and Richard E. Hardy (1972). *Vocational Rehabilitation: Profession and Process.* Springfield, IL: Charles C. Thomas, Publishers.

Dyer, L. (April, 1973). "Job Search Success of Middle-Aged Managers and Engineers," *Industrial and Labor Relations* Review, 26.

Edwards, L.A. & Wells, G.K. (1979). *Shaping the Future: A Systems Approach to Human Resources Development in Vocational Rehabilitation Agencies.* Richmond, Virginia.

Elliott, Timothy & Paul Letung. "Vocational Rehabilitation: History and Practice."

Enelow, W. S. & Goldman, S. (2005). *Insider's Guide to Finding a Job.* Indianapolis, IN: JIST Publishing, Inc.

*The Enhanced Guide for Occupational Exploration* (1991). Indianapolis, IN: JIST Works, Inc.

Farr, J. M. (1991). *Getting the Job You Really Want: A Step-By-Step Guide.* Indianapolis, IN: JIST Works, Inc.

Farr, J. M. (1990). *Job Finding Fast.* Mission Hills, CA: Glencoe/McGraw Hill. Educational Division.

Farr, J. M. (2006). *Job Search Basics.* Indianapolis, IN: JIST Works. Inc.

Farr, J. M. (2005). *The Quick Resume & Cover Letter.* Indianapolis, IN: JIST Works, Inc.

Farr, J. M. (1991). *The Right Job for You.* Indianapolis, IN: JIST Works, Inc.

Farr, J. M. (1991). *The Very Quick Job Search.* Indianapolis, IN: JIST Works, Inc.
Fisher, D. C. (1915). *Hillsboro People.* New York: Henry Holt & Company.
Fogel, W. (1977). "Illegal Aliens: Economic Aspects and Public Policy Alternatives. *San Diego Law Review*, 15.
Freeman, R. "The Evolution of the American Labor Market, 1948-1980," Paper prepared for the NBER, Key Biscayne.
Fullerton, H. Jr. (September, 1987). *Labor Force Projections: 1986-2000.* Monthly Labor Review, 110.
Gale, Z. (1910). *Friendship Village.* New York: The Macmillan Company.
Garland, Hamlin (1899). *Main Traveled Roads.* New York: Harper & Brothers.
Half, Robert (1949). *The Robert Half Way to Get Hired In Today's Job Market.* New York: John Wiley & Sons, Inc.
Hannings, Robert B. (Editor) (1970). *Forensic Psychology in Disability Adjudication: A Decade of Experience: Vocational Experts in the Bureau of Hearings and Appeals.* U.S. Department of Health, Education, and Welfare.
Havranek, J., Grimes, J. W., Field, T. & Sink, J. (1994). *Vocational Assessment: Evaluating Employment Potential.* Athens, GA: Elliott & Fitzpatrick, Inc.
Hassinger, E. W. (1983). "Rural Health Organizations: Social Networks and Regionalizations. "Ames, IA: Iowa State University Press.
Howe, W. (1986). "The Business Services Industry Sets Pace in Employment Growth," Monthly Labor Review, 109.
Hawley, A. E., & Mazie, S. M. (1961). "An Overview" in *Non-Metropolitan American in Transition.* Chapel Hill, NC: The University of North Carolina Press.
Hollingshead, A. B. (1949). *Elmstown's Youth.* New York: John Wiley and Sons, Inc.
Johnson, H. W. (1980). *Rural Health Service: A Book of Readings.* Itasca, IN.
Lingeman, R. (1984). *Caste and Class in the American Town in Small Town America: A Narrative History 1620 - - Present.* New York: G. P. Putnam's Sons.
Lingeman, R. (1983). *The Small Town in America: The Recent Past; the Near Future in Change and Tradition in the American Small Town.* Starkville, MS: The University Press of Mississippi State.
Marks E. and Lewis A. (1983). *Job Hunting for the Disabled.* New York: Barron's Educational Series, Inc.
Mennis, Edmund A. (1999). *How the Economy Works: An Investor's Guide to Tracking the Economy.* Paramus, NJ: New York Institute of Finance.
Myers, J. W., (1983). "Counseling the Older Rural Worker: A Report." *Journal of Employment Counseling*, June.
Norris, P. E. (1990). *The Job Doctor.* Indianapolis, Indiana: JIST Works, Inc.

O'Net Dictionary of Occupational Titles: The Definitive Printed Reference of Occupational Information (2004). Indianapolis, Indiana: JIST Works, Inc.

Peters, T. J. & Waterman, R. H. Jr. (1982). *In Search of Excellence: Lessons from America's Best-Run Companies*. New York: Harper and Rowe, Publishers.

Price, D. Z. & Dunlap, L. J. (1988). "Family Use of Community Services in Economically- Depressed Rural Counties" in *Life Styles: Family and Economic Issues, 9*(4).

Roessler, R. W. (1985). "Self-Starting in the Job Market: The Continuing Need for Job-Seeking Skills in Rehabilitation." *Journal of Applied Rehabilitation Counseling, 16*(2).

Swanson, D. (1991). The Resume Solution. Indianapolis, IN. JIST Works, Inc.

Tew-Washburn, Suzanne. (2001) Job Placement Methods and Models.

Tournier, R. C. (1983). "Small Towns at the Crossroads: Outcome Scenarios in Non- Metropolitan Change" in *Change and Tradition in the American Small Town*. New York: JohnWiley and Sons, Inc.

Salamone, P. R. (1971). "A Client-Centered Approach to Job Placement," Vocational Guidance Quarterly, 266-270.

Tracy, William R., ed. (1994). Human Resources Management & Development Handbook. New York: American Management Association.

Tullier, L. Michelle (2004). Networking for Job Search and Career Success. Indianapolis, IN. Jist Publishing, Inc.

US Department of Labor, Bureau of Labor Statistics (2004-05). *Occupational Outlook Handbook.*

US Department of Labor, Bureau of Statistics. "Occupational Outlook Quarterly." Fall, 2007.

US Department of Labor (1991 Fourth Edition). *Dictionary of Occupational Titles*.

US Department of Labor, Bureau of Statistics. "Outlook: 1990- - 2005." BLS Bulletin 2402. May, 1992.

Vandergoot, D. (1984). "Placement Practices in Vocational Rehabilitation". *Journal of Applied Rehabilitation Counseling, 15* (3).

Vidich, A. J., & Bensman, J. (1958). *Small Town in Mass Society*. Garden City, New York: Doubleday and Company.

"Vocational Expert Handbook" (2003). Social Security Administration, Office of Hearings and Appeals, Philadelphia Region.

Wall, Janet E. (2006) *Job Seeker's Online Goldmine: A Step-by-Step Guide to Government and No-Cost Web Tools*. Indianapolis, IN. Jist Publishing, Inc.

Weed, Roger and Timothy Field (2001) Rehabilitation Consultant's Handbook. Elliott & Fitzpatrick, Inc. Athens, Georgia

Wegmann, R. (1989). *Work in the New Economy: Careers and Job Seeking into the 21st Century* Indianapolis, IN: JIST Works, Inc.

Wells, G. K. *Caste and Code in the American Village: 1870 - - 1920.* Columbia, SC: (An unpublished dissertation) University of South Carolina, December, 1972.

Wells G. K. (1994). *Finding Jobs on Main Street: A Managed Approach to Job Placement*. Athens GA: Elliott & Fitzpatrick, Inc.

White, W. A. (1937). *Forty Years on Main Street.* New York: Farrar & Rinehart, Inc.

Wolfinger, Anne. (2007). *Best Career and Education Web Sites: A Quick Guide to Online Job Search.* Indianapolis, IN. JIST Publishing, Inc.